How did the events of the early modern period affect the way gender and the self were represented? This collection of essays attempts to respond to this question by analyzing a wide spectrum of cultural concerns – humanism, technology, science, law, anatomy, literacy, domesticity, colonialism, erotic practices, and the theater – in order to delineate the history of subjectivity and its relationship with the postmodern fragmented subject. The scope of this analysis expands the terrain explored by feminist theory, while its feminist focus reveals that the subject is always gendered – although the terms in which gender is conceived and represented change across history. *Feminist readings of early modern culture* not only explores the representation of gendered subjects, but in its commitment to balancing the productive tensions of methodological diversity, also speaks to contemporary challenges facing feminism.

FEMINIST READINGS OF EARLY MODERN CULTURE

Self-Portrait at the Easel, Sofonisba Anguissola (*c.* 1556).

FEMINIST READINGS OF EARLY MODERN CULTURE

Emerging subjects

EDITED BY

VALERIE TRAUB

University of Michigan

M. LINDSAY KAPLAN

Georgetown University

DYMPNA CALLAGHAN

Syracuse University

CAMBRIDGE
UNIVERSITY PRESS

Published by the Press Syndicate of the University of Cambridge
The Pitt Building, Trumpington Street, Cambridge CB2 1RP
40 West 20th Street, New York, NY 10011–4211, USA
10 Stamford Road, Oakleigh, Melbourne 3166, Australia

First published 1996

Printed in Great Britain at the University Press, Cambridge

A catalogue record for this book is available from the British Library

Library of Congress cataloguing in publication data

Feminist readings of early modern culture: emerging subjects /
edited by Valerie Traub, M. Lindsay Kaplan, Dympna Callaghan.
p.   cm.
Includes bibliographical references and index.
ISBN 0 521 55249 4 (hardback). – ISBN 0 521 55819 0 (paperback)
1. English literature–Early modern, 1500–1700–History and
criticism. 2. Feminism and literature–England–History–16th
century. 3. Feminism and literature–England–History–17th
century. 4. Women and literature–England–History–16th century.
5. Women and literature–England–History–17th century. 6. Gender
identity in literature. 7. Subjectivity in literature. 8. Sex role
in literature. 9. Renaissance–England. I. Traub, Valerie, 1958–
II. Kaplan, M. Lindsay. III. Callaghan, Dympna
PR428.F45F46   1996
942.05'082–dc20   95–52637   CIP

ISBN 0 521 55249 4 hardback
ISBN 0 521 55819 0 paperback

Contents

List of illustrations   *page* ix
Notes on contributors   xii
Preface   xv

 1   Valerie Traub, M. Lindsay Kaplan, Dympna Callaghan:
     Introduction   1

 2   Denise Albanese: Making it new: humanism, colonialism, and
     the gendered body in early modern culture   16

 3   Valerie Traub: Gendering mortality in early modern
     anatomies   44

 4   Cynthia Marshall: Wound-man: *Coriolanus*, gender, and the
     theatrical construction of interiority   93

 5   Rosemary Kegl: "The world I have made": Margaret
     Cavendish, feminism, and the *Blazing-World*   119

 6   Frances E. Dolan: Reading, writing, and other crimes   142

 7   Kim F. Hall: Culinary spaces, colonial spaces: the gendering
     of sugar in the seventeenth century   168

 8   Jyotsna G. Singh: Caliban versus Miranda: race and gender
     conflicts in postcolonial rewritings of *The Tempest*   191

 9   Laura Levine: Rape, repetition, and the politics of closure in
     A Midsummer Night's Dream   210

10   M. Lindsay Kaplan: Subjection and subjectivity: Jewish Law
     and female autonomy in Reformation English marriage   229

11   Theodora A. Jankowski: "Where there can be no cause of
      affection": redefining virgins, their desires, and their
      pleasures in John Lyly's *Gallathea*   253

12.   Dympna Callaghan: The terms of gender: "gay" and
      "feminist" *Edward II*   275

Illustrations

Self-Portrait at the Easel, Sofonisba Anguissola (*c.* 1556). Reproduced by courtesy of the Museum Zamek, Lancut, Poland.   *frontispiece*

2.1 "Untitled" (History Portrait, no. 224), Cindy Sherman (1990). Reproduced by courtesy of Metro Pictures, New York.   *page* 23

2.2 "Untitled" (History Portrait, no. 225), Cindy Sherman (1990). Reproduced by courtesy of Metro Pictures, New York.   24

2.3 "Untitled" (History Portrait, no. 211), Cindy Sherman (1990). Reproduced by courtesy of Metro Pictures, New York.   25

2.4 *Weroan or Great Lorde of Virginia*, Theodor de Bry from Thomas Harriot, *A Briefe and True Report of the New Found Land of Virginia* (London, 1590). Reproduced by courtesy of the Folger Shakespeare Library.   26

2.5 *The True Picture of One Picte*, Theodor de Bry from Thomas Harriot, *A Briefe and True Report of the New Found Land of Virginia* (London, 1590). Reproduced by courtesy of the Folger Shakespeare Library.   27

3.1 Self-demonstrating corpse, from Charles Estienne, *La dissection des parties du corps humain* (Paris, 1546). Reproduced by courtesy of the Van Pelt-Dietrich Library, University of Pennsylvania.   55

3.2 *The Dance of Death*, from Hans Holbein, the Younger, *Imagini mortis* (Cologne, 1573). Reproduced by courtesy of the Folger Shakespeare Library.   56

3.3 Capital letter, from Andreas Vesalius, *De corporis humani fabrica* (Basel, 1543). Reproduced by courtesy of the Eskind Biomedical Library, Vanderbilt University.   57

3.4 Portrait of Vesalius, from Andreas Vesalius, *De corporis humani fabrica* (Basel, 1543). Reproduced by courtesy of the Eskind Biomedical Library, Vanderbilt University.   58

3.5   Muscleman, from Andreas Vesalius, *De corporis humani fabrica* (Basel, 1543). Reproduced by courtesy of the Eskind Biomedical Library, Vanderbilt University.   59

3.6   Male torso, from Andreas Vesalius, *De corporis humani fabrica* (Basel, 1543). Reproduced by courtesy of the Eskind Biomedical Library, Vanderbilt University.   60

3.7   Female torso, from Andreas Vesalius, *De corporis humani fabrica* (Basel, 1543). Reproduced by courtesy of the Eskind Biomedical Library, Vanderbilt University.   61

3.8   A figure of martyrdom, from Andreas Vesalius, *De corporis humani fabrica* (Basel, 1543). Reproduced by courtesy of the Eskind Biomedical Library, Vanderbilt University.   61

3.9   Anatomist anatomized, from Juan de Valverde de Hamusco, *Anatomia del corpo humano* (Rome, 1560). Reproduced by courtesy of the Folger Shakespeare Library.   62

3.10   Self-demonstrating corpse, from Juan de Valverde de Hamusco, *Anatomia del corpo humano* (Rome, 1560). Reproduced by courtesy of the Folger Shakespeare Library.   62

3.11   Armored cadaver, from Juan de Valverde de Hamusco, *Anatomia del corpo humano* (Rome 1560). Reproduced by courtesy of the Folger Shakespeare Library.   63

3.12   Prone cadaver, from Andreas Vesalius, *De corporis humani fabrica* (Basel, 1543). Reproduced by courtesy of the Eskind Biomedical Library, Vanderbilt University.   64

3.13   Skeleton, from Charles Estienne, *La dissection des parties du corps humain* (Paris, 1546). Reproduced by courtesy of the Van Pelt-Dietrich Library, University of Pennsylvania.   65

3.14   Seated cadaver, from Charles Estienne, *La dissection des parties du corps humain* (Paris, 1546). Reproduced by courtesy of the Van Pelt-Dietrich Library, University of Pennsylvania.   66

3.15   Standing cadaver, from Charles Estienne, *La dissection des parties du corps humain* (Paris, 1546). Reproduced by courtesy of the Van Pelt-Dietrich Library, University of Pennsylvania.   67

3.16   Seated cadaver, from Charles Estienne, *La dissection des parties du corps humain* (Paris, 1546). Reproduced by courtesy of the Van Pelt-Dietrich Library, University of Pennsylvania.   68

3.17   Skeleton, from Charles Estienne, *La dissection des parties du corps humain* (Paris, 1546). Reproduced by courtesy of the Van Pelt-Dietrich Library, University of Pennsylvania.   69

3.18   Martyred figure, from Charles Estienne, *La dissection des
       parties du corps humain* (Paris, 1546). Reproduced by courtesy of
       the Van Pelt-Dietrich Library, University of Pennsylvania.   70
3.19   Female reproductive figure, from Charles Estienne, *La
       dissection des parties du corps humain* (Paris, 1546). Reproduced by
       courtesy of the Van Pelt-Dietrich Library, University of
       Pennsylvania.   71
3.20   Female reproductive figure, from Charles Estienne, *La
       dissection des parties du corps humain* (Paris, 1546). Reproduced by
       courtesy of the Van Pelt-Dietrich Library, University of
       Pennsylvania.   72
3.21   Pregnant figure, from Charles Estienne, *La dissection des
       parties du corps humain* (Paris, 1546). Reproduced by courtesy of
       the Van Pelt-Dietrich Library, University of Pennsylvania.   73
3.22   Seated figure, from Charles Estienne, *La dissection des parties
       du corps humain* (Paris, 1546). Reproduced by courtesy of the
       Van Pelt-Dietrich Library, University of Pennsylvania.   74
3.23   Frontispiece, from Johann Remmelin, *Catoptrum
       microcosmicum* (Ulm? 1619). Reproduced by courtesy of the
       National Library of Medicine.   75
3.24   Second plate with cut-out flaps, from Johann Remmelin,
       Catoptrum microcosmicum (Ulm? 1619). Reproduced by courtesy
       of the National Library of Medicine.   76
3.25   Second plate with cut-out flaps, from Johann Remmelin,
       Catoptrum microcosmicum (Ulm? 1619). Reproduced by courtesy
       of the National Library of Medicine.   77
3.26   Detail from woodcut of devil pitching humans, *The Kalender
       of Sheepehards* (London, 1503). Reproduced by courtesy of the
       Folger Shakespeare Library.   78
4.1   *Wound-man*, from *Anathomia* (*c.* 1450). Reproduced by courtesy
       of the Wellcome Centre Medical Photographic Library,
       London.   105
12.1   Front cover of Jonathan Dollimore's *Sexual Dissidence:
       Augustine to Wilde, Freud to Foucault*, featuring *Station of the Cross,
       Vatican City*, Rotimi Fani-Kayode (Clarendon Press, 1991). By
       permission of Oxford University Press.   276

Notes on contributors

DENISE ALBANESE is Associate Professor of English at George Mason University in Fairfax, Virginia. She teaches and writes about Renaissance literature, critical theory, and the culture of science. Her book, *The New Science and its Others*, was published in 1995 by Duke University Press; she is now completing *Consuming Pastness*, a study of Shakespeare and the Renaissance in twentieth-century mass culture.

LAURA LEVINE is a 1995–96 Folger Fellow at the Folger Shakespeare Library. Her first book, *Men in Women's Clothing: Anti-Theatricality and Effeminization from 1579 to 1642* (Cambridge University Press, 1994), examines anxiety about the stage in Renaissance England. She is at work on a book on Renaissance witchcraft and "magical thinking." She has taught at Brown University, the Department of Performance Studies at New York University, and Wellesley College where she was the recipient of the Pinanski teaching prize.

CYNTHIA MARSHALL, Associate Professor of English at Rhodes College in Memphis, is the author of *Last Things and Last Plays: Shakespearean Eschatology* and of recent articles on Shakespeare in *English Literary Renaissance*, *Studies in English Literature*, and *Shakespeare Quarterly*.

VALERIE TRAUB is Associate Professor of English at the University of Michigan, Ann Arbor. She has published *Desire and Anxiety: Circulations of Sexuality in Shakespearean Drama* (Routledge, 1992), and has articles in *Erotic Politics* (Routledge, 1992), *Body Guards* (Routledge, 1992), *Queering the Renaissance* (Duke University Press, 1993), *Cross-Cultural Performances* (University of Illinois Press, 1993), as well as in *Shakespeare Quarterly* and *Shakespeare Studies*. Her current project, under contract with Cambridge University Press, is on the terms of gendered embodiment in early modern culture.

FRANCES E. DOLAN is an Associate Professor of English at Miami University of Ohio, and an affiliate of the History Department and the Women's Studies Program. She is the author of *Dangerous Familiars: Representations of Domestic Crime in England, 1550–1700* (Cornell University Press, 1994). The project on which she is now working is tentatively entitled "Sinister Competence: Catholicism, Women, and the Law from the Gunpowder Plot to the Popish Plot."

ROSEMARY KEGL is Associate Professor of English at the University of Rochester. She has published essays on Marvell, Puttenham, Shakespeare, and two seventeenth-century Quaker women, Katharine Evans and Sarah Chevers. She is the author of *The Rhetoric of Concealment: Figuring Gender and Class in Renaissance Literature* (Cornell, 1994) and is currently at work on a study of theatrical practices and the gendering of intellectual activity of sixteenth- and seventeenth-century England. The essay in this volume was written with the support of a Newberry Library/National Endowment for the Humanities Fellowship.

KIM F. HALL is Associate Professor at Georgetown University, where she teaches English and Women's Studies. She is the author of *Things of Darkness: Economies of Race and Gender in Early Modern England* (Cornell University Press, 1995). Her articles include "Guess Who's Coming to Dinner?: Colonization and Mescegenation in *The Merchant of Venice*" and "Sexual Politics and Cultural Identity in *The Masque of Blackness*." The essay in this volume is part of her next book project, tentatively titled, *A Taste of Empire: Women, Food and Colonization*.

M. LINDSAY KAPLAN is Assistant Professor of English at Georgetown University. Her book manuscript, *The Culture of Slander in Early Modern England*, is currently under consideration; she has published essays in *Renaissance Drama* and *Early Modern France*.

JYOTSNA G. SINGH is Associate Professor of English and Cultural Studies at Southern Methodist University in Dallas, Texas. She has coauthored a book with Dympna Callaghan and Lorraine Helms entitled *The Weyward Sisters: Shakespeare and Feminist Politics* (Blackwell, 1994). Her essays have appeared in such books as *Re-Considering the Renaissance* (SUNY Press, 1992) and *Women, Race, Writing in the Early Modern Period* (Routledge, 1993), as well as in *Renaissance Drama* and *Theater Journal*.

THEODORA A. JANKOWSKI is a faculty member at Washington State University. She is the author of *Women in Power in the Early Modern Drama* (University of Illinois Press, 1992) and articles on Shakespeare, Webster, Lyly, and Heywood. The essay on *Gallathea* in this collection derives from her current book-length project on the threatening nature of the discourse of virginity in early modern drama English drama.

DYMPNA CALLAGHAN is Associate Professor of English at Syracuse University in Syracuse, New York. She is the author of *Woman and Gender in Renaissance Tragedy: A Study of "King Lear", "Othello", "The Duchess of Malfi" and "The White Devil"* (Humanities Press International, 1989) as well as coauthor, with Jyotsna G. Singh and Lorraine Helms, of *The Weyward Sisters: Shakespeare and Feminist Politics* (Blackwell, 1994).

Preface

As *Feminist readings of early modern culture* makes its way through the publishing house and out into the world, the editors wish to acknowledge some of the circumstances of its production. In the first instance, we were impelled to come together out of a sense of excitement over our collective scholarly projects. The authors included in this volume are not gathered here solely for the purpose of this volume; we have a history of intellectual and personal camaraderie and, in various combinations, have had a self-consciousness of ourselves as each others' best critics.

In the second instance, we are part of a generation that has benefited from the efforts of the academy to diversify itself. The contributors to the volume are lesbian, heterosexual, African-American, Indian, Jewish, WASP, publicly and privately educated in the United States, Britain, and India. We recognize the complex, and sometimes contradictory, constellation of factors – from global capitalism to transnational feminism – that have contributed to our own sense of intellectual possibility.

Finally, we wish to acknowledge that we are all women. In this we emphasize not an essential womanhood or shared sisterhood, but the significant similarities we share as female subjects involved in North American institutions of higher education. These factors are not just the empirical dimensions of our working lives; they also structure our institutional, political, intellectual, and personal engagements.

CHAPTER I

Introduction

Valerie Traub, M. Lindsay Kaplan and Dympna Callaghan

Sofonisba Anguissola's self-portrait, reproduced in the frontispiece of this book, depicts the artist flourishing her brush in a self-conscious articulation of professional identity. As the first Italian woman to gain international recognition as a painter, Anguissola's gesture of self-definition, her apparently confident assertion of identity as a Renaissance artist, also betrays the alienation of women in general from the privileged cultural identity of the humanist subject. Anguissola was celebrated as a novelty, and only as such could she successfully evade the censure and suppression that befell other talented women, such as Lavinia Fontana and Fede Galizia, who strived to emulate her.[1]

Feminist readings of early modern culture: emerging subjects explores the multiple ways that subjects were constructed within the highly contested terms of sixteenth- and seventeenth-century culture. As such, the essays in this volume implicitly enter into a dialogue initiated by scholars who have argued that the modern subject was "invented" in the early modern period.[2] The influence of this claim in the field of early modern studies has been enormous, contributing to the rise of distinct movements and methodologies (cultural materialism, new historicism) which have interacted and conflicted with related critical projects, such as feminism. In the past, however, histories of the subject have rarely been specifically concerned with gender, while feminist work on gender has only minimally taken up, in historical terms, the claim of a new subjectivity.[3] Because the essays in our volume are centrally engaged with the production of gendered subjects, this Introduction begins with a brief description of the discourses that have informed the conceptual possibility of this book.

In response to the so-called "Renaissance birth of the subject," David Aers and Lee Patterson have pointed out that various forms of interiority preexisted the social transformations of the sixteenth century.[4] If Aers and Patterson overstate the case by privileging articulations from a single discourse, theology, over all others, they nonetheless persuasively argue that claims to the modernity of the Renaissance subject have depended in large part upon an ahistorical othering of the medieval period. What's more, they suggest the practical futility, and conservatism, of the search for an originary moment, a search that tends to unify artificially historical periods, and, we would add, individual subjectivities.

We – the editors of this volume – would like to suggest that it is less that the modern subject *came into being* in the early modern period than that the terms of the subject's intelligibility were reconfigured during two hundred years of economic, political, epistemological, and social upheaval.[5] Rather than police the boundaries between premodern, early modern, modern, and postmodern, we wish to pursue the specificity of representation and experience as they are constituted in particular moments in time and space. By replacing ontological claims with more deliberately historical ones, we hope to underscore the point that the subject, in both social and psychological terms, is always in the process of emerging; such an emergence is never whole or complete. And in focusing on the subject as gendered, we echo Judith Butler's assertion that "[t]o claim that the subject is itself produced in and as a gendered matrix of relations is not to do away with the subject, but only to ask after the conditions of its emergence and operation."[6] At the same time, we maintain that philosophical critiques such as Butler's must be augmented by a historical specification of the local matrices through which the defining terms of individual subjects emerged. That which signifies the subject's emergence takes place within the highly contested terms of cultural struggle. Thus, different subjects are marked differently: like Sofonisba Anguissola, they may or may not be accorded interiority, agency, and status; like her as well, they can make claims for cultural recognition only through available means. At the same time that we stress the historicity of the subject, we also emphasize the psychodynamics of cultural fantasy and projection, for in psychoanalytic terms, as Alan Sinfield argues, "the human subject is never full, and hence may, at any moment, appear unformed."[7]

The subject's ongoing struggle for emergence in the early modern period influences, and is influenced by, similarly complicated and contradictory transformations in a range of cultural domains: economic, national, familial, religious, and scientific. The move from an agrarian economy to market relations in a national system of exchange created a bourgeois class of urban dwellers, many of whom were cut off from traditional networks of kin and community. With the decline of face-to-face exchanges in a marketplace designated by a cross, economic relations for a greater number of people became increasingly abstract. Buyers and sellers increasingly were separated by time and distance, and the self-understanding required to enter into this system of transaction was different from that fostered by the immediacy of bargaining in a pre-capitalist market economy.[8] During the same period, Tudor and Stuart efforts to consolidate the nationalist state not only initiated the central-ization of power, but began to fashion subjects with a simultaneously more direct and more conflictual relation to the crown. Concurrent with this development of the state as *patria* was the deployment of the familial model as the defining relation between ruler and subject and an empha-sis on the family as the elemental governing unit.[9] The inculcation of this ideology attempted to foster obedience while conferring a sense of the importance of social responsibility, hence serving to pull individual members of the polity into closer relation to the state.

If the ruler was imaged as a parent, the parent was also given the rights and responsibilities of a ruler. In order for the subject to enact the monarch's will, he or she required a measure of authority in his or her own right. While husbands officially had rule over wives, both parents had rule over other members of the household, such as children and ser-vants, male and female. Thus, the analogy of state to family effected the structural subordination of its subjects while it simultaneously imparted to (at least some of) them a measure of authority.

The advent of the religious movements we unify under the rubric of the Reformation contributed to this contradictory development by stressing obedience to consolidated secular and sacred authorities in the Church of England, while also developing a more activist role for indi-vidual conscience which could justify resistance to these authorities. As A. G. Dickens indicates, the Elizabethan settlement not only gratified "the general demand for a centralized Church coterminous with the nation, [but] also left room for some real divergences of outlook."[10] Protestant ideology provided a cohering function for the English state, as it asserted the state's divine imperative for intervention in the religious struggles on the continent, even as Puritan emphasis on conscience and personal agency in salvation authorized the radical dissent which threat-ened to divide England during the civil war.

The results of, and further impetus to, nation building were the mer-cantile and imperialist ventures that would lead to the subjugation of various peoples around the globe. Diverse as individual travelers' responses to the New World may have been,[11] the quest for national identity depended upon the construction of native peoples as radically different from Europeans, with tropes of exoticism and deficiency – cultural, intellectual, and moral – increasingly becoming privileged as the governing terms of national otherness. Such colonialist projects helped to further, and were furthered by, the new science. Advances in astronomy, optics, and anatomy pushed the scientist's gaze not only outward to the stars and inward to the body's viscera, but across the ocean to peoples inhabiting different climes. Travel, exploration, and colonization were reconfigured through scientific discourses.

The reorganization of scientific knowledge was mirrored in the formalization of a more internalized mode of behavior, as protocols of bodily decorum began to produce the subject as increasingly "civilized."[12] New textual genres (conduct books, pedagogical manuals) and material objects and technologies (forks, handkerchiefs, privies) began to intervene in the body's contact with itself. This "civilized body" was constituted out of, and carried with it, transformed relations of class and politics, property and privacy.[13] Hence, just as the subject emerged as an increasingly bounded, private self, various social mechanisms arose which also compelled its subjection.

If, over the course of this period, multiple cultural projects were initiated which formed the conditions of possibility for a recognizably modern subject, some of these projects were mundane while others were spectacular in their emergence. The terms of gender were reconfigured over the course of two centuries, sometimes subtly in the diurnal round of domestic relations, and sometimes dramatically, as in the instance of witch persecutions. That the terms of gender were a matter of intense social debate is evinced by the range of domains in which gender struggle was played out – village ritual, stage plays, conduct books, broadsides, pamphlet wars, and law courts. In light of such multiple and ongoing struggles, we maintain that the subject is always, although not essentially, gendered at any given historical moment. Because of its provisional and contradictory nature, gender itself continually must be reproduced. Through this expenditure of cultural energy, the terms of gender change over time. We thus reject the now prevalent argument, based on the theory of physiological homology between the sexes, that there existed only one gender in early modern culture.[14] Rather, gender exists as a term of definition even when it is not specifically articulated; it operates according to the exigencies of various discursive domains, and relates to and interacts with other axes of social formation.

The essays in *Feminist readings of early modern culture* plot specific rubrics through which gendered subjects gained cultural intelligibility. The focus is less on inwardness per se (although several contributors discuss the production of interiority), than on the psychic and material technologies, the disciplines and discourses, through which subjects became invested with various modes of signification, a range of material embodiments, and new forms of authority. The social conditions through which subjectivities accrued meaning in terms of gender, race, sexuality, class – and through which they were othered, oppressed, or empowered – include a wide spectrum of cultural events: humanism, technology, science, anatomy, literacy, domesticity, colonialism, erotic practices, the theater and its audience. In order to gain access to these phenomena, our contributors have read and analyzed a broad range of texts: cookbooks, marriage manuals, popular pamphlets, legal depositions, anatomy books, visual arts, theological, and political treatises, and stageplays.

Analysis of this variety of texts makes clear that during the early modern period, various frames of reference and diverse kinds of knowledges – popular, domestic, theatrical, legal, scientific, medical, moral – constituted the terms of subjectivity in distinct and differing ways. Whereas much of the influential scholarship of the past fifteen years has derived its claims about the subject (and, by extension, interiority, subjugation, and agency) from the evidence of only one discursive domain – whether philosophy or medical texts[15] – we believe that processes of interpellation are variable and often at odds. Thus, we strive in this collection to delineate the possibility of multiple agencies, specifiable within discrete historical moments and according to the logics of various discourses and localities. The point in drawing from diverse materials is not merely to render more visible and varied the *histories* of early modern subjects, but to provide a *critique* of modes of subjectivity.

In recognizing the span of time that separates our own situation from that of early modern subjects, we seek to maintain a recognition of the past's alterity while specifying the resonances that exist between early modern and postmodern cultures. As Margaret Hunt has pointed out:

The European Renaissance presents us with a series of societies sufficiently different from our own as to destabilize a number of received assumptions about, among other things, gender, sexuality, politics, religion, language, and identity. Yet it is also a period to which twentieth-century people almost reflexively appeal when they wish to validate whatever passes at any given time for "mainstream values."[16]

In resisting this conservative recourse to the early modern period, we insist on the status of "the Renaissance" as a nineteenth-century, retrospectively painted portrait. As a legitimating apparatus, "the Renaissance" offers the illusion of a totalized historical period coextensive with objective truth. In contrast, we underscore its depencence upon various exclusions and misrecognitions: of the experience of women and the laboring poor, of important events in Islamic and Jewish culture, and of colonialism in the New World. Such exclusions have important ramifications for the historical production of the subject, as Hunt suggests:

The classical, Renaissance, and early modern antecedents of what came to constitute a modern "identity" included a self-affirming public voice (often called "citizenship"), an identification with a vocation (e.g., he is a carpenter), personal autonomy, standardly defined in the Renaissance and early modern period as the ability to deploy the labor, reproductive and otherwise, of inferior family members . . . and some measure of bodily self-control, a central attribute of which was the ability to initiate and to definitively refuse sexual intercourse. All of these were difficult or impossible to attain for married women, slaves, or servants (and these categories cover the overwhelming majority of all women), and most were ontologically incompatible with what a married woman, a slave, or a servant "was."[17]

As several of the following essays imply, however, the absence of investment in a fully articulated, coherent subject may have allowed for the establishment of subcommunities, pockets of resistance, and alliances between subordinated groups. In this regard, it is important to look for resistance in relative terms, rather than to hold early modern women's words and actions up to post-Enlightenment standards of subjective self-consciousness. The condition of a fragmented, diffuse subject makes possible certain challenges to the dominant culture that may not be possible in modernity. For instance, the political status of the family, while reinforcing the subordination of the wife, nevertheless offers women a public role and a proximity to power that is lost in the transformation of the domestic into a private sphere in the eighteenth century.

In hoping simultaneously to mark and bridge the divide between the early modern and the postmodern, we recognize that the past has much of relevance to say because we see the shadows of our own images there. More importantly, we want to resist rewriting the early modern past from the perspective of the Enlightenment. The disfigurements of Enlightenment subjectivity that characterize the postmodern era seem to resemble more closely the emerging subjects of early modernity than does the putatively coherent, unified Englightenment subject who lived in closer historical proximity to our own time.

According to Joyce Chaplin, the term "modern" first was used during the period we call "early modern" to connote distance from the earlier medieval period: "It was derived from the Latin word *hodie,* meaning day. *Hodiern* meant daily, up to date, the way we live now; it is from *hodiern* that the English got the word 'modern' by the early 1500s."[18] To employ the term "early modern" delineates a tension between "us" and "not us": if the postmodern marks a crisis of modernity, the early modern marks the moment when we begin to see the issues of modernity developing. Without asserting that there was a full-blown Enlightenment subject in the sixteenth century or that there was nothing recognizably modern in the medieval subject, we can recognize that the early modern and the postmodern are similar in part because of their transitional status. Despite important differences in the organization of economic and social activity, there remains in certain domains a provocative sense of resemblance between these periods: witness the recent reclamation of "queer" sexuality as coextensive with the dominant terms of Renaissance culture.[19] At the same time, each era has a historical integrity of its own, and focusing only on similarity distorts our understanding of the past. The point is to ask, why the resemblance in one locale and not another?

The dialogue we have staged between early modern and postmodern correlates with our sense of feminism as a dialogic mode of interaction. In response to the effective exclusion of certain women from the predominately white, middle class women's movement – particularly lesbians, sex radicals, women of color, and working-class women – feminism over the last decade increasingly has confronted the possibility and necessity of its own diversity. Through this confrontation, feminists have begun to recognize – if not yet to adequately deal with – the dangers implicit in any univocal assertions in the name of "woman". Beyond that, feminists have recognized that feminism was in its inception founded upon exclusions, particularly in regard to race and class, and that this history has important ramifications for current praxis. It is no historical accident that feminism as a liberal doctrine of equality and rights developed contemporaneously with European imperialism, the slave trade, and full fledged capitalism. Feminism (which unlike earlier defenses of women claimed that the female subject had individual rights) was produced and conditioned by the extensibility of the Enlightenment subject, "Man," which was assumed to represent us all. As Laura Brown recently has asked, "how can we use a feminism that comes out of imperialism?"[20] The answer, we believe, involves remaining aware of the histories from which we – as subjects, as feminists – emerged, an awareness that can be maintained only by continuing a genealogical critique of the conditions of the subject's production, as well as an ongoing resistance to that history. In returning to the period which generated the conditions of possibility for both modern feminism and modern antifeminism, we hope to reconfigure the possibilities of feminism's future. As Denise Albanese asserts in her essay in this volume which analyzes Cindy Sherman's postmodern engagements with the early modern visual past: "In showing how that past was made, they also show how it can be made different."

Part of this process of reconfiguration began when feminist criticism and theory disavowed a "seventies" conception of sisterhood because of its erasure of differences of race, class, and sexuality. However, in doing so, feminist inquiry also abandoned some of the valuable utopian dimensions of feminist praxis which had built on notions of comradeship and solidarity from other leftist enterprises. Believing that the variability of feminist theory and practice depends upon the articulation and interaction of divergent points of view, different methodological choices, and conflicting critical positions, we have envisioned this volume as an ongoing dialogue – among the editors, among the contributors, and between ourselves and our readers. In highlighting the differences between our positions, we are less interested in representing a plurality of possible personal and institutional locations than in registering our status as a collective with a diverse feminist identity. We emphasize the distinction between plurality and collectivity because the former reproduces the very conception of representation inherited from the Enlightenment from which we want to depart, while the latter articulates an oppositional stance relying neither on a permanent group identity nor the erasure of difference. For, while we emphasize the importance of engaging with our differences, we also recognize the strategic importance of consolidating feminist positions. We reject the proposition that we live in a postfeminist age; rather, we believe that it is vital that we not underestimate the power and tenacity of dominant patriarchal structures. Indeed, we emphasize our differences because we also acknowledge the extraordinary flexibility of the dominant ideology and its ability to recuperate radical concepts and practices.

Our dialogic stance is impelled by two additional motives: on the one hand, feminist literary critics and cultural historians mistakenly are assumed by the non-feminist institution to be a single unified school, rather than to represent a spectrum of politics, perspectives, and methodologies. On the other hand, feminist demands for theoretical and methodological unity and consistency, and critical squabbles over the form that unity should take, have served to undermine the political project that feminist scholarship allegedly serves. Our attempt to enact a "nineties" feminist mode of intellectual engagement has much to do with our desire for a positive alternative to an unproductive mode of intellectual interaction prevalent in the United States academy, where scholars offer critiques of others' work more out of a desire to assert their own institutional presence than to contribute to collective inquiry.

Beyond a commitment to an inclusive yet conflictual feminism, this anthology resists advocating for a single method. This is not to suggest that collections organized around a methodological school do not have important roles to play, particularly at foundational moments of a critical project. Rather, the variety of methodological options evident in this volume furthers the understanding that critical categories can obscure those interests, goals, and methods that can draw different critics together. We reject the artificial limit such divisions put on our interactions – in the assumptions, for instance, that straight women shouldn't criticize the work of queer theorists or that lesbians are not interested in what heterosexual feminists have to say; that materialist critics have no interest in psychoanalysis or that psychoanalytic critics have nothing to offer to historical criticism; that new historicists necessarily lack in materialist consciousness or that materialists are overly preoccupied with a totalizing hegemony. Over the course of our scholarly relationships, we recognize that it has been the differences among us that have most fostered our own interpretive practices. Our attempt to foreground, rather than hide, such dissonance promotes a feminism that is as alert to concrete differences in practice as it is to "difference" as a fashionable mode of theory. The "emerging subjects" of our subtitle thus simultaneously refers to the early modern reconfiguration of subjectivities along increasingly salient axes of gender, sexuality, race, ethnicity, and class, and of a contemporary mode of feminist conversation that not only confounds and reconfigures critical boundaries, but exists in continuing dialogic interaction with itself and others.

In an anthology there is a strong temptation to demonstrate not only connections among essays, but also to stress the existence of the volume's coherence and unity. In a dialogic enterprise such as ours, however, such an effort also can be disingenuous. Because we believe that the conflicts between, as much as the intersections among, contributors comprise much of the value of this volume, we resist the temptation to invent a homogenous voice to introduce our work. When we speak of "we," then, we implicitly signal differences as well as our common goals, hoping to invoke not a unified single voice, but an internally conflicted, multiple agency.

In addition to variously defined feminist commitment, the contributors do share an interest in the mutual importance of textuality and history, history and theory. The essays in this volume assume that whereas historical precision must not be sacrificed for theoretical flashiness, historical analysis without theoretical rigor obscures rather than reveals our investments in the past. History is not composed of inert empirical data to be recovered from the archive or the literary text, but is rather a dynamic, complex process that serves (consciously or otherwise) the political needs of the present. The relationship between history and theory in this volume is mutually illuminating: critical theory of various kinds, whether or not explicitly signposted, helps to foreground the difficulties inherent in the project of historicization, while attention to historical events provides the necessary grounding for theoretical speculation.

Many of the essays call into question putative divisions among analytical categories or methodological approaches. Several of them fall within the syncretic, internally conflicted domain of what Laura Brown has called the "new new historicis[m]," taking up "issues of gender and race, feminism and colonialism, working-class culture and male and female homosexual desire."[21] The work included here focuses on the interrelated cultural production of marginalized and dominant identities in order to gain greater analytical purchase on those social processes that foster complicity with dominant structures and those that enable resistance. If the underlying method of this work is careful exposure of forces of social constraint, the end is a refigured political agency. All of the essays address some aspect of emergent female subjectivity. Whereas a number focus on early modern women, others, less predictably, treat masculinity, the nation, and the body as a site of material inscription that is diacritically related to femininity.

The structure of the volume follows a trajectory in which various concerns anticipate, overlap, and extend one another; the essays map out through physical proximity certain arenas of interest, intersection, and conflict. Situating essays in a paratactic manner, we offer a structure in which points of conceptual intersection enable the articulation of multiple perspectives in dialogue and disagreement. Although the necessarily linear quality of the following description suggests most powerfully the linkages among the essays, all of the essays highlight conceptual tensions and methodological positions. The tensions and problems exist both within and between essays. In this sense, it is in the spaces between the essays where much of the work of this volume – the work of feminism – takes place.

Our collection opens with Denise Albanese's examination of the emergence of early modern humanist modes of identification and interpretation, and historicization. Using Cindy Sherman's photographic appropriations of Renaissance "fine art" as a lens through which to read various Renaissance constructions of the past, she demonstrates the extent to which modes of naturalized perception, modes that were codified in the "new Renaissance science," are ideologically frightened by gender and colonialism. Albanese's interest in the relation between representations of the human body and constructions of a historical past is reiterated by Valerie Traub's focus on the visual strategies used to moderate anxieties about the fate of embodiment in early modern anatomical illustrations. As anatomical science attempts to penetrate and expose the visceral interior of the body, it visually encloses and contains the bodily exterior through the imposition of a range of related tropes. Such compensatory gestures seek to assuage fears elicited by the exposure of the flesh, fears that are iconographically mediated through gendered strategies of representation. The representation of corporeal interiority is examined from a more performative, psychoanalytic perspective by Cynthia Marshall, in her analysis of Coriolanus' refusal to display his wounds. Reading Coriolanus' subjectivity as an effect rather than a cause, Marshall interprets his refusal as an exemplary instance of the construction of subjectivity through violence, lack, and vulnerability. She demonstrates how the corporeal "theatrical body" provides a means of access into the audience's experience of a character's subjectivity by showing how the audience's desire for wholeness is a measure of its own psychic fears.

Although Renaissance science was a crucial site of the masculinized discipline of knowledge, its discourses were also available for female appropriation. Rosemary Kegl's analysis of Margaret Cavendish, the Duchess of Newcastle's pseudo-scientific writings highlights the complex social accommodations made by a woman engaged in intellectual activity. Locating Cavendish's utopian *Blazing-World* within a conflictual model of women's writing and feminist politics, Kegl demonstrates how

Cavendish's narrative of intellectual process implies that intellectual equality between men and women turns on women's obtaining access not only to particular concepts but to contemplative habits. The very literacy skills that enabled Cavendish's project, however, could represent an ambivalent cultural attainment for women at the bottom of the social scale. Challenging the feminist assumption that a personal voice is inevitably a privileged expression of selfhood, Frances E. Dolan demonstrates how literacy might inhibit as well as promote women's subject status. Examining the case of a woman accused of witchcraft who used her literacy to promote her healing arts, Dolan analyzes how reading and writing could be demonized as transgressive, even criminal, activities.

The social impact of female literacy was felt in realms quite different from the criminalized labor of a "wise woman" or the fantastical/intellectual imaginings of the Duchess of Newcastle. The extent to which women's reading skills were implicated in England's colonialist agenda is examined in Kim F. Hall's essay on cookbooks and the English sugar trade. Placing bourgeois and elite women's culinary activity in the context of colonialist narratives, Hall demonstrates how women's domestic culture could be made to serve imperialist and nationalist ends, at the same time that it allowed certain women a form of creative self-expression. The intersection of gender assertion and colonial oppression is also the subject of Jyotsnua Singh's contribution, as she exposes conflicting investments in gender and race in twentieth-century postcolonial appropriations of *The Tempest*. Singh finds that a logic of reversal structures postcolonial appropriations of Shakespeare's play, leaving undisturbed the exchange of women that underpins colonialism. Singh's emphasis on the marginalization of women's desires is brought back to the early modern period in Laura Levine's examination of the structuring fantasies of *A Midsummer Night's Dream*. Observing that the play obsessively reenacts moments of sexual coercion ostensibly repudiated by its characters, Levine suggests that the play's attempts to avoid or dispel sexual violence generate a further, amplified violence. Her argument ultimately links the play's perpetuation of coercive fantasies to early modern conceptions of the theater as a site of sexual danger. Levine's metatheatrical analysis of how "something like a rape" is transformed into "something like a marriage" reminds us that the meaning of marriage itself was socially contested. M. Lindsay Kaplan's examination of post-Reformation debates about marriage and divorce demonstrates the extent to which they relied on hitherto rejected Jewish conceptualizations of these practices. In advocating the Hebraic idea that marriage could be dissolved, reformers in effect argued for the theoretical possibility of a wife's escape from subjection to her husband. A related interest in the possibilities of female escape from patriarchal structures informs Theodora A. Jankowski's essay on virginity as a mode of female resistance. Differentiating between the social and political uses of virginity, her analysis stages a conflict between the dominant, biological concept of virginity as removed from desire, and an alternative concept of virginity as coincident with desire. Developing an anti-patriarchal definition of virginity, she recovers women's potential for mutual erotic pleasures. Transgressive pleasures are very much at issue in the final essay of the volume, Dympna Callaghan's comparison of critical and dramatic representations of Queen Isabella. Her essay comparing Elizabeth Cary's and Christopher Marlowe's treatments of the history of Edward II initiates a much needed interrogation of the relationship between feminist and queer theory. Suggesting that representations of feminity and homoerotic masculinity are set against one another in patriarchal culture, she sounds a warning note that returns us to the difficult necessity of political debate in the present moment.

NOTES

1 See Merry E. Wiesner, *Woman and Gender in Early Modern Europe* (Cambridge: Cambridge University Press, 1993).

2 See Stephen Greenblatt, *Renaissance Self-Fashioning: From More to Shakespeare* (Chicago and London: University of Chicago Press, 1980) and *Shakespearean Negotiations: The Circulation of Social Energy in Renaissance England* (Oxford: Clarendon Press, 1988); Jonathan Dollimore, *Radical Tragedy: Religion, Ideology, and Power in the Drama of Shakespeare and His Contemporaries* (Chicago: University of Chicago Press, 1984). Catherine Belsey, in *The Subject of Tragedy: Identity and Difference in Renaissance Drama* (London and New York: Methuen, 1985) and Francis Barker, in *The Tremulous Private Body: Essays on Subjection* (London and New York: Methuen, 1984), specifically have equated the interiority expressed in Hamlet's soliloquies with a distinctly modern paradigm of personhood.

3 Exceptions to this are Belsey, *The Subject of Tragedy* and Jean Howard, *The Stage and Social Struggle in Early Modern England* (London and New York: Routledge, 1994).

4 David Aers, "A Whisper in the Ear of Early Modernists; Or, Reflections on Literary Critics Writing the 'History of the Subject,'" in *Culture and History: 1350–1699: Essays on English Communities, Identities, and Writing* (London: Harvester, 1992), pp. 177–202; Lee Patterson, "On the Margin: Postmodernism, Ironic History, and Medieval Studies," *Speculum* 65 (1990): 87–108.

5 Susan Dwyer Amussen, *An Ordered Society: Gender and Class in Early Modern England* (Oxford: Blackwell, 1988); Christopher Hill, *The World Turned Upside Down: Radical Ideas During the English Revolution* (Middlesex: Penguin Books, 1972 and 1975); Lawrence Stone, *The Family, Sex and Marriage in England 1500–1800* (New York: Harper and Row, 1977 and 1979); David Underdown, "The Taming of the Scold: The Enforcement of Patriarchal Authority in Early Modern England," in *Order and Disorder in Early Modern England*, Anthony Fletcher and John Stevenson, eds. (Cambridge and New York: Cambridge University Press, 1985), pp. 116–36.

6 Judith Butler, *Bodies That Matter: On the Discursive Limits of "Sex"* (New York and London: Routledge, 1993), p. 7.

7 Sinfield, *Cultural Politics – Queer Reading* (Philadelphia: University of Pennsylvania Press, 1994), p. 14.

8 Joyce Oldham Appleby, *Economic Thought and Ideology in Seventeenth-Century England* (Princeton: Princeton University Press, 1978).

9 Dympna Callaghan, *Women and Gender in Renaissance Tragedy* (Brighton: Harvest Press, 1989); John Guy, *Tudor England* (Oxford and New York: Oxford University Press, 1988); and Amussen, *An Ordered Society*.

10 A. G. Dickens, *The English Reformation* (New York: Schocken Books, 1964), p. 418.

11 Stephen Greenblatt, *Marvelous Possessions: The Wonder of the New World* (Chicago: University of Chicago Press, 1991); Peter Hulme, *Colonial Encounters: Europe and the Native Caribbean, 1492–1797* (London and New York: Methuen, 1986); Anthony Pagden, *European Encounters with the New World: From Renaissance to Romanticism* (New Haven: Yale University Press, 1993).

12 Norbert Elias, *The Civilizing Process: The Development of Manners: Changes in the Code of Conduct and Feeling in Early Modern Times* (1939), Edmund Jephcott, trans. (New York: Urizen Books, 1978).

13 Gail Kern Paster, *The Body Embarrassed: Drama and the Disciplines of Shame in Early Modern England* (Ithaca: Cornell University Press, 1993).

14 See Greenblatt, *Shakespearean Negotiations* and Thomas Laqueur, *Making Sex: Body and Gender from the Greeks to Freud* (Cambridge and New York: Cambridge University Press, 1994).

15 See Charles Taylor, *Sources of the Self: The Making of Modern Identity* (Cambridge, MA: Harvard University Press, 1989) and Laqueur, *Making Sex*.

16 Margaret Hunt, afterword, *Queering the Renaissance*, Jonathan Goldberg, ed. (Durham and London: Duke University Press, 1994), p. 359.

17 *Ibid.*, p. 364.

18 Joyce Chaplin, *Letters: The Newsletter of the Robert Penn Warren Center for the Humanities* 3 (1995): 2.

19 Gregory W. Bredbeck, *Sodomy and Interpretation: Marlowe to Milton* (Ithaca and London: Cornell University Press, 1991); Jonathan Dollimore, *Sexual Dissidence: Augustine to Wilde, Freud to Foucault* (Oxford: Clarendon Press, 1991); Jonathan Goldberg, ed. *Queering the Renaissance* and *Sodometries: Renaissance Texts, Modern Sexualities* (Stanford: Stanford University Press, 1992); Bruce R.

Smith, *Homosexual Desire in Shakespeare's England: A Cultural Poetics* (Chicago and London: University of Chicago Press, 1991).

20 Laura Brown, "Amazons and Africans: Gender, Race, and Empire in Daniel Defoe," in *Women, "Race," and Writing in the Early Modern Period*, Margo Hendricks and Patricia Parker, eds. (London and New York: Routledge, 1994), p. 136.

21 Brown, "Amazons and Africans," p. 119.

CHAPTER 2

Making it new: humanism, colonialism, and the gendered body in early modern culture

Denise Albanese

HISTORY, THE POSTMODERN, AND THE PROSTHETIC FEMALE SUBJECT

Two sets of images provide an entry into the argument about humanism and historicism that follows. The first set of images is a series of photographs recently taken by the artist Cindy Sherman, and generally referred to as the "History Portraits."[1] The second set is probably more familiar to readers of Renaissance culture, since it comes from Theodor de Bry's much-discussed engraved illustrations to Thomas Harriot's *A Briefe and True Report of the New Found Land of Virginia* (1590). Each set of images makes a problem out of power and knowledge as they function in the telling of history: the juxtapositions between them enable us to map out the complex interrelationships between past and present, European and North American, and mind and body, that may be taken as formative of modernity.

As my symptomatic readings of these images will indicate, historical narratives are predicated equally on imagined relations and tactical silences. Specifically, they demand an ideological adjudication between what may be comprehended as familiar, and what must be suppressed, or investigated, as alien. This is true whether those narratives flag the emergence of the early modern subject of humanism, the "new" world of modernity betokened by colonialism in the seventeenth century, or, as in the case of Sherman, the postmodern representation of identity and estrangement on which the previous two meet.

In fact, my argument starts out of chronological order; by beginning with Cindy Sherman, I trace a backward trajectory in order to foreground (for later use) the problematic nature of historical retrospection. As meditations, belated ones, on the modern project, Sherman's images make visible categories of representation, technology, and the body produced by gender that are only teasingly, evanescently apprehensible in the early modern illustrations of Harriot. In this regard, Sherman's photographs are also the easier of the two sets to read. To be sure, they are complex as images; but they emerge out of a recent critical terrain that has conditioned self-consciousness about apparatuses of social and aesthetic reproduction, and the range of subject positions that emerge from such reproduction. With the necessary correctives, this self-consciousness can usefully be cast backwards. Nevertheless, because the "History Portraits" are something of a departure for Sherman, they have not much been read as I propose to do – as forays into historicity, as skeptical interventions into the presentation and production of historical consciousness of which the Harriot images constitute an earlier instantiation.

Sherman's previous work – primarily the "Untitled Movie Stills" of the late 1970s – exploited and problematized the position of Woman as object of the Lacanian gaze, in a series of portraits that evoked the style and narratives of the genre movies of the 1940s and 1950s. In each of the earlier photographs, the disguised and costumed Sherman is caught by the camera she herself sets up to catch her, situated in some enigmatic yet hauntingly familiar narrative space. Whether reaching for a book, overtaken while walking on dark city streets, or surprised as she ducks out a sliding glass door in a full-length slip, Sherman inhabits the clothing, demeanor, and desirability of stereotypical femininity as produced by Hollywood movie culture.

The twist is of course obvious, and it is this twist that has given this earlier work its totemic status as feminist critique. In her formal control over the circumstances of image production, Sherman both induces a voyeuristic response and challenges one's right to it. Since she can be located on both sides of the camera, her assumption of the pose of movie-woman makes clear that femininity thus defined as object of the gaze is a performance. Further, the tantalizing incompleteness of the narrative space she set up makes something else clear as well – that a lot more is involved here than meets the eye, at least as framed by the classic fetishistic technology of the cinema.

But the neat dovetailing between Sherman's work and a feminist theory that owes much to Lacan and film practice comes to grief in the "History Portraits," photographs that play off of the luster – both formal and ideological – of Old Master paintings. In these portraits, Sherman is no longer posing as the seductive and alluring Woman: not one of these is a Venus, or any other allegorical female in fetching dishabille. Frequently, in fact, her encounter with (art) history does not leave her a woman at all. She is as likely to be a burgher as a madonna, and even quotes Caravaggio's Bacchus in one of the few portraits to set her up as a focus of erotic desire, however, overdetermined (figure 2.1). Moreover, the "History Portraits" make full, even ludicrous use of the prostheses that have otherwise been the subject of her camera (as, for example, in the "Untitled" series of 1984). Fake body parts abound, from breasts (perhaps not surprisingly) to noses to artificially elongated foreheads (figures 2.2, 2.3). The resultant photographs seem at first merely to invite laughter. In fact, so incisive a critic as Laura Mulvey suggests these images "lack the inexorability and complexity of her previous phase," and reads them primarily as efforts to draw attention "to the art-historical fetishization of great works and their value."[2]

Of course, such critique constitutes part of the photographs' agenda: how else to account for the attempt to stage – and to fall short of – the rich patina of oil in the glossy and superficial intransigence of the photograph? But the reason I begin with these photographs lies precisely in their break with the overtly "feminist," and all but decontextualized, career of the photographic image. If the "History Portraits" are not "inexorable" (a position that oddly privileges a linear clairvoyance), it is perhaps because they do not constitute a continued engagement with the problematics of the modern sex-gender system as defined solely within contemporary theories of gender and the gaze. Rather, these uncanny pictures offer a way to begin theorizing the historical beyond the flatness of canonical postmodern usage.[3]

As is well-known, Fredric Jameson has provided an influential account of the period construct that has come to be called postmodernism. In this account, Jameson places the subject of late capitalism in what is effectively a house of mirrors: "the postmodern" relates to the historical past primarily as a crucial absence, a loss which can be charted through, for example, architecture that knows and summons history only through a deracinated and eclectic citation of period style. If seen through this particular grid, Sherman's portraits are merely confirmations of that loss, reproductions of a pastness that cannot be inhabited and understood as the basis for meaningful political action, but only parodied.

I would not be the first to note that Jameson's model – or, for that matter, Jean Baudrillard's more anarchic version of the flight of significance – of postmodernity is totalizing, and so crucially blind to issues of power and representation attendant on non-hegemonic subjectivities. The evacuation of meaning from history that Jameson laments is far from total, and far as well from disabling. On the contrary, when history's master narratives of dominance and opposition (as Jameson recognizes them) both lose their cogency, heretofore marginalized subjects are afforded a space in which to produce an alternative critical understanding of past formations.

This space is the symbolic location of Sherman's photography. In contrast to Jamesonian despair and the loss of authenticity, or Baudrillardian glee and the play of surfaces, Sherman's imitations (forgeries?) of the past announce their false provenance, and so offer a critique of dominant art-historical narratives of subjectivity, embodiment, and gender. What they fake is the non-modern body and its *habitus*; in calling too much attention to the materiality of the signifier, her portraits, whose subject is "history," cannot but inflect the signified.

As a result, the history which Sherman is interested in staging is the imagined history of embodiment, which means that these representations are politicized, like her earlier work. But the "History Portraits" implicate the subject in ways other than the film simulacra had called forth. Sherman's earlier images, with all their suaveness, tended perhaps to duplicate the very ideal object they also critiqued. From the apparently truth-producing glamour of film, Sherman has moved to the recovery of mundane particularity, even ugliness, suppressed by the idealizing and aestheticizing work of Old Master painting. More overtly than ever before, her truck is with the embodied subject, perhaps even with the body "itself" – not merely as observed, but resolutely as constructed, as material historical artifact. Hence the rhetorical efficacy of prostheses, which remind the viewer that different cultural formations produce the apparent truth of the flesh. Hence, too, the gender variability of her subjects. The freedom Sherman affects in inhabiting male subjects as well as female suggests that the photographs work to make a problem of the apparently immutable sex-gender system of modernity that gave her earlier work its point. Apparently immutable because apparently factual: and here the question of medium and technology, both as deployed and as foregrounded, comes into play.

Oil paint works as part of an apparatus of "artistic" representation, and more obviously constructs its subject than the cold lens of the camera claims to do. Although the camera's title to objectivity is readily deconstructed, the photographic lens is the latest development in a technology whose history is successive reproductions of "the real." It seems useful, therefore, to stress the function of the lens within the ideology of scientific objectivity, especially in the lens' medicalized form as an instrument for inquiry into the deep, and so presumably determining, structures of the human body.[4] In a sense, the lens thus conceived competes with an older mode of social reproduction, the portrait in oils.

Although it seems perverse to juxtapose these two moments in the history of social reproduction on the one hand, and representation of images on the other, that is in effect what Sherman has done. Her (self-) portraits, especially those imitating Renaissance models, dramatize moments of discursive coalescence. But they also put those moments into question. Here, they seem at once to assert and deny, is staged the "birth of the individual"; here, too, is staged the "art" that stresses the "exceptional subject," either canonized by religious discourse (all those madonnas) or by bourgeois wealth (the brocaded profiles, for example).

But notice, too, that I suggested the "History Portraits" problematize these moments of formation; this also gets back to my suspensions of their status as self-portraits, a subject I will have more to say about later. Here, again, the prostheses enter in: their arrant artificiality, pre-posterous breasts on madonnas, bizarrely unlikely faces, remind us not just of the artifact that is the body in history, but of the symbolic violence that lies submerged just beneath the humanist call to identify our sub-jectivities with those depicted in "great art." In a sense, that act of inter-pellation effectively disembodies the subject who gazes – a tacit dematerialization that Sherman's inhabitations correct through their insistence on the priority of the body as signifier. Only through the grotesque self-distortion her prostheses represent, she seems to say, can we locate ourselves then and there.

Note that I used the word "seems": the question is whether there is any other way to get there, to read the past, to narrate relation without the collapse into identity. Sherman suggests the gap from here to there is not smoothly negotiated, that we bring along ourselves and our inter-pretive agendas, much as her camera intrudes on bodies meant only for oil. But I disagree with Mulvey in thinking these representations are avowals only of a body fetishism consequent upon loss, a position to which her theoretical engagement with Freud and Lacan enjoins her. After all, the technology of the lens, in providing – constructing – the clinical "truth" of the body, enables the body to be gendered by an all-determining relationship to the phallus, its presence or absence. Only under these historical circumstances does it make sense to think in terms of the female as fetish, at least as constructed within an accomplished theoretical position. The "History Portraits," with their plays at gender mutation, seem to assert that to read past acts of gendering one must also read against the grain of the present that they inevitably – inexorably? –

also must represent. In so doing, the portraits suggest that Sherman temporarily summons up a time-before: before the castrated woman, before the consolidated discourses of subjectivity and interiority, before the technologies of truth that she burlesques in her corporeal motility. A time, it may be said, before the dematerialized but self-knowing Cartesian subject, or the post-Freudian subject of lack, held full sway.

In fact, the dazzling and grotesque play of surface foregrounded by the prostheses accompanies some pretty evacuated faces – or faces, to put the case more usefully, whose task does not wholly seem to be to create the illusions of a rich interiority for public consumption. But this refusal to model a depth model of representation does not converge on another discourse of loss, a loss of the past, to which images devoid of presence constitute a desperate and fetishistic link: they are not, as I have already suggested, Jamesonian. After all, Sherman is there: owing to her prior work of self-representation, one might say her presence is recognizable *because* it is transformed, because, that is, her image foregrounds both the necessity of self-alienation and the inescapability of her present construction as a subject. Given that these photographs are nothing so simple as "self-portraits" – given, in fact, that their avowed sitter is "History" – they may not simply dramatize a ludicrous failure to intersect with the past. Instead, they are invitations (witty ones) to consider a way out of the canonical reconstruction of all species of history, which demands a seamless interpellation, an identity between past and present. As I have already suggested, it is just this structure of identification – which could also be termed exemplarity – that is the legacy of humanism institutionalized, which has determined how literary practitioners construct history.[5] Sherman's visual puns on anachronism, her overt forgeries of the subject of Renaissance painting, provoke the reader of Renaissance texts to consider the material freight of the past.

What the "History Portraits" offer in place of humanist identification is something akin to the Foucaultian project of genealogy. The past must be read as radically different from the present moment of reading; but equally that reading must always and overtly be compounded with all the categorical interests and investments that cannot but be brought to a retrospective hermeneutics.[6] In this light, it may be of interest that, with few exceptions, the styles Sherman imitates are not the works of Italian Renaissance masters. In denying herself the right (which is really a constraint) to inhabit the Mona Lisa, for example, Sherman broadens the horizon, extends what must be taken into account when we consider the hallowed and canonical representations of the past, the burnished exemplars of which hang on institutional walls, or gain familiarity through endless reproduction. And what must be taken into account, here, is corporeal difference, the intransigence of the material body that has since the early modern period been idealized and effectively shunted away from the multiple sites of engagement that determine the modern world.

Sherman provides a critical model for examining the legacy both of a humanist inscription of the past, and of an alternative model of past relation that can, for lack of a better term, be called proto-ethnographic – imaged, respectively, by her investment in art history, and her gleeful rendering of the social body as other. The models of pastness that her "History Portraits" play on share one important trait: whether exemplary or estranged, each constructs a past apprehensible because of a suppressed act of symbolic violence, one that has demanded an increasing disembodiment for its primary subject-positions. How that disembodiment is effected both within the exemplary philology of Renaissance humanism, and the materialized objectification of colonialism, remains to be seen.

THE PRIMITIVE PAST

The critical rediscovery of the body as site of representation and theory, which Sherman's stills have highlighted, curves back to the second set of images, the engravings done by Theodor de Bry (from watercolors by John White) for Thomas Harriot's *A Briefe and True Report of the New Found Land of Virginia*. One of these images shows a *weroan*, or leader, of the Algonkians (figure 2.4); the second, an equivalent representation of a Pict, the authority for which is "assured in an oolld English cronicle" (figure 2.5).[7] Like the other tribal embodiments of English antiquity to be found in de Bry's images, the Pict is appended to Harriot's *Report* on North America in order to compare one place and another. The captions aid in this project, explicitly linking the Indian to the Pict, yet simplifying the complex, and contradictory, representational codes operating in the engravings by recasting them as the ideological propositions of early modernity. The barbarity of the early British is very much to the point, as the text avers, "for to showe how the Inhabitants of the great Bretannie have bin in times past as savage as those of Virginia" (p. 75). And, if anything, the Pict could be deemed even more savage than his New World counterpart, given the trophies of decapitation he brandishes. Further, the extensive body-decoration he sports in lieu of cloth-

Figure 2.1 "Untitled" (History Portrait, no. 224), Cindy Sherman (1990).

Figure 2.2 "Untitled" (History Portrait, no. 225), Cindy Sherman (1990).

Figure 2.3 "Untitled" (History Portrait, no. 211), Cindy Sherman (1990).

A weroan or great Lorde of Virginia. III.

He Princes of Virginia are attyred in fuche manner as is expreffed in this figure. They weare the haire of their heades long and bynde opp the ende of thefame in a knot vnder thier eares. Yet they cutt the topp of their heades from the forehead to the nape of the necke in manner of a cokfcombe, ftirkinge a faier lóge pecher of fome berd att the Begininge of the crefte vppun their foreheads, and another fhort one on bothe feides about their eares. They hange at their eares ether thicke pearles, or fomwhat els, as the clawe of fome great birde, as cometh in to their fanfye. Moreouer They ether pownes, or paynt their forehead, cheeks, chynne, bodye, armes, and leggs, yet in another forte then the inhabitantz of Florida. They weare a chaine about their necks of pearles or beades of copper, wich they muche efteeme, and ther of wear they alfo brafelets ohn their armes. Vnder their brefts about their bellyes appeir certayne fpotts, whear they vfe to lett them felues bloode, when they are ficke. They hange before thē the fkinne of fome beafte verye feinelye dreffet in fuche forte, that the tayle hangēth downe behynde. They carye a quiuer made of fmall rufhes holding their bowe readie bent in on hand, and an arrowe in the other, radie to defend themfelues. In this manner they goe to warr, or tho their folemne feafts and banquetts. They take muche pleafure in huntinge of deer wher of theris great ftore in the contrye, for yt is fruit full, pleafant, and full of Goodly woods. Yt hathe alfo ftore of riuers full of diuers forts of fifhe. When they go to battel they paynt their bodyes in the moft terible manner that thei can deuife.

Figure 2.4 *Weroan or Great Lorde of Virginia*. Theodor de Bry's engraving in Thomas Harriot's *A Briefe and True Report of the New Found Land of Virginia* (1590).

Figure 2.5 *The True Picture of One Picte.* Theodor de Bry's engraving in Thomas Harriot's *A Briefe and True Report of the New Found Land of Virginia* (1590).

ing renders him in some ways "exotic," more estranged from the bodily decorum of the late Renaissance, than the comparatively modest daubings and drapings of the Algonkian.[8]

Despite the apparent clarity of the historical reasoning he embodies, this fantastic English native delivers a mixed message to late Renaissance consumers of the *Report* – as well as to latter-day viewers of the work of Cindy Sherman. Although the Pict is brought in as a proximate avatar for the precursors of the English race, his temporal distance from any site of contemporary reading seems as significant as the common ground upon which he is purported to stand. The opposite is true for the Algonkian: while he shares the temporal frame of those who might gaze upon his reproduced image, he is distanced as much by the status of primitivism attributed to his culture as by geography. Seen from the vantage of the seventeenth century, the English "then" – when savage Picts were the prime inhabitants of Britain – becomes the (North) American "now," and the comparison one of time as much as of space. One might contrast this representation of the English self as formerly other, barbaric, with an alternative, even classical, model of Englishness. As Spenser and others demonstrated, this history could be imaged by a literary pedigree that extended straight from the Trojan Brutus to the Renaissance English.[9] These competing exemplars of past humanity, the quasi-classical and the quasi-ethnographic, begin to hint that the past is made, not found – manufactured according to ideological interests.

The early modern illustrations for Harriot's *Report* convert alien beings into evidence, render cultural difference available for assessment, at the same moment that the contemporary European male body is exempted from scrutiny and removed, in and by theory, to the site at which the possibility of assessment is contemplated. De Bry's versions of the drawings by White provide no depiction that commemorates European interactions with the inhabitants they observe, no place that the Algonkian can be seen to share with the contemporary English explorer. It is as if the explorers, in contemplating their relation to the Virginians, occupy no space at all.[10]

The temporal opposition set up by the illustrations to Harriot's *Report* constructs complex resemblances over both time and geography. When the salient, specific aspects of the latter come to be seen as "space," there has occurred an evacuation of the local and contingent. An isomorphism develops between the manner in which the alien landscape of Virginia becomes both domesticated and universalized, and the regularizing of the material world. Correspondingly, the agenda that underwrites the juxtaposition seems familiarly, because universalizingly, ethnographic: two images – concepts – are put together, the better to establish a relational link between them. Printing the Pict after the Algonkian suggests that radically differing bodies have become equivalents. The sign of that equation is the conventional, highly stylized musculature both images share. By extension, the cultures they inhabit are brought into an equivalent narrative space.[11] But not, of course, to argue for anything like a cultural equivalence in the here-and-now of contemporary reading, since the juxtaposed illustrations use an ideologically loaded notion of temporality to deny the non-European specificity of the Virginia Indian, and to reposition him in relation to European history. Their common musculature is, after all, coded through the European aesthetic tradition. If the differences between the one and the other, Pict and Algonkian, are both made and reduced to the visible by these engravings, then difference is a matter of time. "Time" must therefore mean something new – at once a measure of linear regularity, and a guarantor of relation even where no prior train, of geography, nationality, or other form of consequence, exists.[12]

Oddly, then, relation and alterity are two sides of the same emergent modern formation. As the anthropologist Johannes Fabian has noted, "what could be clearer evidence of temporal distancing than placing the Now of the primitive in the Then of the Western adult?"[13] Although Fabian is speaking of ethnography as an accomplished, post-Enlightenment epistemology, his words also illuminate the hidden presumptions that inform colonialist discourse almost from its onset. The images of the Algonkians consolidate "Englishness" – and, by extension, Europeanness – at the same time they appear to embrace a universalizing narrative of development. That the consolidation of identity is achieved by a recourse to alterity marks the *Report* as a proto-modern document. The twin assertions of distance and relatedness offered by words and pictures propose a Foucaultian conjunction of power and knowledge: this early modern modeling of history is not the pliant and playful "rehearsal" of culture for which the Renaissance has been a recent referent, but the making of one culture through the expenditure of another.[14] During the period I am considering, the present-time of Europe is valorized by such ideological distancing, by such narratives of parallel but unequal development in New World and Old. This use of temporality has much in common with the reinscription of classical time performed by earlier Renaissance humanists, as this essay will go on to suggest. But unlike that other backward-looking formation, this protoenthnographic past lacks the strategic authority of maturity. The absence of a sophisticated present, inevitably configured as advantage, is one mechanism through which modernity is produced.

FORGERY, IDENTITY, AND HUMANIST HISTORY

In order to highlight the ideological effect of a primitivizing past constituted by the *Report*, I want to spend some time examining the model of human history with which it partly competes: the text-based classical past of Renaissance humanism. The phrase designates a complex, even contradictory formation, which encompasses, for example, theories and practices of pedagogy, citizenship, and religion, and an elite bureaucracy that prefigures the class of modern humanities scholars. Obviously, then, a summary account of humanism would be impossible here, although the various theoretical and practical operations I have listed necessarily inflect the discursive field I am about to map out. I offer what follows in the nature of a selective epitome. As a schematic redaction, it seeks to tease out of humanism its ideology of the past – of what may be at stake when early modern European culture constitutes itself against the authority of classical antiquity.

My argument here both reaffirms and recasts one canonical description of Renaissance humanism: that it saw the emergence of what can be called historical consciousness, which is (to describe it reductively) a consciousness that the past was different from the present, and that certain consequences follow from that position.[15] By granting the importance of historicism to the formation of humanism, it becomes possible to acknowledge the ideological valence of humanist philology, its assertion that classical texts are repositories of social value. Humanist reading and writing are crucial evaluative activities, crucial as well to forming the early modern (male, European) subject. When a humanist scholar reproduces, imitates, annotates, or merely studies Roman rhetoricians and Greek poets, he in effect identifies with them to assume their virtues as a function of their language, and so models his subjectivity in relation to theirs.

Such a structure of identification with the past has proven problematic, as my initial discussion of Cindy Sherman's postmodern historiography has already suggested. Indeed, the humanistic identification with the past makes homologous signification a privileged bridge to bygone mentalities: as valorized by humanist philology, the knowledge of classical Greek and, especially, Latin, collapsed the temporal distance separ-

ating the recuperated texts of Greece and Rome from the vernacular
culture of Europe. To put it more simply, humanist learning replaced the
distance of time with the contiguity of language. The closer a text could
get to Cicero's Latin the better, even to the point of parodic contortion –
as Erasmus' *Ciceronianus*, a satire against the many slavish imitators of
Cicero who would only use the verb *tenses* to be found in the master,
demonstrated to witty effect.[16]

A less drastically mimetic example is provided by Petrarch, who is
generally designated the first Renaissance humanist, and so provides a
useful exemplar of humanist practice. When he collected his familiar
letters together in imitation of Cicero, he included "epistles" to such
classical authors as Horace, Livy, and Quintilian, as well as the inevitable
Tully. Such a collocation made the Italian poet's letters a site for the
invention of "familiar" consciousness – the conversation, if not of
coevals, than of folk who by virtue of a common language have a lot in
common. In one letter to a contemporary, in fact, Petrarch insists that
"Cicero" himself has wounded him grievously – Cicero, that is, person-
ified by a volume of his texts, which has fallen from a shelf and bruised
the poet's leg.[17] The conceit – clearly a jest – nevertheless participates in
consolidating an important truth: in Petrarch's phantasmatic collection
of letters to contemporaries and ancients, the correspondence that for
Foucault in *The Order of Things* was the epistemic foundation of the
Renaissance appears to govern the erasure of diachronicity.
Resemblance is both the order of, and the ordering of, the day.[18]

Even the quickened interest in exposing (and manufacturing) forgeries
characteristic of Renaissance philology arose out of a complex attempt
to re-create, reinhabit, the past through linguistic and historical knowledge. In this regard, consider Lorenzo Valla's argument that the so-
called "Donation of Constantine" – a document that ceded Roman
imperial lands to the Papacy – was a fake, based on the humanist's
authoritative dissection of the Latin. Valla's treatise betrays an exquisite
and scholarly sense of the mendacity, the will to deceive, that lies behind
a telltale linguistic anachronism. As a historiographer of language, Valla
appears to be everything that Petrarch is not – distanced, measured, far
from enraptured with the encrustations of past time. Yet his predication
of late antiquity as a time of authentic difference, whose signification
could be known and understood, makes his treatise not so very different
from Petrarch's familiar letters, and the fiction of immediacy they
suggest.[19]

Seen with a slightly different turn of the lens, Petrarch's epistles offer the same recuperation of loss that a forger attempts to remedy. After all, most modern inscriptions of the past, whether in material or discursive practice, are involved with concepts that forgery particularly fore-grounds: knowledge, authenticity, identification, the accuracy of a his-torical empathy. Anthony Grafton has written accordingly that Renaissance forgery arose, not simply to question or defend territorial or property rights, but also to give rein to a more complex nostalgia for the productions of the past:

> [Forgery] aimed above all at recreating a past even more to the taste of modern readers and scholars than was the real antiquity recovered by historical scholar-ship. Many of the early recorders of monuments and inscriptions filled in missing texts in their notebooks just as they would the missing limbs and heads of statues, moved by an exuberant desire to see the ruined past made whole again.[20]

When the fake artifact from the fake past is exposed, certainly it may also expose the impoverished or incomplete technique of any individual forger, owing to such factors as the defaults of technology; hence Valla's scholarly ease of detection. But the failed forgery is more generally reve-latory, since it more generally discloses crucial limitations of historicist thinking. Rather than think of forgeries as an aberrancy, a corruption of an otherwise stable system of truth and value, perhaps they are an inevitable consequence of the desire to enter into and partake of the past that systematically emerges in the early modern period. What I have pre-viously termed humanist history, for instance, effaces the signs of its con-tingent production, the better to provide an exemplary and convincing rendition of a remote time, of a past into which a reader can insert himself because the historian – like the successful forger – already has done so.[21] The moment when the historical narrative fails to sustain (and so needs augmentation or supplanting) is not unlike the moment when the forgery is exposed: a crucial lack is opened up, an absence of identification and sympathetic imagination – or of conviction shared as readily and as naturally by those who consume the past as those who instantiate it.

Thus Renaissance forger and humanist critic were often the same person. The careful scholar who argued for the inauthenticity of one document might well author one much like it – taken, this time, by con-temporary readers to be a work of classical antiquity. Grafton has spoken of a (non-Freudian?) nostalgia for "wholeness" betrayed in the repair of statuary and the filling-in of historical blanks. Yet this apparently indiscriminate desire to reconstitute the whole is perhaps not as self-evident as his words make it appear, not merely a desire to reverse the iconoclasms of time. The present of Renaissance humanism is apparently permeable to the past, bespeaking not so much Grafton's "exuberance" as an incomplete – emergent – sense that historical separation was a definitive constituent of modern ideology. Seen from this position humanism becomes a willed oblivion to the conditions of historical difference, which becomes rearticulated in the familiar universalist ideologies of "liberal" humanism.[22]

In fact, the connection between the humanism of the Renaissance and its later, Enlightenment, avatar is not far to seek. The latter version of humanism materially imbricated in the overt imperialism of the European nation-state, the voluntary (inter) nationality of linguistic isomorphism among Renaissance humanists led them to constitute themselves as a different sort of political federation, a *res publica litterarum*. Although a state without material borders, in effect a state of mind, this republic of letters comprised an elite citizenry with a certain type of literacy – a skill in reading, inhabiting, and reproducing the texts of classical antiquity – that prefigures the systematic education provided to indigenous peoples by later colonial bureaucracies. Most importantly, the imitative practices so important to Renaissance humanism – the effacing of temporal and geographical remoteness in the name of a universally apprehensible language, like classical Latin – underwrite an ideology of the basic similitude among "men," whose infinite glory and upwardly mobile intellects were therefore to be celebrated. Of course, the sign of "man" is only a universal in pretense. As Juliana Schiesari has shrewdly observed in a recent essay, "Humanism's praise of the 'dignity of man' appears predicated upon the abjection of what it considers the 'non-human.'"[23] Men, both ancient and modern, whose sense of human history and possibility was forged through Latin and Greek were the privileged subjects of humanism: all others – artisans, women, the inhabitants of non-European countries – need not apply. Much follows from that exclusion.

THE LADY VANISHES: THE RENAISSANCE PAST AND THE PROBLEMATICS OF GENDER

One thing that distinguishes Renaissance humanism from its later formations is the comparative humility of its practitioners in the face of classical knowledge. Although their culure is enriched because it has

annexed the intellectual property (what may be termed anachronistically the cultural capital) of Greece and Rome, Renaissance humanists initially conceived of themselves as the junior branches of this
incorporated culture. In an epistle to Homer, Petrarch positions himself
literally as the *infans*, deprived of language, eager for nourishment: "Yet
it is with me as with a baby: I love to babble with those who feed me, even
though they are skilled masters of speech."[24] According to the logic of
generation and development that informs Petrarch's response, classical
antiquity represents the maturity of European – which is to say all –
civilization. The moment from which the Italian humanist speaks is the
product of that maturity, but a juvenile one: the difference in sophistication – development – between his present and the past of Cicero and
Homer is represented by a familial cultivation of speech that serves as a
domestication of humanist philological practice.

   Yet the humility to which I have referred does not represent the whole
picture. Nor could it, if we remember the project of de Bry's illustrations, which valorize present-day Europe over the primitive past of the
native inhabitants. What remains to emerge in modernity is the value of
contemporaneity, the worth of the present moment. Contrast Petrarch's
touching faith in the benign authority of his classical *patres* with the
rather more dismissive characterization of antiquity articulated by
Francis Bacon: in his Preface to *The Great Instauration* (1620), Bacon speaks
of "the wisdom . . . derived principally from the Greeks [that] is but like
the boyhood of knowledge, and has the characteristic property of boys:
it can talk, but it cannot generate, for it is fruitful of controversies but
barren of works."[25] The Baconian quotation inverts the familialism of
Petrarch, and seems to put in question the status of philology as a basis of
knowledge. Classical antiquity is not the parent of the present moment,
but instead its infancy, and authoritative eloquence as the generator of
culture is reduced to unproductive childish prattle.

   Bacon's dismissal of texts as repositories of knowledge is, of course, a
corollary of his empiricist project for the rehabilitation of learning. His
preference for the "generative" powers of the present marks him (in R. F.
Jones' influential formulation) as a "Modern" rather than an "Ancient,"
and an originary figure for the emergence of modern scientific ideologies.[26] Hence the proto-ethnography of Harriot and the proto-empiri-
cism of Bacon betoken in nascent form the study of "man" and
"nature," whose accomplished projects and institutions are recognizable
components of the Enlightenment and after. When Bacon valorizes the
productive capacities of the modern European, he echoes the narrative

of development offered by the colonial illustrations. Thus is mapped out the insistent yet fragmentary "modernity" of canonical science.

Both Bacon and Harriot offer important hints for thinking about how the past becomes deprivileged, becomes but one object of study among many in the modern faculty of disciplines. In imaging that past as embryonic, insufficient, these texts suggest that the classical interpellation of the humanist subject must compete with, and be complemented by, a distinctively presentist subjectivity. But a curious ellipsis, most visible in Petrarch's simile, binds together the three (otherwise discrete) instances I have introduced here. What happens to gender when the speakers and feeders, the sources of language and knowledge, are the writers of classical authority, as they are for Petrarch? Or are reduced to impotent boys in Bacon's version of humanism? How is modernity produced as a consequence of a polarity between the supreme male European subject, whether forward- or backward-looking, and the others against which it launches itself?

Petrarch's comparison of himself to a baby in need of speech and food – both are coextensive – would seem, in its cozy familialism, to demand a maternal presence. Such a presence, however, is unlikely in the text-based formation that he inhabits, for more than the historical fact that comparatively few Renaissance women had access to humanist education. Although it is too simple to say that Petrarch's ideal family contains no place for the female because it is an ideal family, a disembodied one, this formulation comes close to describing the status of the feminine. To the extent that questions of gender arise in the production of humanist subjects, they provide a tacit substrate, a quasi-material ground of discourse. Hence the unexpected contiguity between the humanist's narrative of family development and the less domestic one enacted within Harriot's text. In both cases, the idealizing formation of the early modern subject must do its work in relation to those who for reasons of difference are debarred from the project.

Debarred – but not banished. As we have seen in the case of the Algonkian, alterity has its uses for the manufacture of emergent modernity. The same may be said regarding the phantasms of woman in texts like Petrarch's and Bacon's. In fact, the question may be whether there is a relationship between the body of the woman (as over against the body of the Algonkian) and the humanist corpus. Humanism, as a deliberate political culture, achieves legitimacy through imagining a continuity with classical Greece or Rome that suppresses the fact of historical difference (consider the erasure of the Middle Ages). This suppression

then models a more general strategy of domestication available for the
institution and maintenance of humanist subjectivity. Thus one critically occluded term in Renaissance humanism, and in emergent modernity as well, is the female body, as Petrarch attests. The argument can be
extended further, into the very constitution of the humanist educational
program. As Stephanie Jed has argued in her study of humanist interest
in the legend of Lucretia, a reading program based in the classics can
constitute a form of symbolic violence to the subject gendered female.[27]
The violence is both denied and reproduced, as Jed suggests, by the
reiterated dissemination of texts in the Renaissance – when, time and
again, the story of Brutus and the founding of Rome is related as
foundational for Renaissance polity, for which the rape of Lucretia
becomes merely a pretext, a vehicle. Indeed, a gruesome story recounted
by Anthony Grafton offers further suggestive evidence of humanism's
gender trouble. At the same time that the texts of Cicero were being
rediscovered and reproduced, the perfectly preserved remains of his
daughter Tulliola were, apparently, often themselves "discovered," again
and again for more than a century, at gravesites all over Italy.[28] Grafton
offers no further elaboration. Nevertheless, it is tempting to speculate on
the efficacy of these female bodies as found relics for humanism, as
material counterparts for the work done by the endlessly reproduced,
endlessly defiled Lucretia.

Obviously, no sort of innocence can be claimed as characteristic of
humanist immediacy, in contrast to a proto-colonialist distance whose
dominating effect has been widely recognized. Jed's work usefully reposi-
tions humanism's self-articulation, and shows how its collapsing of the
distinction between past and present does ideological work in reproducing familiar structures of domination: witness the unhappy proliferation of Tulliolas. It is useful to compare the multiplication of female
bodies in humanism proper with the rather different discourse of the
feminine accomplished within Baconian science. In *The Advancement of
Learning*, for instance, the relationship between man and nature is explicitly an erotic congress, separated from what is "empty and void," the
better to produce "solid and fruitful" speculations: "that knowledge may
not be as a courtesan, for pleasure and vanity only, or as a bond-woman,
to acquire and gain to her master's use, but as a spouse, for generation,
fruit, and comfort."[29] Here, the oppositional structures of modernity
reveal what is produced by the tropes of normative heterosexuality
within modern science. Only through their erasures from the scene can
Lucretia and Tulliola testify to the male legacy of humanism; the

Baconian program, however, uses the image of fruitful marriage to legitimate its knowledge-seeking agenda, an image that seems at first to
suggest the necessary (if, of course, inferior) company of women. Yet the
text's summoning of the scientific subject to marriage with "knowledge"
offers merely the tropological appearance of inclusion. Women – and
others – may figure "differently," may appear to constitute an element in
the universal project of science; here, too, they become the matter to be
worked upon, assimilated, domesticated.

BODY LANGUAGE

As the Petrarchan quotation indicates, the Renaissance discourse of
humanism speaks soothingly of family ties, of a fantasy of intellectual
nurture in which traditions of gender play no part. The contrast provided by Caliban is well-known: that thing of darkness is taught language in order to know and curse the great Italian father who can barely
acknowledge his complicity in the formation of the slave's consciousness.
The question of language is thus overtly and crudely political – most
critically, perhaps, insofar as it constructs past times in relation to the
present, sees prior temporality in terms of a linear, organic development.
How is the past reprocessed, how does the emergent modernity of late
Renaissance culture renegotiate its parental thrall to classical antiquity?
How did the past come to be undomesticated? The answer, as I have
already suggested, requires an other – an other, whether Algonkian or
feminine, excluded from the full range of humanist subject-positions
because excluded from the signifying process. In that all-defining regard,
the *Report*'s illustrated man is not much different from the female corpses
Renaissance archaeologists called Tulliola. By virtue of their muteness,
each is delimited by the brute fact of embodiment, or else incorporated
through reduction to mere tropological convenience.

    As an experiment in ethnography before the fact, the *Report* competes
with, indeed, comes to supplement as the discourse of the scientific, the
reproduction of the past associated with humanism to which I have
already alluded. There, notions of antecedence are imbued with and
conveyed by textual presence. Classical antiquity speaks to the
Renaissance humanist through a language of contiguity ideologized as
transparent to its origins, while the native, whose linguistic competence
defies humanist philology and therefore defines its limits, is spoken by his
body, his customs, rather than his textual traces. In fact, the "textless-
ness" of native peoples renders them the readier for absorption into a

universalizing narrative of human development. As Samuel Purchas has written, men wanting the "Use of letters and Writing" are "esteemed Brutish, Savage, Barbarous."[30] And, consequently, ephemeral:

by speech we utter our minds once, as the present, to the present . . . but by writing Man seemes immortall, conferreth and consulteth with the Patriarks, Prophets, Apostles, Fathers, Philosophers, Historians, and learnes the wisdome of the Sages which have been in all times before him; yea by translations or learning the Languages, in all places and regions of the World . . .[31]

Purchas' version of humanism extends the temporal mastery of the Renaissance subject by means of the material canonical text. But the lack of such texts places the Algonkian in a temporal suspension, a time without a prior inscription, an evacuated space that can then be reconfigured to suit the ideological needs of European proto-modernism. Like Cicero's daughter, he must be understood by corporeal analogy, by the representation and examination of his body. Indeed, the comparative scarcity of women-authored texts from the early modern period has until recently provided a distant recasting of Algonkian silence. Since women, by and large, were not considered significant (in the full sense of that term) participants in the projects both of Renaissance humanism and modernity, to study "women" was to be forced into valorizing the apparitional, the specular. Hence the early versions of feminist inquiry that could only seek for images of women – versions of the female circumscribed within the hegemonic, humanist project of Man. To demonstrate how different a postmodern, feminist historiography might look from those versions of the past authorized by hegemonic is, at least in part, the project for which Sherman's "History Portraits" can be used.

The passes at ethnography represented by the engravings imagine how the antique might be reprocessed under the sign of an emergent modernity, to be hypothesized as in need of domestication in discourse. So differential a reading of the past, which might be understood as an allegory of origins for the human sciences, is enabled by its encounter with alterity. In the recently translated book *The Writing of History*, the late Michel de Certeau asserts that the structure of modern Western culture is heterological, which is to say a discourse of the other. The "intelligibility" of this modern culture "is established through a relation with the other [that] moves (or 'progresses') by changing what it makes" there.[32] The modernity with which I have been concerned demands a past against which to reinvent itself, a "silent corpse" whose muteness is the precondition of historical discourse. Thus the body of the

Algonkian, which expresses itself through its physicality, and hence is metonymous for the object that cannot be heard to speak itself, identify itself, is one place to consider what has been silenced and effaced.

But another, rather different place, is provided by Cindy Sherman's "History Portraits." As these photographs suggest in all their energetic and grotesque perversity, history in the time of postmodernity has begun to betray our investment in it, has begun to let that long-silent corpse speak, snigger, mock our official accounts. The past may indeed be pro-logue – but it may also, inevitably, be a parody of the present. As I have earlier suggested, forgery functions as the mirror image of humanist history, which is to say historicism as it has generally been practiced. As if through a distorted glass, forgery shows us the hopes and desires of histo-rians who, since the Renaissance emergence of the discipline, have wanted access to the past "as it really was," to provide an authoritative because truly representative rendering of bygone affairs, events, persons, texts.

Sherman's pictures are anything but such forgeries, and so are any-thing but historiography played straight. Again and again, they raise the issue of originals and imitations, of true and false, only to dismiss them as ludicrous, as deceptive manifestations of a will to assimilate the past, mistaken both in its predication and its pretense of universal knowledge. What the "History Portraits" offer instead is a clamorous reappropria-tion of the canonical past, wholly suitable for postmodern feminist work in the Renaissance. In showing how that past was made, they also show how it can be made different.

NOTES

1 These are a series of more than thirty images made between 1988 and 1990, according to Thomas Kellein, "How Difficult are Portraits? How Difficult are People!," in *Cindy Sherman 1991*, Thomas Kellein, ed. (Kunsthalle Basel, 1991), p. 10.

2 Laura Mulvey, "A Phantasmagoria of the Female Body: The Work of Cindy Sherman," *New Left Review* 188 (July/August 1991): 137–50; the passage cited is from p. 147.

3 See Fredric Jameson, *Postmodernism, or, The Cultural Logic of Late Capitalism* (Durham: Duke University Press, 1991); Jean Baudrillard, "The Ecstasy of Communication," in *The Anti-Aesthetic: Essays on Postmodern Culture*, Hal Foster, ed. (Seattle: Bay Press, 1983), pp. 126–34. For a critique of Jamesonian postmodernism that echoes mine in its attentiveness to feminist art practice, and that deftly argues for its suspicion that such postmodernism conceals "a regret at the passing of the fantasy of the male self" (p. 243), see

Jacqueline Rose, "*The Man Who Mistook His Wife for a Hat* or *A Wife Is Like an Umbrella* – Fantasies of the Modern and Postmodern," in *Universal Abandon? The Politics of Postmodernism*, Andrew Ross, ed. (Minneapolis: University of Minnesota Press, 1988), pp. 237–50.

4 See Ludmilla Jordanova, *Sexual Visions: Images of Gender in Science and Medicine Between the Eighteenth and Twentieth Centuries* (Madison: University of Wisconsin Press, 1989); and Barbara Maria Stafford, *Body Criticism: Imaging the Unseen in Enlightenment Art and Medicine* (Cambridge, MA: MIT Press, 1992).

5 This characterization of literary history obviously leaves out the recent practices of new historicism and cultural materialism. Each of these has rendered problematic traditional (i.e., humanistic) narratives by inserting marginalized knowledges and forms into its accounts of early modernity. However, neither practice has offered an extensive analysis of the modes and institutions by means of which Renaissance humanism became an aspect of the dominant political culture.

6 See Michel Foucault, "Two Lectures" in *Power/Knowledge: Selected Interviews and Other Writings 1972–1977*, Colin Gordon, ed., trans. Colin Gordon, Leo Marshall, John Mepham, Kate Soper (New York: Pantheon, 1980), pp. 78–108.

7 Thomas Harriot, *A Briefe and True Report of the New Found Land of Virginia* (1590), introduction by Paul Hulton (New York: Dover, 1972), p. 75.

8 On the other hand, this may be the epidermal version of Elizabethan sumptuary laws – a displaced aristocratic body whose very extravagance of decoration confirms the racial superiority of the early British. I owe this point to discussions with Leonard Tennenhouse.

9 Richard Helgerson's recent book, *Forms of Nationhood: The Elizabethan Writing of England* (Chicago: University of Chicago Press, 1992), offers a more complicated account of the scripting of national consciousness in Renaissance England; he isolates a functional dialectic between antiquity and the Middle Ages as models for the narratives constituting the state.

10 Consider the complementary negotiation of history in those Renaissance collections called "wonder-cabinets." In the prototypical wonder-cabinet, the classical past of Renaissance humanism is seen as coextensive with its fragmentary material trace and compacted into it, and installed in a space of equivalence with the evidentiary oddments of colonial ventures and proto-scientific ambitions. When thus denatured and set within this purview, "the past," so constructed, is clearly less a source of authority than a demystified relic, an object of curiosity rather than a site of primary investment. "Antiquities" are not antiquity, and what is to be learnt from them is not identity, but perhaps "history," in the modern sense of the term.

    Collections of the sort I have been describing, however, insist increasingly on the past as a complex production: certainly the past is partly the familiarity of classicism, but it is also partly reconfigured as the exotic, the primitive, the curious. The ever greater number of "other" objects in the wonder-cabinet allows for the possibility that the primary humanist model of the classical past has been deaccessioned, changed over from the source of authorizing value to an object of study among many. The juxtaposition of classical fragments with the signs of modernity, as configured by globes, lenses, microscopes, and botanical specimens, reproduces a moment of flux, where dominant forms of apprehending European culture compete with those in emergence.

11 The genealogical connection between the illustrations is suggested (although not problematized) by Stephen Orgel in his edition of *The Tempest* (Oxford and New York: Oxford University Press, 1987), pp. 34–35.

12 I should here note that in general sixteenth- and seventeenth-century discussions of the inhabitants of the Americas speak of them as savages, rather than, strictly speaking, as "primitives." Apprehension of the other took place through a hypothesized privation from civilization, which had its benign form in fantasies of the "Golden World," where, as Pietro Martire insisted, "there is no mine and thine . . . ." For a further discussion of the proto-primitive, see Hayden White, "The Forms of Wildness: Archaeology of an Idea," in *Tropics of Discourse: Essays in Cultural Criticism* (Baltimore and London: Johns Hopkins University Press, 1978), pp. 150–82.

13 Johannes Fabian, *Time and the Other: How Anthropology Makes Its Object* (New York: Columbia University Press, 1983), p. 63.

14 I am alluding to Steven Mullaney's deft, influential, and problematic account of wonder-cabinets and, by extension, other productions of alterity and science in the English Renaissance; see *The Place of The Stage: License, Play, and Power in Renaissance England* (Chicago: University of Chicago Press, 1988), pp. 60–87. For a trenchant critique of Mullaney's description of the wonder-cabinet as filled with "things on holiday," see Amy Boesky, "'Outlandish-Fruits': Commissioning Nature for the Museums of Man," *English Literary History* 58 (1991): 305–30.

15 Eugenio Garin, *Italian Humanism: Philosophy and Civic Life in the Renaissance*, trans. Peter Munz (New York: Harper and Row, 1965). Although Anthony Grafton, in *Forgers and Critics: Creativity and Duplicity in Western Scholarship* (Princeton: Princeton University Press, 1990), has argued that both forgery and scholarship give evidence of historical consciousness as a historical constant, he acknowledges that the apprehension of the past acquires a different inflection in the Renaissance. For a documentation of Garin's thesis, see Peter Burke, *The Renaissance Sense of the Past* (New York: St. Martin's Press, 1969).

16 Erasmus, *Dialogus Ciceronianus*, Pierre Mesnard, ed., in *Opera Omnia*, 2 vols. (Amsterdam: North Holland Publishing Company, 1971), vol. I.2 especially pp. 624–30. See also Francis Bacon, *The Advancement of Learning, Book I*, in *Francis Bacon: A Selection of His Works*, Sidney Warhaft, ed. (New York: Odyssey Press, 1965), p. 223.

17 *De rebus familiaribus* XXI.10, to Neri Morando; in *Letters from Petrarch*, selected and trans. Morris Bishop (Bloomington: Indiana University Press, 1966), pp. 170–71.

18 Michel Foucault, *The Order of Things: An Archaeology of the Human Sciences*, a translation of *Les mots et les choses* (New York: Random House, 1970), pp. 3–45.

19 See Anthony Grafton, ed., *Rome Reborn: The Vatican Library and Renaissance Culture* (Washington, DC: Library of Congress, in association with the Biblioteca Apostolica Vaticana [Rome], 1993), pp. 112–15.

20 Grafton, *Forgers and Critics*, p. 26.

21 For a revealing analysis of forgeries from a sociological and curatorial perspective, see Mark Jones, with Paul Craddock and Nicholas Barkers, eds., *Fake? The Art of Deception* (London: British Museum, 1990).

22 Although the terms Renaissance humanism and liberal humanism have been used as effectively interchangeable by cultural materialist critics like Catherine Belsey and Jonathan Dollimore, much historical work remains to be done examining the transition from one to the other. Lisa Jardine and Anthony Grafton, in *From Humanism to the Humanities* (Cambridge, MA: Harvard University Press, 1986), offer some valuable hints about the shape of the argument in examining the institutionalization of humanism. The role of, for example, John Locke and the British empiricists would also have to be added to the account of emergent universals I offer here, as would a notion of symbolic economies.

23 Juliana Schiesari, "The Face of Domestication: Physiognomy, Gender Politics, and Humanism's Others," in *Women, "Race," and Writing in the Early Modern Period*, Margo Hendricks and Patricia Parker, eds. (London: Routledge, 1994), pp. 55–70. The quotation appears on p. 70.

24 From *De rebus familiaribus* XXIV.12, in *Petrarch's Letters to Familiar Authors*, trans. Mario Cosenza (Chicago: University of Chicago Press, 1910).

25 See preface to *The Great Instauration* in Bacon, *Francis Bacon*, Warhaft, ed., pp. 302–03.

26 R. F. Jones, *Ancients and Moderns: A Study of the Rise of the Scientific Movement in Seventeenth-Century England*, 2nd edn (1961; rpt. New York: Dover, 1982).

27 Stephanie Jed, in *Chaste Thinking: The Rape of Lucretia and the Birth of Humanism* (Bloomington: Indiana University Press, 1989), speaks of the ideological division between Lucretia's "'violated body' and her 'innocent mind'" (p. 13) as productive in separating philology from the political and the historical. This division has implications for literature as a transcendent category, as something apart from (eccentric to?) the main political work of modern Western culture, defined as the reproduction of "liberty."

28 Grafton, *Forgers and Critics*, pp. 26–28.

29 Bacon, *Francis Bacon*, Warhaft, ed., pp. 235–36. The classic account of Baconian gender is Carolyn Merchant, *The Death of Nature: Women, Ecology, and the Scientific Revolution* (San Francisco: Harper and Row, 1980). Since the publication of Merchant's book, the complex relationships between science and gender have been widely discussed. See, among many other sources: Nancy Tuana, ed., *Feminism and Science* (Bloomington: Indiana University Press, 1989); Sandra Harding, *Whose Science? Whose Knowledge?* (Ithacca:

Cornell University Press, 1991); and Page DuBois, "Subjected Bodies, Science, and the State: Francis Bacon, Torturer," in *Body Politics: Disease, Desire, and the Family*, Michael Ryan and Avery Gordon, eds. (Boulder: Westview Press, 1994), pp. 175–91.

30 Samuel Purchas, from *Hakluytus Posthumus, or Purchas his Pilgrimes* 20 vols. (Glasgow: James McLehose and Sons, 1905), vol. I, p. 486; as quoted by Stephen Greenblatt, *Marvelous Possessions: The Wonder of The New World* (Chicago: University of Chicago Press, 1991), p. 10.

31 *Ibid.*

32 Michel de Certeau, *The Writing of History*, trans. Tom Conley (New York: Columbia University Press, 1988), pp. 2–4.

CHAPTER 3

Gendering mortality in early modern anatomies

Valerie Traub

What I would propose . . . is a return to the notion of matter, not as site or surface, but as *a process of materialization that stabilizes over time to produce the effect of boundary, fixity, and surface* . . .

Judith Butler, *Bodies That Matter*[1]

The "unconscious" contents remain here *excluded* but in strange fashion: not radically enough to allow for a secure differentiation between subject and object, and yet clearly enough for a defensive *position* to be established – one that implies a refusal but also a sublimating elaboration.

Julia Kristeva, *Powers of Horror*[2]

THE MATTER OF GENDER

One of the central insights of feminist inquiry in the past ten years is that gender serves not only as a sign of bodily difference, but, in the words of Joan Scott, as "a primary way of signifying relations of power."[3] Thus, the discourse of gender may involve knowledges and disciplines seemingly far removed from the actual experiences of women or men. The following essay proposes to read gender as a rubric for understanding three interrelated historical processes: the emergence of the science of anatomical dissection in Western culture; the negotiation of anxieties implicit in that emergence; and the specific aesthetic and ideological strategies or, to use Butler's phrase, the "process of materialization," whereby gendered differentiations of embodiment were constructed and stabilized under the auspices of the "new science."[4]

The engraved illustrations of early modern anatomy texts offer unique access into early modern ways of perceiving and interpreting corporeal form, function, and meaning. Not only does their visual iconography express a radical shift in modes of somatic representation; it also provides a means of analyzing the politics of intelligibility that govern early modern terms of embodiment. That those terms are

44

gender-inflected is, to the feminist reader of the history of science, unexceptional; however, what has yet to be investigated adequately are the precise ways in which constructions of gender and eroticism function to manage anxieties that originate in the radical shift to empiricism, and thus, stem from the new science itself.

Whereas pre-Vesalian anatomical illustrations, diagrammatic and schematic, depended so heavily on external paradigms to depict the body's interior that the very concept of interiority is belied,[5] Vesalius and his successors attempted to render interior spaces and structures as three-dimensional and objectively apprehendable.[6] Notwithstanding their empiricist intentions, I shall argue that early modern anatomies reveal a pattern of anxieties about the purpose and meaning of human dissection, the practice that comprised the material ground of anatomical inquiry. In addition, whereas important studies have demonstrated the extent to which the female body has been objectified by Western scientific inquiry,[7] little attention has been paid to the ways in which the meaning of gender is negotiated *relationally* through anatomy's visual metaphors. Rather than detail the objectifying visual strategies by which men exert control over women, this essay analyzes anatomy's diacritical semiosis of two mutually constitutive modes of embodiment. For, instead of expressing an essentialized vision of two preexisting and radically incommensurate genders, early modern anatomical illustrations demonstrate the extent to which gender is reciprocally *manufactured* in order to defend against the vulnerability to mortality that all bodies share.

Several compelling accounts of the social function of early modern anatomy have been offered in recent years.[8] Yet, with only two exceptions – Thomas Laqueur's book exploring the homologies imposed upon images of the body's interior and Howard Marchitello's essay on anatomy in Shakespeare's *Othello*[9] – the role of gender in early modern anatomy has gone unexamined. While I propose to foreground gender as an interpretative idiom, I shall do so by analyzing not the representation of the body's inner recesses (as does Laqueur), nor the anatomical tropes of literary texts (as does Marchitello), but patterns of aesthetic representation which are traceable across the surface of anatomical engravings. On the surface of the body's representation are modes of visualization that express cultural anxieties about piercing the protective walls of the flesh; we can see their outlines in the imaging of bodily envelope, external landscape, and ornamentation. In analyzing these surface representations, we gain access to the "process of materialization" that produces "the effect of boundary, fixity, and surface" – an effect that is profoundly gendered, indeed, that partially constitutes the "matter of gender" in the early modern period.

Such an analysis moves beyond the recognition that "woman" often is represented in Western science as a problem of truth (Marchitello) or that images of the gendered body are culturally constructed (Laqueur). It suggests a specification of those representational *strategies* whereby anxieties about the terms of male, as well as female, embodiment are negotiated, managed, and displaced. Central to my argument is that gender is produced by anatomical science as a defense against the body's abjection – the death in life that constitutes the border of one's condition as a living being.[10] In their defensive construction of two visually apprehensible genders, anatomical illustrations function in the way Kristeva describes the mechanism of abjection: because certain unconscious anxieties, of which gender becomes the sign, are never completely excluded, no fixed boundary is secured, no stability of signification is attained. Manifesting what Kristeva calls a "defensive position," anatomies, in their "subliminating elaboration" of the human form, ultimately expose the fear that in death, gender too might die.

DISSECTING ANATOMICAL PRACTICE

For centuries, Western European states legislated against the practice of human dissection; in many cultures, the dismemberment of a corpse, even in the interest of furthering medical knowledge, transgressed deeply held religious and cultural beliefs. Anatomists intent on verifying or challenging the work of scholastics procured material for dissection by robbing graves,[11] appropriating the corpses of the destitute, and secretly cutting down bodies from scaffolds. In the sixteenth century, anatomists continued to attain corpses through illicit means, even though a compromise had been reached whereby the bodies of executed criminals were legally provided for the purpose of public dissection.[12] Jonathan Sawday argues that this collusion between anatomists and the violence of the state gave rise to compensatory visual representations whereby anatomists assuaged any anxiety they may have felt over their complicity with the executioner; the frequently used image of the acquiescent, self-demonstrating cadaver, Sawday argues, inverts the power relations between corpse and dissector and obscures the anatomist's participation in an economy of violent death (figure 3.1).

Recently, Katharine Park has challenged the premise that Western medieval and Renaissance cultures held deep-seated taboos about the violation of corpses, taking particular umbrage against the idea that the practice of dissection was considered to be essentially punitive. The "myth of medieval resistance to dissection," she argues, imposes "a false unity on the long millennium between Augustine and Vesalius and ascrib[es] to the people of that period modern anxieties and a modern sensibility essentially alien to their own."[13] Pointing out that from the early twelfth century, the opening of the corpse was a common funerary practice and, from the fourteenth century, autopsies often were requested by aristocratic families concerned to ascertain the cause of death in order to protect their lineage, Park argues that it was not until the sixteenth century that there occurred a rise in suspicion concerning dissection; this concern was not a result of "age-old taboos," but of "dramatic new anatomical practices" which increased the populace's fear that they would "come under the anatomist's knife."[14]

In her attempt to historicize such practices, Park suggests that Northern European cultures expressed a "differing investment in the fate of the dead body" from their Italian counterparts, which had an impact on their views toward dissection.[15] Italians, it seemed, viewed death as "a quick and radical separation of body and soul," while their Northern counterparts saw death as a gradual process extending over the first year of the corpse's decomposition.[16] For Italians, the corpse was inert and inactive; for Northerners, it continued to be semianimate. Dissection in Northern countries thus was more likely to be seen as an attack on personal identity, whereas dissection in Italy was viewed with relative equanimity, as long as it did not take place through illegal means or violate familial honor.

Park's careful historical research is compelling. However, the evidence that taboos against the corpse's violation were neither universal nor historically constant does not altogether dissociate the practice of dissection from anxiety. From the sixteenth century on, discomfort with the idea of dissection was expressed by many religious and moral authorities, especially those in the North, as well as by members of the lower class (who saw themselves as most vulnerable to violations sanctioned by the state). Whether suspicion about dissection stemmed from beliefs about the corpse's vitality or from the material practices of intemperate anatomists, whether such fears were bound by geography or class, and whether they also coexisted with a popular appetite for anatomy as spectacle, such anxieties *are manifest* – in anatomies themselves. They appear, however, not in the anatomical narrative or in the functional description of body parts, but in the visual tropes by which these texts figure the anatomical project.[17] Whereas anatomical narratives compel support for dissection, anatomical illustrations contradict this surety, expressing instead profound unease about opening and exploring the body in the pursuit of truth. Doubt and dismay about the procedures and products of anatomical knowledge reveal themselves in the imaginatively nuanced impression of the body. It is as though a repressive intentionality at the heart of the anatomical project gives rise to an array of aesthetic strategies whose purpose is to displace anxiety away from the practice of dissection onto the figuration of the body.

The epistemological end of anatomy is to organize and render intelligible, by revealing, deciphering, and transposing onto a text, the seeming chaos of the body's interior – in short, to make the incommensurate commensurate. Corresponding to this epistemological purpose is, as Marchitello suggests, an ontological ambition: "anatomy ask[s] not only how and what we can know about bodies, but what is the *essential* nature of the body, and how are we to understand the relationship between the body and the identity it in some manner houses."[18] The relationship between body and identity, of course, has been profoundly gendered; and, it is at the intersection of epistemological and ontological concerns that gender is most at issue – indeed, gender demonstrates the instance of their intersection. For the epistemological and ontological projects of Western science and philosophy have been not only to map "the feminine" onto "matter" and "matter" onto "the feminine," but to so constitute these terms that they are unintelligible alone.[19] Such mappings come to comprise the obverse of scientific knowledge which, despite the personification of "scientia" as female, was increasingly figured as a masculine enterprise. Indeed, it is partially under the auspices of anatomy that knowledge in the West assumes its masculine habit – an assumption later consolidated by Bacon and Descartes.

At the same time, however, the anatomical attempt to reconcile the pursuit of knowledge with the materiality of the flesh brings into conflict those gendered terms (masculinity/femininity) that are produced as discrete and distinct, and upon which other crucial social distinctions rely. The violence inherent to anatomy, the dearticulation of the flesh which exposes our common fleshly inheritance, compels a recognition of the impossibility of a total separation of the terms that govern gender. At the same time, anatomy elicits an identification between the subject and object of dissection. Although the replacement of barber-surgeons by university physicians in the actual practice of anatomy elevated the social status of dissection, it also involved in the activity of dissection academicians who previously had been uncontaminated by direct contact with the flesh. With his hands inside another's body, the anatomist was newly in danger of becoming not only physically intimate with, but identified with, the inert matter lying on the dissecting table.[20] Both the recognition of this identification and its disavowal are exposed in the visual strategies of anatomical illustrations.

Elisabeth Bronfen has argued that the visual pleasure derived from witnessing aesthetic representations of death stems from the recognition that it is the *other* who has died:

Even as we are forced to acknowledge the ubiquitous presence of death in life, our belief in our own immortality is confirmed. There is death, but it is not my own. The aesthetic representation of death lets us repress our knowledge of the reality of death because here death occurs *at* someone else's body and *as* an image.[21]

Anatomical representations, however, complicate this psychic strategy, as the anatomist functions as the absent presence authorizing the display of the dissected corpse. Whether represented visually or not, the anatomist hovers over the scene of anatomy. Implicated in dissection's epistemological successes and failures, the anatomist is implicated as well in the mortality that anatomy exposes and disavows.

On the one hand, anatomy's discovery (and inscription) of a hidden structure depends upon the systematic violence of stripping away, penetrating, and fragmenting the body.[22] By dismembering the individual corpse, anatomy spatializes, externalizes, and conceptually rebuilds a generic body, a "corpus of mental categories," a "body-as-knowledge."[23] On the other hand, the limits on that conceptual resurrection, and the reminder of mortality, insufficiency, and inadequacy it elicits, threaten to undercut the will to knowledge that propels anatomical inquiry, as reason itself is subjected to the suspicion that the interior density and mystery of the body exceed and defy scientific mastery. Despite the revelation of viscera and the rearticulation of the skeleton, one can never anatomize to the point of ultimate truth; one can never dissect to the ground of being. Despite the anatomist's skillful surgery, physical matter is, in the end, mute, opaque, resistant to revelation.

Rather than explore "woman" as the figuration of this metaphysical problem as other commentators have done, I seek to articulate, through a close reading of both representative and idiosyncratic texts published between 1543 and 1619, the various ways that anatomy genders the

composition and decomposition of the body. The visual texts of four
anatomists – Andreas Vesalius, Juan de Valverde de Hamusco, Charles
Estienne, and Johann Remmelin – display a transcontinental conver-
gence of gendered conventions and codes supplemental to, yet deeply
implicated in, the pursuit of scientific knowledge. As the scientific will to
mastery hits up against the fear that ultimate corporeal knowledge is
unattainable, and as invasive, penetrating bodily procedures fail to
render transparent the opacity of physical matter, these texts deploy a
gendered idiom of representation that both furthers and impedes
anatomy's goals. Whereas representing the body always depends on the
use of metaphor, the particular task during the early years of dissection
of "visibilizing the invisible," in the words of Barbara Maria Stafford,
put into play a specific semiosis born of a complex dialectic of mastery
and misgiving. Such semiotic codes both reflect and produce gendered
understandings of the meaning and significance of the body, as they
negotiate the anxiety that processes of decomposition will efface not
only status, wealth, ambition, and knowledge – as the fifteenth- and sixteenth-century pictorial tradition of the Dance of Death asserts (figure
3.2) – but gender difference as well.[24]

If, in death, the male body's pretensions to physical, intellectual, and
spiritual mastery are rendered obsolete, so too, in dissection, is that same
body rendered open, vulnerable, the object of a (masculine) gaze that it
cannot evade or control. If gender *is* a social construction and not an
essential state of being, then the destruction of gender implicit in death's
disfigurement is implicit in the practice of anatomy as well. It is within
such an ontological, epistemological, and political context that the oft-
noted fetishization of the female cadaver lying prone on the dissecting
table can be understood in its complexity – not merely as the anatomist's
necrophiliac eroticization of a defenseless female object, but as a defensive reinscription of gender in the face of gender's destruction through
death. If death in the early modern period is figured as the great leveler of
age, status, and rank, it is also that which exposes the cultural composition
of gender itself. That male and female bodies are figured, in the dominant
medical paradigm, as homologous only underscores the extent to which
their difference is precariously attained and defensively secured.[25]

THE CLASSICAL ANTIQUE

The representational strategies of Vesalius' *De corporis humani fabrica*
(1543) are complex and various. For instance, Vesalius gleefully reports

his daring and often deceptive efforts to procure bodies, and the grotesque capital initials repeated throughout the *Fabrica* simultaneously poke comic fun at, and dispel anxiety about, his and his students' exploits.[26] Putti are represented robbing graves, lowering corpses from the gallows, gathering heads from the executioner, and boiling bones (figure 3.3).[27] But, in a more serious vein, the anatomical dialectic of male power and potential powerlessness is manifested in the construction of a visual dichotomy between visual depictions of the subject and object of dissection. As codified by Vesalius, anatomical science represents itself to itself in the form of a powerful, impartial seeker of truth who masterfully wields knife or pointer, or carefully handles veins and muscles – as depicted, for instance, in the contemporary portrait of Vesalius which graces his *Fabrica* and *Epitome* (figure 3.4).[28] This image of masculine self-assurance contrasts sharply to representations of the open, vulnerable, fetishized female cadaver, as well as to the violently flayed male object of dissection displayed throughout the work of Vesalius and subsequent anatomists.

Twentieth-century anatomy books generally isolate the body part under discussion, excising it from its organic context in order to highlight diagrammatically its morphology and function. Whereas Vesalius' *Fabrica* includes many plates of individual parts, what is astonishing from a contemporary perspective is the extent to which the body is displayed in corporeal and environmental context, as it is granted not only a sense of unity and totality, but individual dynamism, expression, and will. Vesalius' so-called "musclemen," for instance, who depict the musculature in progressive stages of dissection, not only gesture with their arms, but are environed by the classical topoi observable in the Italian countryside: decaying architectural monuments (figure 3.5).[29] Even those plates that don't display the body in its entirety nonetheless contextualize them, as in the engravings dedicated to male viscera and female reproductive organs; the body is attenuated at the thighs, arms, and neck, presenting a well-defined torso copied from antique statuary (figures 3.6, 3.7).[30]

This formal use of Grecian iconography functions in various ways. It does not merely partake of the Renaissance excitement in matters Greek, nor point to the ancient origin of anatomical knowledge, nor place contemporary work on a par with that of Hippocrates and Galen. Nor was Vesalius simply repeating the available images of his culture. Rather, as Glenn Harcourt argues, the use of the classical antique functions as a bulwark against anxiety. It provides a way of bracketing *in representation* the simple fact that anatomical knowledge is constituted through the violation and destruction of its proper object in practice. The idealized, classical forms of the figures, the fact that they do not read as actual cadavers, sets up a foil within the structure of the illustrations that mitigates the deadening, objectifying force of the accompanying narrative.[31]

Vesalius' strategy of classicization appropriates a widespread motif for particular ends: it imposes a grid of intelligibility that orders the internal disruption of the dissected body, while evacuating the anatomist from the scene of violation. The coordinates of this grid, I want to suggest, are, on the one hand, the mutually constitutive processes of monumentalization and decay and, on the other hand, the mutually constitutive bodily canons of the classical and the grotesque. As critics from Mikhail Bakhtin to Peter Stallybrass have argued, the classical body presents an image of corporeal integrity, unity, coherence, and enclosure.[32] Vesalius' use of the classical antique works to contain, through the imposition of beautifully proportioned outer forms, the inner mess of organs, veins, nerves, and bones, mitigating the discomfort posed by a gaping, vulnerable body by enclosing the gap within the bounded density of a figure cut in stone. This sense of stasis and insulation is heightened in those plates that depict the dissected figure as if it were lying inertly on the ground. Likewise, Vesalius' "musclemen" exist within a monumental context that gives meaning and authority to the display of their innermost regions while displacing interest away from the fact that these figures are pictured as if they had been flayed alive. The Renaissance imposition of order and proportion – suggested by the title of Vesalius' *Fabrica* – not only asserts the harmony of man made in God's image, but attempts to manage the uncomfortable suspicion that the internal structure and workings of the body do not always express a beautiful, or what's worse, fully knowable, design.

Vesalius' attempt to reify the anatomized body as a classical relic from an idealized past is not, however, unequivocally successful. The effects of these images of monumentality and decay are complex and contradictory: on the one hand, the decrepit, monumental environment of the muscle figures works simultaneously as a reminder, in the tradition of *momento mori*, of the vanity and futility underlying all human endeavor, while registering nostalgia for a culture long lost.[33] This reminder of mortality is reiterated at a more personal, less abstract level by the anatomical figures themselves. The gaping yet active "muscleman" and the disintegrating statue simultaneously signify integrity and instability, composition and decomposition, the classical and the grotesque, exposing the frailty of the body at the same time that they defend against it.

On the other hand, the representation of these *momento mori* images within a discourse of anatomy (rather than, for instance, religion or philosophy) locates the jeopardy of the body in the anatomist's own pursuit of knowledge. By employing the broken form of, for instance, the Belvedere Apollo,[34] not as it originally was sculpted, but as it could be imagined lying abandoned in the Italian countryside, the *Fabrica* specifically registers anatomy's destructive force. The reality of violence is made even more emphatic as Vesalius' myological figures progressively expose deeper and deeper layers of tissue, eventually self-destructing into allegorical emblems of martyrdom and execution (figure 3.8). The visual logic of these images is structured around an insurmountable contradiction which the *Fabrica* both confronts and evades: the anatomist, someday, will be anatomized – if not by a fellow surgeon then by the inevitable processes of disintegration. Oscillating between anatomy and monumentalization, the grotesque and the classical body, these representations defensively compensate for the recognition that anatomy – an attempt, after all, to conceptually recompose the human body – is implicated in the body's decomposition. The academic revelation of bodily interiority depends upon the physical violation of bodily integrity.

Despite anatomy's efforts to construct a firm divide between subject and object, mastery and fragility, it also deploys visual tropes that not only identify the anatomist with, but conflate him with, the corpse. Such a conflation parleys the recognition that the mortal, material body that is the site of empirical inquiry is also the precarious ground of the anatomist's own being. The identification of the anatomist with the anatomized reaches a gruesome climax in Juan de Valverde de Hamusco's *Anatomia del corpo humano* (1556): here, the anatomist is anatomized – a logical extension of the fantasy of maintaining scientific control even as one becomes the disembodied and disempowered object of scientific inquiry (figure 3.9). Although Valverde's text is primarily a reprint of Vesalian images, his additions to the Vesalian corpus heighten the apprehension of anxiety: they include not only the anatomist anatomized, but a self-demonstrating corpse (figure 3.10) and a flayed man holding his own skin aloft.[35] Perhaps most strikingly, Valverde adds an image of the dissected male body encased in military armor (figure 3.11); this military figure embodies the simultaneous destruction and preservation of the classical male body, taken to its most defensive extreme.

I am not alone in arguing that fears about violence and mortality, and identifications between anatomist and cadaver, are registered in anatomical illustrations. However, critics generally ignore the extent to which anxiety about dissection, and the strategies used to manage it, are informed by gendered tropes and understandings.[36] Like almost every other early modern anatomist, Vesalius depicted the generic body as male; the female body is employed only as its reproductive supplement. As such, the female body functions as a marginalized, fetishized object whose own singularity puts into relief the incessant exposure of the male body. That the endless variety of decomposition is figured through the martyrdom of male flesh not only heralds the male figure as normative, but suggests that masculinity is forced to bear the weight of contradiction implicit in anatomy. In lifting an arm, for instance, after all muscular ability to do so has been destroyed, these male figures embody the physical impossibility that simultaneously is confronted and evaded by anatomical illustration. Likewise, images of a statue lying prone, his head graced with a full, masculine beard, offer up the dissected male body as if in peaceful sleep, the rupturing of his chest only a temporary (if impossible) inconvenience (figure 3.12). These perversely gendered, yet dismembered, objects of inquiry hold within their masculine likeness the fate of the anatomist himself.

Whereas both male and female bodies are represented through the paradigm of the classical antique, it is crucial to recognize that throughout the early modern period, the classical body was overwhelmingly associated with what were presumed to be male powers of agency, rationality, and impermeability. The female body, on the other hand, was represented in political theory, conduct books, humoral theory, and stageplays as naturally grotesque – permeable, transgressive, always in need of enclosure and containment.[37] Yet, the macabre male figures of Vesalius and subsequent anatomists suggest that when mortality is at issue, the grotesque bodily canon effectively signifies the vulnerability to which men, despite their gender privilege, are also susceptible. Cultural associations between vulnerability, violation, and effeminization suggest that the canon of the grotesque body, whether represented in the male or female form, is the cultural reservoir of anxiety about the body's openness – to dissection, to disease, to death. More importantly, the cross-identifications and compensatory relations between bodily canons demonstrate the extent to which the classical and grotesque, and male and female terms of embodiment, are mutually constitutive, diacritical, the presence of the one requiring and depending upon the other.

As the male body is represented as progressively torn apart, the tropes that organize it and give it meaning begin to elide into the tropes that culturally figure the female. And yet, it is not so much that the fractured male figure is feminized, but that his gender ultimately is effaced: part by part, the body slips progressively into a representational realm where gender difference holds no meaning. The terms of intelligibility that figure gender difference as an absolute and non-negotiable certainty in living creatures dissipate into the elusive ungendering of death.

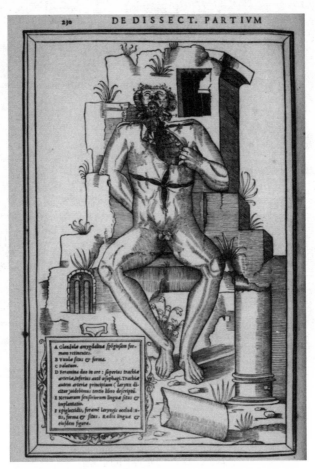

Figure 3.1 Self-demonstrating corpse. From Charles Estienne,
La dissection des parties du corps humain (1546).

Figure 3.2
Woe! woe! inhabitants of Earth,
Where blighting cares so keenly strike,
And, spite of rank, or wealth, or worth,
Death – Death will visit all alike.
The Dance of Death. From Hans Holbein, the Younger, *Les simulachres & historiees faces de la mort* (1538). Reproduced in *Imagini mortis* (1573).

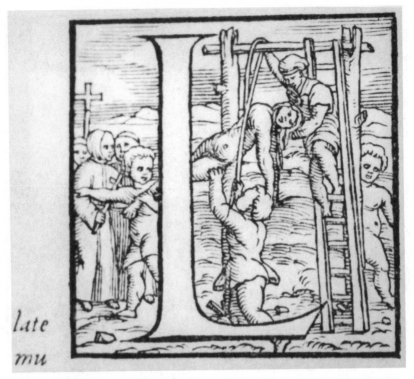

late
mu

Figure 3.3 Capital letter. From Andreas Vesalius, *De corporis humani fabrica* (1543).

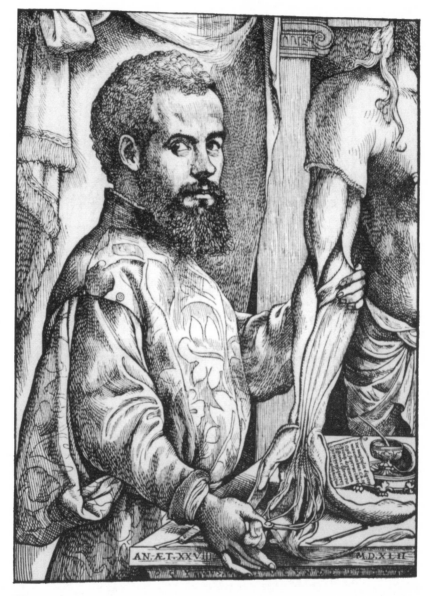

Figure 3.4 Portrait of Vesalius. From Andreas Vesalius, *De corporis humani fabrica* (1543).

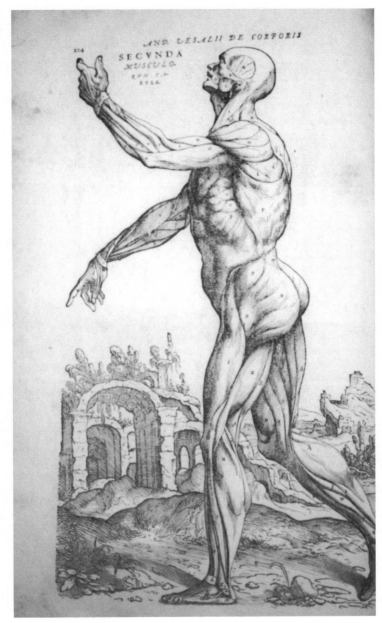

Figure 3.5 Muscleman. From Andreas Vesalius, *De corporis humani fabrica* (1543).

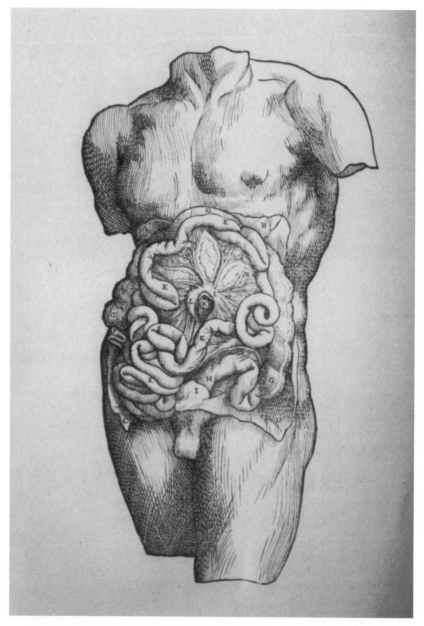

Figure 3.6 Classicized male torso. From Andreas Vesalius, *De corporis humani fabrica*
(1543).

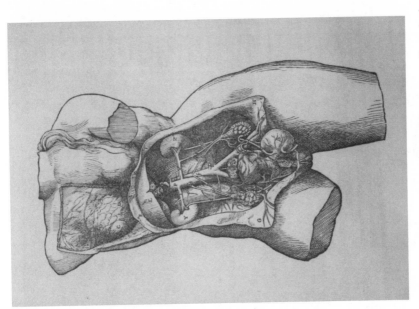

Figure 3.7 Classicized female torso. From Andreas Vesalius, *De corporis humani fabrica* (1543).
Figure 3.8 A figure of martyrdom. From Andreas Vesalius, *De corporis humani fabrica* (1543).

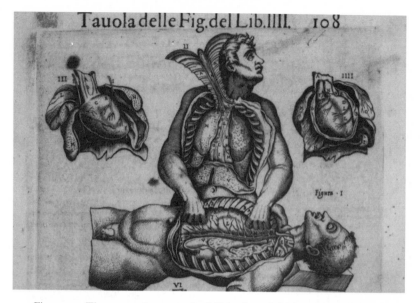

Figure 3.9 The anatomist anatomized. From Juan de Valverde de Hamusco,
Anatomia del corpo humano (1560).

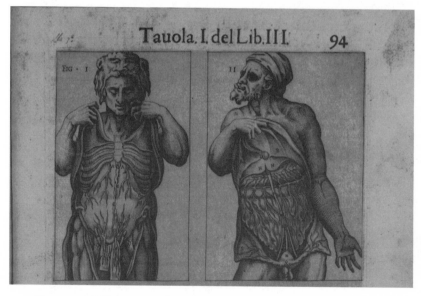

Figure 3.10 Self-demonstrating corpse. From Juan de Valverde de Hamusco,
Anatomia del corpo humano (1560).

Figure 3.11 Cadaver armored in military dress. From Juan de Valverde de Hamusco, *Anatomia del corpo humano* (1560).

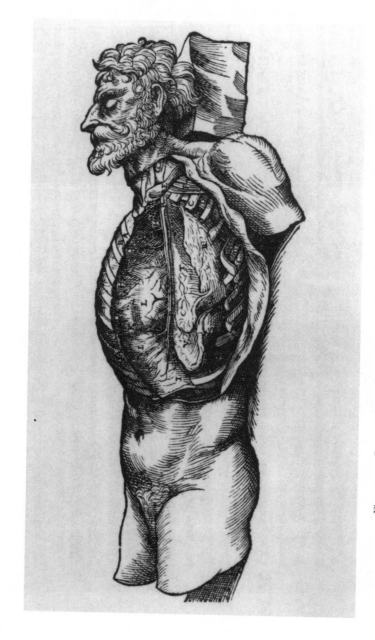

Figure 3.12 Prone cadaver. From Andreas Vesalius, *De corporis humani fabrica* (1543).

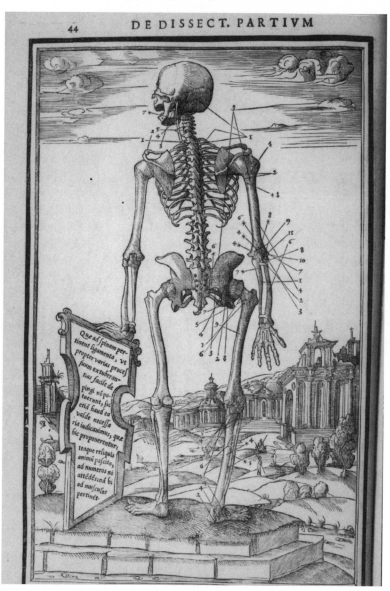

Figure 3.13 Skeleton on a plinth. From Charles Estienne,
La dissection des parties du corps humain (1546).

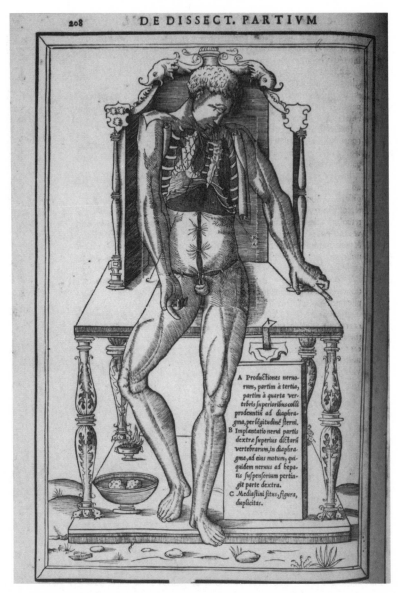

Figure 3.14 Cadaver seated on a throne. From Charles Estienne,
La dissection des parties du corps humain (1546).

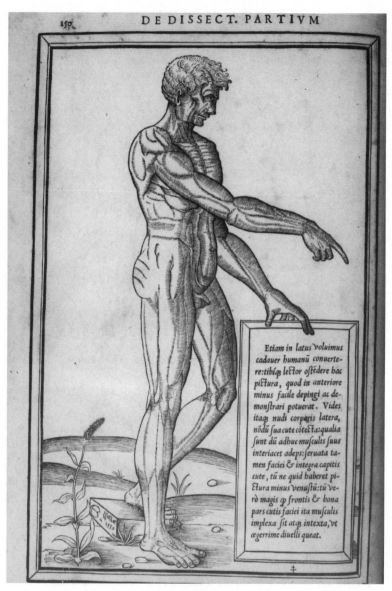

Figure 3.15 Cadaver pointing to anatomical information. From Charles Estienne, *La dissection des parties du corps humain* (1546).

68 VALERIE TRAUB

Figure 3.16 Cadaver holding informative scroll. From Charles Estienne,
La dissection des parties du corps humain (1546).

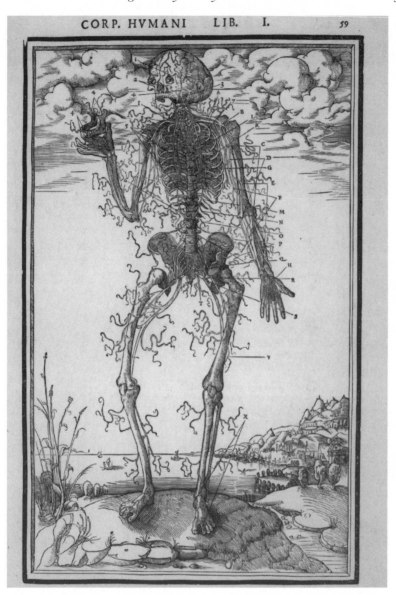

Figure 3.17 Skeleton holding its jaw. From Charles Estienne,
La dissection des parties du corps humain (1546).

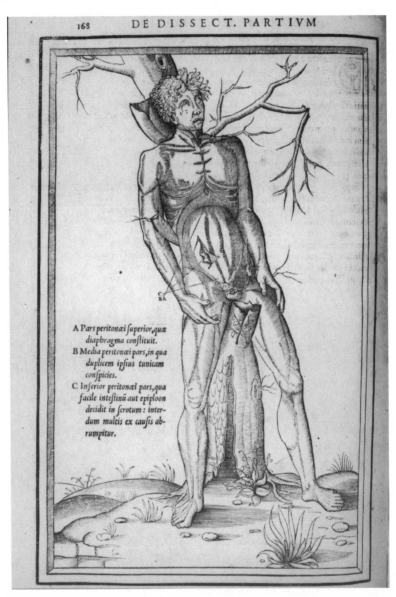

Figure 3.18 A figure of martyrdom. From Charles Estienne,
La dissection des parties du corps humain (1546).

Figure 3.19 Female reproductive figure in her boudoir. From Charles Estienne,
La dissection des parties du corps humain (1546).

Figure 3.20 Female reproductive figure in her boudoir. From Charles Estienne,
La dissection des parties du corps humain (1546).

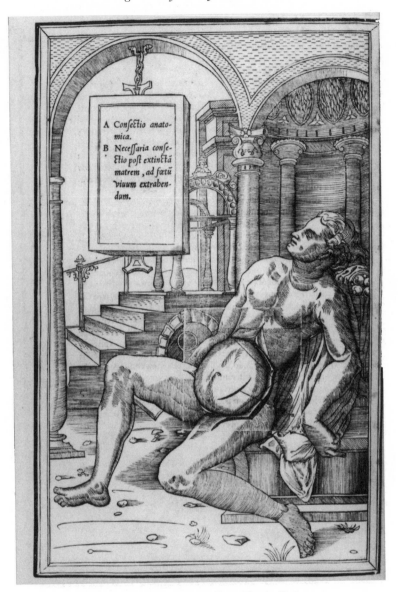

A Confectio anato-
mica.
B Neceffaria confe-
Etio poft extinctã
matrem , ad fœtũ
viuum extrahen-
dum.

Figure 3.21 Pregnant corpse. From Charles Estienne,
La dissection des parties du corps humain (1546).

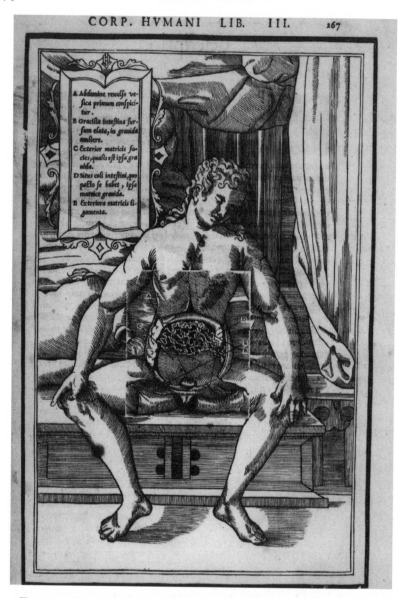

Figure 3.22 Female reproductive figure in her boudoir. From Charles Estienne,
La dissection des parties du corps humain (1546).

Figure 3.23 Frontispiece. From Juohann Remmelin, *Catoptrum microcosmicum* (1619).

Figure 3.24 Second plate with devil's face above and below. From Johann Remmelin, *Catoptrum microcosmicum* (1619).

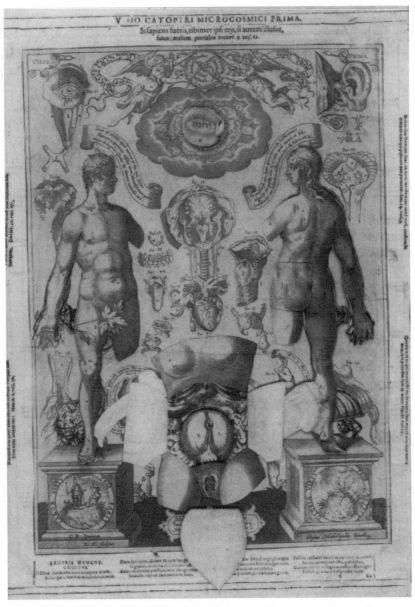

Figure 3.25 Second plate with genital flaps open. From Johann Remmelin,
Catoptrum microcosmicum (1619).

Figure 3.26 Detail from woodcut of devil pitching humans, with devil's face over genitals. From *The Kalender of Sheepehards* (1503).

DISSECTING DESIRE

Those gendered tropes and bodily canons that are figured obliquely in Vesalius' use of the antique are reiterated and transfigured in the engravings of other anatomists. Indeed, in *La dissection des parties du corps humain* (1546) by French surgeon Charles Estienne, the oscillation between the classical and the grotesque, the monumental and the anatomical, is taken to an extreme.[38] If Estienne's grand visual compendium – comprised of twelve "generic" skeletons; forty-two male figures depicting ligaments, nerves, muscles, veins; and ten female figures representing reproductive anatomy – seems exceptional or aberrant, his system of representation is not.[39] *Du corps humain* exhibits many of the same anxieties and employs some of the same strategies that are more conventionally figured in Vesalius and his followers. But, even more revealing of anatomy's exigencies is Estienne's strategic divergence in the treatment of his female figures from the terms of visibility canonized in the *Fabrica*.

Like Vesalius' musclemen, Estienne's male figures are located in vast pastoral scenes, accoutered in and surrounded by conventions of classical antiquity. They stand atop hills, plinths, overlooking cities (figure 3.13); sit on chairs, thrones, benches, tree stumps, and columns (figure 3.14); stand near or lean against trees, architectural monuments, on top of books. They grasp or gesture with swords and staffs, holding or pointing to informative scrolls (figures 3.15, 3.16). Only one plate shows a man located inside a building, looking out a window, and only two plates position a male figure lounging or groveling on the ground. Classical architecture and beautifully carved thrones – in contrast to Vesalius' images, these material objects are completely intact – lend an impressive air of monumentality; books and scrolls suggest the preeminence of reason, while staffs and swords metonymize phallic power. Nature, present in the form of diminutive flowers and solitary trees, is subsumed by and subservient to man's control. The confluence of images of fertility and power surrounding Estienne's male figures suggests that this classical body emblematizes both controlling reason and controlled reproduction. The problem of male reproductive anatomy, often the site of anxiety about generational continuity, is displaced onto symbols of male virility – the fertile, yet non-human presence of plants. Within nature, yet elevated above it, the male body becomes the visual emblem of reason controlling nature, science mastering the flesh.

Yet, as in the *Fabrica*, the representation of the classical male body is destabilized; as the plates continue, Estienne's figures become increasingly distorted and grotesque. Within the textual chronology of the plates, the first indication of anxiety is a depiction of a skeleton holding its jaw, with nerves angrily wiring out of his body (figure 3.17). Textual distress becomes more pronounced in the section dedicated to the display of internal organs, with depictions of male figures whose torsos are opened, the skin peeled away; who are leaning against thorny trees in an iconographic reminder of St. Sebastian or the crucifixion (figure 3.18); who have been scalped, with their scalps gruesomely hanging on the limbs of a nearby tree. In contrast to Vesalius' figures who passively hold a skull or gesture toward the heavens, Estienne's figures actively rend their own flesh, exposing their viscera to view (figure 3.1). The self-demonstrating cadaver, as Sawday has argued, indicates the corpse's complicity with and acquiescence to his own vivisection. And yet, the self-violation here also heightens the visual assault on the reader, forcing the uneasy recognition that underneath, the classical male body *is* the grotesque body: deformed, mutilated, macabre.

Historians of art and medicine routinely marginalize Estienne's *œuvre*, while expressing discomfort with his male figures. Charles Singer remarks that "The chief defect of Estienne is the distorted ugliness of his figures,"[40] while Saunders and O'Malley suggest that Estienne's plates "have the distinction of being without doubt the most hideous ever published . . . The vast amount of non-essential delineation serves no purpose but confusion."[41] While it is true that Estienne's emphasis on the full physical form subordinates and obscures anatomical detail, I want to suggest that it is in part because his aesthetic strategies are *not* so anomalous that his work has been discredited: his images take the logic of Vesalian tropes to an extreme, the effect of which is to heighten the sense of masculine vulnerability that all of these anatomies share.

As if to compensate for and assuage this visual violence, the section of *Du corps humain* dedicated to female reproductive anatomy revitalizes Estienne's classicism, as female anatomical figures are composed as sensual goddesses, offered up for visual and erotic pleasure. In Estienne, the reproductive interior of woman takes its place within the Italian and French traditions of the "Loves of the Gods" and pornographic engravings, which situate nude women inside the boudoir (figures 3.19, 3.20). As their shared iconography suggests, Estienne's anatomy owes much to the erotic engravings of such artists as Perino del Vaga – whose "Love of the Gods" series sensualized Greek goddesses – and the "postures" of Guilio Romano, which were engraved and published with Pietro Aretino's sexually explicit *Sonneti Lussuriosi*.[42] Like the portraits of courtesans available in commercial catalogues,[43] these female figures seem always ready for sexual activity. Estienne's women rarely stand; instead they sit or lounge with legs gracefully curved or spread wide. Located in private domestic spaces – bedrooms, bathhouses, and halls – they recline on or near beds or couches, sensuously encircled by curtains, pillows, or columns. The few female figures positioned outside are firmly enclosed, either by the exterior walls of the town, or by pillows and furniture. Unlike the male figures, they never hold scrolls, point to informative text, or touch anything other than their own bodies. They are not situated in nature; rather, they represent nature domesticated, made available for man's use. In contrast to the distress accompanying the male exposure of viscera, these female figures, in an attribution of agency that seems primarily male fantasy, are represented as taking exhibitionistic pleasure in the viewer's gaze.[44]

Ostensibly dedicated to rendering female reproductive anatomy intelligible, the progression of the plates recapitulates the telos of heterosexual intercourse. The first plate depicts a pregnant woman, her belly the visual center of the illustration (figure 3.21); the second plate focuses on the womb, with the woman's legs spread wide, her vulva completely exposed (figure 3.22); other plates show the woman carrying within the womb a fetus or twins. Yet, despite (for perhaps along with) this progression, the visual logic of these plates is governed by tropes of pornography and prostitution. Estienne's text distances the viewer from the object, locating sexual activity within the safe, two-dimensionality of artifice. Emphasizing the sensuality of the reproductive body helps to mitigate anxieties about physical reproduction at the same time that the text narratively insists upon the dangers of generation: the text accompanying the first plate, for instance, informs the reader where to make an incision to remove the fetus of a pregnant woman who is dead.

By beginning his compendium of female figures with a dead pregnant nude, Estienne offsets the effect of the previous illustrations of male figures who, in their grotesque mobility, appear all too alive. This pregnant figure of stasis and immobility amplifies the qualities shared by all of Estienne's "goddesses": constancy of object, acquiescence, experimental possibility.[45] The attractiveness of the female nude is defined by the same qualities inherent in visual artifice. Insofar as anatomy was the representational field in which the uncovering of the female body was taken to its physical limit – beginning with nudity, progressing through multiple layers of tissue, and ending with the skeleton – it is both logical and revealing that anatomy, as an emerging "scientia sexualis," would appropriate for its own use images from the illegitimate, yet widely available, *ars erotica*. Indeed, the *ars erotica* offer a way to compensate for the grotesque exposure of the male figures: with the classical male body viscerally violated, the representation of the female figure carries the burden of asserting the stability and comfort of a body visually contained and socially controlled. The psychic safety provided by pornographic conventions attempts to reconstitute the experience of reading anatomy by translating the reader's anxiety into arousal.

DEATH'S BODY

A pornographic idiom also underlies Johann Remmelin's *Catoptrum microcosmicum* (1619) which, in contrast to *Du corps humain*, depicts the female body as a grotesque site upon which are fixated theological anxieties about the exposure of the flesh.[46] This early seventeenth-century precursor to the anatomical pop-up book employs cut-out flaps to conceal and reveal multiple segmented layers.[47] The physical make-up of this book, which enjoins the reader to lift and reveal successive body parts, also constitutes anatomy *as* pornography; but rather than being enticed to an experience of pleasures legitimated by the text, the reader is coerced into an experience of sin and transgression.

Although the frontispiece is devoid of the cut-outs that distinguish this book in the history of printing, the sumptuous display of this engraving encapsulates the concerns of the *Catoptrum* as a whole (figure 3.23). Visually, the plate is segmented into thirds, with the title and publication information centered within a bounded cartouche surrounded by elaborate ornamentation: men of medicine, surgical instruments, skulls, and the inscription, *"momento mori"* – all fairly conventional title-page fare. Slightly less conventional for a scientific text is the smaller scene located above the title, where a fiery devil and his broken pitchfork are theologically countered by the image of a chained savior, beaming refulgent rays of light. This representation of immortal combat is glossed in the motto above, which proclaims Christ's promise of eternal life.

These images of struggle between the fire of damnation and the light of God's grace, between eternal death and eternal life, serve to adumbrate and gloss the more earthly tension between the realms of religion and science. The visual hierarchy organizing the frontispiece expresses the necessity to subordinate anatomy to theological purpose. Those images of death that in anatomy books conventionally signify both the pressing need for cadavers and the product of anatomical pursuits (in the form of the articulated skeleton) are recuperated here, via Christian faith, as images of a temporary passage into eternity. The corporeal body is represented as transient, while the status of anatomy is bounded by its purposeful revelation of God's purpose.

Despite the religious victory asserted in this engraving, subsequent illustrations belie such moral certitude, where a wealth of images express mistrust about what will be revealed by the anatomist's gaze. The physical layers of the body, painstakingly engraved on separate sheets and precisely ordered one on top of the other, attempt to display the body as a three-dimensional whole at the same time that the discrete segments literally fragment the body. Yet, the very proliferation of these layers, as well as their necessary two-dimensionality, suggests that corporeal nature is resistant to the anatomist's piercing look. Despite the readers' direct access to representations of the body's hidden recesses, and the implied invitation to lift away muscles, veins, hearts, and lungs, we can never behold the body in its totality. The anatomist's assertion of visibility is countered by the reader's sense of frustration and futility.

The anxiety generated by this resistance to corporeal visibility is, in the second plate, fixated upon the female reproductive body. There, two symmetrically arranged male and female figures gaze at each other across the central space of the engraving;[48] between these figures, and perspectively twice their size, is a female torso, its genitals overwritten with the face of a devil (figure 3.24).[49] At the top center of the plate is the Hebrew Tetragrammaton, the sacred four-letter name for God, encircled by winged cherubs blowing breath into God's word (figure 3.25).[50] The Tetragrammaton is inscribed over a circular cut-out which covers three subsequent layers: first the face of an angel, then the face of a patriarch, and finally the hideous face of another devil. The shock the reader experiences in this progression lies in its suggestion that, if we delve far enough into the nature of matter, and in particular, if we anatomize the secrets of the body, we find, not the persistent presence of God, but sin, error, and damnation. The face of the devil not only overlays the (always-about-to-be-exposed) female genitals, but also underlies the (in-the-process-of-being) dissected word of God, compelling two related equations: between the female body and matter, and between religious transgression and dissection. Not only do such correspondences blame the female body as the source of sin, but they project onto it both the ontological problem of meaning posed by physical matter and the epistemological failure of dissection to resolve it. Less a metaphorical image than an allegory of evil, less an "illustration" than a construction of matter as gendered and gender as matter, Remmelin's headless "Eve" fixes woman's body as the mortal site of primal sin and worldly knowledge.[51] What is exposed in such textual (dis)locations is the crafting of femininity as a defensive reinscription, as that which shores up a masculine sense of coherence and immunity to mortality.

The representation of the devil's face covering genitalia was a conventional folk motif present throughout late medieval and early modern Europe – represented, for instance, in a woodcut from the popular *The Kalender of Sheepehards* (1503) (figure 3.26).[52] Yet, Remmelin's appropriation of this commonplace creates more complex effects than the theological equation of sin with female sexuality; the death that is discovered at the core of the female form in Remmelin's use of this trope reanimates and redirects the effects of this iconographic tradition.[53] For, implicated in the desires and anxieties exposed in Remmelin's anatomy is not merely the scientific practice of dissection, but also the reader of anatomy. Insofar as the *Catoptrum* compels the reader not only to turn its pages, but to lift bodily flaps and handle muscles and organs, the reader, in order to gain knowledge, must also dissect. The effect of the *Catoptrum* on the dissecting reader is thus not limited to the abjection of woman. For, in enticing the reader to take part in a kind of textual strip-tease, the text promises to reveal one thing (the empirical ground of being) while delivering something else: the source of all error is located in the dissecting hand of the reader. Concealing as much as it reveals, the text engages in a kind of visual sado-masochism: the reader's desire to apprehend knowledge empirically is chastised and disciplined via a confrontation with the fated failure of empiricism. This epistemological problem is encoded as the ontological reality of the flesh, while both epistemology and ontology are layered onto the female body. That the intended reader of Remmelin's anatomy is male suggests the dual purpose of the *Catoptrum*'s disciplinary function: not just to fixate sin on the body of woman, but to implicate within her abjected body the transgressive touch of man.

Different as their iconographic repertoires are, these anatomies each stage a gendered contradiction between word and image, demonstrating the risks to the subject inherent to anatomy's project. Vesalius' *Fabrica* endeavors to allay the anxiety of dissection by imposing a framework of the classical antique, while Valverde's *Anatomia* exhibits an amplified need for defense by taking recourse in military tropes. In contrast to Valverde's armoring of the male body, Estienne's *Du corps humain* attempts to mitigate the terrors of its flayed musclemen by prostituting its female figures, thereby implying that anatomy *is* pornography. This psychic safety net is manipulated further by the *Catoptrum microcosmicum*, which seduces the reader into the ambivalent pleasures of a gaze and a touch that carry with them a history of violation, error, and futility.

Whether for particular readers these depictions incite primarily desire or anxiety, whether the pleasure experienced in the pursuit of knowledge overrides displeasure about knowledge's disciplining and deferral or, indeed, whether these psychic reactions can be separated, I can't say. But perhaps such closure is beside the point. More important than apprehending the final response elicited by anatomy on individual readers is to recognize that these are *motivated*, *invested* representations, existing within, and helping to produce, a new regime of science and the gendered body. It is no accident that the widespread dissemination of anatomies was coterminous with efforts to exclude women from the practice and increasing prestige of medicine. The gendering of scientific knowledge as masculine – the emergence of medicine as a modern science through the creation of a male subject and a female object of knowledge – depended not only upon anatomists' claims to objectivity, but on the professionalization and regulation of midwifery, the success of which eventually led to the exclusion of women from all branches of medicine.[54] However exceptional their individual publishing histories, these anatomies materially intervened in the intellectual opportunities and physical health of countless women.[55]

Posed between desire and anxiety, fraught with instability and incoherence, early modern anatomies exist as figurations of the abject – reminding the reader of both the possibilities and the limits of disciplines of bodily knowledge. If the history of science has tended to emphasize epistemological gains, these texts remind us that the limits of knowledge are also lodged within constructions of a gendered body. Anxieties about the relation between gender and matter, matter and knowledge, knowledge and transgression remain palpably discernible to the reader who turns their pages.

NOTES

Heartfelt thanks to Georgianna Ziegler of the Folger Shakespeare Library for her generosity in locating various editions of anatomy texts during a summer fellowship provided by the Folger Library. I would also like to thank William Engel for sharing his expertise in iconography, emblems, and Latin. Karen Newman, Mark Schoenfield, and my co-editors gave incisive responses to early versions of this paper, and Brenda Marshall offered important editing advice. Arleen Tuchman updated me on the history of science, and Adriane Stewart did an excellent job translating Estienne's text. I also appreciate the questions and suggestions of the members of the Early Modern Studies Group of Vanderbilt University and the financial assistance of the Vanderbilt University Research Council, which not only provided me with summer research support, but underwrote much of the cost of slide reproduction. Thanks finally to Lisa Cullum for her expert assistance in preparing the manuscript for publication.

1 Judith Butler, *Bodies That Matter: On the Discursive Limits of "Sex"* (New York: Routledge, 1993), p. 9.
2 Julia Kristeva, *Powers of Horror: An Essay on Abjection* (New York: Columbia University Press, 1982), p. 7.
3 Joan Wallach Scott, *Gender and the Politics of History* (New York: Columbia University Press, 1988), p. 42.
4 Science, of course, was neither a singular nor unified entity – in this period or in ours. Constructed out of various and often conflicting knowledges and practices, "science" in my useage exists as a shorthand for the early modern commitment to empirical modes of investigation and verification.
5 While Vesalius represents a radical break in the conceptual regime of anatomical representation, it is important to note that pre-Vesalian images provide some of the tropes – in particular, the "wound man" and the "gravida" – that will be redeployed later.
6 The work of illustrating these anatomies seems to have been collaborative: anatomist, artist, and engraver all worked together to compose the engraving. I thus use the names "Vesalius," "Valverde," "Estienne," and "Remmelin" less in reference to a historical personage than the combination of agency that produced these texts.
7 Ludmilla Jordanova, *Sexual Visions: Images of Gender in Science and Medicine Between the Eighteenth and Twentieth Centuries* (Madison: University of Wisconsin Press, 1989); Londa Schiebinger, *Nature's Body: Gender in the Making of Modern Science* (Boston: Beacon, 1993).
8 Francis Barker, *The Tremulous Private Body: Essays on Subjection* (London: Methuen, 1984); Luke Wilson, "William Harvey's *Prelectiones*: The Performance of the Body in the Renaissance Theater of Anatomy," *Representations* 17 (1987): 62–95; Glenn Harcourt, "Andreas Vesalius and the Anatomy of Antique Sculpture," *Representations* 17 (1987): 28–61; Jonathan Sawday, "The Fate of Marsyas: Dissecting the Renaissance Body," *Renaissance Bodies: The Human Figure in English Culture c. 1540–1660*, Lucy Gent and Nigel Llewellyn, eds. (London: Reaktion, 1990), pp. 111–35. Traditional analyses of Renaissance anatomy focus on describing the background of, influences on, and disputes among the "great men" of anatomy; celebrating the replacement of scholastic reiteration of ancient knowledge with empirical observation based on human dissection; judging the scientific precision of anatomists' observations and depictions; and, for the more iconographically inclined, placing anatomical illustration within the context of

Renaissance conceptions of Man and Art. See Ludwig Choulant, *History and Bibliography of Anatomic Illustration*, Mortimer Frank, ed and trans. (Chicago: University of Chicago Press, 1920); Charles Singer, *The Evolution of Anatomy* (New York: Knopf, 1925); C. M. Saunders and Charles D. O'Malley, *The Illustrations from the Works of Andreas Vesalius of Brussels* (Cleveland: World Publishing Co., 1950); Harvey Cushing, *A Bio-Bibliography of Andreas Vesalius*, 2nd edn. (Hamden: Archon Books, 1962); Charles D. O'Malley, *Andreas Vesalius of Brussels, 1514–1564* (Berkeley: University of California Press, 1964). For an explanation of a renewed interest in anatomy in the 1980s and 1990s, see Nancy Sirasi, "Early Anatomy in Comparative Perspective: Introduction," *Journal of the History of Medicine and Allied Sciences* 50.1 (January 1995): 3–10.

9 Thomas Laqueur, *Making Sex: Body and Gender from the Greeks to Freud* (Cambridge, MA: Harvard University Press, 1990); Howard Marchitello, "'Vesalius' *Fabrica* and Shakespeare's *Othello*: Anatomy, Gender and the Narrative Production of Meaning," *Criticism* 35.4 (Fall 1993): 529–58.

10 Kristeva, *Powers of Horror*, pp. 1–18.

11 The exhuming of corpses was also associated with witchcraft.

12 For the difficulties of obtaining corpses in England, see Frances Valadez, "Anatomical Studies at Oxford and Cambridge," in *Medicine in Seventeenth Century England*, Allen Debus, ed. (Berkeley: University of California Press, 1974), pp. 393–420. For a general account of the development of anatomy in the fourteenth and fifteenth centuries, see Nancy Sirasi, *Medieval and Early Renaissance Medicine: An Introduction to Knowledge and Practice* (Chicago: University of Chicago Press, 1990).

13 Katharine Park, "The Criminal and the Saintly Body: Autopsy and Dissection in Renaissance Italy," *Renaissance Quarterly* (Spring 1994): 1–33, quote 4.

14 *Ibid.*, 4, 18.

15 Katharine Park, "The Life of the Corpse: Division and Dissection in Late Medieval Europe," *Journal of the History of Medicine and Allied Sciences* 50.1 (January 1995): 111–32, quote 118.

16 *Ibid.*, 115.

17 The only statements by anatomists that indicate discomfort castigate others for their abhorrence of anatomical procedures, as when Jacopo Berengario da Carpi writes: "the dissection and handling of the members are vile and repulsive to many" (cited in Harcourt, "Andreas Vesalius," 35).

18 Marchitello, "Vesalius' *Fabrica*," 537.

19 See, in addition to Judith Butler, *Bodies That Matter*, Susan Bordo, *The Flight to Objectivity: Essays on Cartesianism and Culture* (Albany: SUNY Press, 1987) and Luce Irigaray, *This Sex Which Is Not One*, trans. Gillian Gill (Ithaca: Cornell University Press, 1985).

20 Although several critics allude to the identification of the anatomist with the dissected corpse, Luke Wilson performs the most searching and detailed examination of this dynamic, arguing that, in Harvey's "performance" of

dissection, the cadaver paradoxically is represented as an agent while the anatomist's body is cadaverized. I would suggest that such cross-identification depends upon a concept of corporeal rather than psychical interiority, the integrity of which was newly endangered by scientific practices.

21 Elisabeth Bronfen, *Over Her Dead Body: Death, Femininity, and the Aesthetic* (New York: Routledge, 1992), p. x. Although our work shares an interest in the relation between death and femininity, Bronfen's psychoanalytic method insists on a universalized connection that I would argue is historically produced.

22 See, in addition to Barker, *Tremulous Private Body*, Wilson, "Harvey's *Prelectiones*," Harcourt, "Andreas Vesalius," and Sawday "Fate of Marsyas,", Devon Hodges, *Renaissance Fictions of Anatomy* (Amherst: University of Massachusetts Press, 1985) and Barbara Maria Stafford, *Body Criticism: Imaging the Unseen in Enlightenment Art and Medicine* (Cambridge, MA: MIT Press, 1991).

23 Wilson, "William Harvey," 63.

24 Originally painted on church murals, the motif of the *danse macabre* was widely disseminated by Hans Holbein the Younger. See *The Dance of Death: Forty-One Woodcuts by Hans Holbein the Younger*, introduction by Werner Gundersheimer (New York: Dover, 1971), a facsimile of the original 1538 French edition of *Les simulachres & historiees faces de la mort*. The translation of Holbein's French verse is by Frederick H. Evans. For a cogent description of the iconography of death, see William Engel, *Mapping Mortality: The Persistence of Memory and Melancholy in Early Modern England* (Amherst: University of Massachusetts Press, 1995).

25 For the homology of the body in early medical paradigms, see Laqueur, *Making Sex*.

26 For an analysis of the capital letters of the *Fabrica*, see Samuel W. Lambert "The Initial Letters of the Anatomical Treatise, *De Humani Corporis Fabrica*, of Vesalius," in *Three Vesalian Essays to Accompany the Icones Anatomicae of 1934*, Samual W. Lambert, Willy Wiegand and William Ivins, Jr., eds. (New York: Macmillan, 1952).

27 Andreas Vesalius, *De corporis humani fabrica* (Basel, 1543). Vesalius' attempts to procure bodies are discussed in Saunders and O'Malley', *Illustrations* Sawday, "Fate of Marsyas", and Park, "Life of the Corpse."

28 Andreas Vesalius, *Epitome* (Basel, 1543).

29 It is generally agreed that the background of the "musclemen" plates, if set side by side in their proper chronology, form a continuous, panoramic landscape. The site has been variously identified as Rome or south-west of Padua.

30 In the *Fabrica*, the external bodily envelope is differentially depicted according to its location within the various "books" of the body: skeleton, musculature, veins and arteries, organs, and pulmonary system all possess their own codes of representation. The plates dedicated to the skeletal, musculature, venous and nervous systems generally show the entire body from head to foot. Occasionally, these plates excise the arms or render only one side of

the body. Whereas the skeleton and muscle plates locate the figure within a specific locale, showing it engaged in dramatic activities and thereby granting it an individual identity, the plates depicting veins and nerves show the figure completely decontextualized and devoid of affect.

31 Harcourt, "Andreas Vesalius," 34–35.

32 See Mikhail Bakhtin, *Rabelais and His World*, trans. Helene Iswolsky (Bloomington: Indiana University Press, 1984) and Peter Stallybrass and Allon White, *The Politics and Poetics of Transgression* (Ithaca: Cornell University Press, 1986).

33 For an analysis of monumentalization in early modern drama, see my *Desire and Anxiety: Circulations of Sexuality in Shakespearean Drama* (London: Routledge, 1992) and Abbe Blum, "'Strike All that Look upon with Mar[b]le': Monumentalizing Women in Shakespeare's Plays," *The Renaissance Englishwoman in Print: Counterbalancing the Canon*, Anne M. Haselkorn and Betty S. Travitsky, eds. (Amherst: University of Massachusetts Press, 1990), pp. 99–118.

34 See Sawday, "Fate of Marsyas," p. 127.

35 Juan de Valverde de Hamusco, *Anatomia del corpo humano* (Rome: 1556, 1560). Similar images of the flayed man appear in Helkiah Crooke's *Microcosmographia, A Description of the Body of Man* (London, 1615), his *Somatographia anthropine* (London, 1616), and Thomas Bartholin's *Anatomia reformata* (London, 1651). Bartholin's title-page is designed around the trope of using the skin of a flayed man as material upon which to inscribe the title.

36 The exception to this trend is Marchitello, whose reading, in "Vesalius' Fabrica," of dissection in terms of the Eve figure in Vesalius' *Epitome* and the title-page of the *Fabrica* are focused primarily on gender implications. The title-page of the *Fabrica*, which shows Vesalius performing a dissection of a nude female, often has been read in gendered terms, although the focus has been not dissection per se, but the representation of the female body. See Karen Newman's consideration of the illustrations in Vesalius, Crooke, and Geminus in chapter 1 of *Fashioning Femininity and English Renaissance Drama* (Chicago and London: University of Chicago Press, 1991). Wendy Wall, in *The Imprint of Gender: Authorship and Publication in the English Renaissance* (Ithaca and London: Cornell University Press, 1993), views the Vesalius frontispiece as emblematic of "the general erotic imagery that pervades book preliminaries" as well as of a "gendered program" of a "visual blazon" that positions the reader as voyeur, pp. 202–03.

37 See, in addition to Stallybrass and White, *Politics and Poetics of Transgression*, Gail Kern Paster, *The Body Embarrassed: Drama and the Disciplines of Shame in Early Modern England* (Ithaca: Cornell University Press, 1993).

38 Charles Estienne, *La dissection des parties du corps humain* (Paris, 1546).

39 Estienne's text was written prior to Vesalius', but was published three years after the *Fabrica*; its effect was eclipsed as Vesalius' more accurate representations were canonized.

40 Singer, *Evolution of Anatomy*, p. 100.

41 Saunders and O'Malley, *Illustrtions from the Works*, p. 24.

42 For a short discussion of Estienne's reliance on Perino del Vaga, see Pierre Huard and Mirko Drazen Gremek, *L'Œuvre de Charles Estienne et l'Ecole Anatomique Parisienne* (Paris, 1965). Romano's drawings were engraved by Marcantonio Raimondi, and published with Pietro Aretino's *Sonneti Lussuriosi* in 1525. They are available as *I Modi: The Sixteen Pleasures, An Erotic Album of the Italian Renaissance*, ed. Lynne Lawner (Evanston: Northwestern University Press, 1988).

43 See Lynne Lawner's analysis of these catalogues in her introduction to *I Modi*.

44 Estienne's pornographic representations belie Jordanova's contention, presumably drawn from Vesalius, that early modern anatomies represent reproductive organs as "disembodied parts" devoid of eroticism.

45 I am grateful to Suzanne Bost for her formulation of the relation between artifice and object in "The Undead Queen: Monumentalization in *The Duchess of Malfi* and *The Winter's Tale*," presented at the Group for Early Modern Cultural Studies Conference, Rochester, Fall 1994.

46 Johann Remmelin, *Catoptrum microcosmicum* (Ulm?, 1619).

47 Remmelin's strategy of layering body parts via the "pop-up" method had its precursor in the so-called "fugitive sheets" of Vesalius' *Epitome*, in which cutouts of the venous system were to be placed over the surface anatomy of a female nude.

48 The two figures are basically symmetrical, although the male has two layers that the female figure lacks, and the female's buttocks open to reveal muscles and fat. Both follow the general schema of revealing first a representation of the veins, then several layers of muscles, then the bones. Their genitals are covered by drapery, although the male genitals, in danger of exposure because of the frontal view, are additionally clothed with a non-removeable fig-leaf. Both stand on pedestals, and the iconography surrounding them is explicitly gendered. Partially hidden behind the male figure's plinth is a king, crowned and holding a scepter. Behind the female figure is a death's head with a funereal spade. Near the male figure's right calf is Atlas – the stable man bearing the globe – while at the female figure's foot, fickle Fortuna holds her sail aloft the winds of fate. Located in the surrounding margins of the plate are biblical verses referring to the fear of God, the creation, and the resurrection; inscriptions on the plinths instruct man to bring forth and woman to nourish.

49 The devil is inscribed *invidia ogre diabole neanias*. Subsequent layers depict the vulva, the womb and fallopian tubes, the veins, and finally a fetus, surrounded by the back wall of the womb. This fetus within the womb is reiterated on the surface of the plate with an infant attached to a suspended placenta. The breasts also open to reveal veins and tissue. Because subsequent plates represent all of these organs, and the plate individually depicting the female includes her reproductive anatomy, the point of this additional image is to give special attention and weight to the pregnant female body.

50 Above this, a sword and a quill are crossed by angels. At the very center of the illustration between the male and female figures lies an image of the heart, the neck, the skull; in the upper left corner is an eye; in the upper right is an ear.

51 The subsequent two plates of the *Catoptrum* can be read through the logic provided by the previous plate. The frontispiece for the second book delineates the male frontal view. Surrounded by various organs and veins suspended in air, the male figure stands with one foot resting on a skull, jauntily gesturing with his left arm. A large plant serves the function of fig-leaf covering the genitals, which are additionally hidden by winding drapery. A snake winds through the skull's orifices. To the right of the skull is a small Christ on the cross, surrounded by Hebrew letters that translate as "This is the head of your savior/salvation." The figure's torso opens to reveal multiple layers of muscles, veins and organs, which are illustrated on both sides.

The frontispiece for the third book delineates the female frontal view. Like her male counterpart, she stands with one foot on the ground, the other on top of a skull, surrounded by various veins and organs. Winding through the skull is a snake, only this time it holds an apple on a stem in its mouth. Hebrew letters wind around the snake. Instead of a plant, at the bottom center is a phoenix rising out of a funeral pyre; the smoke billows up to cover the figure's genitals which are also covered by a layer of drapery. Underneath the genital drapery is a clear rendition of the vulva. Belly and breasts open to reveal multiple layers of veins and organs, some of which insert into others.

52 *The Kalender of Sheepehards*, an anonymous text, was first translated into English in 1503 and reprinted throughout the sixteenth century. *The Kalender of Sheepehards: A Facsimile Reproduction*, S. K. Heninger, Jr., ed. (Delmar, New York: Scholars' Facsimiles and Reprints, 1979).

53 Remmelin's text, republished with the same plates in 1660, was translated into English and published in London as *A Survey of the Microcosm or the Anatomy of the Bodies of Man and Woman* in 1675 and 1702. In the translated editions, reengraved plates have excised all theological symbology. The image of God's name is replaced by a title surrounded by a fleur-de-lis; devils, angels, and biblical verses are gone. Such a stripping away of theological commentary may register national differences between post-Reformation Germany and England, as well as a lessening of theological anxieties about dissection by the end of the seventeenth century.

54 For the past twenty years, the history of midwives has focused on the decline in women's activities and status after the "invasion" of man-midwives. See Jean Towler and Joan Bramall, *Midwives in History and Society* (London: Croom Helm, 1986). This history is now being challenged by those who would focus on the ways midwives developed apprenticeship relations, self-regulated their practices, and defended their skill and legitimacy in different ways across Western Europe. See Hilary Marland, ed. *The Art of Midwifery: Early Modern Midwives in Europe* (London and New York: Routledge, 1993).

55 The relevance of continental anatomies to English culture should not be underestimated. Partly because the advancement of native English anatomy lagged behind that of Italy and France, continental anatomies, including those of Estienne and Remmelin, were widely available in London. Vesalian illustrations were even more widespread in Latin editions as well as in many popular London publications: Thomas Geminus' Latin *Compendiosa totius anatomie delineatio* (London, 1545) and his "Englished" version, *A Compendious Delineation of the Whole Anatomy* (London, 1553); Thomas Raynald's *The Byrth of Mankynde* (London, 1545) (a translation of Eucharius Roesslin's *Rosengarten*, a popular midwifery); Helkiah Crooke's *Microcosmographia, a Description of the Body of Man* (London, 1615); and Thomas Bartholin's 1651 English translation of his father's Latin *Institutiones anatomicae* (London, 1641).

CHAPTER 4

Wound-man: Coriolanus, gender, and the theatrical construction of interiority

Cynthia Marshall

Feminists have frequently pointed out the unhappy ramifications for women of Cartesian dualism. Inscribed within the separation of mind and body is a further implicit division based upon gender, since the traditional association links men with the mind, while women's more visible reproductive capacities have enforced their identification with the lower realm of the body or bodiliness. So deeply engrained is the dualistic mode of thinking that its traces appear virtually everywhere, not least in our critical practice. Those who would challenge traditional sex and gender systems have advanced a great deal of exciting work on the material conditions of the early modern theater, considering its relevance to social codes and conditions more generally, its ability to arouse erotic energies, and its various physical effects, such as the prosthetic devices used to mime gender.[1] In general, recent feminist approaches to the early modern period have been informed by or allied with forms of materialist analysis and have openly embraced an association with the body as a subversive tactic. However, there may be reasons to question how successful such a subversion can be. Philosopher Elizabeth Grosz points out the problems with reductionist attempts to disavow the "unbridgeable gulf between mind and matter":

> To reduce either the mind to the body or the body to the mind is to leave their interaction unexplained, explained away, impossible . . . Rationalism and idealism are the results of the attempt to explain the body and matter in terms of mind, ideas, or reason; empiricism and materialism are the results of attempts to explain the mind in terms of bodily experiences or matter . . . Both forms of reductionism assert that either one or the other of the binary terms is "really" its opposite and can be explained by or translated into the terms of its other.[2]

I agree with Grosz that the mind–body problem can neither be denied nor dissolved by an insistence on the priority of one of its two terms, and I offer the essay that follows as an effort to bring into dialogue two modes of inquiry that normally remain separate. The essay takes up a classically humanist question: the origin and qualities of inwardness, of an inner and truer selfhood. But rather than approaching this topic solely in terms of literary or linguistic tokens of selfhood, I have pondered the phenomenal or material effects that might produce such an intuition. As an attempt to bring together discourses of "mind" and "body," this represents only a tentative step, but I hope at least to suggest a productive direction for thinking about the ways selfhood, with gender as (perhaps arguably) its central term, was indicated in the early modern theater and continues to be indicated in various settings today.

Does a developed selfhood presuppose masculinity? Or might masculinity in some way impede the complexity necessary for an inner dimension? I have chosen to write about Shakespeare's Coriolanus because in him characterological problems are so insidiously entwined with questions of gender. In Coriolanus we glimpse the emergence of the heroic masculinity that has become our culture's dominant ideal of male identity, but it appears here in a form that seems, with historical hindsight, flawed and incomplete. Moreover, the attention paid in Coriolanus to the troubled surface of the hero's body – wounded, yet insistently masculine – challenges us to rethink the terms through which identity is linked to physical being. We might begin by examining Coriolanus' alleged deficiencies as a dramatic character.

Coriolanus lacks something. That has been the complaint of critics who repeatedly, even obsessively, invoke a rhetoric of absence in responding to the hero of this late Shakespearean play. Jonathan Goldberg, for instance, notes that Coriolanus' emotional privation constitutes a "crucial lack," and Michael Goldman observes his "lack of inwardness." Paul Cantor finds all the play's characters to be deficient in this way ("In Shakespeare's portrayal, the Romans lack inwardness"), a perception that may be related to Stanley Cavell's sense of the play's generic "lack or missing of tragedy." Janet Adelman notices how the lack extends to the audience: "We are made as rigid and cold as the hero by the lack of anything that absolutely commands our human sympathies."[3] These testimonies to absence are made particularly striking by their appearance alongside another generalized perception of the play, typified by A. C. Bradley's remark that "if Lear's thunderstorm had beat upon [Coriolanus'] head, he would merely have set his teeth"[4] – that it is unusually physical in both word and action. With its plot involving hungry multitudes and its hero extraordinarily interested in martial valor, it is little wonder that Coriolanus insists on the inescapability of the body. As Zvi Jagendorf observes, "everywhere we encounter legs, arms, tongues, scabs, scratches, wounds, mouths, teeth, voices, bellies, and toes together with such actions as eating, vomiting, starving, beating, scratching, wrestling, piercing, and undressing."[5] This apparent paradox – vivid physical presence existing simultaneously with an eroding sense of lack – has implications for our understanding of how the early modern theater embodied its meanings and in particular for the success of bodily signifiers in producing a sense of characterological presence and plenitude.

Shakespeare's plays have been the site of much recent inquiry into the ways what we call subjectivity began to be constructed in early modern England. This work has for the most part progressed through attention to the verbal texture of the plays – in isolation, that is, from a performance emphasis. Yet we need to consider the specifically theatrical effects that produce an impression of subjective identity and of its fullest dramatic achievement, character depth. Such a consideration will begin to position subjectivity in the lived theatrical experience of the audience, rather than limiting it to the author or the actors of the plays. We can theorize performance by approaching the play-texts as documents of playhouse practice; we might ask, for instance, what psychological or semiotic mechanisms convey an impression of subjectivity to an audience. Where in the theatrical dynamic does the experience of psychological plenitude reside? How, conversely, is "lack" conveyed in the theater? And how does gender inflect theatrical constructions of subjectivity?

Coriolanus emphasizes the part played by the audience in the formation of character, by underscoring conflicts between verbal and embodied forms of meaning and by withholding the usual means (soliloquy and direct address) of establishing intimacy between characters and audience. Coriolanus himself presents particular difficulties, since his excessive fixation on violence, his evident sense of class superiority, and his refusal to explain or reveal himself render him an unknowable character. In these theatrical difficulties, I want to suggest, we can trace the violence through which subjective identity is achieved. The play both models the violent birth of identity in its staged action and extends this process to the audience. *Coriolanus* demonstrates the appropriateness of available models of subject formation – Foucault's, Althusser's, Lacan's – that entail a wrenching of possibility, a violence of loss and conscription into a symbolic order. Here I will use Julia Kristeva's model of identity formation, because its dialectic offers a means to avoid the opposing perils of studying character by means of performance theory. I want to avoid, on the one hand, ascribing ready-made interiority to Coriolanus (the assumption humanist critics have typically made) or, on the other hand, essentializing the audience by universalizing my own responses. Kristeva's dynamic model locates identity in the space between semiotic and symbolic, between the body and language; this is the space that demands our attention in the theatrical interaction.

This essay focuses on the episode (in II.iii) in which Martius Coriolanus refuses to show his wounds to the assembled populace. Shakespeare alters this scene from his Plutarchan source, in which Coriolanus unproblematically reveals his wounds. In the play, the scene establishes both the hero's fate – his rejection by the plebeians – and his characterological presence – his pride, stubbornness, irascibility. Thus the scene offers a central locus for issues of verbal and physical revelation of character. It suggests how Shakespeare negotiates the spatial, symbolic, and psychic spaces between actor and audience, and how he seems intent on bringing those spaces into the viewer's consciousness.

While not disputing the psychoanalytic perception that Coriolanus' wounds figure vulnerability, I will concentrate here on a prior question, the semiotic one of how (rather than what) the wounds signify in the theater. This is the question Shakespeare raises when he has Coriolanus refuse to show his wounds: the hero attempts to halt the process of signification. Considering wounds as signifiers involves questions of gender and power in the dynamic of theatrical experience. I will suggest that the phenomenology of performance incorporates but challenges the Lacanian notion of the phallus as master (or even sole) signifier. Readers of Lacan, of course, will suspect that what is at issue in the complaints of "lack" is the hero's masculine identity. In Lacan's terms, Coriolanus lacks what a subject must always lack: the phallus that could guarantee identity. Certainly his failure to achieve a fully realized subjectivity is all the more interesting given the hyper-inscription in his character of easily recognizable codes of Roman masculinity – glorification of violence, preference for male relational bonds, and denial of emotional dependency. In our culture, subjectivity has typically presupposed maleness – in Marjorie Garber's concise terms, "to be a subject is to have a phallus, to be male literally or empowered 'as' male in culture and society."[6] But I think we can more fully understand how character is created in the mind of the reader or viewer by releasing the equation of theatrical potency with phallic signification (that is, with what is, or can be, shown) and hence with masculinity. *Coriolanus* derives its peculiar, troubling power from its scrambling of the elements in this equation. For if a feminizing attention to his wounds undermines the hero's power, he also gains complexity and interest and perhaps even interiority from what, on a certain level of imaginative creation, he lacks.

What is at stake in considering how the theater produces effects of characterological depth? At the end of her essay "Women's Time," Kristeva calls for an "*interiorization of the founding separation of the socio-symbolic contract.*" This often-quoted phrase presents real problems for feminist praxis – how might the goal of interiorizing violence be effected? and what are the implications of introducing 'its cutting edge into the very interior of every identity"?[7] Like most poststructuralist theorists, Kristeva sees identity as multiple and diffuse, such that a single subject contains various and potentially opposing roles. For Kristeva, the subject is imbued with violence from its moment of origin: in *Powers of Horror*, she describes the originary crisis of identity as one of separation; the subject in a sense gives birth to itself when it first distinguishes "self" from "not-self." Further, the subject's negotiations with the symbolic realm are continually problematic, and because these negotiations are never completed, it remains always a subject-in-process. Kristeva politicizes this understanding for feminism by insisting that "violence be conceived in the very place where it operates with the maximum intransigence . . . in personal and sexual identity itself."[8] Without the recognition that violence is a condition of subjective identity and therefore located "within" each subject, it will (continue to) be projected onto scapegoats by those with the power to do so.[9]

Kristeva's semiotic theory has particular relevance for the study of drama, since her concern with the means of signification accords with the problematic status of the real within theatrical practice. Kristeva's essay on "The True-Real" ("Le vréel"), for instance, ponders an aesthetic that might close the gap between language and body by formulating a truth that would also be the real (in the Lacanian sense). "In this economy," Kristeva writes, "there are no *images* or *semblances*." Against the customary distinction of sign and referent, here "the signifier is the (sole) truth, it is the body and vice versa."[10] She finds the collapsing of meaning into the real to characterize modernist thought and art as well as the discourse of psychotics, and she names Antonin Artaud (who belongs to both categories) as an exemplar of "concretization" of the signifier.[11] The notion of a truth that exists in the real, without image or signifier, haunts *Coriolanus*. Terry Eagleton, for example, writes that the hero "confers value and meaning on himself in fine disregard for social opinion, acting as signifier and signified together."[12] But before considering the specific conjunction of Kristeva's ideas with this particular play, I should discuss more generally the connection between violence and theatrical interaction, and how interiority is implicated in this connection.

Kristeva's interest in Artaud may account for the parallel between the "cutting edge" of her feminist theory and what Derrida calls the "permeating" effects of Artaud's theater of cruelty.[13] Although Artaud's goal was the "exteriorization . . . of latent cruelty"[14] and Kristeva's "an *interiorization of the founding separation*," the apparent opposition collapses when the dialectical positions of interior/exterior in each formulation are taken into account. Each theorist locates violence within the subject. Each would enact a form of violence – Artaud's theatrical, Kristeva's rhetorical – in order to demonstrate an inner or "latent cruelty." And most importantly, in each case the boundaries of subjective identity are called into question. Artaud sought to demonstrate latent cruelty by breaking down the distinction between "real" and "theatrical" violence. An audience is implicated when violent physical acts are actually performed on stage; such a theater disallows comfortable distancing of violence into aesthetic or mimetic remoteness. Analogously, the position of agency is blurred in Kristeva's quest to "introduc[e] . . . into the very interior of every identity" the "cutting edge" on which subjectivity is founded. Her rhetoric breaks down the positions of subject and object in order to demonstrate "potentialities of *victim/executioner* which characterize each identity, each subject, each sex."[15] That the theater of cruelty can "permeate" an audience's consciousness suggests the vulnerability of audiences to certain experiences. Processes of identification enable extreme theatrical engagements: one's own safety and bodily integrity are cast into doubt by the dramatized action. But (how) can the interiorization of violence Kristeva calls for occur as a theatrical effect? Can "interiorization" be forced, induced, or even encouraged? And who is it that interiorizes in a theatrical dynamic – actor? director? audience member? critic?

The ambiguity about what interiority might mean in the theater is compounded when the text at issue dates from the early modern period. Recent inquiries into the historical construction of subjectivity have understood "interiority" as a mode of gesturing, through words, toward an inner self – as in the paradigmatic example, Hamlet's claim to "have that within which passeth show."[16] Lyric poems, especially sonnets (and especially Shakespeare's sonnets), have provided the strongest evidence of an interiorized early modern subjectivity.[17] Interiority may even be thought of as a purely verbal construction – an assumption which seems justifiable, if not obligatory, from an evolutionary standpoint, and one which accords in a developmental sense with the Lacanian idea that entry into the symbolic creates the subject. Language is inextricably bound to whatever we mean by the human self, so we understandably recognize and endorse verbal claims to interiority.

But in the theater, and so in the study of play-texts, the matter is quite a bit more complicated. Considering the possibility of interiorization as a specifically *theatrical* effect requires that we understand subjectivity in a more transactional way than is customary, for the theatrical dynamic can usefully direct attention to *how* interiority is figured. Hamlet's claim, for instance, is built upon a theatrical tension between what might be shown and what remains hidden "within"; as Douglas Lanier suggests, only the possibility of display allows Hamlet to posit "that within" which remains private.[18] Further, in the theater words are compellingly attached to the actor who utters them, and an actor may, or may not, impress an audience as conveying a sense of inner depth, quite independently of whatever words he or she speaks, through such means as physical presence, gesture, and expression. Production decisions will certainly influence the extent to which characters will be developed along the interior dimension, and in fact whether they will be developed in this way at all. Yet it is axiomatic that whatever impression of a character an audience gains in the theater will be attached to the body of the presenting actor. Dissonance may mark the relationship – a viewer may be troubled by a poor casting decision or by memories of other theatrical embodiments of the same character; a play-text may even advertise the poor fit between a presented character and the view others hold of him. Yet, at least for the duration of the performance, the locus of a given character will be in the physical self of the presenting actor.

If interiority has a necessarily physical dimension in the theater, the connection was particularly strong in early modern culture, when inwardness was regularly conceived in a "corporeal way," as Katharine Eisaman Maus phrases it.[19] Anne Ferry documents the use of the same words to describe what we think of variably as either "inward" or "outward" experiences: "the very lack of consistent distinctions between literal and figurative uses of language for what is in the heart shows that man's inward and outward experiences were viewed as closely parallel and that no great separation was consistently or systematically conceived to exist between them."[20] The corporeality of inwardness did not render it discernible, however, since it was the bodily interior – in Maus' terms, "still mysterious in a way perhaps hard to recapture in an age of medical sophistication"[21] – that housed, or figured, psychological depth. Interiority as a whole was not attached to a particular bodily site – certainly not to the brain, where today scientists and lay folk alike locate the self, with some nostalgic competition from the heart. Bodily organs were understood to be the seats of various feelings and behaviors. The established abilities of the kidneys (reins) to signify passion, the womb (mother) to denote hysterical emotion, and the heart to figure (as it still does) romantic love seem not to have been immediately threatened by anatomists' uncovering of those organs as simply body parts.[22] The significance attached to bodily interiors was especially resilient in the theater, because it reiterated the phenomenal limits of drama. Lear's wish to "anatomize Regan" and "see what breeds about her heart" conflates two literalizing possibilities: that Lear might actually find what "makes these hard hearts" (III.vi.74–76) and, more horribly, that he might demonstrate his discovery to the audience. The latter possibility ceases to be so remote when Gloucester is blinded on-stage.

Although Lear could never (I want to hope) actually anatomize Regan in the theater, the representation of a wounded body on-stage has considerable power to suggest, demonstrate, or even create a character's inner dimension. Rupturing the bodily surface that houses or contains the mysterious inner self, wounds serve as tokens of that self, even as gateways to it. Theatrical wounds are most obviously markers of extreme and memorable experience. On-stage, a wounded character is marked semiotically, taking possession of wounds that are distinctively "hers" or "his," evident and unassailable facts of personhood. Once wounded, a character indeed takes on a new identity, in a psychological as well as a physical way, since a wound asserts its own agenda and tells its own story, requiring the sufferer's accommodation to it as a bodily fact – as, for example, with the blinded Gloucester. Moreover, as Elaine Scarry argues, wounds (and scars) visibly record the collision of individual bodies with political forces through war or other social conflict,[23] and theatrical wounds frequently carry this sort of demonstrative significance. In these various ways, wounds as signifiers construct the individual while deconstructing his or her body.

Leo Kirschbaum many years ago observed how Shakespeare and his contemporaries used stage blood to excite a primal horror in the theatrical audience.[24] But beyond the generalized effects of thrill and terror, we should note that particular identifications will determine an audience member's response to a bloody spectacle. It matters a great deal, for instance, whether one identifies primarily with the perpetrator or the victim of violence. The role of imagined pain in such a theatrical engagement generally has been undertheorized, and needs more attention as a component of audience identification. Even Scarry, who argues forcefully that other people's pain remains in accessible to us and who insists that "living" pain not be equated with its verbal representation, is prepared to make an exception for Artaud's theater of cruelty. She believes "some ultimate and essential principle of reality" is exposed by "the mime of cruelty."[25] Artaud himself saw a continuity between Jacobean drama and the form of theater he wished to create.[26] We can more thoroughly consider the material effect of Shakespeare's drama by exploring its capacity to break down metaphysical distance between audience and actors through the representation of pain.

Although a wounded character invites sympathetic identification wordlessly through an appeal to the audience's appeal to the audience's own bodily vulnerability, the power of wounds on stage also derives from a paradox of subjective effect. Because theatrical wounds are always on one level false, they call into question exactly that which they would prove: the felt experience and subjective identity of the wounded character. The disruption of created illusion that occurs when an audience "knows" a wound is illusory but "believes" in it as real can serve to promote theatrical construction of character, by challenging the audience's involvement and requiring it to paper over gaps in the presented subject. In W. B. Worthen's estimate, Shakespeare's "interactive stage" thrived on audience participation in the creation of character. Whereas modern American theater has produced a theory of character that assumes "'truth,' interior fidelity, subtextual vitality, character coherence, and so forth," the theater of Shakespeare's day assumed a diffuse and disrupted version of individual character. Worthen observes that "epilogues, soliloquies, and various versions of direct address to the audience imply" that "'character' in the Renaissance may have been a more collaborative or even collusive activity, one in which the seam between actor and character may well have been visible . . ."[27] Coriolanus' wounds, testifying at once to the artifice of the stage and to the felt subjectivity of the character, present such a seam; they require collusion of several sorts from an audience.

In *Coriolanus*, an inordinate amount of attention comes to bear on the hero's wounds. His mother, Volumnia, expresses the overdetermined Roman attitude toward martial violence: blood, she says, "more becomes a man / Than gilt his trophy" (I.iii.39–40). She "thank[s] the gods for't" on hearing that her son has been hurt (II.i.120), and proudly discusses the locations and number of his wounds (Menenius says "Now it's twenty-seven" [II.i.154]). The spectacle of a bleeding Martius Coriolanus is reiterated throughout the battle scenes early in the play: "*Enter Martius, bleeding, assaulted by the enemy*" (I.iv. 61 stage direction); "Who's yonder, / That does appear as he were flay'd?" (I.vi.22–23); ". . . blood / Wherein thou seest me mask'd" (I.viii.9–10); "from face to foot / He was a thing of blood" (II.ii.108–09). Most crucially in terms of the plot, Roman custom in the play requires that anyone seeking public office display his wounds to the people assembled in the marketplace. When Martius Coriolanus refuses the custom, his downfall begins. The play, bound up as it is with assessment of Martius' character, turns not simply on the matter of his having wounds but on the semiotic issues of showing and interpreting them.

The significance Shakespeare granted to the episode in the market-place is apparent from his deviation from the source text. In the corresponding scene in Plutarch's *Life of Caius Martius Coriolanus*, Martius readily displays himself: he "showed many wounds and cuts upon his body, which he had received in seventeen years' service at the wars . . . So that there was not a man among the people but was ashamed of himself to refuse so valient a man . . ."[28] In Shakespeare's play, when Coriolanus appears in the "napless vesture of humility" (II.i.232) he first offers "I have wounds to show you, which shall be yours in private" (II.iii.76–77). But when challenged by the plebeians, he retreats from accommodation to defiance: "I will not seal your knowledge with showing them" (II.iii.107). The change provides clearer motivation for the people's rejection of Coriolanus and gives stronger point to the character's pride and stubbornness. But this is not all: it also generates complex theatrical meanings through the conflicting testimonies of the actor's body and the character's wounds. We need to attend to these "surface" meanings before assigning characterological depth to Martius Coriolanus, lest we mistakenly attribute causal force to what is in fact a theatrical effect.[29]

For Shakespeare's Coriolanus, the question of exposing his wounds is less one of compliance to ceremony or conformity to public expectation than of allowed knowledge, of the extent to which his wounds cease to be his own and become more generally available – whether, as he puts it, they "shall be yours." Semiotic issues take precedence over historical or even motivational ones, since the question of who really knows Martius is intrinsically linked to his wounded body. The character's identity is radically determined by the wounds that speak of his heroism, the same wounds that speak of his ultimately tragic defiance of the people. When Menenius says "the wounds become him" (II.i.122), he refers to their enhancing value, but in the Roman symbolic economy Martius indeed seems on the verge of "becoming" his wounds. He depends upon them to validate his identity as warrior, but the wounds prove unstable and appropriable as signifiers. Rather than guaranteeing his identity, the wounds disfranchise it. An interesting visual analogue for Martius Coriolanus is the wound-man illustration popular in late medieval medical textbooks, which pictures various types of wounds and other physical ailments on a single figure (see the example in figure 4.1). Despite their iconographic debt to St. Sebastian, wound-men typically did not evince a unified theme or represented identity. Instead, the sheer variety of wounds, together with the inclusion in the picture of causal weapons, renders a wound-man a visual encyclopedia of possible complaints, not a patient any practitioner might encounter and certainly not a wounded hero. What is missing is the acknowledgement of pain that would establish the wound-man as a suffering person. Instead, the individual's identity is subordinate to that of his wounds – precisely the fate to which Coriolanus is liable, and for the same reasons.

In denying the people sight of his wounds, it seems that Coriolanus attempts to retain control as "author of himself" (v.iii.36). Through interpretive fiat, critics regularly assign Martius' motivation for his refusal, in the process granting him an inner dimension of considered action. Certainly the representation of decision can be a powerful indicator of subjective identity in drama.[30] The soliloquy in which Brutus ostensibly decides to join the conspiracy to kill Caesar, for instance, conveys a sense of Brutus' reasoning abilities, his inner dimension. But Martius' thought processes are not represented when he decides against displaying his wounds, so to provide reasons for his decision is actually to create an inner dimension in the name of reading it. Critics have been quick to do this. Vivian Thomas, for instance, notes here the "unyielding" character of Coriolanus, who "finds this [showing the wounds] unbearable"; Alexander Leggatt writes that "he imagines himself losing his social position, his physical strength, and his sexual identity, in a loss of self more specific and detailed than anything Antony feared."[31] Psychoanalytic readings that focus on the symbolic significance of the wounds are even more specifically insistent in their discovery of motives. Janet Adelman maintains that Coriolanus fears showing the wounds would reveal "through the persistent identification of wound and mouth, that he too has a mouth, that he is a feminized and dependent creature."[32] Madelon Sprengnether similarly sees him as reluctant "to expose his incompleteness, his implicitly castrated condition"; and in

Charles K. Hofling's view, "being placed in the passive position" is the "most intolerable" aspect of the situation to Coriolanus.[33] Coppélia Kahn recently has complicated the gendered emphasis of classic psychoanalytic readings, maintaining that for Coriolanus "his wounds function like a fetish: he must mention them, but only to prevent mention of them. Even as they evoke the female aperture, they deny it."[34] Despite her sensitivity to the culturally inscribed codes of identity in the play, Kahn does not hesitate to presuppose Coriolanus' psychological depth.

Each of these readings, in fact, presupposes a model of psychological complexity and considered action that inspires a search for what Kaja Silverman calls "an illusory 'wholeness.'"[35] When we pay attention to the theatrical phenomenology enacted here, it becomes evident that Martius Coriolanus' refusal creates the need for a multidimensional hero and constructs the place for such a character to occupy. An unfolding sense of the historical development of subjectivity underlies this claim: Shakespeare did not come upon a ready-made concept of interior self-hood, but participated in its creation; here we see a step in the process of that creation. If, from our historically belated position, we make a prior assumption of characterological unity, the consequent attempt will be to account for Martius' action by ascribing depth or complexity of motivation to him. But the play does not document any Hamlet-like access of self-understanding in Martius when he finds himself at variance with local custom. He proceeds in this scene with customary bluntness. The advent of complexity is rather a theatrical effect: an audience witnessing Martius rejecting social expectation sees "difference" portrayed on-stage. The audience's perception is crucially altered here: the moment of refusal functions as the theater's equivalent of the Kristevan "founding separation of the socio-symbolic contract." It is the split on which (our notion of) Martius' subjectivity is founded.

We can better understand why this is the case by remembering how the play implicates an audience's own desire to see Martius Coriolanus' wounds and its own propensity to attach meanings to his hurt body. The character repeatedly uses theatrical metaphors to explain his unwilling-ness to be put on display: "It is a part / That I shall blush in acting" (II.ii.144–45); "Would you have me / False to my nature? Rather say I play / The man I am" (III.ii.14–16). The division between the "I" and the actor, which makes it necessary for "the man I am" to be "play[ed]," implies the character's subjective consciousness. The splitting off of the theatrical other, the "part" to be played or rejected, defines the

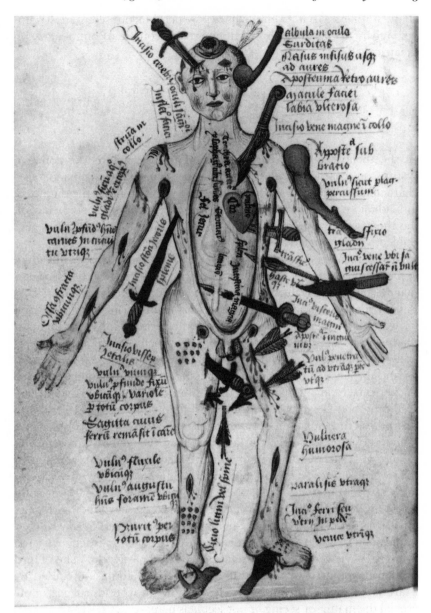

Figure 4.1 *Wound-man.* From pseudo-Galenic *Anathomia* (*c.* 1450).

characterological self. Even the lines in which Martius seems most compellingly to acknowledge his own inner truth contain a commentary on
theatrical effect:

> I will not do't,
> Lest I surcease to honour mine own truth,
> And by my body's action teach my mind
> A most inherent baseness.

(III.ii.120–23)

At the theatrical level, the "body's action," the actor's position and
gesture, necessarily instructs, even creates, the meaning attributed to the
character's "mind." Against the character's demand that the dignity of
individual "truth" be properly "honour[ed]" by appropriate behavior,
the theatrical dynamic posits the body's truth as likewise "inherent."
Subjectivity is initiated through splitting and division.

In the theater, the "body's action" is often more trustworthy than
verbal claims to inner truth. And in the theater, it is less the character
than his physical self that is at issue in the episode in the marketplace. As
Philip Brockbank points out, "making Coriolanus shrink from displaying
his wounds to the people . . . focuses further action and spectacle upon
the hero's body."[36] This focus reveals a gap between the hero and his
body, reiterated in the theater by the analogous gap between the character and the actor's body. Rather than fixing the meaning of this event in
the personal motivation of the hero, or presuming the ability to read correctly the body's symbolism, we should follow Shakespeare's lead and
realize that the issue is precisely semiotic – the point within the play and
therefore within the theater is how, and why, the wounds are read, not
merely what such reading might render. Martius seeks to "stand / As if a
man were author of himself" (v.iii.35–36), but the crowd wishes itself to
authorize him; as the Third Citizen says, "if he show us his wounds and
tell us his deeds, we are to put our tongues into those wounds and speak
for them" (II.iii.5–8). As I have suggested, such lines serve reflexively to
implicate an audience, since "speaking for" wounds is exactly what, as
responsive viewers or interpreters, we customarily do. The Third
Citizen's subjunctive "if" as well as the general confusion caused by
Martius' reiterated broken promises to show his wounds suggests how
crucial the matter of seeing or not seeing is here:

> SECOND CIT. He mock'd us when he begg'd our voices.
> THIRD CIT.   Certainly,
> He flouted us downright.

FIRST CIT.   No, 'tis his kind of speech; he did not mock us.
SECOND CIT.   Not one amongst us, save yourself, but says
               He us'd us scornfully: he should have show'd us
               His marks of merit, wounds receiv'd for's country.
SICINIUS.   Why, so he did, I am sure.
ALL.   No, no; no man saw 'em.
THIRD CIT.   He said he had wounds which he could show in
               private . . .

$$(\text{II.iii.157–64})$$

The ceremony in the marketplace would ostensibly frame and limit the meaning of the wounded body to the citizens' requirements, to the "tongues" they would put into the wounds – a feat Antony accomplished in *Julius Caesar* with his display and interpretation of Caesar's wounded body. Martius' resistance – "I will not seal your knowledge with showing them" (II.iii.107) – challenges his various audiences by refusing exposure and condemning the viewers' power. He indicts the desire to see that any theater audience shares with the plebeians.

Most tellingly, Shakespeare reminds the audience of the privileged position of our own view of Martius and his wounds. After the siege at Corioles, Martius "appear[s] as he were flay'd" (I.vi.22); one commentator compares the description of Marsyas in Golding's Ovid, "Nought else he was than one whole wounde."[37] Witnessing this scene, a theater audience is granted visual intimacy and hence, in the play's terms, a knowledge of Martius that is subsequently denied to the plebeians in the marketplace. Martius himself does not admit pain, and even attempts to "reconfigur[e] . . . blood as healthy sweat."[38] Nevertheless, an audience's identification with him is encouraged in the play's early scenes, and his presence is sufficiently gruesome that it will carry a component of imagined pain. Through its ability to "permeate," in Artaud's sense, the consciousness of the audience, theatrical violence effects a phenomenological link. Precisely because theatrical violence and theatrical pain are illusions, they have subjective content only in the presence of a responsive audience. If the actor playing Martius, that is, "feels" the pain from his hidden wounds, he will do so only by way of his efforts to convince an audience. The viewer who imagines the wounds completes the theatrical circuit and, in a certain sense, creates the character by incorporating his or her thoughts and feelings; hence no ready division separates the character's consciousness from the viewer's. Martius' inner self could even be said to exist within individual audience members rather than within the presenting actor, so that in the battle scenes, the pain of Martius' wounds is felt primarily by the audience.

The formalized ritual of showing the wounds, however, reinstates the distance between audience and hero – or simply instates it. When Coriolanus is put on display and objectified in II.iii, the theater audience is placed in parallel identification with the viewing populace; the citizens become our on-stage doubles, seeking knowledge of Martius that he now insists is "private." A fissure in the audience's awareness is created, as we first identify with a wounded Martius and then are denied full view of him and reminded of our place as audience. We are jolted from an empathic to a scopic relationship with Martius Coriolanus, from a semiotic to a symbolic economy. This disruption of theatrical effect mimes the dispute within the play over Martius' character and his position in relation to Rome. By extending to the audience the issue of judging Martius, the play fixes his identity on the split through which he is objectified.

As an instance of what Garber terms the "literature of male sexual and martial initiation," *Coriolanus* documents the sense that "to be a subject is to have a phallus."[39] Martius' failure to be "author of himself," his shrinking from displaying the signs of martial combat, his final capitulation to the wishes of his mother – all this suggests that Martius lacks coherent masculine identity, a convincing name (-of-the-father), or on the symbolic level, the phallus. In the linguistic register, the uneasy foundation of Martius' masculine identity is emblematized by the shifting of his name(s). Although the addition of the honorific "Coriolanus" seems initially to record his attainment of coherent identity, the name depends on his political loyalty to Rome, and eventually the exiled Martius rejects it:

> "Coriolanus"
> He would not answer to; forbad all names:
> He was a kind of nothing, titleless,
> Til he had forg'd himself a name o'th'fire
> Of burning Rome.   (v.i.11–15)

For the audience, any reference by name to a hero who forbids "all names" will involve a choice; Jarrett Walker nicely observes that "to call him anything is to tilt our perception either toward the realm of the voice, the linear time of natality and death implied by 'Caius Martius,' or toward the realm of the body, where one violent action can overwhelm time and record itself in eternity."[40] Corporeal identity takes on a heightened precedence with a character so resistant to verbal signification. But despite the character's drive to define himself in action, the play teaches that not only action but the body itself is subject to interpretation.

The stability of Coriolanus' claim to "honour [his] own truth" is punctured as the play demonstrates the negotiated terms of any human truth. The sliding signification of the hero's wounds vividly documents this fact: initially the signs of heroism and valor, they come to be associated with shame and vulnerability, an association fulfilled in his less than heroic death. Like a wound-man, Coriolanus is unable to claim his wounds as his own; he is unable to restrict their meaning to martial codes. His inability to control the signifying capacity of his wounds emblematizes a generalized erosion of power. In the marketplace, Martius is positioned as the object of the gaze, a position that erodes the claims of masculinity. As Susan Bordo observes, "orthodox masculinity dreads being 'stripped' of whatever armor it has constructed for itself, dreads being surveyed and determined from without."[41] Converted from active heroic subject to spectacularized object, Coriolanus is not only demasculinized but feminized. What eludes him is the signifying phallus that would guarantee his self-affirmation.

Overtly, of course, *Coriolanus* is an extremely masculine play – few by Shakespeare are more so. The Rome envisioned here is a hard, tough, unaccommodating world, in which women as well as men value military valor over domesticity, and in which the hero's strongest emotional enthusiasm is directed toward his rival Aufidius. But the heavily macho quality of Martius' persona (given visual emphasis by the black leather favored in recent stage productions) suggests an element of self-parody: in Lacan's terms, "virile display itself appears as feminine."[42] In its radical dependence on an audience, display testifies to an anxiety about self-authorization, an uneasiness about the possession of signifying power. By this logic, we might understand Coriolanus' refusal to display his wounds as a rejection of femininity. At this moment of claiming his "own truth," he embraces masculinity as a construct – but acknowledges in the process his lack of self-guaranteed identity. Judith Butler elaborates usefully on the Lacanian position: "The having of the phallus as a site of anxiety is already the loss that it fears, and it is this recognition of the masculine implication in abjection that the feminine serves to defer. The threat of a collapse of the masculine into the abjected feminine threatens to dissolve the heterosexual axis of desire; it carries the fear of occupying a site of homosexual abjection."[43] This perception helps explain the play's intersection with discourses of homosexuality, whether feared or embraced, as well as suggesting my point that what is at stake is the uneasy ground of masculinity, or, in Butler's words, "the masculine implication in abjection." Since abjection has traditionally been coded in our culture as exclusively feminine, it is no wonder critics of *Coriolanus* complain of a "lack": the play advertises masculinity but extends to its audience an identification with a feminized hero. Yet femininity functions here not as the simple opposite of masculinity, but in the wider and more complicated sense Silverman has advanced: to "designat[e] a number of conditions that are constitutive of all subjectivity, although they are antipathetic to conventional masculinity."[44] Coriolanus' objectification punctures his masculine armor as it deepens his represented subjectivity.[45]

By a peculiar paradox, Coriolanus' wounds exert enormous power in the marketplace scene, although they remain hidden on-stage. Their continued influence limits the applicability of a theory of identity founded on specularity. Lacanian theory accounts for the displacement of meaning that we might imagine to plague Coriolanus – or, roughly speaking, his lack of the phallus. But specularity fails to account for the peculiar potency of the undisclosed wounds. In order to explain the dynamic through which meaning is constructed, through which interiority is not merely figured by, but contained within, the body, we need Kristeva's semiotic theory. The wounds code the impossibility, and the destructiveness, of philosophy's appeal to the body as a ground of truth: the symbolic truth of the wounds is their sliding signification, for they serve contradictorily as symbols of valor and of vulnerability, and their meaning can be all too readily manipulated by the tribunes. Against Lacan's privileging of the visual, evidenced in his claim that "there can be no possible symbolic use for what is not seen, for what is hidden,"[46] the play rejects the notion of a stable physical base for truth. Although Kristeva shares with Lacan a sense that "significance is indeed inherent in the human body,"[47] her version of subject formation displaces the father's all-important role. It is not identification with the father, spokesman for the symbolic order, that inaugurates individuality, but the prior effort, which Kristeva sees as an action of the subject-in-process, to differentiate from the semiotic bond with the mother.

Whereas Lacan's model is predicated on, and hence ensures, the primacy of the phallus, Kristeva sees the drama of identification as occurring somewhere else, semiotically, between mother and child. This developmental crisis of separation is "logically and chronologically" prior to the "mimesis" by which identity as we know it is fashioned: "Even before being *like*, 'I' am not but do *separate, reject, ab-ject*."[48] Martius' difficult and imperfect separation from Volumnia models this process. His insistence on being "the man I am" discloses the self-assertion of an identity in the making. *Coriolanus* focuses strongly on the mother–son relationship and excludes the hero's father (those who apply a Freudian paradigm in effect reinscribe the lost father, granting him status as the crucial [missing] link). The play thus presents a version of the Kristevan developmental model: Coriolanus' attempt to define himself in relation to his mother and, by extension, to Rome. Although he has incorporated Volumnia's ethos, his identity is predicated on the abjection of his mother/Rome. He enacts a struggle "to release the hold of *maternal* entity even before ex-isting outside of her, thanks to the autonomy of language. It is a violent, clumsy breaking away, with the constant risk of falling back under the sway of a power as securing as it is stifling."[49] The warrior-identity collapses when he falls "back under the sway" of Volumnia's power, acceding miserably to her claim in v.iii. The psychoanalytic readings of Adelman, Kahn, and Sprengnether likewise emphasize the centrality of the mother-son relationship, but Kristeva's attention to semiotic processes suggests the complexity within the signifying systems.

Martius Coriolanus functions as the Kristevan subject-in-process. The challenge the character extends to systems of unity and coherence and presence indicates the problems this model creates for a humanist aesthetic. A "violent, clumsy," and ultimately unfinished creation of identity is not only modeled within the play's fiction but enacted in its presentation: an audience struggles to know Coriolanus as he struggles to differentiate "the man I am." With this play, to know is to reject: separation from a full and satisfying space of meaning occurs in several spheres. The plebeians, guided by the tribunes, realize Martius' distinctive identity and reject him with one movement. Similarly, audiences and critics know Martius Coriolanus by rejecting him, not by identifying with him. Fixing him as an insufficient or imperfect hero amounts to the critical abjection of Martius Coriolanus.[50]

Kristeva's revision of Lacan's model of phallic signification not only advances a different story of development, one in which semiotic mother replaces phallic father, but has the further result of producing a different theory of meaning, one in which the "signification of the phallus . . . [is] never guaranteed."[51] Since there is no founding moment of phallic certainty, no originary and no final point of revelation, signs (like subjects) remain forever in process, indeterminable in an absolute sense. But rather than signaling a lurch toward abstraction and the endless deferral of meaning, for Kristeva the indeterminacy of signs acknowledges their "materiality." In the words of Cynthia Chase, "they *can be signs* precisely because they may or may not be significative. That is what is called a text."[52] The very condition of textuality guarantees the instability of Martius' wounds as signifiers; their meaning is disputed, veiled, and contested, both within the play's fiction and within the theatrical economy. This textualizing of the hero's wounds delivers a powerful and unsettling challenge to the notion of phallic certainty. As compensation, perhaps, for the "lack" in masculinity, the play gestures toward another form of textuality that eventually takes form as the interiorized self. *Coriolanus* shows masculinity to be, like the actor's body, a construction of surface effects that may become permeable. It shows interiority, on the other hand, to begin with permeability and to achieve meaning through the textual system in which it is read.

I will conclude this essay with an example of how the model of phallic masculinity has shaped discussions not only of the male body, but of "the body" in general. Stanley Cavell, whose reading of *Coriolanus* details the significance of language, brilliantly connects the hero's refusal of speech with his rejection of the way human society entails "mutual partaking, incorporating one another," a form of dependency "symbolized, or instanced, by speaking the same language."[53] Cavell's essay shows how the psychological issues in the play ultimately become political. Further, through his explicit interest in the part of the audience he grants political suasion an immediate and recognizable manifestation. Yet the status of the real in connection to *Coriolanus* apparently continued to trouble Cavell, for the second publication of his essay concludes with a "Postscript" that documents the centrality of the play's body politics as well as Cavell's own anxieties about the implications of this focus on bodiliness.

In the "Postscript," Cavell questions the stability of his original approach by offering "a different way of characterizing [Coriolanus'] reason for alarm" with his human condition, "one that rather literalizes the parable" of the belly.[54] This reading focuses on anality. As if relieved to find his interest echoed in the "masterful" essay of Kenneth Burke, Cavell quotes Burke's remarks about "'the fecal nature of invective'" and the significance of the final two syllables of Coriolanus' name. Cavell finds Burke "immensely tactful"[55] and the concern with tact is one of several signals of discomfort as Cavell, ordinarily so fluent a stylist, refers to "unprotected prose" and to being "shamed into making [his] embarrassment . . . more explicit." Why this paroxysm of critical self-abjection? Cavell maintains that "to avoid risking one's critical balance in traversing this play is to avoid a measure of participation in the play's assessments of the balance civilization exacts."[56] He accordingly documents the physical, one might almost say primal, embarrassment with which he himself confronts *Coriolanus*.

Given this no-holds-barred critical performance, with Cavell taking *Coriolanus* "to raise the question . . . what it is to know that others, that we, have bodies," his conclusions are decidedly odd. For Cavell, acknowledging our bodiliness means

to know that, and perhaps know why, the body has (along with the senses) two openings, or two sites for openings, ones that are connected, made for each other, a top and a bottom, or a front and a back, outsides and insides.[57]

There is an obvious omission from this anatomical model – it fails to recognize differences in the sexed body. Cavell is not insensitive to such omissions: in the preface to *Disowning Knowledge* he contemplates the "male inflection" of his essay on *King Lear*.[58] But it seems as if the pressure of the dualisms (self/other, mind/body) within which he has constructed his argument betray Cavell's effort to confront the disconcerting fact of being a bodily creature, so that the body – any body – becomes a single entity with "two sites for openings." The body Cavell recognizes here differs from the one at issue in *Coriolanus*, since the hero's body is not the smooth, classically male body marked by "two openings" for entrance and exit. It is, rather, a body riddled with apertures and vulnerabilities – the body of a wound-man. The emphasis on the sheer multiplicity of Coriolanus' wounds (as, for instance, at II.i.145–55) enforces this physical dispersion.

Yet the omissions from Cavell's argument paradoxically demonstrate his thesis: *Coriolanus* is not only "about" the condition of living in a body with needs, desires, and vulnerabilities, but the play forces its audience into a confrontation with that difficult fact[59] – or rather, with that body. Ultimately "the body" at issue will not be Coriolanus', or the actor's, or Kenneth Burke's, not even each of our own, but the body next to us – that is, the experiential fact of the diversity of physical beings among whom we live. The real surprise in Cavell's "Postscript," given that his main theme has been skepticism, is the failure of so scrupulous a critic to recognize here the limits subjectivity necessarily places on what he himself might "know" about having, about being, a body among other bodies. As the play shows, the temporal priority and the final inescapability of a body that inevitably fails to conform perfectly to the shapes embraced by identity – a body constantly changing and inter-acting with its environment – undercuts any claim for subjective iden-tity's coherence.

Without our culture's notion of closed and completed masculinity, Coriolanus would not, I suspect, be seen as lacking, so it is useful to con-sider the notion as an evolved one. In Grosz's view, the temporal nature of subjective experience, its quality of becoming, effectively decon-structs the polarity between presence and absence by "surpassing . . . the model of lack": "In place of plenitude, being, fullness or self-identity is not lack, absence, rupture, but rather becoming."[60] Significantly, of course, Lacan writes of the mirror *stage* and Kristeva of the subject-in-*process*, both giving emphasis to the unfolding of lived experience. A developmental model has particular relevance to drama, a genre whose meanings unfold within the temporal dimension and whose characters, while necessarily present in one sense, are never self-identical. Drama is a mode of becoming in large part because its meanings are created through, with, and upon the bodies of actors. Coriolanus' interiority, written as it is on the actor's body, is anything but a psychic dimension. When human identity is understood as inescapably bound up with an unruly and vulnerable body, notions of the free, whole, and coherent self are impossible to support. "To read for and affirm confusion, contradic-tion is to insist on thinking in the body in history,"[61] writes Jane Gallop. We might also turn this statement around, for to insist on the body is to affirm the confusion that identity – however gendered – is heir to.

NOTES

1 To cite only a few works on each topic: on social codes and conditions, see Jean Howard, "Scripts and/versus Playhouses: Ideological Production and the Renaissance Public Stage," *Renaissance Drama*, new series 20 (1990): 31–49; Carol Thomas Neely, *Broken Nuptials in Shakespeare's Plays* (New Haven: Yale University Press, 1985); Gail Kern Paster, *The Body Embarrassed: Drama and the Disciplines of Shame in Early Modern England* (Ithaca: Cornell University Press, 1993); on erotic energies, see Lisa Jardine, *Still Harping on Daughters: Women and Drama in the Age of Shakespeare*, 2nd edn (New York: Columbia University Press, 1989); Valerie Traub, *Desire and Anxiety: Circulations of Sexuality in Shakespearean Drama* (London and New York:

Routledge, 1992); Stephen Orgel, "Nobody's Perfect: Or Why Did the English Stage Take Boys for Women?," *South Atlantic Quarterly* 88.1 (1989): 7–29; on physical effects, see Peter Stallybrass, "Transvestism and the 'Body Beneath': Speculating on the Boy Actor," in *Erotic Politics: Desire on the Renaissance Stage*, Susan Zimmerman, ed. (London and New York: Routledge, 1992), pp. 64–83.

2 Elizabeth Grosz, *Volatile Bodies: Toward a Corporeal Feminism* (Bloomington: Indiana University Press, 1994), p. 7.

3 Jonathan Goldberg, *James I and the Politics of Literature: Jonson, Shakespeare Donne, and Their Contemporaries* (Baltimore: Johns Hopkins University Press, 1983), p. 187; Michael Goldman, *Shakespeare and the Energies of Drama* (Princeton: Princeton University Press, 1972), p. 118; Paul Cantor, *Shakespeare's Rome: Republic and Empire* (Ithaca: Cornell University Press, 1976), p. 109; Stanley Cavell, *Disowning Knowledge in Six Plays of Shakespeare* (New York: Cambridge University Press, 1987), p. 143; Janet Adelman, "'Anger's My Meat': Feeding, Dependency, and Aggression in *Coriolanus*," in *Shakespeare: Pattern of Excelling Nature*, David Bevington and Jay L. Halio, eds. (Newark: University of Delaware Press, 1978), p. 119.

4 A. C. Bradley, *Coriolanus: The British Academy, Second Annual Shakespeare Lecture* (New York: Oxford University Press, 1912), p. 5.

5 Zvi Jagendorf, "Coriolanus: Body Politic and Private Parts," *Shakespeare Quarterly* 41.4 (1990): 458.

6 Marjorie Garber, "Spare Parts: The Surgical Construction of Gender," in *The Lesbian and Gay Studies Reader*, Henry Abelove, Michèle Aina Barale, and David M. Halperin, eds. (New York: Routledge, 1993), p. 322.

7 Julia Kristeva, "Women's Time," in *The Kristeva Reader*, Toril Moi, ed. (New York: Columbia University Press, 1986), p. 210.

8 *Ibid.*, p. 209.

9 The violent metaphor she employs in calling for introduction of the socio-symbolic's "cutting edge" into each identity typifies the central problem Kristeva has presented for feminists: she sometimes seems to evidence the very faults she would diagnose. Without wishing to diminish the importance of maintaining a clear stand in the face of repressive political systems, I would stress that the power of Kristeva's work often derives from the risks she is willing to take. Her problematic use of violence indicates an effort to confront theory's intersection with the phenomenal world.

10 Julia Kristeva, "The True-Real," *The Kristeva Reader*, p. 236.

11 Toril Moi, ed., *The Kristeva Reader*, p. 214.

12 Terry Eagleton, *William Shakespeare* (New York: Blackwell, 1986), p. 73.

13 Derrida sees the theater of cruelty as obliterating the illusion of safe havens of existence by implicating the audience in the theatricalized violence. Cruelty that breaks what Artaud calls "the surface of a spectacle" encroaches on the minds (and bodies?) of those present (Antonin Artaud, *The Theatre and Its Double*, trans. Mary Caroline Richards [New York: Grove Press, 1958], p. 37). In Derrida's terms, "cruel representation must permeate

me" (Jacques Derrida, *Writing and Difference*, trans. Alan Bass [Chicago: University of Chicago Press, 1978], p. 237).

14 Artaud, *Theatre*, p. 92.

15 Kristeva, "Women's Time," p. 210.

16 *Hamlet*, 1.ii.85. Quotations from Shakespeare's plays other than *Coriolanus* follow *William Shakespeare: The Complete Works*, Alfred Harbage, ed. (Baltimore: Penguin, 1969); quotations from *Coriolanus* follow Philip Brockbank's New Arden edition (New York: Methuen, 1976).

17 See Margreta De Grazia, "The Motive for Interiority: Shakespeare's *Sonnets* and *Hamlet*," *Style* 23.3 (Fall 1989): 430–44.

18 Douglas Lanier, "'Stigmatical in Making': The Material Character of *The Comedy of Errors*," *English Literary Renaissance* 23.1 (Winter 1993): 89.

19 Katharine Eisaman Maus, "Proof and Consequences: Inwardness and Its Exposure in the English Renaissance," *Representations* 34 (1991): 39.

20 Anne Ferry, *The "Inward" Language: Sonnets of Wyatt, Sidney, Shakespeare* (Chicago: University of Chicago Press, 1983), pp. 65–66.

21 Maus, "Proof," 39.

22 Michael Neill has recently pointed out parallels between the development of anatomy theaters and popular playhouses – parallels that Shakespeare and other Jacobean dramatists exploit through references to particular parts of the discovered bodily interior ("The Stage of Death," Shakespeare Association of America Meeting, April 1993).

23 Elaine Scarry, *The Body in Pain: The Making and Unmaking of the World* (New York: Oxford University Press, 1985), pp. 63–64.

24 Leo Kirschbaum, "Shakespeare's Stage Blood and Its Critical Significance," *PMLA* 64 (1949): 517–29.

25 Scarry, *Body*, pp. 11–12, 34. Scarry proposes pain as emblematic of the skeptical condition: "'hearing about pain' may exist as the primary model of what it is 'to have doubt'" (p. 4).

26 Goldberg, *James I*, p. 154.

27 W. B. Worthen, "Deeper Meanings and Theatrical Technique: The Rhetoric of Performance Criticism," *Shakespeare Quarterly* 40.4 (Winter 1989): 454, 455.

28 *Shakespeare's Plutarch*, T. J. B. Spencer, ed. (New York: Penguin, 1964), p. 319.

29 Harry Berger, Jr., discussing *2 Henry 4*, makes a similar claim: "speakers *as characters* are the effects rather than the causes of their language and our interpretation" ("What Did the King Know and When Did He Know It? Shakespearean Discourses and Psychoanalysis," *South Atlantic Quarterly* 88.4 [Fall 1989]: 813).

30 For an astute discussion of the place of characterological interiority in post-structuralist criticism, see Alan Sinfield, *Faultlines: Cultural Materialism and the Politics of Dissident Reading* (Berkeley: University of California Press, 1992), pp. 56–66. Sinfield writes that "interiority is projected by an audience or reader as the place where discourses intersect" (p. 64).

31 Vivian Thomas, *Shakespeare's Roman Worlds* (New York: Routledge, 1989), p.

161; Alexander Leggatt, *Shakespeare's Political Drama: The History Plays and the Roman Plays* (New York: Routledge, 1988), p. 194.

32 Adelman, "Anger's My Meat," p. 115. Adelman goes on to suggest in a note that "Coriolanus's unwillingness to show his wounds may derive partly from a fear that in standing 'naked' (2.2.137) and revealing himself to the people as feminized, he might be inviting a kind of homosexual rape" (p. 124n).

33 Madelon Sprengnether, "Annihilating Intimacy in *Coriolanus*," in *Women in the Middle Ages and the Renaissance: Literary and Historical Perspectives,* Mary Beth Rose ed. (Syracuse: Syracuse University Press, 1986), p. 101; Charles K. Hofling, "An Interpretation of Shakespeare's *Coriolanus*," in *Twentieth Century Interpretations of* Coriolanus: *A Collection of Critical Essays,* James E. Phillips, ed. (Englewood Cliffs: Prentice-Hall, 1970), p. 91.

34 Coppélia Kahn, "Mother of Battles: Volumnia and Her Son in Shakespeare's *Coriolanus*," *differences: A Journal of Feminist Cultural Studies* 4.2 (1992): 163.

35 Kaja Silverman, *Male Subjectivity at the Margins* (New York: Routledge, 1992), p. 50.

36 Philip Brockbank, *Coriolanus*, Introduction, p. 46.

37 Rodney Poisson, "*Coriolanus* I. vi. 21–24," (*Shakespeare Quarterly* 15 [1964]: 449), cited by Brockbank, *Coriolanus*, p. 135n.

38 Paster, *Body Embarrassed*, p. 96.

39 Garber, "Spare Parts," p. 322.

40 Jarrett Walker, "Voiceless Bodies and Bodiless Voices: The Drama of Human Perception in *Coriolanus*," *Shakespeare Quarterly* 43.2 (1992): 171.

41 Susan Bordo, "Reading the Male Body," *Michigan Quarterly Review* 32.4 (Fall 1993): 717.

42 Jacques Lacan, "The Meaning of the Phallus," in *Feminine Sexuality: Jacques Lacan and the Ecole Freudienne,* Juliet Mitchell and Jacqueline Rose, eds., trans. Jacqueline Rose (New York: Norton, 1982), p. 85.

43 Judith Butler, *Bodies That Matter: On the Discursive Limits of "Sex"* (New York: Routledge, 1993), pp. 205–06.

44 Silverman, *Male Subjectivity*, p. 389.

45 Paul Smith writes of the failures of male bodily experience to conform perfectly with phallic organization of the symbolic. Masculinity leaves "hysterical residues," with the hysterical "marked by its lack of containment . . . and by its task of carrying what is strictly the unsayable of male experience" (*Clint Eastwood: A Cultural Production* [Minneapolis: University of Minnesota Press, 1993], pp. 155, 170).

46 Jacques Lacan, *The Seminar of Jacques Lacan, Book II: The Ego in Freud's Theory and in the Technique of Psychoanalysis 1954–55,* Jacques-Alain Miller, ed., trans. Sylvana Tomaselli (New York: Norton, 1988), p. 272. Mikkel Borch-Jacobsen traces "the profound misogyny of the symbol" to Lacan's overreliance on visual forms to represent identity; for Lacan, "the phallus, erected and majestic, is the statue of the ego" (*Lacan: The Absolute Master,* trans. Douglas Bush [Stanford: Stanford University Press, 1991], pp. 217, 218).

118   CYNTHIA MARSHALL

Julia Kristeva, *Powers of Horror: An Essay on Abjection*, trans. Leon S. Roudiez (New York: Columbia University Press, 1982), p. 10.
48 *Ibid.*, p. 13.
49 *Ibid.*
50 Adelman similarly observes that "the nature of our involvement in the fantasies embodied in this distant and rigid hero does not permit any resolution: it also separates and limits" ("Anger's My Meat," p. 119).
51 Cynthia Chase, "Desire and Identification in Lacan and Kristeva," in *Feminism and Psychoanalysis*, Richard Feldstein and Judith Roof, eds. (Ithaca: Cornell University Press, 1989), p. 81.
52 *Ibid.*, p. 83.
53 Cavell, *Disowning Knowledge*, p. 165.
54 *Ibid.*, p. 169.
55 *Ibid.*, p. 174.
56 *Ibid.*, p. 175.
57 *Ibid.*, p. 176.
58 *Ibid.*, p. x.
59 Similarly, Jonathan Goldberg's paper on "The Anus in *Coriolanus*," which builds on Cavell's and Burke's arguments, seems to me less radical in its confrontation with bodiliness than it appears to be. Critical of Cavell for failing to understand anality ("it would seem as though to Cavell the anus exists only in language,") Goldberg explores the question of the play's anal erotics, explicitly identifying an important aspect of the play's male homoeroticism and focusing particularly on the phrase "fisting each other's throat" (IV.v.126). Yet in presenting his paper at the 1994 meeting of the Shakespeare Association of America, Goldberg delivered an aggressive performance: the paper was punctuated with phrases such as "fuck buddy" and "Menenius hurls shit," and was concluded with distribution of an illustration evocative of fisting which clearly shocked some members of the audience. Although the acknowledgment of anality implicitly carries with it an awareness of what I have been calling penetrability, Goldberg resorted to a phallic form of assertion – the same form that fails Coriolanus in the play.
60 Grosz, *Volatile Bodies*, p. 165.
61 Jane Gallop, *Thinking Through the Body* (New York: Columbia University Press, 1988), p. 132.

CHAPTER 5

"The world I have made": Margaret Cavendish, feminism, and the Blazing-World

Rosemary Kegl

May 30, 1667: After dinner I walked to Arundell-house . . . where I
find much company, endeed very much company, in expectation of
[Margaret Cavendish,] the Duchesse of Newcastle, who had
desired to be invited to the [Royal] Society . . . Anon comes the
Duchesse, with her women attending her; among others, the
Ferrabosco of whom so much talk is, that her lady would bid her
show her face and kill the gallants. She is endeed black and hath
good black little eyes, but otherwise but a very ordinary woman I do
think; but they say sings well. The Duchesse hath been a good
comely woman; but her dress so antick, and her deportment so
unordinary, that I do not like her at all, nor did I hear her say anything that was worth hearing, but that she was full of admiration, all
admiration. Several fine experiments were shown her . . . among
others, of one that did while she was there turn a piece of roasted
mutton into pure blood – which was very rare – here was . . . a very
pretty black boy that run up and down the room, somebody's child
in Arundell-house. After they had shown her many experiments,
and she cried still she was "full of admiration," she departed, being
led out and in by several Lords . . .

The Diary of Samuel Pepys[1]

Margaret Cavendish's *The Description of a New World, Called the Blazing-
World* narrates the adventures of a gentlewoman from another world
who is abducted by a merchant and made empress of the new world into
which she sails. As empress, she establishes schools and societies for
virtuosos and debates with them the results of their experiments and
speculations. She enlists the soul of Margaret Cavendish to serve as her
scribe and sends her own soul, with Cavendish's, to travel to England
where both souls dwell briefly in the body of Margaret's husband,
William. The *Blazing-World* was first published in 1666 as an appendix to
Cavendish's scientific treatise, *Observations upon Experimental Philosophy*. It
was reprinted twice in 1668 – once again appended to the *Observations*

and once in a separate edition whose revised epistle was addressed not "To the Reader" but "To all Noble and Worthy Ladies."

Biographers, literary critics, and historians often cite the excerpt from Pepys' diaries with which I preface this essay in order to illustrate the limited intellectual authority that could be claimed even by those seventeenth-century English women, like Cavendish, whose social status – "being led out and in by several Lords" – afforded them some access to academic institutions or to professional and scientific societies.[2] Pepys, of course, was by no means alone in dismissing Cavendish's "deportment" and her intellectual authority in the same breath. Yet, given this larger response to Cavendish's work, Pepys suggests more precisely that Cavendish's interest in science is motivated by her fascination with rarities: she is "full of admiration, all admiration." In other words, Pepys draws upon an available, but by no means stable, distinction between professional and amateur scientists.[3] And, perhaps not surprisingly, he also casts Cavendish as herself an object of analysis rather than an analyzer – depicting her and her entourage as purported rarities which, like the liquified mutton, prove, on closer inspection, to be remarkably ordinary after all. But even more important for the purposes of this essay, Pepys emphasizes the formal symmetry of Cavendish's visit to the Royal Society: "After they had shown her many experiments, and she cried still she was 'full of admiration,' she departed, being led out and in by several Lords . . ." In this way, he denies Cavendish her characteristic narrative of intellectual *process*. For example, in her prefatory remarks to the *Observations*, Cavendish emphasizes the consequences of women's limited educational opportunities by referring to the process by which she learned to master those "hard Words and Expressions" that had initially made "the Philosophical Works of other Authors" inaccessible to her.[4] And, unlike those authors, she promises her readers an annotated list of key terms and concepts – a list which she expands in the treatise's second edition.

The *Blazing-World* interests me because of its author's longstanding prominence within feminist paradigms about seventeenth-century English women's intellectual activity. Cavendish is cited in Mary Astell's and Bathsua Pell Makin's seventeenth-century proposals for educating women, and, several hundred years later, Virginia Woolf devotes a not entirely complimentary chapter of the *Common Reader* to her work. More recently, Cavendish's attempts to claim intellectual authority through her writing and through her visit to the Royal Society have prompted critics to ask how we should evaluate a feminist agenda which is

advanced by a seventeenth-century woman writer who was also an aris-
tocrat, a royalist, and a notorious rack-renter – a woman writer who
undoubtedly agreed with her husband that "when Moste was Unletterd,
it was much a better world."⁵ Within this framework, critics often have
turned to the *Blazing-World* in order to assess those seventeenth-century
feminist, utopian impulses that Cavendish's writing might have pro-
duced.⁶

Two scholars are particularly helpful for sorting through these issues.
The first, Hilda Smith, has argued that Tory and Anglican women who,
like Cavendish, numbered among the gentry and aristocracy actually
were best able to formulate a seventeenth-century feminist politics.
These women, she explains, were ideally positioned to experience their
own limited access to education as an instance of oppression which
affected them precisely because they were women. Drawing upon forms
of rationalism and skepticism that were associated with the new science,
they demonstrated their own intellectual equality with men and, in so
doing, demonstrated more generally that contemporary methods of
educating women were insufficient. I find Smith's model useful for
understanding what might have motivated the conjuncture of gender,
science, and intellectual activity in much of Cavendish's writing, including the *Blazing-World.* This is particularly crucial given Cavendish's
notoriously contradictory claims about women's intellectual potential
and her explicit emphasis not upon collective struggle but upon her individual accomplishments. Smith does acknowledge the limitations of the
sort of feminism which these Tory and Anglican women advanced – its
reluctance to address women's political and economic oppression and its
related inability to address the concerns of the majority of English
women who were members of neither the gentry nor the aristocracy. Yet
she also assumes that a social position like Cavendish's provided the only
viable site for an emerging feminist politics – an assumption governed, in
part, by Smith's effort to establish a continuous and, I would argue,
largely non-conflictual feminist tradition.⁷

Margaret Ezell claims that attempts to establish a continuous tradition of women's writing too often have led scholars to focus "on the
extraordinary individual instead of surveying the general pattern of
women's participation in the intellectual life of the century." Ezell advo-
cates, instead, that we consider those forms of published writing which,
by virtue of their subject matter, are often overlooked and that we consider the widespread production and circulation of unpublished manu-
scripts. I find Ezell's argument a useful counterpart to Smith's. As I have

explained, Smith does situate Cavendish's writing within a larger seventeenth-century feminist project and thus challenges what Ezell refers to as the more common tendency to view Cavendish as an "isolated eccentric." Yet Ezell's use of the category "intellectual life" suggests how we might situate that larger project within a more conflictual model both of women's writing and of feminist politics. Most explicitly, of course, the category is designed to draw our attention to a range of often neglected forms of women's writing. But more important, in Ezell's critical practice, it emphasizes the range of social conditions under which that writing took place. In other words, by using this category, Ezell does not seek to define what did or should count as intrinsically "intellectual" activity; instead, she seeks to understand how seventeenth-century women's writing might have produced competing accounts of gender relations and competing models for social change.[8]

Because I am interested in what sort of feminist agenda for social change might have been produced by the conjuncture of gender, science, and intellectual activity in Cavendish's writing, it might seem somewhat counterintuitive *not* to focus on the *depiction* of that intellectual activity in Cavendish's one explicitly utopian text. Yet I would argue that to do so would be to follow in Pepys' footsteps and to deny the formal imperative of Cavendish's work – the narrative of intellectual process which she so carefully constructs and through which, in her words, she appended the *Blazing-World* "to my *Philosophical Observations*, and joined them as two Worlds at the ends of their Poles."[9] In fact, I would argue further that an analysis of those feminist worlds that Cavendish would make it possible, and *im*possible, for us to imagine requires both keeping in mind the narrative of intellectual process that characterizes her writing and keeping in play that narrative's unevenly related, often overlapping formal registers. This essay will consider why Cavendish's model of intellectual activity takes this precise narrative form and will inquire into its logic.

As these introductory remarks suggest, I am interested in specifying not only the accomplishments of Cavendish's version of seventeenth-century feminism but also its limitations. For example, in the longer study from which this essay is excerpted, I examine Cavendish's tendency to equate her intellectual process with her published corpus. This equation would make unimaginable, for Cavendish's seventeenth-century readership and for twentieth-century critics such as Woolf, the range of social conditions under which, as Ezell notes, many of Cavendish's female contemporaries produced and made public their writing – contemporaries who included her husband's daughters, Jane Cavendish and Elizabeth Brackley.[10] This sort of emphasis on a published corpus, while not unique to Cavendish, has had a disproportionate influence on feminist accounts of English women's writing in the early modern period. Its afterlife might best be measured by what Ezell has astutely described as the tendency for those accounts to "collapse creativity into publication." In this way, Ezell argues, critics have too quickly equated print with authorship; have too readily overestimated the importance of the "persistent prejudice" against publication, particularly during the seventeenth century; and have too often overlooked the significance and highly public nature of genres such as formal manuscript debates.[11] In the next section of this essay, I refine what Smith has told us about Cavendish's contribution to a larger seventeenth-century feminist project: Cavendish's narrative of intellectual process suggests that intellectual equality with men might turn on women's obtaining access not only to particular *concepts* but also to contemplative *habits*. In assessing the limitations of this contribution, I refer once again to Cavendish's principles of exclusion – including, in this case, her tendency to categorize as non-intellectual the tasks performed by her female printers.

Yet to assess the limitations of Cavendish's feminist narrative of intellectual process solely by noting such patterns of exclusion would tend to foster a too-restricted understanding of Ezell's category of "intellectual life." If that category is useful precisely because it draws our attention to the range of social conditions under which Cavendish's writing took place, then it also prompts us to consider more carefully the range of social conditions that her model of intellectual equality might have helped to produce. In other words, to press Ezell's category, locating the *Blazing-World* within "the intellectual life of the century" also entails locating its narrative within that kind of intellectual activity, not restricted to readers and writers, through which Cavendish and her English contemporaries imagined their relationship to the world in which they lived. It is in this context that I find the *Blazing-World's* governing metaphor – the joining of "two Worlds at the ends of their Poles" – particularly intriguing. This metaphor is one version of the feminist narrative of intellectual process that I argue is pervasive throughout Cavendish's work. In the final section of this essay, I analyze its aesthetic imperative in order to demonstrate how the same metaphor that figures women's intellectual equality with men also helps to shape an English experience of merchant's capital, of female desire, and of racial difference.

A MUSING, CONSIDERING, CONTEMPLATING MANNER

One of the female correspondents in Cavendish's *CCXI. Sociable Letters* notes that "for the most part Women are not Educated as they should be, I mean those of Quality, for their Education is only to Dance, Sing, and Fiddle, to write Complemental Letters, to read Romances, to speak some Language that is not their Native, which Education, is an Education of the Body, and not of the Mind."[12] Cavendish attributes her own escape from the fate shared by most women "of Quality" to a fairly idiosyncratic breeding that included access not only to particular *concepts* which tended to be made available primarily to men, but also to those contemplative *habits* of both body and mind which might allow a woman to substitute her writing for the "Needle-works, Spinning-works, Preserving-works, as also Baking, and Cooking-works, as making Cakes, Pyes, Puddings" which women more typically "use to pass their Time withall."[13] For example, in her *A True Relation of the Birth, Breeding, and Life of Margaret Cavendish, Duchess of Newcastle*, Cavendish writes that she was "addicted from my childhood to contemplation rather than conversation, to solitariness rather than society, to melancholy rather than mirth, to write with the pen than to work with a needle," and that, unlike most aristocratic women, she "had rather sit at home and write, or walk, as I said, in my chamber and contemplate" – being more "delighted with thoughts than in conversation with a society, insomuch as I would walk two or three hours, and never rest, in a musing, considering, contemplating manner." In Cavendish's account, this inclination was encouraged by the unorthodox education offered to her by her mother, and by the similar "humour" displayed by her brothers and sisters.[14] Eight years later, she explains how her husband fostered this habit of contemplation: "It may be said to me, as one said to a Lady, *Work Lady, Work, let writing Books alone, For surely Wiser Women ne'r writ one*; But your Lordship never bid me to Work, nor leave Writing . . .; the truth is, My Lord, I cannot Work, I mean such Works as Ladies use to pass their Time withall . . ."[15]

Antonio Gramsci's remarks on education suggest how Cavendish's "musing, considering, contemplating manner" might have contributed to the larger seventeenth-century feminist project that Smith has described. Gramsci writes:

[Studying] is a process of adaptation, a habit acquired with effort, tedium and even suffering . . . Undoubtedly the child of a traditionally intellectual family acquires this psycho-physical adaptation more easily. Before he ever enters the class-room he . . . is already in possession of attitudes learnt from his family environment . . . This is why many people think that the difficulty of study conceals some "trick" which handicaps them – that is, when they do not simply believe that they are stupid by nature. They see the "gentleman" – and for many, especially in the country, "gentleman" means intellectual – complete, speedily and with apparent ease, work which costs their sons tears and blood, and they think there is a "trick."[16]

By emphasizing her contemplative manner, Cavendish's narrative of intellectual process demonstrates that women might acquire not only those concepts but also those habits that are central to intellectual life. Women are not "stupid by nature." And yet, like Gramsci's "gentleman," Cavendish also helps to restrict the scope of what sort of activity might be recognized *as* intellectual. For example, Cavendish's attempt to define her intellectual habits extends to her supposed unwillingness to edit her writing: "As for my Work, *The World's Olio*, they may say some Words are not Exactly Placed, which I confess to be very likely . . . for I leave the Formal, or Worditive part to Fools, and the Material or Sensitive part to Wise men."[17] Among those "Fools" who might have attended to her "Worditive parts" were two seventeenth-century widows who inherited their husbands' printing shops – Alice Warren, who printed the 1662 edition of Cavendish's *Plays*, and Anne Maxwell, who, beginning with the 1666 version of the *Observations* and *Blazing-World*, printed all of the new and revised English editions of Cavendish's work until Cavendish's death in 1673. Although Warren seems to have retained her husband's printing shop for less than two years, Maxwell directed her husband's business for at least ten years.[18] Where would the activity of these propertied widows be located within Cavendish's narrative of intellectual process?

Although, by 1666, English women were allowed to serve as apprentices in the Stationer's Company, most continued to enter the printing trade as the wives, widows, or daughters of male stationers. For example, a 1668 survey after the London fire lists Maxwell as one of four remaining female printers, all of whom inherited printing shops after their husbands' deaths. It is somewhat more difficult to say precisely what sorts of tasks these women's roles as printers might have entailed. Studies of seventeenth-century women printers in England, France, Germany, and Italy suggest that their training varied according to the needs of the fathers and husbands in whose shops they generally learned their trade and according to the pressures exerted by male journeymen who intermittently feared that the women's labor might reduce their own opportunities for employment. Although these women tended not to work the presses and although many of those who owned a printing shop might have relinquished its management to a male supervisor, others do seem to have been involved in setting the type, in correcting the finished sheets, in supervising employees and apprentices who performed these tasks, and in negotiating contracts with authors or publishers who commissioned their services.[19] Yet, more important for the purposes of this essay, whatever decisions Cavendish actually might have made about her printers, her model of intellectual activity certainly granted them no authority in helping to shape her literary, scientific, or social projects – a role, incidentally, which *was* granted, even to women, under the seventeenth-century censorship regulations of Roger L'Estrange, on the one hand, and under the seventeenth-century political practices of radical sectarians, such as the Quakers, on the other.

In the remainder of this essay, I focus on one instance of Cavendish's feminist narrative of intellectual process – the *Blazing-World*. That text refines Cavendish's larger narrative by outlining the very particular demands that scientific study places on contemplative habits. In the *Blazing-World's* preface, Cavendish considers the intellectual process that leads her to "join a Work of Fancy to my serious Philosophical Contemplations." Arguing against an absolute distinction between fancy and reason, she explains that the "Rational search and enquiry into the causes of Natural Effects"

requires sometimes the help of *Fancy*, to recreate the Mind, and withdraw it from its more serious Contemplations.

And this is the reason, why I added this Piece of *Fancy* to my *Philosophical Observations*, and joined them as two Worlds at the ends of their Poles . . . But lest my Fancy should stray too much, I chose such a Fiction as would be agreeable to the subject I treated of in the former parts . . .[20]

In keeping with this prefatory promise, the *Blazing-World is* "agreeable to the subject" of her *Observations*. Following the Royal Society's practice in the middle of the 1660s, the *Blazing-World's* empress divides her investigators into committees – assigning each a particular scientific task. Her responses to their findings are abbreviated versions of Cavendish's responses, in the *Observations*, to her contemporaries' views on optics, anatomy, astronomy, pathology, pneumatics, mathematics, meteorology, and alchemy. And most notably, of course, the very *existence* of the Blazing World marks what Cavendish describes in the *Observations* as the practical limits of experimental philosophy and its deceiving "Glasses." Yet, when Cavendish's prefatory remarks are read alongside the opening narrative of the *Blazing-World*, it is clear that she is stressing not merely

that the *Observations* and the *Blazing-World* are thematically connected –
metaphorically "joined . . . as two Worlds at the ends of their Poles" – but
that moving between these poles is part of the scientist's necessary intellectual journey.

The first few pages of the *Blazing-World* clarify the spatial logic of
Cavendish's metaphor. After describing the fortuitous deaths of the
Lady's merchant abductor and his fellow sailors, Cavendish writes:

> At last, the Boat still passing on, was forced into another World; for it is impossi-
> ble to round this Worlds Globe from Pole to Pole, so as we do from East to West;
> because the Poles of the other World, joining the Poles of this, do not allow any
> further passage to surround the World that way; but if any one arrives to either
> of these Poles, *he is either forced to return, or to enter into another World* . . . (pp. 2–3, my
> emphasis).

In other words, Cavendish prefaces the *Blazing-World* by suggesting that
fancy is not merely contemplation's disposable by-product but, instead,
at least for the scientist, one of its essential components. She represents
this essential relationship between fancy and contemplation as a joining
of the *Blazing-World* to the *Observations* as "two Worlds at the ends of their
Poles." The spatial logic of her metaphor casts the decidedly fanciful
Blazing-World as a necessary step in the process of studying natural philosophy – that "hardest of all Human Learning, by reason it consists
onely in Contemplation."[21] In this way, the *Blazing-World*'s narrative of
intellectual process demonstrates not only that women might acquire
both the *concepts* and the contemplative *habits* that are central to intellectual life but, even more precisely, that women – or at least one woman –
might acquire those concepts and contemplative habits that are central
to scientific study.

The final section of this essay analyzes the aesthetic imperative of
what I have been arguing is the *Blazing-World*'s governing metaphor for
intellectual process – the joining of "two Worlds at the ends of their
Poles." As I explained in my introductory remarks, Cavendish's work has
long been central to feminist accounts of seventeenth-century English
women's intellectual activity – the terms in which those women claimed
intellectual equality with men and the conditions under which they produced and circulated their writing. In those remarks and in this first
section of the essay, I considered how Cavendish's feminist narrative of
intellectual process distinguished among its female subjects. It seems
particularly crucial in a volume whose essays address the "emerging subjects" of early modern culture and of contemporary feminist analysis
also to consider how that same narrative participated in another kind of

intellectual activity, not restricted to readers and writers, through which both men and women positioned themselves as subjects in seventeenth-century England.

IT SEEMED BUT OF ONE PIECE

The text of the *Blazing-World* is joined to that of the *Observations* much as the Blazing World into which the Lady sails is joined to that world from which she is abducted; the reader is no more likely to confuse those two texts than the Lady is to confuse those two worlds. Yet if recent critics are any indication, readers are *entirely* likely to confuse the world from which the Lady is abducted with that world in which Margaret Cavendish resides. To a degree this confusion is built into Cavendish's writing. For example, in the Blazing World, there is one religion and "one language . . . nor no more but one Emperor, to whom they all submitted with the greatest duty and obedience, which made them live in a continued Peace and Happiness; not acquainted with Foreign Wars or Home-bred Insurrections" (p. 10). Unlike the Blazing World, Cavendish's world and that of the Lady are divided into "several Nations, Governments, Laws, Religions, Opinions" which tend to dissolve into "Factions, Divisions and Wars" (pp. 102, 103). Moreover, the text describes London as the "Chief City of *E*," and it describes the Lady's "Native Countrey" as "ESFI" – an acronym which I take to refer to an imperial Britain which would include England, Scotland, Ireland, and, based on England's longstanding claims, France (pp. 152, 143).

What then distinguishes Cavendish's world from that of the Lady? Cavendish's world, we are constantly reminded, is one to which the Blazing World's material objects – and in particular its precious metals and precious stones – *can*not be transported. The Lady's world is one to which those objects *will* not be transported. For example, Cavendish devises underwater vehicles that allow the Lady to transport a large naval force through the narrow passage "out of the *Blazing-World*, into the World she came from" (p. 126). The Lady uses this opportunity for large-scale transportation in order to rescue her native country from a foreign war – eventually securing for ESFI a monopoly over maritime trade and thus an absolute dominion over its neighbors. Yet the Lady refuses to transport gold or jewels to that world "for, said she . . . all the World, their Natures are such, that much Gold, and great store of Riches makes them mad, insomuch as they endeavour to destroy each other for

Gold or Riches sake" (pp. 147–48). The Lady quickly assures Cavendish that if "there could a Passage be found out of the Blazing-world, into the World whence you come," she would "willingly give you as much Riches as you desir'd" (p. 148). Although grateful to her friend, Cavendish predicts "that there will be no Passage found into that World" – at least none that would allow for the transport of "whatsoever is Material" (pp. 148, 149). In short, the impossibility of moving the Blazing World's material objects to the Lady's world takes the form of an imperial prohibition. The impossibility of moving those objects to Cavendish's world takes the form of a physical barrier.

The significance of this distinction between imperial prohibition and physical barrier might best be explained by considering the role of gold and jewels in the Blazing World and, in turn, that world's characteristic aesthetic. Cavendish explains: "None was allowed to use or wear Gold but those of the Imperial race, which were the onely Nobles of the State; nor durst any one wear Jewels but the Emperor, the Empress and their Eldest Son; notwithstanding that they had an infinite quantity both of Gold and precious Stones in that World . . ." (p. 14). Thus, in spite of their abundance, the Blazing World's gold and jewels are subject to restrictive sumptuary laws that govern their proper use. By virtue of this prohibition, the emperor constructs his ships, chariots, stables, and, in fact, his entire imperial city, Paradise, out of gold. Cavendish emphasizes that such imperial objects are *aesthetically distinct* from those of the Blazing World's other inhabitants. For example, unlike their wooden and leather counterparts, the emperor's golden boats "were so well sodder'd, that there was no fear of Leaks, Chinks, or Clefts" (p. 8). In other words, like the cliffs that surround the entrance to the imperial city, the emperor's boats "seemed to be all one piece, without partitions" (p. 9).

That same aesthetic characterizes what is, in the Lady's account, one of the Blazing World's most remarkable architectural achievements: "Amongst the rest, the Imperial Room of State appear'd most magnificent; it was paved with green Diamonds (for there are in that World Diamonds of all Colours) so artificially, as it seemed but of one piece . . ." (p. 12). This description recalls John Evelyn's 1664 translation of Roland Freart's *A Parallel of the Antient Architecture with the Modern.*[22] In his prefatory epistle to Charles II, Evelyn characterizes his translation as a contribution to England's "publick Work[s]" through which, he suggests, the king might reinforce his absolute authority and thus secure his "*Empire*

Universal." Evelyn's "An Account of Architects & Architecture" is appended to Freart's treatise. In the final pages of that essay, Evelyn recommends one form of architecture whose combination of artistry and conspicuous wealth was quite popular among "the *Antients*":

> *Emblema* . . . where not only the *Pavement*, but likewise all the *Walls* are most richly incrusted with all sorts of precious [stones] cut and lay'd . . . in the shape of *Birds, Flowers, Landskips, Grotesks* and other *Compartiments* most admirably Polished, a glorious and everlasting magnificence: But where it is made of lesser *Stones*, or rather morsels of them, assisted with small *Squares* of thick *Glass*, of which some are *Gilded*, it is call'd *Mosaic-work* . . .

I am not suggesting that Evelyn's "*Mosaic-work*" is identical to the diamond mosaic with which, in a world where "precious Stones were Rocks" (p. 14), the Emperor's apartment is paved. Yet when Evelyn laments the dearth of this form of architecture in England, he does claim that it is *best* approximated by the Queen Mother's parquet floors. More important, however, in the logic of Cavendish's text, such "*Mosaic-work*" is associated with absolute rule, with "*Dominion* of the *Ocean*," and with an "*Empire Universal*" not only through its "everlasting" display of artistry and conspicuous wealth but also through its very aesthetic. Like the Blazing World, whose inhabitants are united under one religion, one language, and one absolute monarch, such mosaics "seemed but of one piece."

What might Cavendish's insistence upon this aesthetic tell us about the imperial prohibition through which the Lady restricts "Gold, and a great store of Riches" from entering her world, and what might it tell us about the physical barrier that prevents those material objects from entering Cavendish's world? I would note, first, that the Lady's prohibition assumes that gold, as an object, possesses inherently desirable qualities; this desirability is depicted as self-evident and identical whether we are visiting the Lady's world, Cavendish's world, or the imperial city in the Blazing World. In other words, in Cavendish's narrative, the value of gold is detached from the social relations, and in particular from the human labor, involved in its extraction and refinement. Second, I would note that Cavendish distinguishes the role of gold in her own world and that of the Lady, on the one hand, from its role in the Blazing World, on the other. In so doing, she suggests that the desire for gold would be much less socially disruptive if bullion were not allowed to serve as money. It is not surprising that Cavendish might associate imperial prohibitions concerning the transport of gold with arguments about money.

In the years immediately preceding the publication of the *Blazing-World*, the English controversy over the export of gold and silver bullion provided one forum for defining the nature of money. Writers like Samuel Fortrey, Thomas Mun, and Cavendish's husband, William, promised that increasingly large stores of bullion would enter England *if* bullion were not hoarded but, instead, allowed to circulate as a commodity within the country's lucrative import, re-export, and triangular trades – including, by the middle of the seventeenth century, the West African slave trade.[23]

At first glance, the Lady's prohibition and, even more crucially, the Blazing World's fantastic rejection of the money form, might seem to be incompatible with these accounts of English commerce. For example, the Lady remarks that gold is "so fixt a Metal, that nothing has been found as yet which could occasion a dissolution of its interior figure" (p. 40). A piece of gold can be divided or reconstituted, she explains, but its essence is vulnerable neither to alteration nor to convincing imitation. In other words, the Lady highlights *precisely* those properties which make it likely that gold might be assigned what Marx calls the "formal value" of money – a commodity's social usefulness when it is selected to serve as the generalized equivalent of congealed human labor. And yet, although the Blazing World's economy is elsewhere characterized by a global division of labor and although "all their Traffick was by exchange of several Commodities," Cavendish stresses that the inhabitants of that world "used no Coyn."[24] In fact, as I have explained, the Blazing World's sumptuary laws prohibit *any* use of gold by those who are not members of the "Imperial race." Instead, as the text's early passages on shipbuilding suggest, the very properties that otherwise might have characterized gold in its money form are cast as those properties that define the *aesthetic* of imperial objects forged from gold: they "seemed but of one piece." As I began to suggest earlier, both the elimination of money and the attendant aestheticization of the money form tend to naturalize the value of gold, to naturalize the relationship between gold and money, to assume that money itself produces those social relations that it is called upon to mediate – in short, to elide the structural role of congealed human labor in the production of value. In other words, I am arguing that, in its particular vision of a moneyless society, the *Blazing-World* actually registers and reinforces the very relationship to commodities and, even more particularly, to money, that was fundamental to England's experience of seventeenth-century commercial capital.

Presumably Cavendish's fantasy of direct barter entails some nostalgia for a more transparent or immediately accessible experience of social relations. It is quite curious, then, that she insists repeatedly that the relationship between the Blazing World and her world could never be characterized by even this system of commodity exchange – reminding us that a physical barrier precludes transporting "whatsoever is Material" between those worlds. This is particularly striking since the one object, whose materiality is admittedly in question, that *does* manage to move between these worlds is the soul of Margaret Cavendish in the *Blazing-World*'s depiction of the conjunction between an ideal female intellectual life and the women's desire. Before summoning Cavendish's soul to visit her on the model of a platonic lover and serve as her scribe, the Lady asks her spiritual interlocutors whether such souls are, like spirits, immaterial. They respond that her question mistakes "the purest and subtilest parts of Matter for Immaterial Spirits" (p. 78). *They* are spiritual and immaterial, they explain; Cavendish's soul is spiritual and subtly material. Yet, in spite of what is a fairly lengthy clarification, Cavendish's text is far from consistent on this issue. For example, upon the arrival of Cavendish's soul in the Blazing World, "the Empress imbraced and saluted her with a Spiritual kiss" (p. 89). Upon its departure, "the Empress's Soul embrac'd and kiss'd the Duchess's Soul with an Immaterial Kiss, and shed Immaterial Tears, that she was forced to part from her, finding her not a flattering Parasite, but a true Friend; and in truth, such was their Platonick Friendship, as these two loving Souls did often meet and rejoice in each others Conversation" (p. 123).

In order to account for this inconsistency, I return once more to Cavendish's aesthetic imperative. As seventeenth-century readers of popular travel narratives would have recognized, the Blazing World's characteristic mosaic-work numbers among the commonplaces about Constantinople upon which Cavendish draws when describing her fanciful imperial city, Paradise – the narrow and winding waterway through which travelers generally entered Constantinople, the hills that surrounded that entrance, the precious stones that lined the sultan's throne and the walls of his "appartment for State," the eunuchs who served as the sultan's "Priests and Governors" (p. 14), and, finally, Constantinople's Roman architecture, including most notably the marble "*Mosaik* painting" of Sancta Sophia. For example, the sixth edition of *Sandys Travailes*, published in 1658, explains that Sancta Sophia is "adorned with *Mosaik* painting" – "[a]n antique kind of work, composed of little square pieces of Marble; gilded and coloured according to the place that they are to assume in the figure or ground: which set together, as if imbossed, present an un-expressible statelinesse, and are of a marvellous durance." During the sixteenth and early seventeenth centuries, English commentators generally perceived the military and mercantile strength of the Ottoman empire as a threat to England. In keeping with this perception, English travel writers tended to prefigure the self-destruction of that empire – including its control over lucrative trade routes and its system of absolute rule – by describing the decay of the "un-expressible statelinesse" and "marvellous durance" of Sancta Sophia. "The speciall obiect of Antiquities, I saw within this City," William Lithgow reported in 1632, "was the incomparable Church of Saint *Sophia,* whose ornaments and hallowed vessels, were innumerable, in the time of *Justinian* the Emperour, who first builded it; but now converted to a *Moskuee,* and consecrate to *Mahomet,* after a diabolicall manner." According to Sandys, that conversion was accomplished by "*Mahomet* the Great" who, "upon the taking of the City, threw down the Altars" and "defaced [church] Images (of admirable workmanship, and infinite in number)" – most memorably, as Thomas Smith would explain several years after the publication of the *Blazing-World,* "several figures" from "sacred history" that were represented within Sancta Sophia's mosaic-work – and who located Sancta Sophia's buildings "neer unto the fore-front of his seraglio." As the reports of Lithgow, Sandys, and Smith suggest, English travel narratives tended to attribute the decay of Sancta Sophia, and by extension of the Ottoman Empire, to the irrationality of Islam or to sultans who were too preoccupied with sexual pleasure to govern effectively. For example, travellers reported as "depraved" and distinctly non-English the "inordinate passion" and "libidinous pleasures" experienced between the sultan and his male and female slaves and subjects, between women in the seraglio, and between the infrequent female rulers and their female advisors.[25]

   The *Blazing-World* contributes to these narratives about the racial, religious, and sexual identities that are properly characteristic of the Ottoman empire and of England. When the Lady, visiting Cavendish's world, speculates that the "*Grand-Seignior*" must be the greatest of all monarchs "for his word was a Law, and his power absolute," Cavendish champions the superior civility of English royalty and cautions that, in an Islamic state, "the Law and Church do govern the Emperor, and not the Emperor them" (pp. 104, 105). And when the souls of the Lady, Margaret Cavendish, and William Cavendish reside temporarily in William's body, Margaret writes, "And then the Duke had three Souls in one Body; and had there been some such Souls more, the Duke would have been like the *Grand-Signior* in his *Seraglio*, onely it would have been a *Platonick Seraglio*" (p. 110). In fact, although initially made jealous by the conversation between William and the Lady, Margaret reasons "that no Adultery could be committed amongst *Platonick* Lovers" (p. 110).

This reasoning goes some way toward explaining the *Blazing-World*'s depiction of the "Platonick Friendship" between the Lady and Margaret Cavendish – those "two loving Souls" whose "meeting did produce such an intimate friendship between them, that they became *Platonick* Lovers, although they were both Femals" (pp. 123, 92). In spite of the spirits' warning about the "subtil and insinuating" nature of platonic lovers, the women's husbands evidence no jealousy about this conjunction of female intellectual activity and platonic love. I would argue that, in the logic of Cavendish's text, the repeatedly emphasized physical barrier between the Blazing World and that of Cavendish precludes the possibility of physical contact between women and thus allows for the continued representation of the mobility of their desire – including their desire for one another. The relationship between Cavendish and the Lady is by definition "immaterial," in the sense that it is not experienced as a threat to the women's conjugal contracts and thus is not experienced as relevant. Yet this analysis does not entirely account for what I described earlier as the text's inconsistency about what it would mean for Cavendish's soul to *be* "material" and thus about the platonic nature of the women's love. Rather than attempt to resolve that inconsistency, I would suggest that its *ir*resolvability registers Cavendish's more general method of constructing what it means to be English by depicting the Blazing World both through and in tension with the Ottoman empire.[26]

An equally irresolvable inconsistency characterizes the *Blazing-World*'s construction of racial difference. During her entrance into the Blazing World, the Lady encounters men and women of "several Complexions" who form a human "*Mosaic-work*" – joined together through one language and under one absolute monarch. Cavendish hastens to add that none of these complexions are "like any of our World." Later, after describing the "Imperial race" into which the Lady marries and whose complexions, like that of the Lady, remain unremarked upon, Cavendish elaborates:

[A]nd as for the ordinary sort of men in that part of the World where the Emperor resided, they were of several Complexions; not white, black, tawny, olive- or ash-coloured; but some appear'd of an Azure, some of a deep Purple, some of a Grass-green, some of a Scarlet, some of an Orange-colour, &c . . . The rest of the Inhabitants of that World, were men of several different sorts, shapes, figures, dispositions, and humors . . .; some were Bear-men, some Worm-men, some Fish- or Mear-men, otherwise called Syrens; some Bird-men, some Fly-men, some Ant-men, some Geese-men, some Spider-men, some Lice-men, some Fox-men, some Ape-men, some Jack daw-men, some Magpie-men, some Parrot-men, some Satyrs, some Gyants . . .; and of these several sorts of men, each followed such a profession as was most proper for the nature of their Species . . . (pp. 14–15)

In light of this description of the Blazing World's inhabitants, it is useful to recall one of the few passages that Cavendish adds to her 1666 version of the *Observations* when issuing a new edition in 1668. Arguing that heat and cold actually might be reduced to a common principle, Cavendish asks, by way of analogy, "Were all *Blackmoors*, who seem a kind or race of men different from the White, produced from *Adam*?" In her lengthy answer to this question, Cavendish helps to consolidate one available, but by no means dominant, English scientific discourse of racial difference – eventually asserting that the *racial* difference between "*Blackmoors*" and "White men" might best be understood as a difference in *species*: "For, if there were no differences in their productions, then would not onely all men be exactly like, but all Beasts also; *that is, there would be no difference between a Horse and a Cow, a Cow and a Lyon, a Snake and an Oyster*" (p. 120, my emphasis). In the logic of Cavendish's argument, that species difference gives precedence to the "White men" who descended from Adam.

As the passage that I cited earlier suggests, the *Blazing-World* is similarly interested in distinguishing its "several sorts or kinds" of inhabitants according to a difference of species. And yet in the *Blazing-World* these "men of several different sorts, shapes, figures, dispositions, and humors" are precisely those inhabitants whose resemblance to geese or bears or spiders *distinguishes* them from "the ordinary sort of men in that part of the World where the Emperor resided" – from the men "of several Complexions." In other words, unlike the *Observations* to which it is appended, the *Blazing-World* draws a distinction between difference based on species or complexion, understood as "humors," on the one hand, and difference based on complexion, understood as "colour," on the other.

This inconsistency between the *Observations* and its appendix might be attributed not only to the flexibility of race as a category during the seventeenth century but also to the varied and shifting ways in which "colour" – particularly "blackness" – functioned as a significant variable in defining difference. For example, if we recall for a moment the quotation from Pepys with which I introduced this essay, the "blackness" of the

Italian Ferrabosco might not locate her among Cavendish's *"Blackmoors,"* yet Pepys does represent the fact that she "is endeed black and hath good black little eyes" as distinctly out of the "ordinary." In fact, that "blackness" seems to be involved in the potentially lethal allure – "so much talk is, that her lady would bid her show her face and kill the gallants" – that secures her a place among the rarities in Cavendish's entourage. And if the varied and shifting meanings of "blackness" make somewhat obscure Pepys' description of a "very pretty black boy that run up and down the room, somebody's child in Arundell-house," it is not at all obscure that the child's "blackness," however it is to be understood, contributes to the rarity of the scene that Pepys is setting.

Of course, the simplest explanation for the inconsistency between the *Observations* and its appendix is offered by the text – that none of the Blazing World's "ordinary sort of" inhabitants are *"Blackmoors"* or "White men." In fact, their various complexions are not "like any of our World" and thus have no social force either in England or in the Ottoman empire. Yet this explanation does not take into account Cavendish's tendency to depict the Blazing World both through and in tension with the Ottoman empire and, in the process, to construct what it means to be English. For example, her description of the Blazing World's inhabitants is remarkable for the care with which she introduces her readers to the colors of their complexions. In other words, precisely by aestheticizing differences based on color into a human, and presumably egalitarian, *"Mosaic-work,"* this passage asserts that such differences are, in some way, a significant variable. The philosophy to which at least one traveller attributed the success of Ottoman imperial rule offers a way of understanding that significance. Confronted by advisors who wish him to "root . . . out" the empire's Jewish merchants, Soliman the Great

bad them look upon a Flower-Pot, that held a quantity of fine Flowers of divers colours . . . and bid them consider whether each of them in their colour, did not set out the other the better; and that if any of them should decay, or be taken away, whether it would not somewhat spoil the Beauty of the rest. After every one had heard the *Sultan*'s Opinion, and did allow of it to be true; the Emperour did begin to explain this, and said, The more sorts of Nations I have in my Dominions under me, as *Turks*, *Moors*, *Grecians*, *&c.* the greater Authority they bring to my Kingdoms, and make them more famous. And that nothing may fall off from my Greatness, I think it convenient, that all that have been together so long hitherto, may be kept and tolerated so still for the future . . .[27]

To read the *Blazing-World*'s human *"Mosaic-work"* as a similar sort of imperialist fantasy would make more intelligible Cavendish's otherwise perplexing claim that *all* of the Blazing World's inhabitants "tender'd [the Lady] all the Veneration and Worship due to a Deity" (p. 13).

This essay is not meant to offer a conclusive reading of the *Blazing-World* but a suggestive one – designed to underscore what might be gained by attending to the unevenly related, often overlapping, formal registers through which Cavendish's larger feminist narrative of intellectual process operates. This line of inquiry has allowed me to consider how Cavendish's version of seventeenth-century feminism has helped to shape our assumptions about the conditions under which early modern women produced and circulated their writing, how it participated in contemporary debates about women's educability, and how the same metaphor through which Cavendish figures women's intellectual equality with men figures in the *Blazing-World's* understanding of merchant's capital, female desire, and racial difference. It is, I would conclude, precisely by insisting upon the *im*perfect relationships among Cavendish's feminist worlds, and among the subject-positions that those worlds would offer, that we might begin the larger project of locating women's writing within a much less restrictive account of "the intellectual life of the century."

NOTES

I am grateful to Dympna Callaghan, M. Lindsay Kaplan, Erin Mackie, Lynn Meloccaro, John Michael, and Valerie Traub for their thoughtful responses to earlier versions of this essay.

1 *The Diary of Samuel Pepys*, Robert Latham and William Matthews, eds., 11 vols. (Berkeley and Los Angeles: University of California Press, 1974), vol. viii, pp. 242–43.
2 Sylvia Bowerbank, "The Spider's Delight: Margaret Cavendish and the 'Female' Imagination," *English Literary Renaissance* 14.3 (Autumn 1984): 398–405; Douglas Grant, *Margaret the First: A Biography of Margaret Cavendish, Duchess of Newcastle, 1623–1673* (London: Hart-Davis, 1957), pp. 15–26; Kathleen Jones, *A Glorious Fame: The Life of Margaret Cavendish, Duchess of Newcastle, 1623–1673* (London: Bloomsbury, 1988), pp. 154–65; Sara Heller Mendelson, *The Mental World of Stuart Women: Three Studies* (Amherst: University of Massachusetts Press, 1987), pp. 45–61; Carolyn Merchant, *The Death of Nature: Women, Ecology, and the Scientific Revolution* (San Francisco: Harper and Row, 1980; paperback edition, 1983), pp. 268–73; Gerald Dennis Meyer, *The Scientific Lady in England, 1650–1760: An Account of Her Rise, with Emphasis on the Major Roles of the Telescope and Microscope* (Berkeley and Los Angeles: University of California Press, 1955), pp. 1–15; Samuel I. Mintz, "The Duchess of Newcastle's Visit to the Royal Society," *The Journal of English and Germanic Philology* 51 (1952): 168–76; and Henry B.

Wheatley, *The Early History of the Royal Society* (Hertford: Stephen Austin, 1905), pp. 43–45.

3 For one excellent analysis of this distinction, see Michael Hunter, *Science and Society in Restoration England* (Cambridge: Cambridge University Press, 1981), pp. 59–86.

4 Margaret Cavendish, *Observations upon Experimental Philosophy. To which is added, The Description of a New Blazing World*, 2nd edn (London, 1668), first three pages of the unnumbered prefatory address "To the Reader." All subsequent citations refer to this edition, unless otherwise noted.

5 Thomas P. Slaughter, ed., *Ideology and Politics on the Eve of Restoration: Newcastle's Advice to Charles II* (Philadelphia: American Philosophical Society, 1984), p. 20.

6 Bowerbank, "Spider's Delight," 402–05; Catherine Gallagher, "Embracing the Absolute: The Politics of the Female Subject in Seventeenth-Century England," *Genders* 1 (Spring 1988): 32–33; Kate Lilley, "Blazing Worlds: Seventeenth-Century Women's Utopian Writing," in *Women, Texts and Histories 1575–1760*, Clare Brant and Diane Purkiss, eds. (London: Routledge, 1992), pp. 119–29; Merchant, *Death of Nature*, pp. 271–72; Lisa T. Sarasohn, "Science Turned Upside Down: Feminism and the Natural Philosophy of Margaret Cavendish," *Huntington Library Quarterly* 47.4 (Autumn 1984): 301–302; Hilda L. Smith, *Reason's Disciples: Seventeenth-Century English Feminists* (Urbana: University of Illinois Press, 1982), p. 81; Janet Todd, *The Sign of Angellica: Women, Writing, and Fiction 1660–1800* (New York: Columbia University Press, 1989), pp. 67–68; Marilyn L. Williamson, *Raising Their Voices: British Women Writers, 1650–1750* (Detroit: Wayne State University Press, 1990), p. 40.

7 Smith, *Reason's Disciples*.

8 Margaret J. M. Ezell, *The Patriarch's Wife: Literary Evidence and the History of the Family* (Chapel Hill, NC: University of North Carolina Press, 1987), pp. 62–100, and *Writing Women's Literary History* (Baltimore: The Johns Hopkins University Press, 1993), pp. 1–65. The quotations are from *Patriarch's Wife*, pp. 62–63.

9 *The Description of a New World, Called The Blazing-World*, in *Observations* (1668), second page of unnumbered epistle "To the Reader." For these – and all subsequent – citations from the *Blazing-World*, I will use the 1668 edition. The two versions of the 1668 edition of the *Blazing-World* are (with the exception of their epistles) identical, including in pagination. The 1666 edition is paginated differently, and its text differs slightly.

10 This argument emerges from my analysis of Cavendish's attention to the production and circulation of her writing and from my analysis of her remarks in the *Observations*, in the collections of plays that she published in 1662 and 1668, and in the "Catalogue" and "Observations upon the Opinions of some Ancient Philosophers" that appear in the 1666 edition of the *Observations*. The former portion of the analysis focuses on two of her booksellers, Allestry and Martyn; one of their printers, Thomas Roycroft;

their bookshop, the Bell; and the practices surrounding the editing and distribution of Cavendish's presentation copies. For a discussion of the manuscript collections compiled by Jane Cavendish and Elizabeth Brackley, see Ezell, *Patriarch's Wife*, p. 67.

11 Ezell, *Writing Women's Literary History*, pp. 32, 36.

12 *CCXI. Sociable Letters* (London, 1664), p. 50 (letter 26).

13 *CCXI. Sociable Letters*, first page of unnumbered epistle "To His Excellency The Lord Marquess of Newcastle."

14 *A True Relation of the Birth, Breeding, and Life of Margaret Cavendish, Duchess of Newcastle* (1656), Egerton Brydges, ed. (Kent, 1814), pp. 27, 29, 29–30.

15 *CCXI. Sociable Letters*, first page of unnumbered epistle "To His Excellency The Lord Marquess of Newcastle."

16 Antonio Gramsci, *Selections from the Prison Notebooks*, Quintin Hoare and Geoffrey Nowell Smith, eds. and trans. (New York: International Publishers, 1971), pp. 42–43.

17 *CCXI. Sociable Letters*, first and second pages of "The Preface" addressed to "Noble Readers."

18 Henry R. Plomer, *A Short History of English Printing 1476–1898* (London: Kegan Paul, Trench, and Trübner, 1900), pp. 208, 225, and "A Dictionary of the Booksellers and Printers who were at Work in England, Scotland and Ireland from 1641–1667," in *Dictionary of the Printers and Booksellers who were at Work in England, Scotland and Ireland 1557–1775*, Plomer, H. G. Aldis, G. H. Bushnell, E. R. McC. Dix, A. E. Esdaile, R. B. McKerrow, and others, eds., reprinted in compact form in one volume (Ilkley, Yorkshire: The Grove Press for The Bibliographic Society, 1977) pp. 125, 188–89.

19 Alice Clark, *Working Life of Women in the Seventeenth Century*, Reprints of Economic Classics (London: G. Routledge and Sons, 1919), pp. 161–70; Natalie Zemon Davis, "Women in the Crafts in Sixteenth-Century Lyon," in *Women and Work in PreIndustrial Europe*, Barbara A. Hanawalt, ed. (Bloomington: Indiana University Press, 1986), pp. 167–97; Margaret Hunt, "Hawkers, Bawlers, and Mercuries: Women and the London Press in the Early Enlightenment," *Women and History* 9 (Spring 1984): 41–68; Deborah Parker, "Women in the Book Trade in Italy: 1470–1620," lecture delivered at the Newberry Library, Chicago, June 4, 1994; Merry E. Wiesner, *Working Women in Renaissance Germany* (New Brunswick: Rutgers University Press, 1986), pp. 139, 149–63. For the 1668 survey and a listing of each woman's apprentices and employees, see Plomer, *Short History of English Printing*, pp. 224, 226–27.

20 *Blazing-World*, in *Observations* (1668), second and third pages of unnumbered epistle "To the Reader."

21 *Blazing-World*, in *Observations* (1668), second page of unnumbered epistle "To the Reader." In fact, even Cavendish underscores this essential relationship in the epistle "To all Noble and Worthy Ladies" with which she prefaces the 1668 version of the *Blazing-World* that was issued without the *Observations*.

22 Roland Freart, *A Parallel of the Antient Architecture with the Modern*, trans. John

Evelyn (London, 1664). The next several citations are from the treatise's six-page (unnumbered) prefatory epistle "To the Most Serene Majesty of Charles the Second," and from pp. 141–42. I am grateful to Andrew Morrogh, who suggested that Evelyn's work might be helpful for a reading of the *Blazing-World*'s architecture.

23 William Cavendish, *Advice to Charles II*, pp. 35–42; Samuel Fortrey, *Englands Interest and Improvement* (1663; rpt. Baltimore: The Lord Baltimore Press, 1907); Thomas Mun, *England's Treasure by Forraign Trade* (1664; rpt. Oxford: Basil Blackwell, 1928). C. G. A. Clay, *Economic Expansion and Social Change: England 1500–1700*, 2 vols. (Cambridge: Cambridge University Press, 1984), vol. II, pp. 154–213, and E[phraim] Lipson, *The Economic History of England*, 3 vols. (London: A. & C. Black, 1931), vol. III, pp. 62–153, discuss triangular trade, the balance of trade, and English commercial policy and maritime practices. The citation is from Mun, *England's Treasure by Forraign Trade*, p. 5.

24 Karl Marx, *Capital*, trans. Ben Fowkes, 3 vols. (New York: Vintage Books, 1977), vol. I, pp. 162–280, and *Capital*, trans. David Fernbach, 3 vols. (London: Penguin Books in association with New Left Review, 1981), vol. III, pp. 431–55.

25 For instance, see Peter Heylyn, *Cosmographie*, 4th edn (London, 1666), pp. 794–96; William Lithgow, *The Totall Discourse* (London, 1632), pp. 132–35, 138–39, 147–56; Paul Rycaut, *The Present State of the Ottoman Empire* (London, 1667), pp. 1–11, 33–40; and *Sandys Travailes*, 6th edn (London, 1658), pp. 24–25, 39–40, 58. For an example of the trajectory of writing about the Ottoman Empire as the century progresses, see Thomas Smith, *Remarks Upon the Manners, Religion And Government Of the Turks* (London, 1678), pp. 277, 288–90, 307–09. The quotations are, in order, from: Sandys, p. 24; Lithgow, p. 135; Sandys, p. 25; Smith, p. 308; Sandys, p. 25; Rycaut, p. 35; Rycaut, p. 33; and Lithgow, p. 158.

26 Although my analysis of the *Blazing-World* is indebted to Valerie Traub's "The (In)Significance of 'Lesbian' Desire in Early Modern England," in *Queering the Renaissance*, Jonathan Goldberg, ed. (Durham: Duke University Press, 1994), pp. 62–83, I am suggesting that Cavendish's narrative offers a less absolute distinction between women's desire for one another and the institutional prerogatives of heterosexual marriage than Traub finds represented on the Renaissance stage. I should add that the instability of the distinction between what is "material" and "immaterial" is even more pronounced in the 1668 version of the *Blazing-World* from which Cavendish deleted a 1666 passage about the absolute difference between material and immaterial "Creatures" (*Observations upon Experimental Philosophy* [London, 1666], pp. 70–71).

27 "Dr *Leonhart Rauwolff*'s Itinerary into the *Eastern* Countries," trans. Nicholas Staphorst, in *A Collection Of Curious Travels & Voyages*, John Ray ed., 2 vols. (London, 1693), vol. I, pp. 62–63. Rauwolff entered Turkey on May 18, 1573. The booksellers explain in their epistle "The Booksellers to the Reader" that Rauwolff's manuscript account of his travels had long been popular among

scholars yet, until this Royal Society publication was issued, existed in England only in the Arundellian Library at Gresham College and only in its original High Dutch. Although Cavendish would not have been able to read the manuscript in High Dutch, it is plausible, given her connections to scientific and intellectual communities, that she might have become aware of its contents through family members or family friends either during her exile in Antwerp or after her return to England.

CHAPTER 6

Reading, writing, and other crimes

Frances E. Dolan

In Salisbury in the 1650s, an eighty-year-old cunning-woman named Anne Bodenham was accused of witchcraft, and ultimately convicted and executed. As an old woman whose work as an occult practitioner eventually exposed her to criminal prosecution, Bodenham was certainly not unique, even as late as the middle of the seventeenth century. Yet, at first glance, Bodenham's story, as narrated in Edmond Bower's pamphlet, *Doctor Lamb Revived, or, Witchcraft Condemn'd in Anne Bodenham, a Servant of His* (1653), distinguishes itself, even among the diverse and sensational discourses of witchcraft, through the emphasis it places on the accused's ability to read and write. Anne Bodenham sometimes wore spectacles, "taught divers young Children to read," and claims to have learned about "white" witchcraft by reading books she found in the notorious Dr. Lambe's rooms. Furthermore, she depended on both reading and writing in her practice of magic: raising spirits "by reading in her Books"; employing written charms; and compelling a young serv-ingmaid to sign her name in blood in a red-bound book that was "worth thousands of other books, and can doe more."[1]

Contrary to the widespread assumption, then and now, that early modern English witches were illiterate and untutored, this case (to which I will return later) suggests that some women might have acquired occult knowledge from books. On the one hand, some pamphlet accounts of witchcraft prosecutions disseminated the belief that "this silly sex of women can by no means attaine to that so vile and damned a practise of sorcery, and Witchcraft, in regard of their illiteratenesse and want of learning."[2] According to this view, while men might follow Dr. Faustus' lead in reading their way into heresy and diabolism, women stumbled into witchcraft only through inarticulate rage. On the other hand, other commentators on the phenomenon of witchcraft, recognized the dangers of women's unregulated access to print. John Stearne, assistant to the witchfinder Matthew Hopkins, for instance, listed those "addicted to the reading and studie of dangerous books, inticing to the practice of hidden mysteries, of Magick and Inchantments" among those particularly vulnerable to the devil's temptation.[3] If witchcraft could be associated with either "illiteratenesse and want of learning," *or* "the reading and study of dangerous books," then the issue is not whether women could read but whether their ability to do so altered misogynous assumptions and practices such as those that enabled witchcraft prosecutions.

Given the uneven and inadequate evidence regarding early modern literacy, we need not assume that most English women could neither read nor write; yet that assumption has governed most of the scholarship on early modern literacy. David Cressy, who bases his influential study *Literacy and the Social Order* on the analysis of signatures, argues that "women were almost universally unable to write their own names for most of the sixteenth and seventeenth centuries," although he acknowledges some variations by class and region. For instance, women's, servants', and apprentices' rates of literacy were higher in London, and some (exceptional) elite women achieved quite high levels of literacy. Yet Cressy stresses throughout his study that "in all sources and in all areas and periods, the literacy of women lagged behind that of men."[4] Although all scholars of early modern literacy agree that men probably attained higher levels of literacy than women, many have challenged Cressy's definition of literacy as narrow and exclusive, and his methods as likely to underestimate literacy rates, especially among women and laboring men. As Keith Thomas argues, "in early modern England there were so many kinds of written word, such a diversity of scripts, typefaces, and languages, that a simple contrast between 'literacy' and 'illiteracy' fails to register the complexity of the situation."[5] Refusing that simple distinction makes it possible to see that reconsidering definitional categories may be more important than proving that women belonged in one category rather than the other.

Thomas demonstrates, for instance, that it was easier to read blackletter than roman-type, and easier to read either kind of type than to read script. Thus, many people who could not read handwriting might be able to read print. Since writing was taught separately from and subsequent to reading – after that point in the curriculum at which most girls and many boys (especially those whose labor was needed) left school – many who could read could not write.[6] For instance, the pamphlet *Blood for Blood, or, Justice Executed for Innocent Blood-Shed* (1670), which recounts Mary Cook's murder of "her own and only beloved Child," depicts Cook as unable to sign her examination (or confession) – she makes "a cross instead of her name" – but as able to read "Books suitable to her present condition . . . which she seemed diligently to improve her time in."[7]

It certainly is not my purpose here to provide an historical justification for the habit of "equating femininity, consumption, and reading, on the one hand, and masculinity, production, and writing on the other," a habit that Tania Modleski challenges.[8] As I will show, women's reading might itself be productive: Anne Bodenham, for instance, supported herself by means of the occult arts she learned from books; women readers might also have appropriated what they read in inventive, unpredictable ways that made consumption a kind of production, as Roger Chartier has argued.[9] Further, many women of various social and economic positions could and did write. Considering reading and writing as separate skills, however, enables us to understand how estimates of literacy based on signature collection might underestimate, even exclude, women. It also operates as a useful reminder that the more we learn about education and literacy, the less we can be sure who possessed which skills and to what extent. I assume rather than seek to prove that many women could read and/or write. My question is: what difference did – and does – their literacy make?

Diverse representations of criminal women, including plays and pamphlet accounts of actual cases, suggest not only that women of widely various social positions could read and/or write, but also that women's literacy figured significantly in the processes of crime and punishment. Stage villainesses, for instance, read and write: Lady Macbeth enters reading a letter, and later writes and reads while sleep-walking; Alice Arden, the adulterous, murderous wife in *Arden of Faversham*, exchanges letters with her lover, and pores over her prayer book when she is feeling remorseful, or wishes to appear so.[10] Representations of crime not only warn that women could use their reading and writing skills to learn and practice witchcraft, plot murder and adultery, or conspire in treason; they also demonstrate that state and church could exploit women's literacy to punish and reform them. Women's writing skills might leave damning evidence of their guilt – thus aiding in their apprehension, condemnation, and punishment; their ability to read and write might help a minister lead them to repentance, then enable them, once contrite, to witness to other sinners more persuasively. The widely different, even contradictory, values assigned to women's literacy in the discourses of crime, even within a single text, suggest that, as Margaret W. Ferguson has argued, "literacy, in theory and in practice, constituted a major site of social conflict in the early modern period."[11] In the conflicts fought out on this site, the stakes for criminal(ized) women such as Anne Bodenham were the highest possible: acquittal or conviction, life or death, salvation or damnation. Yet the advantages that female combatants might gain by seizing control over the written word were unpredictable.

THE BENEFITS OF LITERACY

In English common law, an offender's literacy might enable him both to perpetrate speech crimes and to seek pardon (and avoid execution) for certain felonies. The law held the authors, and in some cases the printers, distributors, or readers, of prohibited works criminally accountable for exercising their writing and reading skills. The hangman publically burned books determined to be libelous or seditious. Yet reading ability also provided a gendered route to pardon; in early modern England, men could avoid execution for certain offenses by means of a legal fiction linking them to the clergy. In the Middle Ages, clerics had the right to be tried in ecclesiastical rather than royal courts for certain offenses. Proving that they were clerics by demonstrating their ability to read Latin, they could escape punishment in secular courts. In practice, this came to mean that those men who could read could achieve formal pardon and escape hanging for certain offenses (such as theft and murder).[12] The high incidence of men successfully claiming benefit of clergy suggests that judges employed flexible definitions of "literacy" and varied their testing methods as it suited them. Perhaps many convicts could read, or could at least recite the brief "neck-verse" (Psalm 51, verse 1) from memory. But benefit of clergy assumed that literacy, even the fiction or ephemeral performance of it, and criminality were curiously incompatible – the latter cancelling the former – for men.

Until 1624, women's ability to read was legally irrelevant. For instance, in Robert Yarington's *Two Lamentable Tragedies* (1601), two servants who conceal their master's crime meet very different fates when their complicity is discovered. One, a man, receives benefit of clergy and is branded in the thumb, then released. The other, a woman, is not so lucky. "But wretched Rachels sexe denies that grace, / And therefore dooth receive a doome of death / To dye with him whose sinnes she did conceale."[13] Legal reforms in 1624 and 1691 acknowledged that the claim to clerical status and its benefits had become so obviously a legal fiction that it might as well be extended to women. The first reform extended benefit of clergy to women accused of stealing goods worth less than ten shillings. Until 1691, when women were granted the privilege on equal terms to men, women accused of stealing goods worth more than ten shillings or of any violent crime could not claim this benefit. Prior to 1691, benefit of clergy was largely restricted to men because, even at the level of legal fiction, it was unimaginable in post-Reformation England that women might be clerics. In this legal fiction, which confers on men the ultimate material benefit for their literacy, the legal system institutionalized until the late seventeenth century its assumption that women's literacy could not cancel out their criminality. Only women's maternity could do that. If a convicted woman pleaded that she was pregnant, and the judge and a jury of matrons chose to believe her, she too might postpone punishment and escape the gallows, temporarily, or in some cases, permanently.[14] She could never achieve formal pardon by this means, however. Like benefit of clergy, benefit of belly could only be claimed once. Both pleas allowed the judge considerable discretion; although the convicted woman was supposed to be visibly pregnant with a "quick" or moving fetus, the plea was sometimes accepted in cases when the pregnancy could not be proved. But the judge's discretion did not extend to accepting the plea from women past child-bearing age. Obviously, an elderly woman such as Anne Bodenham, literate but post-menopausal, and accused of a crime more serious than petty theft, was denied access to either gender-inflected (and, in the case of women, age-biased) means of postponing or avoiding execution. The legal system enacted the assumption that her post-reproductive female body, which could not possibly house a fetus whose life might confer (temporary) value on her own, was not worth saving; her reading ability could not compensate for that lack.

WHAT CRIME IS IT TO WRITE HOME? WRITING AND/AS EVIDENCE

Although criminal women's reading ability did not confer the same legal benefits that men's did, their writing ability carried equal risks: in court, the prosecution could use handwritten documents to incriminate them. Letters provide tangible evidence in many seventeenth-century trials, although the accused often dispute their authorship of all or part of the correspondence attributed to them. In his *Great Britaines, Great Deliverance, from the Great Danger of Popish Powder* (1606), William Leigh warns the conspirators in the Gunpowder Plot (after the event) that "Your owne Letters shall discover the treason, and the writing of your owne hands shall betray the mischief of your owne hearts."[15] Since covert correspondence could prove dangerous if it fell into the wrong hands, those engaged in illicit activities of any kind assiduously destroyed the evidence. One informer against supposed conspirators in the Popish Plot of 1679, Thomas Dangerfield, alias Willoughby, explained that Catholics burned all correspondence "for they were cunning enough to keep no Papers by them of any Importance, as being liable to Searches that were likely to be made there on the least suspicion." If this had not been their habit, he "could have been able to have proved the whole Matter upon them, by their own Hand-writings."[16] In *Malice Defeated* (1680), Elizabeth Cellier's autobiographical account of her trial and acquittal for treason, Cellier explains what made her suspicious of Dangerfield, the chief witness against her, whom she successfully disqualifies.[17] He insisted on receiving a letter in her "own writing": "By this I perceiv'd he was already a Rogue, and endeavouring to get something of my writing, to make ill use of."[18] In the context of suspicion, accusation, and prosecution, one's "own Hand-writings" are taken as such irrefutable evidence that they are the goal of all investigations, the "last word."

As a result, any kind of writing becomes suspicious. In accounts of various legal proceedings associated with the Popish Plot, servants testify to "seeing *Mrs. Cellier* and others often writing," as if this were damning in itself.[19] In another Popish Plot trial, the accused (Edward Fitzharris) was forced to surrender the notes he was consulting as he conducted his own defense; in another, the spectators were reminded that it was forbidden for a "known Roman Catholick" to take "Notes of the Evidence," presumably because these notes might aid the defense or contribute to a pro-Catholic narrative of the trial.[20] But Cellier challenges this pervasive assumption that Catholic literacy is transgressive or dangerous in itself. When questioned whether she wrote home while in Newgate, Cellier responds, "Pray my Lord, what Crime is it to write home?"[21] Throughout her text, Cellier depicts how difficult it is for Newgate inmates to correspond with those outside the prison; yet she insists that their clandestine correspondence is legal. As a Catholic implicated in the byzantine accusations and counter-accusations that constituted the Popish Plot and the Mealtub Plot, Cellier depended on correspondence to monitor the treatment of Catholic prisoners and to connect them to their coreligionists. Smuggling prohibited writing materials in for herself and other inmates, and scheming to get letters into and out of the prison, Cellier helped to foster a Catholic network in a time of profound crisis. Cellier always wrote on the assumption that her letters would be intercepted and scrutinized. Although prison officials routinely copied her correspondence throughout her stay in Newgate, the copies they produce as evidence cannot prove much other than the existence of this Catholic network which, while suspicious, is not illegal: "but I had Committed no Crime, and therefore nothing but Innocence could be found in my Letters."[22]

Although Cellier was acquitted of the treason charges, ultimately the state did hold her criminally accountable for her writing. Because of her claim in *Malice Defeated* that Catholic prisoners were tortured, she was convicted of libel and sentenced to the pillory, where she was brutally treated by the crowd. The "proof" offered by handwriting was also under debate in Cellier's libel trial. Cellier could deny her authorship of *Malice Defeated* because the manuscript in the prosecution's possession was not in her writing, which was "a scrambling ugly hand, far different from the Manuscript."[23] Witnesses for the prosecution undermined this line of defense by testifying that Cellier employed copyists to whom she dictated. Accounts of Cellier's libel trial thus highlight the double-bind of literacy for women. Cellier's authorship of the book is questioned – priests must have ghost-written it – yet her accountability for the book is never in doubt.[24] Cellier is acknowledged as an author only to the extent that it will justify her prosecution and conviction.

Accounts of both Cellier's treason and libel trials suggest that she was acutely aware of the dangerous connection between literacy and evidence. Although her abilities to read and write were central to her political activities – she fostered a correspondence network and she was a polemicist – she left scant evidence. Not only did she use fire and dictation to limit the documents that could be connected to her through her "own writing," but she also employed, as her courier to and from Newgate, a servant who could not later testify to the letters' contents. As the servant explains: "I know not, for I cannot read written hand."[25] The court accepted the servant's demurral, which both curtailed the testimony she could offer and shielded her from implication. In this case, her status as a servant probably helped to lend credibility to her claim that she could not read script and that she had simply acted as an innocent, ignorant messenger.

In other instances, third parties to correspondence – that is, those who neither wrote nor received the letters in question – could be found guilty simply for being "privy" to a letter's contents. Domestic tragedies, representations of recent, local crimes, betray a particular interest in this phenomenon. In *A Warning for Fair Women* (1599), Anne Sanders is convicted as an accessory to her lover's murder of her husband on the assumption that she was "privie of" a letter from her lover to another conspirator.[26] Although Anne denies knowledge of the letter, the audience has seen her consent to both adultery and complicity in the murder. In *Arden of Faversham*, in contrast, the innocent Bradshaw is convicted for the murder of Arden, although he knew nothing about it; he simply carries a letter written by Master Greene to Alice Arden. When he asks Alice Arden to admit whether he was "privy" to the conspirators' intent, she replies wearily, "I dare swear thou knewest not the contents." In Holinshed's account of the case, he also claims that Bradshaw was "never made privy" to the conspirators' schemes; his conviction and execution "proceeded wholly by misunderstanding of the words contained in the letter which he brought from Greene."[27] Bradshaw's wrongful conviction, then, reveals the limits of what a document's "hard" evidence can prove. It also points to the risks of literacy. In dramatic and non-dramatic representations of both these famous cases, the defendant's literacy qualifies, even defeats, his or her claim to innocence. If Anne Sanders and Bradshaw had not been able to read, they could not have been convicted and executed.

Contests regarding the veracity, meaning, and ownership of written evidence also occurred outside of the courtroom. In the domestic settings (crowded with spectators) in which most possession cases were observed and diagnosed, exorcised, cured, or exposed as frauds, victims of demonic possession violently fought to control documentation of their condition. When a possessed young woman, Joyce Dovey, saw a man who wished to record his observations of her

with the paper in his hand, shee fell upon him very violently, and would have taken the paper from him, but he contended with her very toughly, and after a long conflict, gave her the repulse, who having kept the paper without tearing, onely a little corner, but not a word torne off, he voluntarily threw it downe on the ground, saying, Devill thou hast not power to take it up, and so took it up himselfe and departed.[28]

In another case, the possessed, while in a fit, gestures that she wishes to write. When she is given paper and a pen, she spells out the names of those whom she accuses in abbreviated form;

whilst she was writing these words, she was blowne up ready to burst, shrinking with her head, as if she feared blowes: then would she be drawne, as in convulsion fits, till she got that writing from them that had it, and either burne it in the fire, or chew it in her mouth, till it could not be discerned. Let any one snatch the paper from her and hide it as private as he could, she would have gone to the party and place, still in torment till she got it, and either burne it, or chewe it, that none could discerne one word she had wrote, then immediately she would have ease.[29]

Beliefs about demonic possession, as recorded in these pamphlets and as disseminated across oral and print cultures in early modern England, assume that the devil (or some other evil spirit) manifests his presence through the possessed's exaggerated *bodily* symptoms and behaviors, but prohibits the *written* documentation of possession. Working through the possessed, the devil seeks out and destroys any such textual evidence, whether an observer or the victim herself produces it. In presenting even the devil as fearing and suppressing documents, such pamphlets demonstrate the extraordinary, inculpatory power attributed to the written word.

Given that women's writing might testify against them, and that legal and popular representations of criminal women associate their reading and writing skills with their disorderly, illegal, or violent acts, I do not intend to "celebrate" these women's acquisition and deployment of literacy. After all, those who determined literacy's moral and social value were largely those who prided themselves on their own alphabetic accomplishments.[30] Furthermore, early modern persons did not necessarily need "alphabetic literacy" to achieve professional or social success because written and oral, literate and illiterate cultures interacted and overlapped.[31] Indeed, representations of crime frequently testify to the startling array of literacies, competencies, and knowledges on which women might draw.

As with so many other cultural changes, the wider distribution of printing and literacy was a mixed blessing for women (and for non-elite men). On the one hand, the most fully literate persons also attained the freest access to privileges and opportunities from which they would otherwise have been excluded. Attending to the particulars of early modern English social order, Cressy demonstrates "how well the ranking based on literacy agreed with the ordering by status and esteem, and also the degree to which literacy was commensurate with alternative rankings by occupation and wealth."[32] More generally, Pierre Bourdieu argues that "speakers lacking the legitimate competence are *de facto* excluded from the social domains in which this competence is required, or are condemned to silence."[33] Literacy (to whatever degree) provided entrance into more privileged social domains, and escape from the increasingly stigmatized status of the "illiterate." In literacy, women and lower-class men attained not only a powerful tool for economic advancement, social mobility, and self-assertion, but also "a double-edged sword" which they might wield for "'unlicensed' ends."[34] On the other hand, the acquisition of literacy often meant the disciplining as much as the empowerment of the dominated, their induction into an unaccommodating system of social and linguistic distinction which did not operate in their favor and which could use the written word as yet another mechanism of control.[35]

WITCHCRAFT BY THE BOOK: THE CASE OF ANNE BODENHAM

The events that ended in Anne Bodenham's execution for witchcraft began with a routine visit to a local cunning-woman. A maid, Anne Styles, visited Bodenham at her mistress' request to procure protection against the attempts her mistress, Mrs. Goddard, thought her step-daughters were making to kill her. Ultimately, Bodenham got caught in the crossfire between mother and stepdaughters; the stepdaughters accused her of attempting to murder them via witchcraft. I have discussed elsewhere the complex, distressed relations between stepmother and stepchildren revealed by this case.[36] Here, I wish to explore Edmond Bower's emphasis on reading and writing, and the shifting valuations of women's literacy, in his account of the case in *Doctor Lamb Revived*.[37]

As soon as Anne Styles approached her, "the Witch put on her Spectacles, and demanding seven shillings of the Maid which, she received, she opened three Books."[38] Bodenham puts on a lot more than her spectacles at this moment. She performs her ability to see what her client cannot: both the alphabetic literacy that enables her to comprehend the three books she opens and the occult vision on which cunning-persons depended, a vision into the future and beyond or outside of the natural world. Throughout her encounter with Styles, Bodenham combines these two kinds of vision. By "reading in a book," for instance, she causes apparitions to appear, then disappear (sig. B4); she also consults a "glass" or mirror. Simultaneously donning her glasses and demanding payment, Bodenham announces the market value and usefulness of her double vision. As supernaturally empowered spectator/reader and knowledgeable professional, she has both agency and authority.

In response to Mrs. Goddard's desire for "some Charm, or writing under her own hand, that should keep her from ill, and preserve her from danger, . . . the Witch took Pen Ink and Paper, and wrote something, and put some yellow powder therein." She advises Styles that her mistress "must never look in it" but should wear it in her bosom by day and place it under her head as she sleeps (sig. B4v). Anne Bodenham's reliance on writing was not unique among cunning-women or so-called "white" witches, who often depended on written charms and incantations to procure positive effects, such as reversing bewitchments or offering protection.[39] In her testimony describing her first encounter with the witch, Anne Styles links Bodenham's literacy to knowledge, knowledge presented simultaneously as valuable and as criminal. In the context of Bodenham's prosecution, Styles testifies that Bodenham's occult knowledge is threatening, transgressive, potentially violent. Yet, from the perspective of a servant who cannot read or write herself, Styles also associates the cunning-woman's sought-after supernatural knowledge and marketable skills with her mastery of the alphabet – which, in itself, is as mysterious to the maid as anything that Anne Bodenham knows.

According to Styles' testimony, on which the prosecution depends, Bodenham exceeds the limits even of a cunning-woman's questionable uses of literacy. Bodenham convinces Styles to sign her name in a book, that is, to make a covenant with the devil. Since Styles cannot write, Bodenham guides the pen dipped into Styles' blood. Styles confesses that "this hand of mine write my name in the Devils book, this finger of mine was pricked, here is yet the hole that was made, and with my blood I wrote my own Damnation" (sig. D). In this confession, Styles gains credibility by claiming to have participated in demonic literacy; yet she also downplays her own complicity by transferring accountability to Bodenham, against whom she testifies.

According to published accounts of witchcraft, many accused women confessed to making such contracts with the devil.[40] Keith Thomas argues that a diabolical compact or covenant did not figure importantly in witchcraft trials until the seventeenth century: "No reference in a trial to an oral compact with the Devil is recorded before 1612; and not until the investigations of Matthew Hopkins, the professional witch-finder who was active in the late 1640s, was there sworn evidence testifying to a written covenant."[41] Both the timing and the association with Hopkins suggest that the new interest in diabolical compacts corresponded to debates regarding evidence in witchcraft trials. In a climate of uncertainty, a written covenant promised irrefutable evidence of witchcraft. In such a case, the accused's participation in literacy – even if this is testified to (by herself or another) rather than documented – works to damn and incriminate her.

Although Bower's text presents Anne Styles as having signed the contract, she is not tried as a witch, nor is she even called one. Bodenham, playing the role of Mephistophilis, the demonic facilitator, rather than Faust, is the one who stands trial. Bodenham belongs neither in the familiar tradition of Faust, the learned, curious, questing male scholar, doomed yet admirable, nor in the counter-tradition that Phyllis Mack describes, in which women's occult knowledges and practices reinforce rather than transcend constructions of the feminine in terms of the permeable, fluid, submissive, and receptive body.[42] Nor does Bodenham hold either of the two positions in relation to medical knowledge that Mary Ellen Lamb maps out: Bodenham's participation in a demonized "primarily female oral tradition" does not expose her to prosecution; but neither does her reliance "on a body of written knowledge compiled by male authors" protect her "from charges of witchcraft by validating male authorities."[43] Drawing on these various gender-inflected traditions, Anne Bodenham yet stands apart from them as a result of her persistent association with books.

When she describes her successful career as a cunning-woman, Bodenham begins with her studies under Dr. Lambe: ". . . she reading in some of his Books, with his help learnt her Art, by which she said she had gotten many a penny, and done hundreds of people good."[44] Through her study, Bodenham achieved material advantages: People "always called her Mris. *Boddenham*" (sig. E2), and paid her for her skills. Bodenham's account of how she attained her valuable skills simultaneously demystifies and diabolizes this process: "If those that have a desire to it, doe read in books, and when they come to read further then they can understand, then the Devil will appear to them, and shew them what they would know; and they doing what he would have them, they may learn to doe what they desired to do, and he would teach them" (sig. E4v). Bodenham's confession, which Bower presents as shocking and incriminating, might also be read as inspirational and instructive. She teaches *her* readers to push beyond the obstacles raised by their own ignorance. Depending on the devil as tutor, they "may learn to doe what they desired to do"; they may improve their lives materially, as she did.

Bodenham attributes concrete use-value to her books, and the occult power to which they give her access also translates into cultural capital, which enables her to earn a living and achieve respect in her community. These books accrue further value in *Doctor Lamb Revived* because Edmond Bower himself expresses so much interest in them and goes to such lengths to get hold of them. In response to his interest, Bodenham offers to let him have her books "if [he] would keep them secret" and "accept of them" (sig. E v). Bodenham assumes that he wants the books not as evidence against her but as conduits of marketable knowledge. According to Bower, she confides to others that he is himself a witch who will "doe many notable things with her books" (sig. E2). Her sense of the books' significance confirmed by Bower's acquisitive interest, Bodenham directs her husband to take Bower to their house and "to deliver [him] her Books." Although Bower plans to present the books to the Assize judge as evidence against Bodenham, the books disappoint him because "they were nothing concerning her art" (sig. E v). He wants the "red book," in which the names are signed in blood (in large part because it would incriminate all the supposed signers). Bodenham promises it to him, teasing him with shifting explanations for its elusiveness – it is hidden where even her husband cannot find it; if he grants her "liberty to goe home" (sig. E v), she will teach him a charm from the book which will enable him to discover a fortune buried in the garden at Wilton – but she never produces it. In addition to withholding the "red book," Bodenham decides not to bequeath any of her other books to Bower after all.

Despite the fact that Bodenham is in prison under sentence of death throughout these negotiations, that Bower has many, if not all, of Bodenham's books in his possession, and that Bower marshalls her words and her books as evidence against her, Bodenham clings to the belief that her books belong to her and that she can bequeath them as she chooses. Bower explains Bodenham's decision to leave the books to a grocer who also visits her this way: "because I did prosecute her, and informed the Judge what she told me, she would not teach me any thing; but because (as she said) Mr. *Langley* seemed to be a good honest man, she would let him have her books, and teach him her Art" (sigs. E4v–F). Bodenham assumes that even her prurient, harassingly godly visitors will want her books. She also assumes that even as a married woman and a convicted witch she has the right to make a will and distribute her property as she chooses: "And she said, she had made her Will, and given Legacies to many of her friends" (sig. F v). Bower warns her that "her Husband might choose whether he would let them have" these legacies. In response, Bodenham threatens: "If he doe not, the Devill shall never let him be quiet" (sig. F v). Having denied throughout any alliance with the devil, Bodenham invokes him at last to help her outwit the legal and social restrictions on a married woman's autonomy; she acts like a witch when reminded that she is a wife.

In addition to scrambling to find someone who will accept and appreciate her books, Bodenham worries over the future of the other source of her expertise as a cunning-woman, her garden. Just as other sorcerers might destroy their books, Prospero by "sinking" and Dr. Faustus by burning, Bodenham directs "that the Women that shrowded her should goe into her Garden, and gather up all her herbs, spoyl all her flowers, and tear up the roots" (sig. F v). Even in the context of criminal prosecution and impending execution, even in a rather unsympathetic account in which her voice is, at best, mediated, Anne Bodenham is presented as exerting control over her death and over those things she valued in life: the sources of her knowledge and her livelihood, her herbs and her books.

While Anne Bodenham exerts an unusual degree of control over her dying, and especially over her books, she does not perform her literacy on the scaffold, as many convicts did, but rather, according to Bower, appears defiant, undignified, and drunk. Many condemned persons read Bible verses or their own confessions on the scaffold; they might even request that their hands be untied that they might unfold and hold their notes.[45] In contrast, Anne Bodenham makes no reference to the abilities that played such a crucial role in bringing her to the scaffold. Impious and disorderly, she attempts to "turn her self off" after the noose is on her neck – a shocking, if suicidal self-assertion, where penitent submission is expected – and refuses to forgive the hangman. Her last words are: "Forgive thee? A pox on thee, turn me off" (sig. F2v). No longer wearing her spectacles, Bodenham dies making a spectacle of herself.

READING, WRITING, AND REPENTING

In *Doctor Lamb Revived*, Bower represents reading as exculpatory, as well as incriminating. Although he identifies Anne Bodenham's literacy with her criminality, he construes Anne Styles' inability to read as evidence of her low social class, ignorance, ungodliness, and vulnerability to temptation. Thus, either literacy or illiteracy can lead women to witchcraft. As part of her repentance, Anne Styles promises to learn to read: "I am not yet too old to learn, I will learn to read, sure, if God will be pleased that I shall, though I break my sleeping time to learn" (sig. F4v). Other Protestant advisers on godly conduct such as John Dod and Robert Cleaver, similarly, promote literacy as "a great helpe in the course of this life and a treasure of much greater account then mony."[46] In depicting

literacy as an important aid to spiritual comfort, repentance, and salvation, Bower contributes to the stigmatization of illiteracy, which sometimes was associated with vagrancy, laziness, godlessness, and
irresponsibility.

Bower depicts Bodenham's work as a reading teacher ambiguously. On
the one hand, her teaching incriminates her as surely as her addictions to
gossip and Popery, her storytelling, and her occult practices (sig. B). On the
other hand, her teaching provides a respectable front behind which she
conducted her more sinister work; Bower accuses her of "*pretending* to get
her livelyhood by such an employment" (sig. B, emphasis mine). Finally,
Bower obviously assumes that those who read his pamphlet will benefit.
He even reveals that reading (or misreading) has shaped his own attitudes
and practices: He remembers "a Story which I had before read in Mr.
Scot's *Discovery of Witchcraft*" about the efficacy of bringing accused and
accuser into confrontation and imitates this method (sig. D2v).[47]

Other accounts of trials and executions dwell on the crucial role that
literacy plays in convicts' repentance and proselytizing. For instance,
mothers anticipating execution bequeath texts to the children who will
survive them.[48] At the end of the play *A Warning for Fair Women*, for
instance, the condemned Anne Sanders leaves to each of her children,
"a booke / Of holy meditations, *Bradfords* workes" (lines 2702–03). As
depicted in *Fair Warning to Murderers of Infants* (London, 1692), a pamphlet
account of widow Mary Goodenough's murder of her illegitimate
newborn, Goodenough laments that she was unable to see her living
children before her death and must resort to writing to them.
Goodenough depends on literacy despite the limits of her own writing
and her children's reading ability, both of which require her to beg assistance. "I am now forced to take this way of Writing, and to beg the help
of another Hand, my own Hand being as my Heart is, trembling; and
my confused Head uncapable of expressing what I desire to impart to,
and impress upon you" (sig. B v). A postscript enjoins the children:

Read this Paper, or get it Read to you by my Neighbour *Thomas Bolt*, or Mrs.
Mary Rose, or such others as will teach you to Understand and Improve, not to
Contemn and Neglect it. Read it over, or a good Part of it every Lords Day; be
not asham'd of my Dying Confessions or Advice; for they are the best Remains
of your Dying Mother, the only Legacy she has to leave you, and if well
Improv'd, they will indeed yield you a Goodly Heritage. (p. 14)

The painfully composed letter replaces the mother's body in all its sinfulness and criminality – guilty of fornication, bastardy, and infanticide,
ignominiously executed on the public scaffold – as her "best Remains."

The author of *Fair Warning to Murderers of Infants* blames Mary Goodenough's neighbors for their failure to offer the struggling mother the charity that might have prevented her desperate crime. S/he suggests that the community can rectify their past errors by taking "care her Children learn to read, learn the Catechism; read to them and press upon them this their Mothers Last Will concerning them. Don't stick at a little charge or trouble to do them good" (sig. A3).[49] This account of a criminal woman depicts documents as an appropriate legacy from mother to child, and reading as a means by which children can become godly, law-abiding subjects.

Rather than urging books on others, a convict might herself refuse to read. A literate Catholic prisoner, for instance, might refuse to read the Bible, thereby defying the Protestant emphasis on Scripture and the authority of a combined church and state. When in custody, Margaret Vincent, a convert to Catholicism who killed her children rather than raise them as Protestants, "proved her selfe to be an obstinate Papist, for there was found about her necke a Crucifixe, with other reliques which she then wore about her: that by the Justice was commanded to be taken away, and an English bible to be delivered her to read, the which she with great stubbornesse threw from her, not willing as once to look thereuppon, nor to heare any divine comforts, delivered thereout for the succour of her Soule" (sig. B). She "refused to looke upon any protestant booke, as Bible, Meditation, Prayer booke and such like, affirming them to be eronious, and dangerous for any Romish Catholique to looke in" (sig. B v).[50] The account of Margaret Vincent's crime and punishment, *A Pitilesse Mother* (1616), like *Fair Warning to Murderers of Infants*, depicts reading as the means by which murderous mothers might repent, prepare for death, and offer instruction to their surviving children. In laboriously dictating a letter, and urging her children to learn to read, Mary Goodenough enacts her penitence. Conversely, by refusing to read, Margaret Vincent reveals herself to be a hardened sinner. Although both texts depict criminal women's reading as potentially instructive and reforming, they also reveal literacy as a site of struggles with profound consequences for body and soul.

Margaret Vincent's preference for "reliques" over books seems to confirm the rarely-questioned assumption that Catholic religious practice centered on objects, images, and rituals, whereas Protestantism centered on the Word and therefore promoted wider-spread literacy. Based on this assumption, historians still claim that those women who remained Catholic did so because Catholicism was more congenial to their illiteracy.[51] While this may have been partially true, it does not take into account learned converts. More important, the contrast between Catholic gentlewoman Margaret Vincent's refusal rather than inability to read and Protestant Mary Goodenough's humble, earnest, but unskilled attempts to write a letter complicates any simple association of Catholicism with illiteracy and Protestantism with literacy. Many of the women whose literacy I have discussed here either identified themselves as Catholic or were accused of "papistrie." Perhaps Catholic women were not less likely to be able to read and/or write, but more likely to recognize that they might be incriminated by demonstrating their skills.

The first step in employing gender as a category of analysis with reference to the history of literacy involves challenging narrow, exclusive definitions of literacy, and asking which women could read or write under which conditions rather than assuming that few could at all. As scholars have reconsidered the research protocols that long led them to overlook or ignore evidence of women's reading and writing, they have uncovered that evidence in abundance. Much work remains to be done in the important project of uncovering and assessing evidence of women's roles as producers and consumers of the written word. While the discourses of crime provide further documentation of early modern Englishwomen's literacy, these discourses also open up to question what kind of difference women's literacy made to them or should make in scholars' understanding of them.

Histories of early modern literacy generally chart the progressive spread of reading and writing skills outward from an elite center. In accord with this expansion of literacy, it is widely assumed that by the eighteenth century more women, across a wider range of social, economic, and geographical locations, would have been able to read and/or write than could have done so in the fourteenth century. Certainly, many more women write and publish in the eighteenth century than in the sixteenth. It is difficult to prove, however, that women's relationship to education and literacy steadily *improved*. For instance, while the Reformation promoted literacy, even for women, it abolished an institution that had previously fostered women's education: the convent.[52] Even if the percentage of women who could read and/or write increased in the course of the early modern period, more is not inevitably better.

Women's increased access to literacy did not necessarily improve their status or expand their rights, although it may have helped lay the groundwork for changes in both these arenas in subsequent centuries. In published accounts of crime and punishment, literacy accrues value when it facilitates legal and spiritual surveillance and discipline: when it teaches a criminal woman's children *not* to follow her example; when it helps an implicated maid dissociate herself from witchcraft and become more godly; when it fosters a convict's sense of her own humility, inadequacy, and sinfulness; when it provides evidence.[53] Such texts criminalize women's literacy, however, when that literacy enables women to plan and enact crimes, to attain and employ occult knowledge, to outwit and defy legal and religious authority.

In relation to literacy, most early modern women could not win. While we might expect to find literacy criminalized in texts about crimes, scholars have argued that women's reading was policed and their writing prohibited or marked as transgressive even when they were not engaged in other criminal activities.[54] In the extreme case of criminal women, we can see clearly a dual evaluation of literacy – as virtuous when it aided social control and as criminal when it aided self-determination – that must have frustrated and constrained even those women whose literacy did not lead them into print, let alone to the scaffold or pillory. Divided from their own accomplishments and thus against themselves, literate women at every social level encountered in the written word not just a tool for self-expression and self-assertion, not just access to knowledge and work, but also a means to incriminate and expose themselves.

The double-bind to which literacy subjected women corresponds to the double-bind of women's competence more generally. Early modern English culture often required that women in extraordinary circumstances assume responsibility for themselves: most notably, a woman accused of treason had to conduct her own defense; less dramatically, widows or women whose husbands were absent were expected to manage their estates, run households, and defend their rights by bringing suit when necessary. The exceptional circumstances of the civil war, for instance, compelled many royalist women to petition, sue, and strategize to protect or reclaim their property. While early modern culture assumed, even depended on, women's competence, it criminalized particularly visible enactments of that competence as scandalous or sinister.

Although women's literacy did not necessarily alter their status or rights, it did provide an avenue to agency, however criminalized, for some women. Anne Bodenham's literacy enables her not only to find a profession and advance her social status, but to contest the accusations against her, defy the conventions governing accused and convicted persons, and control the distribution of her possessions. Elizabeth Cellier's literacy enables her to defend herself successfully against treason charges and to publish her own account of the proceedings. But literacy was not a necessary condition for achieving agency, nor was it without costs. Literacy was not even an absolutely necessary material condition for authorship; the first autobiography in English was "written" – in this case, dictated – by a woman who could neither read nor write, Margery Kempe.[55]

As subjects for feminist analysis, literate early modern women do have one distinct advantage: they leave more evidence. If subjects are, in part, discursively constituted – constructed and recognized when they speak and when that speech is registered and regulated – then historians of early modern subjectivity, like the early modern legal system, depend on voluble (and therefore visible) subjects and the written evidence they leave.[56] Scholars can only study early modern women's speech, and the processes of subject-formation of which it was so crucial a part, in those cases in which we have *records*.[57] Women did not have to keep such records themselves; the voices of many women, from mystic Margery Kempe to convicted criminals, survive to us through the transcriptions and mediations of male scribes, often employed by church or state. But more, and more reliable, evidence survives regarding the subjectivities of women who kept the records themselves. The ground of my arguments here – discourses of crime and punishment in which "evidence" serves to convict women – tempers my glee in discovering literate women's self-documentation. The evidence I seek is often the incriminating evidence early modern women wisely and busily burned.

I suspect that, like the learned elite of early modern England, I am more likely to recognize literate women as subjects. I most readily attend to those skills on which I depend professionally: the abilities to speak persuasively, to read, interpret, and write. While my focus on those arenas of competence and agency with which I am most familiar may be understandable, such a focus could lead me to overemphasize literacy at the expense of other competencies. My disciplinary privileging of literacy could also foster the assumption that women's literacy inevitably facilitated their self-expression and self-determination. Such assumptions – that literacy was a much more valuable skill than others, or that it offered a reliable avenue to self-assertion – are as restrictive and misleading as the assumption that women could not read or write. To the extent that literacy was a factor in the discursive constitution of gendered, class-inflected subjects to whom voice, consciousness, and agency were attributed, it operated to subordinate as well as to empower the subjects it helped to construct, thus providing a cautionary reminder that, then as now, the process of subject-formation for women and men was a process of disciplining as much as, or more than, a process of liberation and affirmation.

NOTES

I am grateful to Mark Thornton Burnett, Dympna C. Callaghan, J. S. Cockburn, Mary Jean Corbett, Laura Mandell, Susan Morgan, Scott Cutler Shershow, and Valerie Traub for their helpful comments on earlier drafts of this essay. I would also like to thank my colleagues in the Miami University Department of History, and members of the Ohio State and Harvard Departments of English, for the opportunity to present my work-in-progress, and for their thought-provoking questions.

1 Edmond Bower, *Doctor Lamb Revived, or, Witchcraft Condemn'd in Anne Bodenham, a Servant of His . . . By Edmond Bower an eye and ear Witness of her Examination and Confession* (London, 1653), sig. E v.

2 *A Most Certain, Strange, and True Discovery of a Witch* (London, 1643), rpt. in *Reprints of English Books, 1475–1700*, J. A. Foster, ed. (Ingram, PA, np. 1939), p. 2

3 John Stearne, *A Confirmation and Discovery of Witchcraft* (London, 1648), sig. B2.

4 David Cressy, *Literacy and the Social Order: Reading and Writing in Tudor and Stuart England* (Cambridge: Cambridge University Press, 1980), pp. 145, 128–29. At some points, Cressy seems to hold women accountable for their low levels of literacy: "The truth is that most mothers were useless for the transmission of literacy because most of them were themselves unable to write. Some could read who could not write, but even these could hardly have taken their children much beyond the ABC. Close to ninety percent of the women in seventeenth-century England could not even write their names, so few of them could have made satisfactory teachers" (Cressy, p. 41).

5 Keith Thomas, "The Meaning of Literacy in Early Modern England," in *The Written Word: Literacy in Transition*, Gerd Baumann, ed. (Oxford and New York: Oxford University Press, 1986), pp. 97–131, esp. p. 99.

6 On the dissociation of these two skills, see also Cressy, *Literacy and the Social Order*, chapter 2; and Margaret Spufford, "First Steps in Literacy: The Reading and Writing Experiences of the Humblest Seventeenth-Century Spiritual Autobiographers," *Social History* 4.3 (1979): 407–34, especially 414. This disparity between reading and writing skills obviously compromises signature collection as an index of reading ability. Cressy's research methods, for instance, underestimate all those who could read print but not sign their names (Spufford, "First Steps in Literacy," 414). Furthermore, census-type documents such as the Protestation Oath of 1641–42 on which historians of literacy depend, underestimate women, who were not required

to take such oaths, and recusants (such as Elizabeth Cellier), whom the oaths were designed to root out. See R. S. Schofield, "The Measurement of Literacy in Pre-Industrial England," in *Literacy in Traditional Societies*, Jack Goody, ed. (Cambridge: Cambridge University Press, 1968), pp. 310–25, esp. pp. 319–21.

7 N. Patridge, *Blood for Blood, or, Justice Executed for Innocent Blood-Shed* (London, 1670), pp. 20, 37.

8 Tania Modleski, *Feminism Without Women: Culture and Criticism in a "Postfeminist" Age* (New York: Routledge, 1991), p. 26.

9 Roger Chartier, "Culture as Appropriation: Popular Cultural Uses in Early Modern France," in *Understanding Popular Culture: Europe from the Middle Ages to the Nineteenth Century*, Steven L. Kaplan, ed. (Berlin: Mouton, 1984), pp. 229–53.

10 Renaissance drama is full of contests between patriarchs and subordinates regarding the possession of documents: Gloucester grabs Edmund's letter in *King Lear*; York grabs Aumerle's letter in *Richard II*; Arden grabs Michael's letter in *Arden of Faversham*. In each case, the domestic superior (father or master) assumes an inferior has no right to a privately conducted correspondence. In each case, the letter *is*, in fact, crucial to the subordinates' conspiracy against his father, master, or king's interests. Such texts suggest that, in the family, patriarchal authority depends on monopoly of the written word.

11 Margaret W. Ferguson, "A Room Not Their Own: Renaissance Women as Readers and Writers," in *The Comparative Perspective on Literature: Approaches to Theory and Practice*, Clayton Koelb and Susan Noakes, eds. (Ithaca: Cornell University Press, 1988), pp. 93–116, esp. p. 115.

12 J. H. Baker, *An Introduction to English Legal History*, 3rd edn (London: Butterworths, 1990), pp. 586–89; J. S. Cockburn, "Trial By the Book?: Fact and Theory in the Criminal Process 1558–1625," in *Legal Records and the Historian*, J. H. Baker, ed. (London: Royal Historical Society, 1978), pp. 60–79, esp. pp. 76–79; Cynthia B. Herrup, *The Common Peace: Participation and the Criminal Law in Seventeenth-Century England* (Cambridge: Cambridge University Press, 1987), pp. 48, 143, 175; and J. A. Sharpe, *Crime in Early Modern England, 1550–1750* (London: Longman, 1984), pp. 67, 147.

13 Robert Yarington, *Two Lamentable Tragedies* (London, 1601, rpt. in *A Collection of Old English Plays*, A. H. Bullen, ed., 4 vols. (London: Wyman & Sons, 1885), vol. IV, IV.ix, p. 86

14 Almost half of convicted female felons pleaded the belly, and a large percentage of those who did so were successful and may ultimately have secured pardons. J. S. Cockburn, *Calendar of Assize Records: Home Circuit Indictments. Introduction* (London: Her Majesty's Stationers Office, 1985), pp. 121–23; and James C. Oldham, "On Pleading the Belly: A History of the Jury of Matrons," *Criminal Justice History* 6 (1985): 1–64, especially 19–20, 32.

15 William Leigh, *Great Britaines Great Deliverance* (London, 1606), sig. C2v.

16 *Mr. Tho. Dangerfeilds [sic] Particular Narrative, of the Late Popish Design to Charge*

those of the Presbyterian Party with a Pretended Conspiracy against His Majesties Person, and Government (London, 1679), sigs. B2v, D.

17 Dangerfield had been convicted of theft, but had received benefit of clergy: "He said he was a Clark, and desir'd the benefit of the Book, which was granted; and he read, and was (according to Law) *Burnt in the Hand*" (Cellier, *Malice Defeated: Or a Brief Relation of the Accusation and Deliverance of Elizabeth Cellier* [London, 1680], sigs. K2–K2v). He had also been convicted of other offenses. Although he had been pardoned so that he could inform and testify against Cellier (among others), Cellier proved that the King's pardon did not cover all of his offenses, so he was not qualified as a "good witness" in a treason trial. Her acquittal results directly from her success in blocking Dangerfield's testimony.

18 *Ibid.*, sig. E2.

19 *Mr. Tho. Dangerfeilds Particular Narrative*, sig. Q.

20 John H. Langbein, "The Criminal Trial before the Lawyers," *The University of Chicago Law Review* 45.2 (1978): 263–316, especially 309; *The Tryall of Richard Langhorn* (London, 1679), pp. 18–19. According to Langbein, Fitzharris was required to give his notes to his wife.

21 Cellier, *Malice Defeated*, sig. G. *This is a Short Relation of Some of the Cruel Sufferings (For the Truths Sake) of Katharine Evans & Sarah Chevers, In the Inquisition in the Isle of Malta* (London, 1662) similarly depicts female prisoners' strategies to secure writing materials, and to smuggle their own writings out of the prison and into circulation. Conflicts over women's possession of books and writing materials might occur at home as well as in prison. Peter Clark quotes from a lawsuit describing a man who assaulted his wife "when she had been reading and leaving her book in some place . . . he would catch the book out of her hands and tear it in pieces or otherwise fling it away." "The Ownership of Books in England, 1560–1640: The Example of Some Kentish Townsfolk," in *Schooling and Society: Studies in the History of Education*, Lawrence Stone, ed. (Baltimore: Johns Hopkins University Press, 1976), pp. 95–111, passage quoted on p. 97.

22 Cellier, *Malice Defeated*, sig. F.

23 *The Tryal of Elizabeth Cellier* (London, 1680), p. 3.

24 *The Tryal and Sentence of Elizabeth Cellier; For Writing, Printing, and Publishing, A Scandalous Libel, Called Malice Defeated* (London, 1680), p. 30.

25 Cellier, *Malice Defeated*, sigs. E2, L.

26 *A Warning For Fair Women* (1599), Charles Dale Cannon, ed. (The Hague: Mouton, 1975), line 2332. See also Arthur Golding's narrative of Sanders' crime and punishment in *A Briefe Discourse* (1573, rpt. 1577), which Cannon reprints.

27 *Arden of Faversham* (1592), Martin White, ed. (London: Ernest Benn, 1982), scene 13, lines 2–9. The quote from Holinshed's chronicle of the case appears on p. 111 of White's edition.

28 James Dalton, *A Strange and True Relation of a Young Woman Possest with the Devill* (London, 1647), rpt. in *Reprints of English Books*, Foster, ed., pp. 5–6.

164   FRANCES E. DOLAN

29 Mary Moore, *Wonderfull News from the North. Or, a True Relation of the Sad and Grievous Torments, Inflicted upon the Bodies of Three Children of Mr. George Muschamp, late of the County of Northumberland, by Witchcraft* (London, 1650), sig. B3.
30 Cressy, *Literacy and the Social Order*, p. 1; Thomas, "The Meaning of Literacy," pp. 116–17.
31 Harvey J. Graff, *The Legacies of Literacy: Continuities and Contradictions in Western Culture and Society* (Bloomington: Indiana University Press, 1987), p. 11. On the interconnections between oral and written cultures, see: Roger Chartier, "Texts, Printing, Readings," in *The New Cultural History*, Lynn Hunt, ed. (Berkeley: University of California Press, 1989), pp. 154–75, esp. pp. 169–70; David Cressy, *Literacy and the Social Order*, chapter 1; Natalie Zemon Davis, *Society and Culture in Early Modern France* (Stanford: Stanford University Press, 1975), chapter 7; Graff, *The Legacies of Literacy*, chapter 5; Thomas Laqueur, "The Cultural Origins of Popular Literacy in England 1500–1850," *Oxford Review of Education* 2.3 (1976): 255–75, esp. 267–78; Keith Thomas, "The Meaning of Literacy," p. 98; and D. R. Woolf, "The 'Common Voice': History, Folklore and Oral Tradition in Early Modern England," *Past and Present* 120 (August 1988): 26–52.
32 Cressy, *Literacy and the Social Order*, p. 118.
33 Pierre Bourdieu, *Language and Symbolic Power*, trans. Gino Raymond and Matthew Adamson, John B. Thompson, ed. (Cambridge, MA: Harvard University Press, 1991), p. 55, see also p. 54; Richard Halpern, *The Poetics of Primitive Accumulation* (Ithaca: Cornell University Press, 1991), chapter 2. Similarly, Richard Hoggart argues that literacy is useful not only to those who acquire it, but to the dominant classes and institutions that seek to control them (*The Uses of Literacy: Changing Patterns in English Mass Culture* [Fair Lawn, NJ: Essential Books, 1957]); Natalie Davis argues that if printing could open up new avenues to knowledge, it could also "make possible the establishment of new kinds of control on popular thought" (*Society and Culture*, pp. 224–25); and David Levine challenges historians who assume that prudence, morality, and intelligence belong only to the literate ("Illiteracy and Family Life During the First Industrial Revolution," *Journal of Social History* 14.1 [1980]: 25–44).
34 Ferguson, "A Room Not Their Own," p. 115. Cressy also argues that literacy was "a double-edged tool": "If reading could bring enrichment and advantage it could also imperil the soul, damage the mind and subvert the moral bases of society" (Cressy, *Literacy and the Social Order*, p. 8).
35 Lawrence Stone argues that increased access to education and literacy contributed to the Revolution of the 1640s, and that contemporaries' perception of a link between literacy and radicalism contributed to greater ambivalence about a literate populace by the end of the century. "The Educational Revolution in England, 1560–1640," *Past and Present* 28 (July 1964): 41–80, esp. 73–80.
36 *Dangerous Familiars: Representations of Domestic Crime in England, 1550–1700* (Ithaca: Cornell University Press, 1994), chapter 5.

37 As a visitor to Anne Bodenham, Edmond Bower was motivated by curiosity and officiousness rather than by any official role, legal or spiritual, in the proceedings. When he zealously collects evidence and badgers the accused – to the point that, on the day of her execution, the minister attending to her objects – he works on his own initiative and in his own interests.

38 Bower, *Doctor Lamb Revived*, sig. B v. Subsequent citations will refer to this text, cited in full above, and will appear parenthetically.

39 In *Religion and the Decline of Magic* (New York: Scribner's, 1971), Keith Thomas explains that written charms might even be worn by illiterate people (pp. 182–83). See also Karen Newman, *Fashioning Femininity and English Renaissance Drama* (Chicago: University of Chicago Press, 1991), p. 68.

40 See, for instance, *The Witches of Huntingdon, Their Examinations and Confessions* (London, 1646), which describes how Elizabeth Weed signs a Faust-like covenant with her own blood.

41 Thomas, *Religion and the Decline of Magic*, p. 444. On the legal debates regarding admissible proofs of witchcraft, see Barbara J. Shapiro, *Probability and Certainty in Seventeenth-Century England: A Study of the Relationships Between Natural Science, Religion, History, Law, and Literature* (Princeton: Princeton University Press, 1983), chapter 6.

42 Phyllis Mack, *Visionary Women: Ecstatic Prophecy in Seventeenth-Century England* (Berkeley: University of California Press, 1992), p. 48, see also pp. 75–77.

43 Mary Ellen Lamb, "Women Readers in Mary Wroth's *Urania*," in *Reading Mary Wroth: Representing Alternatives in Early Modern England*, Naomi J. Miller and Gary Waller, eds. (Knoxville: University of Tennessee Press, 1991), pp. 210–27, esp. p. 224.

44 On Bodenham's notorious mentor, Dr. Lambe, see the *Dictionary of National Biography* and *A Briefe Description of the Notorious Life of John Lambe* (Amsterdam, 1628). Lambe was associated with the Duke of Buckingham. When a London crowd attacked him in 1628, they referred to him as "the duke's devil." Lambe's career seems to have inspired a play in the 1630s, *Dr. Lambe and the Witches*, no longer extant. Many years later, Bower still uses Bodenham's association with Lambe to discredit her and increase his pamphlet's sensational value and marketability.

45 See the account of Adam Sprackling's execution in *The Bloody Husband* (London, 1653); and the account of Giles Broadway's execution in Cobbett's *Complete Collection of State Trials*, Thomas B. Howell, ed., 33 vols. (London: R. Bagshaw, 1809–26), vol. VI, columns 419–26.

46 John Dod and Robert Cleaver, *A Godly Forme of Houshold Government* (London, 1612), sig. Q4v.

47 As a skeptic committed to questioning the existence, let alone prosecution, of witches, Scot did not seek to instruct and encourage witchfinders like Bower. However, in cataloguing and critiquing popular beliefs and practices, Scot also codified them.

48 As scholars such as Mary Beth Rose and Wendy Wall have argued, impend-

ing death often licensed women to write, as it were from beyond the grave. Mary Beth Rose, "Where Are the Mothers in Shakespeare? Options for Gender Representation in the English Renaissance," *Shakespeare Quarterly* 42.3 (1991): 291–314, especially 312; and Wendy Wall, "Isabella Whitney and the Female Legacy," *ELH* 58.1 (1991): 35–62.

49 *Fair Warning to Murderers of Infants* (London: 1692), sig. B v, Postcript (p. 14), and sig. A 3.

50 *A Pitilesse Mother. That Most Unnaturally At One Time, Murthered Two of Her Owne Children* (London, 1616). See also *An Account of the Seducing of Ann, the Daughter of Edward Ketelbey, of Ludlow, Gent. to the Popish Religion* (London, 1700). Carol Karlsen and Jane Kamensky both discuss a similar phenomenon in relation to witchcraft in colonial New England. "Martha Godwin had no trouble reading Catholic or Quaker books, Cotton Mather explained, or books that argued that witches did not exist. But she could not get near the Bible, books that argued for the existence of witches, or Puritan catechisms for children without falling into what he described as 'hideous Convulsions'" (Karlsen, *The Devil in the Shape of a Woman: Witchcraft in Colonial New England* [New York: Norton, 1987], p. 247). Also see Jane Kamensky, "Words, Witches, and Woman Trouble: Witchcraft, Disorderly Speech, and Gender Boundaries in Puritan New England," *Essex Institute Historical Collections* 128.4 (October 1992): 286–307.

51 See, for instance, John Bossy, *The English Catholic Community, 1570–1850* (London, 1975), p. 158.

52 On Medieval women's literacy, see also: Rita Copeland, "Why Women Can't Read: Medieval Hermeneutics, Statutory Law, and the Lollard Heresy Trials," in *Representing Women: Law, Literature, and Feminism*, Susan Sage Heinzelman and Zipporah Batshaw Wiseman, eds. (Durham, NC: Duke University Press, 1994), pp. 253–86; Joan Kelly, "Did Women Have a Renaissance?" in *Women, History, and Theory* (Chicago: University of Chicago Press, 1984), pp. 19–50, esp. p. 35; Angela M. Lucas, *Women in the Middle Ages: Religion, Marriage and Letters* (New York: St. Martin's Press, 1983), chapters 9 and 10; Susan Schibanoff, "Taking the Gold Out of Egypt: The Art of Reading as a Woman," in *Gender and Reading: Essays on Readers, Texts, and Contexts*, Elizabeth A. Flynn and Patrocinio P. Schweickart, eds. (Baltimore: Johns Hopkins University Press, 1986), pp. 83–106, esp. p. 100; and Shulamith Shahar, *The Fourth Estate: A History of Women in the Middle Ages* (London: Methuen, 1983), pp. 50–52, 154–61, 214–17.

53 Writing often played a role in punishments, as well as crimes. For instance, Thomas Potts' *The Wonderfull Discoverie of Witches in the Countie of Lancaster* (London, 1613) recounts that, for her participation in witchcraft, Margaret Pearson was sentenced to stand in a pillory in the open markets at Clitheroe, Paddiham, Whalley, and Lancaster, on four market days, "with a paper upon [her] head, in great Letters, declaring [her] offence" (sig. U4v). Such punishments obviously assumed that, by transforming the convict into a billboard, the "paper" would simultaneously shame her and edify spectators.

54 Even elite women's literacy was policed; they were not free to read whatever they chose. As Mary Ellen Lamb argues, "Renaissance educators represented the chastity of women readers as highly contingent upon the nature of their reading, which was strictly circumscribed to exclude any works, especially chivalric narratives or books of love, that did not advance a woman's spiritual state" (*Gender and Authorship in the Sidney Circle* [Madison: University of Wisconsin Press, 1990], chapter 1, esp. p. 9). See also Lamb, "Women Readers in Mary Wroth's *Urania*," pp. 212–14; Caroline Lucas, *Writing for Women: The Example of Woman As Reader in Elizabethan Romance* (Milton Keynes, PA: Open University Press, 1989), esp. chapter 1; and Diane Willen, "Women and Religion in Early Modern England," in *Women in Reformation and Counter-Reformation Europe: Public and Private Worlds*, Sherrin Marshall, ed. (Bloomington: Indiana University Press, 1989), pp. 140–65, esp. pp. 144–46. It was not just that there were good and bad texts and hence good and bad readers. A reader might also read the "right" things in the "wrong" way. See Roger Chartier, "Culture as Appropriation," pp. 229–53; and Davis, *Society and Culture*, pp. 191–92, 225–26.

55 Women could also outwit literacy as a condition of authorship or readership by dictating a confession and assuring its publication and distribution; or by having others read aloud to them. See my "'Gentlemen, I Have One Thing More to Say': Women on Scaffolds in England, 1563–1680," *Modern Philology* 92.2 (1994): 157–78.

56 My conception of subjectivity has also been informed by Louis Althusser, "Ideology and Ideological State Apparatuses (Notes Towards an Investigation)," in *Lenin and Philosophy and Other Essays*, trans. Ben Brewster (New York: Monthly Review Press, 1971), pp. 127–86; Teresa de Lauretis, "Eccentric Subjects: Feminist Theory and Historical Consciousness," *Feminist Studies* 16.1 (1990): 115–50, esp. 115, 191; Joan Scott, "The Evidence of Experience," *Critical Inquiry* 17 (Summer 1991): 773–97; and Paul Smith, *Discerning the Subject* (Minneapolis: University of Minnesota Press, 1988).

57 Karen Newman, *Fashioning Femininity*, p. 69.

CHAPTER 7

Culinary spaces, colonial spaces: the gendering of sugar in the seventeenth century

Kim F. Hall

In 1602, naturalist Hugh Plat published one of the more popular domestic manuals, *Delightes for Ladies*, with an opening verse that foregrounds his sense that he has switched to a "feminine" genre. Speaking of his previous books on husbandry and agriculture: "Of these and such like other new found skills, / With painful pen I whilome wrote at large, / Expecting still my countries good therein, / And not respecting labor, time or charge," he characterizes those efforts as selfless, laborious gifts to the nation.[1] However, with this book, Plat makes clear his sense that he is working with a "feminine" genre; in expressing that anxiety in the language of sweetness and preserving, he gives a more historical resonance to anthropologist Sidney Mintz's argument that "sweet things are, in both literal and figurative senses, more the domain of women than of men":[2]

> But now my pen and paper are perfumed,
> I scorn to write with coppress or with gall
> Barbarian canes are now become my quills,
> Rosewater is the ink I write withall:
> Of sweets the sweetest I will now commend,
> To sweetest creatures that the earth doth bear:
> These are the Saints to whom I sacrifice
> Preserves and conserves, both of plum and pear.
> Empaling now adieu, tush[!] marchpane walls
> Are strong enough, and best befits our age:
> Let piercing bullets turn to sugar balls,
> The spanish fear is hushed and all their rage. (sig. A2v)

Writing now with "perfumed" paper and "Barbarian canes," Plat explicitly equates this project with the feminine and the foreign. Moreover, these qualities are insistently connected to sugar: women and their productions are both "sweetest" and rhetorically made almost indistinguishable. Food here also becomes ritual: homely "preserves and conserves" are sacrificial offerings to his female audience. Plat's "perfumed" paper and "rosewater" ink announce his movement from masculinist and heroic texts to a more homely genre. His somewhat oblique reference to the Armada victory, England's primal moment of national pride ("Let piercing bullets turn to sugar balls, / The spanish fear is hushed and all their rage"), suggests that the English home may be another arena for English self-definition.

I would like to use this seemingly trivial verse to remind the modern reader that, in making "preserves and conserves," seventeenth-century women participated in a growing movement from a Mediterranean to an Atlantic economy, and made the English home an important part of what Immanuel Wallerstein has called the modern world system.[3] While it may look odd to read both nationalism and a developing world system in the same cultural enterprise, in this case it seems precisely the tension between a changing world economy and attempts to define the boundaries of individual national identities that produces such ambivalent (and often contradictory) notions of the foreign and the domestic in English texts. Seventeenth-century cookbooks are filled with spices, pepper, sugars, nuts, as well as more obviously precious substances such as gold and ambergris which were the stuff of world trade: when an English woman made a confection from a cookbook like Plat's, she implicitly helped foster watershed changes in England's economy. For a popular recipe such as marzipan, she would have used rosewater made from her own roses and almonds imported from the Middle East by way of Italy. She also used a great deal of sugar, first produced in a Portuguese (and later English) sugar colony, refined in Antwerp, and then sold by London merchants. This demonstration of her family's status and her own culinary expertise thus depended on England's increasingly colonial trade practices. Plat's verse, while seemingly looking inward from the English seas to the English home, actually links his English woman reader to a broader colonial context.

This essay is the beginning of a larger project which attempts to understand the ways in which women participated in England's colonial expansion in the seventeenth century. Looking at sugar, which is a product associated with both white women and African slavery, reveals the importance of women and gender ideologies in the growing consumption of "foreign" luxury goods in England. Specifically, it asks: what is the function of gender in sugar's change from a foreign luxury good to a taste that now seems closely associated with the English?

Asking this question should involve broadening not only the sense of women's roles in national and international arenas, but also our sense of what it means to study "women" in early modern England. It also means considering the ways in which women as producers (which would include white women as producers of confectionary and Afro-Caribbean women as producers of sugar and future slave labor) helped reshape the political economy of England. Reconceptualizing the study of women in this manner means charting larger economic and cultural movements through a somewhat artificial yoking of the realms of consumption and production, as well as setting aside traditional disciplinary and temporal boundaries. In the first half of this essay, I will focus specifically on a particular part of the English meal – the banquet, or "void" – and its links to women and emergent nationalism. I then turn to England's first sugar island, Barbados, and examine the ways in which the ideology of the cookbook may have influenced the first English treatise on the sugar trade, Richard Ligon's *A True and Exact History of the Island of Barbados* (1657). Together, these sections not only will make evident the links between English culinary and colonial history; but, more specifically, will suggest that the shaping of the English woman's role in the household was necessary, not only for maintaining domestic order, but for the absorption of the foreign necessitated by colonialism. While we are familiar with the search for new territories and precious substances that fueled colonial expansion, the more mundane byproducts of this trade – the exposure to new foodstuffs and the gradual incorporation of those foods into European diets – is often accepted as a "natural" occurrence rather than one which is often contested and must be prepared for ideologically.

The cookbook played a relatively unheralded role in the formation of European nationalism. One of the earliest printed books, close to the Bible in popularity,[4] the cookbook appeared *en masse* throughout Europe and thus participated in the emergence of print capitalism and the spread of vernacular languages that were the hallmarks of national consciousness in early modern Europe.[5] While the first printed cookbooks appeared in Germany in the early fifteenth century, printed English cookbooks and domestic manuals began to proliferate in the middle of the sixteenth century. The works I discuss here might more properly be called domestic manuals since they also had medicinal and ornamental functions and were thus much more than a compilation of food recipes. It is only in the late seventeenth century that cookbooks become a more specialized genre; nevertheless, I will use the term "cook-book" throughout because I am primarily interested in that function (although it will become apparent that the idea of a "domestic manual" is important to the overall essay).[6]

In Continental Europe, production and use of cookbooks were a masculine affair. In England, however, male authors both dedicated their cookbooks to, and assumed their books would be read by, women.[7] Gervase Markham's *The English Housewife* (first published in 1615) hints at the gender coding of English cookbooks when it assures its female readers that it can help them master cookery despite masculine (and obfusticating) encroachments: "though men may coin strange names, and feign strange art, yet be assured she that can do these, may make any other whatsoever."[8] As owned objects, recipe books in the vernacular give evidence of a national consciousness played out in the realm of the feminine just as the books themselves teach wives and mothers the expected attributes of the English household. As guides and historical documents, recipe books give testimony to an established – and growing – form of women's artistic and literary production. Unfortunately, these ephemeral creations – the decorative sweetmeats and sculptures, along with their accompanying poems and epigrams – are largely lost to modern readers.[9]

Even though the basic English meal, particularly for the rural poor, remained the same for centuries, elaborate meals and culinary innovation were an important part of aristocratic life. Thus, printed cookbooks and domestic manuals have specific class, as well as gender, valences. Like other forms of courtesy literature, they preserve the fiction that they are writing for aristocratic audiences, offering their upwardly-mobile women readers a peek into the status competitions and consumption patterns that they wished to emulate. Sociologist Jack Goody notes, "these manuals helped them to breach the hierarchical organization of cuisine, since the 'secrets' of rich households were now revealed and sumptuary laws prohibiting imitation were no longer effective."[10] Throughout the seventeenth century, the titles of cookbooks – *The Ladies Cabinet Enlarged and Opened* (1655), *The Queen-Like Closet*, or *Rich Cabinet* (1684), *Rare and Excellent Receipts* (1690) – promise to reveal the hidden ways of the aristocracy in a "period of unprecedented economic mobility among the middle landowning groups."[11] The rhetoric of the cabinet not only marks the role of these books in conspicuous display, it also links the cookbook to colonial trade. The cabinet, a comparatively recent architectural fashion, was a sign of wealth which kept both confections and exotic New World trifles.[12] The revelatory promises of these cook-books are also akin to the rhetoric of early colonialist texts which simi-larly offer to reveal the hidden secrets of feminized foreign lands.[13]

Sugar played a key role in this status competition: with the develop-ment of the Atlantic sugar trade in the seventeenth century, it came into England in increasing quantities and with dropping prices. Although sugar is an important ingredient in earlier cookbooks and always played a role in the conspicuous consumption in court culture, it was not until the late sixteenth and seventeenth centuries that sugar use began to spread beyond the wealthiest classes, presumably by those wanting to emulate a social elite.[14] Although it was the somewhat later habit of putting sugar into tea during the eighteenth century that spread across social lines and really fueled Britain's imperial appetites, earlier cooking practices also gave sugar a notable symbolic and culinary importance that swelled the demand for it; in the words of Sidney Mintz, sugar in the seventeenth century was "*transformed* from a luxury of kings into the kingly luxury of commoners – a purchased luxury that could be detached from one status and transferred in use to another."[15]

In the earliest cookbooks, sugar appears primarily as a spice, a preser-vative, and as "medicine," not necessarily as a sweetener or confection. However, by the end of the seventeenth century, its original use as a spice seems so forgotten that, in his recipe for mustard, Sir Kenhelm Digby had to caution his readers to "put a good spoonful of Sugar to it (which is not to make it taste sweet, but rather quick, and to help the fermenta-tion)."[16] Concurrent with the perception of and rise in sugar's use as a sweetener is the increasing elaboration of "banqueting stuffs" in aristo-cratic meals. The word "banquet" in the seventeenth century designated not only what we might call a "feast," an elaborate meal consisting of many courses, but what was dubbed the "void": "the serving after a meal, or sometimes between meals, of decorative sugar molds and sweetmeats (confectioned flowers, nuts, spices and fruit)."[17] Culinary his-torian C. Anne Wilson explains the evolution of this course:

the origins of banquets of this type go back to the medieval ceremony of the void. This was originally a way of passing the time until the hall or great chamber had been prepared for after-dinner activities, a collation of sweet wine and spices was eaten standing while the table was being cleared or "voided" after a meal. In the later seventeenth century when words of French origin became fashionable, "void" was replaced by a French word of much the same meaning, "dessert" . . . But sometimes it was served in a special room, or in a turret on the roof or a building in the garden, and was known as a banquet.[18]

The banquet or "void" was the part of the English meal that most specifically depended on sugar.[19] It also was the part of the meal least connected to nourishment and more to entertainment and rituals of status, for it involved a process of conspicuous consumption that trickled down from the courtly elite. Although a highly elaborate and abundant meal always involves some degree of status competition, and the sweetmeats and candies that eventually made up the void appeared in earlier ages, during the Jacobean era the void and its sweets become part of watershed changes in English life. The development of a separate "banqueting house" both transformed domestic architecture and helped create aristocratic subjectivity.[20]

Many of these confections were the "marchpanes" (marzipan) which began to hold pride of place in the English banquet. Gervase Markham suggests their importance when he notes that, in arranging a banquet, "March-panes have the first place, the middle place, and the last place."[21] Although subtleties or "soltelties" – decoratively presented foods in the shape of letters, knots, arms, beasts, birds, and other fancies – were the most prominent void food from the fourteenth century on, during the late sixteenth century subtleties were increasingly joined by "marchpanes" which are made almost entirely of refined sugar. Marchpane denotes both the sugar-almond paste and the substances made from it. Plat's *Delightes for Ladies* offers a typical recipe:

Take to every Jordan Almond blanched, three spoonfuls of the whitest refined sugar you can get, searce your sugar, and now and then as you see cause put in 2 or three drops of damask Rose-water, beat the same in a smooth stone mortar, with great labor, until you have brought it into a dry stiff paste, one quarterne of sugar is sufficient to work at once. (sigs. B4v–B5r)

Usually marchpane devices were highly formal and elaborate, representing various mottos and allegories. Plat's work suggests many such "devices," but recommends in particular the making of marzipan "saucers, dishes, bowls, &c." (sig. B7r) as well as rabbits and pigeons from sugar-paste, commenting, "By this means, a banquet may be presented in the form of a supper, being a very rare and strange device" (sig. B4r). Thus, at the end of the actual meal, Plat's banquet offers a metameal, a second meal composed of gilded confections that reminds the feasters of their own luxury and wealth (as well as of the relative novelty of breakable earthenware).[22]

The void was more ritual than entertainment. Patricia Fumerton notes that, after viewing and admiring the banquet, it was customary "not simply to consume but to 'break' and 'spoyle' confectionery," often violently.[23] The banquet after Ben Jonson's *Masque of Blackness* was said to be "so furiously assaulted that down went tables and trestles before one bit was touched."[24] Orazio Bursino describes the banquet following another court entertainment, Jonson's *Pleasure Reconcil'd to Virtue*; the King:

glanced round the table and departed, and at once like so many harpies the company fell on their prey. The table was almost entirely covered with sweet-meats, with all kinds of sugar confections. There were some large figures, but they were of painted cardboard, for decoration. The meal was served in bowls or plates of glass; the first assault threw the table to the ground, and the crash of glass platters reminded me exactly of the windows breaking in a great mid-summer storm.[25]

Bursino's description reveals just how removed the "void" was from nourishment: the object was not to eat, but to destroy the table, suggesting that the action and the more ritualistic aspects of consumption were paramount. Much later, Robert May begins *The Accomplisht Cook, or the Art & Mystery of Cookery* (first published in 1678) with a now notorious description of an even more elaborate entertainment said to have taken place at a Twelfth Night feast:

Make the likeness of a Ship in Paste-board, with Flags and Streamers, the Guns belonging to it of Kickses, bind them about with packthread, and cover them with close paste proportionable to the fashion of a Cannon with Carriages, lay them in places convenient as you see them in Ships of war, with such holes and trains of powder that they may all take Fire; Place your Ship firm in the great Charger; then make a salt round about it, and stick therein eggshells full of sweet water . . . then in another Charger have the proportion of a Stag made of coarse paste, with a broad Arrow in the side of him, and his body filled up with claret-wine; in another Charger at the end of the Stag have the proportion of a Castle with Battlements, Portcullises, Gates and Draw-Bridges made of Pasteboard . . . and covered with coarse paste as the former; place it at a distance from the ship to fire at each other . . . At each side of the Charger wherein is the Stag, place a Pie . . . guild them over in spots, as also the Stag, the Ship and the Castle; bake them, and place them with gilt bay-leaves on turrets and tunnels of the Castle and Pies; being baked, make a hole in the bottom of your pies, take out the bran, put in your Frogs, and Birds, and close up the holes with the same coarse paste, then cut the Lids neatly up . . . before you fire the trains of powder, order it so that some of the Ladies may be persuaded to pluck the Arrow out of the Stag, then will the Claret-wine follow, as blood that runneth out of a wound. This being done with admiration to the beholders, after some short pause, fire the train of the Castle, that the pieces all of one side may go off, then fire the Trains of one side of the Ship as in a battle; next turn the Chargers; and by degrees fire the trains of the other side as before. This done, to sweeten the stink of powder, let the Ladies take the egg-shells full of sweet waters and throw them at each other. All dangers being seemingly over, by this time you may suppose they will desire to see what is in the pies; where lifting first the lid off one pie, out skip some Frogs, which make the Ladies to skip and shriek; next after the other pie, whence out come the Birds, who by a natural instinct flying in the light, will put out the Candles; so that with the flying Birds and skipping Frogs, the one above, the other beneath, will cause much delight and pleasure to the whole company.[26]

May concludes this riotous account with the nostalgic comment, "These were formerly the delights of the Nobility, before good House-keeping had left *England*," perhaps hinting at the drop in conspicuous consumption that accompanied the Puritan revolution, as well as indicating that such banquets were paradoxical signs of domestic order.[27] Even in an entertainment created (we assume) by men, women are an integral part of the spectacle since May scripts female curiosity and cowardice into the void. In making women dispel the cannon smoke by tossing "egg-shells full of sweet waters" at each other, May brings to the fore associations of women with sweetness.[28]

   In fact, the banquet was more exclusively the preserve of women than May's account indicates. The art of creating these sugary delights was specifically attached to female labor and creativity as well as to women's literary productions. Even in households where male stewards were responsible for the main meal, aristocratic women created the devices that composed the void. The numerous recipes for confectionery and preserves as well as the annotations in a manuscript cookbook owned by Lady Elinor Fettiplace suggests that much of the summer and fall would have been spent preparing her speciality – confections – for winter banquets.[29] After praising the "plain country housewife," Sir John Harington, in a poem, "To his Wife of Women's Virtues" (1615), praises a higher-class woman in terms which imply that her standing was characterized by her needlework and her confectionery:

> The next a step, but yet a large step higher,
>   Was civil virtue fitter for the city,
>   With modest looks, good clothes, and answers witty,
> Those baser things not done but guided by her.
>
> Her idle times and idle coin she spends
>   On needle works, and when the season serves
>   In making dainty Junkets and Conserves
> To welcome in kind sort his dearest friends.[30]

While the "plain country" housewife spends her time on household work, the higher-class woman is marked by her removal from such labor. Her skill at making void foods is distanced from the energy needed for their production (just think about Plat's directions to beat sugar and rose water "with great labor") because it is now raised to the status of a leisured art and is made evidence of her hospitality.

Harington's sense that confectionery is a gentlewoman's art is readily confirmed in this description of a feast given in honor of the newly crowned King James on his progress from Scotland:

The tables were newly covered with costly banquets wherein everything that was most delicious for taste proved more delicate by the Art that made it seem beauteous to the eye: the Lady of the house being one of the most excellent confectioners in England, though I confess many honorable women very expert.[31]

Indeed, the lady of that house, Grace Mildmay, was a renowned confectioner who at sixty-two had a portrait done that featured her "receipt book" in the background.[32] Both the praise of Lady Mildmay and Harington's verse suggests that confectionery provided individual English women with a venue for social and artistic self-expression. If, as I have suggested, the English home was an arena for national self-definition, it was also an arena where women asserted their own agency and "hospitality" was visibly a mode of creativity as well as care for others.

One can also regain a sense of women as creative subjects by viewing the void as the female counterpart to the primarily male literary world. Many void confections contained poems or written fancies inside; thus, success at making confections also involved a degree of literary skill. In his *Arte of English Poesie*, George Puttenham describes the use of "Posies" in the banquet: "There be also other like Epigrams that were sent usually for new years gifts or to be Printed or put upon their banqueting dishes of sugar plate, or of marchpanes, & such other dainty meats . . ."[33] His description suggests that women would have had a role in literary production if we assume that the verses used in women's confectionery were in fact written by women. In a different move, poet Emilia Lanyer praises the Countess of Pembroke's translations of the Psalms and uses the language of sweetness to compare her own *Salve Deus Rex Judaeorum* with the Countess' verse:

Though many Books she writes that are more rare,
Yet there is honey in the meanest flowers:
Which is both wholesome, and delights the taste:

Though sugar be more finer, higher prized,
Yet is the painful Bee no whit disgraced,
Nor her fair wax, or honey more despised.[34]

Decorated confections and sweetness, already the province of women, provide a ready metaphor for Lanyer's description of her own poetic art; the truly "lost art" of verses and mottos written by women for the void is preserved in a more recognizably literary form. She here describes women's literary productions in terms of sweets, making herself the "painful Bee" who toils laboriously at producing "unlearned lines" in contrast to the "higher prized" refined sugar of the aristocratic Countess of Pembroke.[35] Her use of the language of sweetness suggests that there would have been a keen awareness of the process of making sugar since the entire metaphor rests on the distinction between honey, a "natural product" and sugar, which results from "human ingenuity and technical achievement" – and African labor.[36] As I shall discuss in more detail later, the opportunities for female expression provided by confectionery came to depend upon colonial enterprises, including slavery.

While the production of confections and the language of sugar itself is connected with the feminine in fundamental ways, looking solely at women's investment in the production of confections gives an incomplete picture of the cultural economy of sugar. The meanings of sugar are also shaped by its production from "barbarian cane." If sugar consumption was particularly associated with aristocratic female labor, sugar production was even more closely linked to African labor since it required slave labor for maximum profitability.[37] From its first appearance in the New World, sugar was connected with slavery. Columbus brought cane to the Americas on his second voyage, along with a proposal to enslave the native population in the establishment of *ingenios* (sugar factories). Over the course of two centuries, sugar moved from "first a sought-after luxury, then a costly everyday rarity, finally a central item in our diet . . ." and that course ran parallel with England's participation in the triangular trade.[38] Sucrose in its raw form – cane – was associated with slavery and colonization in the English mind. As Sidney Mintz affirms, "the aim of acquiring colonies that could produce sugar (among other things) for the metropolis . . . predates the seventeenth century."[39] Although the first sugar refineries were set up in London in the 1550s, England relied on the Dutch for most of its refined sugar until its sugar colonies went into a boom period and Parliament passed the Navigation Acts in the 1660s. In Barbados, England's first sugar economy, slavery did not rise until the island abandoned its unsuccessful attempts at cultivating tobacco and indigo and, with Dutch help, realized its spectacular success with sugar.

These changes in the sources of sugar and the increasing importance of sugar to English trade resonate outside of trade circles and were more than likely an important part of the consumption of sugar. Mintz notes the increase and diversification in references to sugar in literature of the early modern period:

From the seventeenth century onward . . . sugar imagery became ever commoner in English literature . . . This imagery bridges the two very different "meanings" we have discussed: the inside meanings as sugar became commoner, and its employment in social settings by even the least privileged and poorest of Britain's citizens; and the significance of sugar for the empire, for the king, and for the classes whose wealth would be made and secured by the growing productivity of British labor at home and British enterprise abroad.[40]

Just as the increasing references to sugar in literature mark the shift downward and the metamorphosis of sugar's "meanings" later, the diverse lexicography of sugar in seventeenth-century cookbooks indicates a high degree of awareness of sugar production. The categorization of the relative purity of sugars, combined with an emphasis on the site of production, existed to a degree rarely seen today – muscovado, clayed, refined, double refined, Madeiras, Barbados – all suggest that sugar users had a knowledge of the sources of sugar in the same way that a collector of Oriental rugs of necessity becomes aware of the origins of and techniques for producing that luxury commodity.[41] There is a hint of such knowledge in John Evelyn's discussion of sugar use in salads: "Of *Sugar* (by some called *Indian-Salt*) as it is rarely used in *Salad*, it should be of the best refined, white, hard, close, yet light and sweet as the *Madera's*: Nourishing, preserving, cleansing, delighting the Taste, and preferable to Honey for most uses."[42]

This interest in the sources of sugar bridges the realms of consumption and production in a more meaningful way than first may be apparent and argues for, not only broadly economic, but specific cultural links between the English woman at home and England's colonial enterprises. For a more inclusive picture, I turn to Barbados, England's first sugar colony. First colonized in 1627, by the 1660s this island had an extremely productive economy based on sugar and was the benchmark for production on other islands. During the seventeenth century, it went from a producer of poor tobacco to a wealthy colony which was a key coordinate in the triangular trade. Much of what is known of the early history of

Barbados comes from Richard Ligon's influential *A True and Exact History of the Island of Barbados*[43] which gives both the natural history of the island and directions for establishing a sugar plantation. Throughout, Ligon promises the industrious planter great wealth available through "the sweet negotiation of sugar."[44] If Plat's *Delightes for Ladies* gives the aspiring housewife a guide to the conspicuous consumption of sugar, Ligon's gives the ambitious householder a key to the wealth necessary for such consumption. Ligon's treatise and cookbooks such as Plat's provide both sides of England's sugar economy: both are "workbooks" geared to the production of sugar goods. As disparate as the cookbook and this colonial treatise seem, they have in common an eagerness for reproducing exquisite meals and thus insuring the appearance of domestic harmony and luxury.

Like Plat's manual, *A True and Exact History* associates itself immediately with women, although it is clearly meant for potential planters. The dedicatory poem by George Walshe ends by equating the text with the feminine and decorative arts of weaving and needlework:

> The Cane or Mine, (that makes that Spot of ground
> As rich, as any 'twixt the Poles is found)
> Is here So full and happily expressed:
> You Candy that, which does preserve the rest:
> And its Ingenio seems to be a Lecture
> (As 'tis described) of the Art of Architecture.
> The texture of the whole you've wove so nice,
> Your fine spun thread, warped, wooft with Artifice.
> It seems a Landscape in rich Tapestry,
> Embroidered with Nature's Novelty,
> Attiring all in such a lovely Dress,
> Rich, Genuine, and full of Courtliness:
> That as Great Britain sometimes I have seen,
> So you've Barbadoes drawn just like a Queen. (sig. A r–v)

First equating sugar canes with the more immediately profitable mines of gold and silver coveted by the English, Walshe hints at the immeasurable profitability of sugar. Although architecture is part of the male sphere, the other metaphors are overwhelmingly associated with the feminine. He picks up on the increasingly common metaphors of candying and preserving seen earlier in Plat's *Delightes for Ladies*. More significantly, Walshe equates the creation of Ligon's text with the weaving of tapestries and of embroideries and, finally, with aristocratic feminine dress. His language hints at the refinement needed to create sugar from sugar cane. It may also evoke the "refinement" that was also a product of a "woman's art" – the making of elaborate confections or conceits from sugar. This insistence on the domestic and civilized aspects of sugar production may also work to allay status anxieties since owners of sugar plantations make their wealth outside of more traditional channels. Barbados here is not only analogous to "Great Britain," civilized, artificial, and courtly, but also to a Queen, dressed in tapestry and embroidery (in distinct contrast to earlier descriptions of foreign and feminized lands which are usually "open," innocent, and nude).[45]

Ligon's text at first glance would seem to belong to the growing body of English travel writing and ethnography, a genre, as I have argued elsewhere, devoted to the imposing of an English rhetorical order on the cultures encountered through English travel and trade.[46] However, a closer look suggests that *A True and Exact History* has more in common with the domestic manual than the travel guide. A great deal of Ligon's text is devoted to food. Before his exhaustive lists of the meats available on the island, he tells how he transformed its gastronomic habits: "When I first came upon the Island, I found the Pork dressed the plain ways of boiling, roasting, and sometime baking: But I gave them some tastes of my Cookery, in hashing, and fricasseeing this flesh; and they were all much taken with it; and in a week, every one was practicing the art of Cookery" (p. 34).

Indeed, this portion of Ligon's text is shaped by the "art of Cookery," just as the entire book (as Walshe's poem suggests) transforms the land by art. His descriptions of the island are structured around the English meal. In English fashion, he first concentrates on the meats available on the island and continues:

Next to the flesh and fish this Island affords, 'tis fit to consider what *Quelquechoses* there are to be found, that may serve to furnish out a Table of such Viands, as there are to be had; which are eggs several ways, *viz* poached, and laid upon sippits of bread, soaked in butter and juice of limes and sugar, with plumped currants strewed upon them, and cloves, mace, and cinnamon beaten, strewed on that, wth a little salt. Eggs boiled and roasted, fried with Collops, of the fat of Pork well powdered. Buttered eggs, and amulet of eggs, with the juice of limes and sugar, a Froize and a Tansey; Custards, as good as any at my Lord Mayor's Table; . . . as also pickled Herring, and Mackerel, which we have from new England, and from *Virginia Botargo* of which sort I have eaten the best at Colonel Drax's that ever I have tasted. (p. 36)

In this exhaustive catalog, not unlike the lists of ideal meals found in cookbooks, Ligon describes the "*Quelquechoses*" (or Kickshaws) as if they were the raw materials "found" on the island itself.[47] His inclusion of fancy dishes such as "*Quelquechoses*" (literally, "somethings") is significant in that, as a food item, they are associated with ornate, "made" luxury items and are therefore highly artificial. Unlike most travel accounts, which focus more on the edibility of raw materials and their trade value, Ligon's emphasis, like that of the cookbook, is on the duplication of already known (aristocratic) dishes. His overwhelming concern is whether the delicacies found on the English table can be replicated in Barbados.

Whereas the order of travel narratives tends to be geographical or temporal, Ligon's is culinary. Instead of leading his reader through a map, the reader follows a menu. His language, "The next thing that comes in order is drink . . . Having given you a taste of the bread," marks off the transitions in text as transitions in taste. At one point, while describing the fruits available on Barbados, he also offers a choice as to how they could be served: "The fruits that this Island affords, I have already named, and therefore it will be needless to name them twice; you may take your choice, whether you will have them set on the Table before or after meat; they use as they do in *Italy*, to eat them before meat" (p. 37). Even in portions not explicitly devoted to meals, his language is that of the cookbook: "the Fig tree and Cherry tree, which have savory names, but in their natures neither useful, nor well tasted" (p. 69). Like earlier cookbook authors, he gives readers a glimpse of high society though food: "and now you see the provision the Island affords, give me leave to show you what feasts they can (when they will) make for their friends, upon their Plantations, which that I may the better do, I will make two bills of fare; the one for an Inland Plantation, the other for a Plantation near the sea" (p. 38).

The one food item that Ligon does not include in his treatise is confectionery or sweetmeats. The exclusion would not be so remarkable if it were not in a treatise obsessively concerned with food whose stated purpose is delineating the processes of sugar production. Indeed, it is not until the very end of *A True and Exact History* that we actually see the details of making sugar. Sugar production thus holds the same structural position as the "void" in the English meal. After having tasted the meat, fish, and fowl of the island, the reader gets to sample, not the airy artificial trifles that display wealth, but the making of the basis for that wealth. The end product here results not from the labor of white women, but from the labor of the African slaves and indentured servants that were necessary for running a "sugar island."

Like the cookbook, *A True and Exact Description* offers a promise of
bounty that can be achieved with good housekeeping. In *The English
Housewife*, Gervase Markham admonishes his reader:

Let her diet be wholesome and cleanly, prepared at due hours, and cooked with
care and diligence; let it be rather to satisfy nature than our affections, and apter
to kill hunger than revive new appetites; let it proceed more from the provision
of her own yard, than the furniture of the markets, and let it be esteemed for the
familiar acquaintance she hath with it, than for the strangeness and rarity it
bringeth from other countries.[48]

Markham's concern with thrift, self-sufficiency, and good order are the
hallmarks of the genre. In a similar manner, Ligon suggests that his presence – and culinary talents – have brought good husbandry and wealth
to Barbados: "But now at my coming away from thence, it was much bet-
tered, for by the care and good Husbandry of the Planters, there was
greater plenty, both of the victuals they were wont to eat, as Potatoes,
Bonavist, Loblolly, as also of the bone meat" (p. 37).

Interestingly, for a text that eschews "strangeness and rarity,"
Markham includes a great many recipes that rely on foreign and rare
substances like ambergris, pearls, gold, and sugar. In fact, the most
recent editor of Markham suggests that the ingredients of salads were
chosen precisely for their expense and rarity.[49] A later work, Sir John
Evelyn's *Acetaria* (1699), eschews the use of such items in salads when it
nostalgically (and falsely) recalls a previously "pure" culinary state:
"They could then make an honest Meal, and dine upon a Salad, without
so much as a Grain of Exotic Spice."[50] Rather than dismiss this
simultaneous inclusion of, and disdain for, the "strange" as a mere inconsistency, we might use Evelyn's statement to open up the question of
strangeness and the absorption of "foreign" foods into a national diet. It
might be that the woman's "familiar acquaintance" is the very thing necessary to remove the threat of strangeness: as substances pass through
the English home and are transformed from raw material to "food," they
lose their foreign taint. The cookbook may offer just this sort of transformative power: the mere incorporation of such substances into recipes
makes them less strange and unacceptable. In more simple terms, the
"receipt" allows for a kind of *sprezzatura* in the presentation of expensive
items. (In order to truly seem to be one of an elite, one must appear
casual about or indifferent to the expense.) Ligon may be proposing
himself a similar task of making the strange and foreign, domestic and
comfortable. He masters the landscape of Barbados by drawing on the
familiarizing powers of the cookbook; by making everything "food," he

presents the landscape as already tamed and cultivated: "Having given you in my Bills of Fare, a particular of such Viands, as this Island afforded, for supportation of life, and somewhat for delight too, as far as concerns the Table . . ." (p. 101).

As I mentioned earlier, the banquet was also the impetus to an architectural innovation. By the end of the seventeenth century, void foods were usually consumed in a room separated from the feast and often in a wholly separate building designed especially for the purpose. Banqueting houses arose as little "conceited" rooms or buildings dedicated to the void. Thus the void is closely connected to the elaboration of domestic architecture in the seventeenth century.[51] It is perhaps not coincidental that these changes in domestic space took place roughly concurrent with the expansion of Britain's borders in colonies abroad: colonial trade increasingly provided the wealth for the expansion and maintenance of the country estate.[52] We have a hint of this connection when Evelyn uses the language of imperial conquest to condemn the consumption of luxury goods:

there's a Snake in the Grass; Luxury, and Excess in our most innocent Fruitions. There was a time indeed when the garden furnished Entertainments for the most Renowned Heroes, virtuous and excellent Persons; till the blood-thirsty and Ambitious, over-running the Nations, and by Murders and Rapine rifled the World, to transplant its Luxury to its new Mistress, Rome. Those whom heretofore two Acres of Land would have satisfied, and plentifully maintained; had afterwards their very Kitchens almost as large as their first Territories . . ."[53]

As Evelyn's language suggests, the expansion of the boundaries of the "home" through additional peripheral spaces such as banqueting houses resembles the larger national expansion into a colonial periphery. Like the country house, the colonial plantation is a rural, agrarian phenomenon. For Barbados in particular, the move from tobacco to sugar meant a move from small farms to large estates.[54] Treatises such as Ligon's participated in the process of remaking England abroad by extolling the familiarity and attractiveness of the landscape. Richard Eburne, in his popular *A Plaine Path-Way to Plantations* (1624), argues to his countrymen that no plantation land is foreign, "It be the people that makes the Land English, not the Land the People" (sigs. B2v–B3r).[55] The rhetoric around Barbadian settlement complements this process of familiarization, making the land feel as English as possible before the settlers actually arrive. For example, Colonel Thomas Modiford, the island's first colonial governor, comments on the change in Barbados since the adoption of the sugar trade, hinting at the transformative powers of the sugar trade: "the buildings in 1643 were mean, with things only for necessity; but in 1666 plate, jewels and household stuff were estimated at 500,000 pounds, their buildings very fair and beautiful, and their houses like castles, the sugar houses and negroes' huts show themselves from the sea like so many small towns, each defended by its castle."[56] Modiford's description here naturalizes the sugar industry; his nostalgic lens turns the Barbadian landscape into a feudal estate where slave-trading sugar capitalists become benevolent lords of their own castles. His vision promises aspiring gentry "castles" which represent both wealth and paternalistic control over laborers. It also rhetorically eliminates (as Ligon does) the constant threat of slave rebellion.[57]

As sugar saturated the cookbook and the English economy, it perhaps is only fitting that the first English treatise on the production of sugar be intensely concerned with the English household, the order of which is best exemplified by the feast or banquet. The plantation manual must address a central problem: it must attract to a foreign landscape a people who are, as Eburne describes, "wedded to their native Soil like a Snail to his Shell . . . that they will rather even starve at home, then seek store abroad."[58] The cookbook, which articulates the practices that define the English home (and the woman's place within it) offers a possible solution. Whereas earlier narratives of colonization attracted reading audiences by extolling strangeness and novelty, *A True and Exact History of the Island of Barbados* solves its dilemma by removing the strangeness of this new land, subsuming any possibly threatening difference under the good husbandry and sweet domesticity of the English cookbook.

NOTES

This essay was originally a conference presentation for the 1993 Berkshire Conference on the History of Women. Connie M. Razza was instrumental in the research and writing of that presentation and this essay. Special thanks also go to Alison Byerly, Susan Greenfield, Susan Zlotnick, Leona Fisher, Dennis Todd, and Ruth Widmann for their advice and comments.

1 Hugh Plat, *Delightes for Ladies, To Adorne Their Persons, Tables, Closets and Distillatories: With Beauties Banquets, Perfumes and Waters* (London, 1608), sig. A2v. All references are to this third edition and are noted in parentheses in the text.

2 Sidney Mintz, *Sweetness and Power: The Place of Sugar in Modern History* (New York: Penguin Books, 1985), p. 150.

3 Immanuel Wallerstein defines the modern world system in his introduction:

In the late fifteenth and early sixteenth century, there came into existence what we may call a European world-economy . . . It was a kind of social system the world had not really known before and which is the distinctive feature of the modern world system. It is an economic but not a political entity, unlike empires, city-states and nation-states. In fact, it precisely encompasses within its bounds (it is hard to speak of boundaries) empires, city-states, and the emerging "nation-states." It is a "world" system, not because it encompasses the whole world, but because it is larger than any juridically-defined political unit. And it is a "world-*economy*" because the basic linkage between the parts of the system is economic, although this was reinforced to some extent by cultural links and eventually . . . by political arrangements and even confederal structures. (*The Modern World System: Capitalist Agriculture and the Origins of the European World-Economy in the Sixteenth Century* [New York: Academic Press, 1971], vol. I, p. 15).

4 Esther B. Aresty, *The Delectable Past* (London: George Allen and Unwin Ltd, 1964), p. 27.
5 See Benedict Anderson, *Imagined Communities: Reflections on the Origin and Spread of Nationalism* (London and New York: Verso, 1991), pp. 37–46.
6 For a more detailed discussion of the development of the "cookery books" see Lynette Hunter, "'Sweet Secrets' from Occasional Receipt to Specialised Books," in *"Banquetting Stuffe": The Fare and Social Background of the Tudor and Stuart Banquet*, C. Anne Wilson, ed. (Edinburgh: Edinburgh University Press, 1991), pp. 36–59.
7 See Stephen Mennell, *All Manners of Food: Eating and Taste in England and France from the Middle Ages to the Present* (Oxford: Oxford University Press, 1985), pp. 87–89 and Aresty, *The Delectable Past*, p. 43.
8 Gervase Markham, *The English Housewife*, Michael R. Best, ed. (Kingston, ONT: McGill-Queen's University Press, 1986), p. 53. This edition is a collation of the editions published in 1615, 1623, 1631, 1638, and 1668.
9 Much of the work done on cookbooks does not specifically answer the question of how many (and what types of) women were actually able to read them. Mennell brings up the question of literacy in general, but does not address women in any significant way. Traditional approaches to women's histories tend to argue that the rates of female literacy were quite low. David Cressy argues that most domestic work did not require reading, but notes that "several popular books were aimed specifically at a female audience. There were privileged women whose literacy was a social ornament, daughters who learned to read and write to please their fathers, and wives whose literacy matched that of their husbands" (*Literacy and the Social Order: Reading and Writing in Tudor and Stuart England* [Cambridge: Cambridge University Press, 1980], p. 128). He warns against reading such popular manuals as evidence of widespread female literacy and does not distinguish among women by class in charting rates of illiteracy. He nonetheless makes the claim that female literacy rose gradually during the seventeenth century,

particularly in the last quarter, which is when the first cookbooks authored by women began to appear as well (p. 129). R. A. Houston notes that reading and writing were taught separately and that more women and men could read at a rudimentary level than could write (*Literacy in Early Modern Europe: Culture and Education 1500–1800* [New York and London: Longman, 1988], p. 134). This would make it likely that the reading audience for cookbooks was greater than literacy figures might suggest.

Frances E. Dolan challenges Cressy with an approach that is more liberating for this essay. She notes that Cressy's methodology has been questioned and argues against a strict division between literacy and illiteracy: "the more we learn about education and literacy, the less we can be sure who possessed which skills and to what extent. I assume rather than seek to prove that many women could read and/or write" (p. 144). With Dolan, I would like to assume women's literacy, particularly when thinking about the verses and "posies" that were an important part of void foods. This assumption in turn suggests that women might have read manuals such as Puttenham's *The Arte of English Poesie* (1589) for help in composing such verses.

10 Jack Goody, *Cooking, Cuisine and Class: A Study in Comparative Sociology* (Cambridge: Cambridge University Press, 1982), p. 152.

11 Lawrence Stone, *The Crisis of the Aristocracy, 1558–1641* (Oxford: Clarendon Press, 1965), p. 11.

12 Mark Girouard, *Life in the English Country House: A Social and Architectural History* (New Haven and London: Yale University Press, 1978), pp. 129–30. Joy Kenseth argues that Cabinets of Curiosities or *Wunderkammer* "often served as status symbols and sometimes were a means to climb the social ladder" ("A World of Wonders in One Closet Shut," in *The Age of the Marvelous*, Joy Kenseth, ed. [Hanover, NH: Hood Museum of Art, 1991], p. 85).

13 For more on this phenomenon, see Annette Kolodny, *The Lay of the Land: Metaphor as Experience and History in American Life and Letters* (Chapel Hill: University of North Carolina Press, 1975); Patricia Parker, *Literary Fat Ladies: Rhetoric, Gender, Property* (London and New York: Methuen, 1987); and Nancy Vickers, "'The Blazon of Sweet Beauty's Best': Shakespeare's *Lucrece*" in *Shakespeare and the Question of Theory*, Patricia Parker and Geoffrey Hartman, eds. (New York: Methuen, 1985) pp. 95–115.

14 Woodruff Smith, "Complications of the Commonplace: Tea, Sugar and Imperialism," *Journal of Interdisciplinary History*, 23.2 (Autumn, 1992): 259–78 and Mintz, *Sweetness and Power*, pp. 151–52. Richard Sheridan argues that English sugar consumption quadrupled from between 1600 and 1700 and that more and more imports of sugar were retained for domestic consumption (*Sugar and Slavery: An Economic History of the British West Indies* [Baltimore: Johns Hopkins University Press, 1974], pp. 21–22). For more on the history of sugar, see Noel Deer, *The History of Sugar*, 2 vols. (London: Chapman and Hall, 1949). For specific discussions of Caribbean

sugar production, see Sheridan and Richard Dunn, *Sugar and Slaves: The Rise of the Planter Class in the English West Indies* (Chapel Hill: University of North Carolina Press, 1972).

15 Mintz, *Sweetness and Power*, p. 97. Mintz rather lyrically speaks to the importance of sugar to English elites:

> The rich and powerful, however, derived an intense pleasure from their access to sugar – the purchase, display, consumption, and waste of sucrose in various forms – which involved social validation, affiliation and distinction. The blending of sugar with other rare and precious spices in the preparation of food; the use of sugar as a fruit preservative; the combination of sugar with crushed pearls or fine gold in the manufacture of medical "remedies"; the magnificent subtleties giving concrete expression to temporal and spiritual power – all confirm what sugar meant, and how sugar use informed meanings, among the privileged (p. 154).

16 Sir Kenhelm Digby, *The Closet of Sir Kenhelm Digby, Knight, Opened* (1669), Anna Macdonnell, ed. (London: P. L. Warner, 1910), p. 194.

17 Patricia Fumerton, *Cultural Aesthetics: Renaissance Literature and the Practice of Social Ornament* (Chicago: University of Chicago Press, 1991), p. 112.

18 C. Anne Wilson, *The Appetite and the Eye* (Edinburgh: Edinburgh University Press, 1990), p. 9.

19 There is some semantic confusion around the terms "banquet" and "void" which is further complicated by the more modern sense of a banquet as a large, elaborate meal. Although "banquet" did have this sense even in the sixteenth century, that type of meal was usually known as a feast. "Banquet" more frequently referred to the course at the end of the meal which featured wine and the decorative sweet goods commonly known as "banquetting stuffe." In this it is not significantly different from the "void." Mark Girouard notes that the banquet could be served at any time, even to small groups of people, even though it was most common to have it after feasts (*English Country House*, pp. 104–05). I have elected to use the term "banquet" to refer to the actual course and "void" to refer to the ritual of eating, even though, as C. Anne Wilson suggests, the terms encompassed both aspects.

20 For a complete discussion of the relationship between "the void," Jacobean masques, and the evolution of English subjectivity, see Patricia Fumerton, *Cultural Aesthetics*. Much of my discussion of the void relies on her insights.

21 Gervase Markham, *The English Housewife*, p. 121.

22 Hilary Spurling, *Elinor Fettiplace's Receipt Book: Elizabethan Country House Cooking* (London: Salamander Press, 1986), p. 108. It may also call attention to the relatively new practice of having individual place settings "so that a man no longer had to share with others, to draw from a common plate or pot, to use the same instruments" (Goody, *Cooking, Cuisine and Class*, p. 143). See also Fernand Braudel, *The Structures of Everyday Life: The Limits of the Possible* (Berkeley and Los Angeles: University of California Press, 1992), p. 138.

188   KIM F. HALL

23 Fumerton, *Cultural Aesthetics*, p. 132.
24 Quoted in *ibid.*, p. 161.
25 Quoted in *ibid.*, p. 162.
26 Robert May, *The Accomplisht Cook, or the Art & Mystery of Cookery* (London, 1685), sigs. A7v–A8r.
27 *Ibid.*, sig. A8r. Both Jack Goody (*Cooking, Cuisine and Class*, p. 147) and Phillipa Pullar (*Consuming Passions: Being an Historic Inquiry into Certain English Appetites* [London: Hamilton, 1971], pp. 125–29) suggest that English cooking still declined during the Interregnum and that that decline had a lasting impact on English cuisine. Mennell disagrees with the general tendency to blame the Puritans for the decline in English cooking. He particularly faults Phillipa Pullar and argues that the Restoration would have reintroduced continental influences in English cooking. Although I agree with Mennell that the actual Interregnum was much too short to have changed English cooking to the degree that Pullar claims, one must also account for the sense of nostalgia for earlier cooking that permeates some of these cookbooks, as well as for works like the anonymous *The Court and Kitchen of Elizabeth* (London, 1664) which includes with the recipes a bitter attack on Cromwell's wife, Elizabeth, and her seemingly extravagant housekeeping practices (although, in fact, the recipes seem much like the ones found in other cookbooks). The nostalgia could be a marketing ploy which draws on the nostalgia for Elizabeth I's reign, but it is a distinct change from the promises of earlier cookbooks to show new devices and dainty delights. In some ways it may just bring to the surface the nostalgia inherent in any recipe. Even the cookbooks that promise the "new" are based on the idea that the cook can remake a previously created perfect dish.
28 This conversion of militaristic action to banqueting delight is reminiscent of the conversion called for in Plat's earlier verse (see page 166).
29 Spurling, *Elinor Fettiplace's Receipt Book*, pp. 31, 39. Spurling also makes the point that, as property, cookbooks represent a form of matrilineal inheritance "unlike virtually any other form of inheritance" (p. xi). Certainly Laura Esquivel's 1989 novel and subsequent film, *Like Water for Chocolate* (1992), also show the cookbook as a link between women across generations.
30 Sir John Harington, *The Letters and Epigrams of Sir John Harington, together with The Praise of Private Life*, Norman Egbert McClure, ed. (Philadelphia: University of Pennyslvania Press, 1930), p. 291.
31 Quoted in Spurling, *Elinor Fettiplace's Receipt Book*, p. 165.
32 *Ibid.*, p. 165.
33 George Puttenham, *The Arte of English Poesie*, Gladys Doidge Willcock and Alice Walker, eds. (Cambridge: Cambridge University Press, 1936), p. 58.
34 Emilia Lanyer, *The Poems of Emilia Lanyer: Salve Deus Rex Judaeorum*, Susanne Woods, ed. (Oxford: Oxford University Press, 1993), p. 30, lines 195–200.
35 The issue of labor here is a bit more complicated since "refined sugar" relies on secondary and tertiary levels of labor to reach the desired state of purity.
36 Mintz, *Sweetness and Power*, p. 16.

37 W. A. Aykroyd, *Sweet Malefactor: Sugar, Slavery and Human Society* (London: Heinemann, 1967), p. 23. Wallerstein disagrees with the standard belief that sugar and slavery were intimately linked: "The fact is, however, that the first attempts to grow sugar and tobacco in the Caribbean were almost always based on using indentured labor, not slaves. It was only towards the end of the seventeenth century that slaves became the characteristic labor force of the islands, and only in the early eighteenth century can this be said to have become the case for the southern mainland colonies of North America" (*The Modern World System II: Mercantilism and the Consolidation of the European World-Economy, 1600–1750* [New York: Academic Press, 1980], p. 171). He does, however, later note that "Slavery . . . came to sugar plantations earlier than to tobacco plantations and came to the West Indies rather than to the Southern mainland of North America" (p. 172). He also concedes that during the period in question, sugar is associated with "boom periods" and cites Dunn on the effect of the sugar boom between 1640 and 1660. He concludes: "Thus it was that in the extended Caribbean, the new periphery of the period from 1600 to 1750, the basic form in which proletarian labor was organized was slavery rather than wage labor, tenantry, or coerced cash-crop labor. Slavery, given the political conditions of the epoch, was economically optimal for the bourgeois producers who shaped, via the legal system as well as the market, the basic relations of production in the region" (p. 175).

38 Immanuel Wallerstein, "The World that Sugar Made," *Food and Foodways* 2.2 (1987): 110.

39 Mintz, *Sweetness and Power*, p. 37.

40 *Ibid.*, p. 155.

41 See Brian Spooner ("Weavers and Dealers: The Authenticity of an Oriental Carpet," in *The Social Life of Things: Commodities in Cultural Perspective*, Arjun Appadurai, ed. [New York: Cambridge University Press, 1986, pp. 195–235) who argues that "the carpet business involves not just the supply of carpets, as in the cases of other commodities, but also the supply of information about them" (p. 198).

42 John Evelyn, *Acetaria: A Discourse of Sallets* (London, 1699), p. 102.

43 *A True and Exact History* is a key text for historians since it is one of the few early commentaries on the Barbadian settlement; however, it has been largely ignored by scholars of literature, despite its significance in literary history. Peter Hulme (*Colonial Encounters: Europe and the Native Caribbean, 1492–1797* [London: Methuen, 1986]) identifies it as the source for the very popular Inkle and Yarico story in the seventeenth century.

44 Richard Ligon, *A True and Exact History of the Island of Barbados* (London, 1657), p. 96. All references are to this edition and are noted in parentheses in the text.

45 See, for example, Louis Montrose's discussion of Jan van der Straet's drawing of Vespucci's discovery of America (Louis A. Montrose, "The Work of Gender in the Discourse of Discovery," *Representations* 33 [Winter

1991]: 3–6) and Georgianna Ziegler's analysis of the frontispiece of Ortelius's *Theatrum Orbis Terrarum* in "En-Gendering the World: The Politics and Theatricality of Ortelius's Titlepage," in *European Iconography East and West, Selected Papers of the Szeged International Conference, June 9–12, 1993*, Gyorgy E. Szónyi, ed. (Leiden: E. S. Brill, 1996), pp. 128–45.

46 See Kim F. Hall, *Things of Darkness: Economies of Race and Gender in Early Modern England* (Ithaca and New York: Cornell University Press, 1995), chapter 1.

47 May's description of the Twelfth Night feast is along this order as well. See also Hannah Woolley's *The Accomplisht Ladys Delight* (London, 1681), which ends with an address to the reader and several bills of fare:

> I have here presented to thee the order of a Feast, and a Bill of Fare, which was taken out of the Records of the Tower; I have done it the rather, that thou maist see what Liberality and Hospitality there was in Ancient times amongst our Progenitors: like this to *Solomon's* Royal House-keeping, yet he was one that was endued with wisdom from above; by which Liberality his objects were made rich, so that silver was as plenty as Stones in the streets of Jerusalem, and there was peace in all his days: According to his Judgement from his inspired Wisdom, so was his Practice, and so was his Declaration: for food and rainment, is all the Portion that man hath in his life. (Sig. Illr)

48 Markham, *The English Housewife*, p. 8.
49 *Ibid.*, p. xxxvii.
50 Evelyn, *Acetaria*, p. 185.
51 Fumerton, *Cultural Aesthetics*, p. 112.
52 Girouard, *English Country House*, p. 3.
53 Evelyn, *Acetaria*, p. 179.
54 Mintz, *Sweetness and Power*, p. 53.
55 Richard Eburne, *A Plaine Path-Way to Plantations* (London, 1624), sigs. B2v–B3r.
56 *Calendar of State Papers*, American and West Indian, p. 529.
57 This element of control is also important to Ligon's treatise. He is at great pains to insist that the islands are secure and that slave or servant rebellion is not significant, yet he describes an elaborate surveillance and defense system created by the planters and his map of the island features an illustration of a white islander shooting at two escaping slaves. Clearly the fear of rebellion was omnipresent in a white ruling class increasingly outnumbered by slaves and indentured servants.
58 Eburne, *A Plaine Path-Way*, p. 59.

CHAPTER 8

Caliban versus Miranda: race and gender conflicts in postcolonial rewritings of The Tempest

Jyotsna G. Singh

CALIBAN AND DECOLONIZATION

I cannot read *The Tempest* without recalling the adventures of those voyages reported in Hakluyt; and when I remember the voyages and the particular period in African history, I see *The Tempest* against the background of England's experimentation in colonisation . . . *The Tempest* was also prophetic of a political future which is our present. Moreover, the circumstances of my life, both as colonial and exiled descendant of Caliban in the twentieth century is an example of that prophecy.[1]

There is just one world in which the oppressors and oppressed struggle, one world in which, sooner than later, the oppressed will be victorious. Our [Latin]America is bringing its own nuances to this struggle, this victory. The tempest has not subsided. But *The Tempest*'s shipwrecked sailors, Crusoe and Gulliver, can be seen, rising out of the waters, from terra firma. There, not only Prospero, Ariel, and Caliban, Don Quixote, Friday and Faust await them, but . . . halfway between history and dream – Marx and Lenin, Bolivar and Marti, Sandino and Che Guevara.[2]

Since Caliban first appeared on the stage in Shakespeare's *The Tempest* in 1611, he has been theatrically reincarnated in many different forms. Most recently, Prospero's "misshapen knave" and "demi-devil" has been transformed into a third world revolutionary. Revisionary histories of colonialism – especially since the 1960s – frequently evoke the figure of Caliban as a symbol of resistance to colonial regimes in Latin America, the Caribbean, and Africa. These revisions interrogate the so-called "discovery" of the Americas to trace a history of the Caliban myth in the early encounters between the European colonizers and natives. Crucially, they challenge the veracity of Columbus' account of "cannibals" in his diary, suggesting that the term "cannibal" – for which Caliban is an anagram – is itself a deformation of the name *Carib*, an

Indian warrior tribe opposed to the Europeans or a variant of another tribal name, *Kanibna*. Furthermore, they argue that while there is limited and conflicting evidence backing Columbus' association of caribs/cannibals with people who eat human flesh, the image of the cannibal easily elided with Shakespeare's Caliban, ideologically holding in place the European distinction between their own "civilized" selves and the "savage" others they encountered in the New World.[3] Cheyfitz lays down the boundaries of this revisionary reading as follows:

> Whatever the actual linguistic case may be, however, we have cause to wonder, as Columbus himself apparently did from time to time, at Columbus' association of the cannibals with eating human flesh. He did not have any empirical evidence, and his assertion that the Arawaks themselves told him is contradicted by Columbus' own admission that neither the Indians nor the Europeans knew each other's language. If we try to imagine the use of gestures in this case, we have not gotten around the problem of translation, but only embedded ourselves more deeply in it . . . [however] after the association Columbus elaborated in his journal, cannibal . . . [became] a part of a diverse arsenal of rhetorical weapons used to distinguish what they conceive of their "civilized" selves from certain "savage" others, principally Native Americans and Africans.[4]

Such contemporary interrogations of the so-called originary moment of European colonialism in Columbus' "discovery" of the Americas have stirred considerable interest in earlier, native revisions of colonial history. Today, as we question Prospero's heroic qualities within the providential code that had previously designated the play a pastoral romance, we can also recognize why Caribbean and Latin American writers, in the wake of decolonization in the 1960s, imaginatively identify with Caliban in their rewritings of Shakespeare's play. Roberto Fernandez Retamar recalls a history of a variety of Latin American responses to *The Tempest* through this century – some of which valorize Ariel as a native intellectual – and argues that new readings from a genuinely non-European perspective were only enabled by the gradual emergence of "third world" nations.[5] Thus, writing in 1971, Retamar declares

> Our symbol then is not Ariel . . . but rather Caliban. This is something that we, the *mestizo* inhabitants of these same isles where Caliban lived, see with particular clarity: Prospero invaded the islands, killed our ancestors, enslaved Caliban, and taught him his language to make himself understood. What can Caliban do but use that same language – today he has no other – to curse him . . . I know no other metaphor more expressive of our cultural situation, of our reality . . . what is our history, what is our culture, if not the history and culture of Caliban?[6]

These identifications with Caliban, and an accompanying unease about his alien language, typify numerous Latin American and Caribbean responses, especially in their articulations of Caliban's revolutionary potential against Prospero's linguistic authority. The Barbadian writer George Lamming, while assuming his people's identification with Caliban, often returns to the impasse of the colonizer's language in his pioneering essay of 1960:

> Prospero has given Caliban language: with all its unstated history of consequences, an unknown history of future intentions. This gift of language meant not only English, in particular, but speech and concept as a way, a method, a necessary avenue towards areas of the self which could not be reached any other way . . . Prospero lives in the absolute certainty that Language, which is his gift to Caliban, is the very prison in which Caliban's achievements must be realized and restricted.[7]

Writing some years later, the Martinique writer and founder of the Negritude movement, Aimé Césaire, is more unequivocal in his play, *A Tempest*, casting Caliban as a successful revolutionary who persistently repudiates Prospero's (European) version of history:

CALIBAN: . . . I am telling you [Prospero] . . . I won't answer to the name Caliban . . . Call me X. That would be best. Like a man without a name. Or, to be more precise, a man whose name has been stolen. You talk about history . . . well, that's history, and everyone knows it! . . . Uhuru.[8]

These and other such third world identifications with Caliban have clearly occasioned a paradigm shift among Western audiences and critics who in the past "tended to listen exclusively to Prospero's voice; [who] after all . . . speaks their language."[9] And in his stage manifestations too, Caliban has come a long way from appearing as the eighteenth-century primitive or the nineteenth-century Darwinian "missing link" to be accepted as a colonial subject or an embodiment of any oppressed group.[10] Undoubtedly, these anti-colonialist rewritings of Shakespeare's *The Tempest* question the play's seemingly aesthetic concerns, crucially relocating it within a revisionist history of the "discovery" of the Americas and the struggles for decolonization in this region. However, while these historicizations of Prospero's mistreatment of Caliban *make visible* the colonial contexts of Shakespeare's play, they often simply signal a *reversal* of the roles of the oppressor and the oppressed, typically demonstrated by Césaire in *A Tempest* when he depicts the relation between Prospero and Caliban as an endless and inevitable Hegelian struggle between the master and slave. Despite leaving open the possibility of a constant negotiation of power between the two men in alternating roles, the play does little to question the inevitability of hierarchical structures.

Therefore, ironically, Prospero refuses to return to Europe at the end of Césaire's play. He threatens a freed and defiant Caliban: "I will answer your violence with violence," but concludes almost tamely: "Well Caliban, old fellow, it's just us two now, here on the island . . . only you and me," while Caliban shouts: "Freedom Hi-Day, Freedom Hi-Day."[11] Finally, in his anti-colonial version of Shakespeare's play, Césaire leaves Prospero and Caliban at an impasse: locked in a continual, potentially violent struggle while sharing the otherwise uninhabited island.

In Lamming's reading of *The Tempest*, the writer also frequently lapses into psychologizing universals when defining the Prospero/Caliban polarity (in which Miranda has a peripheral role):

[According to Lamming, while] Caliban is [Prospero's] convert, colonised by language, and excluded by language . . . Prospero is afraid of Caliban. He is afraid because he knows that his encounter with Caliban is largely his encounter with himself. The gift [of language] is a contract from which neither participant is allowed to withdraw . . . [yet] Caliban is a child of Nature . . . [and] Miranda is the innocent half of Caliban.[12]

In such formulations, Prospero is the dominant force in a natural psychic struggle between Self and Other, namely, between Prospero and Caliban – and Miranda as the object of desire functions to define and keep this rivalry alive.

Lamming and Césaire exemplify a tendency among the anti-colonial appropriations of *The Tempest* to reverse the roles of oppressor and oppressed. And more importantly, in doing so, they view the identities of the women – of Miranda and of the missing "native" woman, Sycorax – simply as an aspect of the Prospero/Caliban opposition rather than in terms of the complex *sexual ideologies* underpinning colonialism. I wish to look afresh at the relation between Miranda and Caliban, specifically at the way in which Shakespeare's play intersects with postcolonial reappraisals of it, which, I believe, do not adequately address the interactions between race, sexuality, and political struggle. At the center of my concerns lies the *gendering* of these postcolonial discourses of revolution in which Caliban as the prototype of a male revolutionary becomes a convenient, homogenizing symbol for decolonization. What these writers do not acknowledge is that their focus on Caliban "generates a self-conscious, self-celebrating male paradigm" that often posits a utopia in which women are marginalized or missing.[13] Retamar imagines such a male utopia in his vision of a tempest, "halfway between history and dream," which will unify the former oppressors and oppressed: Prospero, Caliban, and Ariel figure alongside Friday, Don Quixote, Marti, and Guevara, among others, but Miranda (as well as her dead mother) and Sycorax are missing.[14]

Postcolonial theorists (both in Western and non-Western locations) have frequently critiqued narratives of "discovery" for the way in which they gender "the New World as feminine, [while] sexualizing . . . its exploration, conquest, and settlement."[15] Some have also traced a history of this feminization of the various non-European cultures, whereby they exude a "full blown . . . sensuality" of a "sweet dream" in which the West had been wallowing for more than four centuries."[16] From these examples it is evident that critics resisting colonialism have been quick to note how gender is crucial in mapping the signification of power relations in the West – especially in relation to its native others. It is surprising, however, that in their rewritings of *The Tempest*, non-Western writers like Lamming, Césaire, and Fanon have created liberationist, third world narratives oddly oblivious to the dissonances between race and gender struggles. Thus, ironically, their anti-colonial discourse produces the liberated "Black Man" via the erasure of female subjectivity. For instance, they acknowledge Miranda, but only as the property of the European masters, and therefore, in this eyes, a desired object to be usurped and claimed in the service of resistance. It is Fanon's alienated black male who best expresses this contradiction in the agenda of decolonization, when he declares: "I marry white culture, white beauty, white whiteness. When my restless hands caress those white breasts, they grasp white civilization and dignity and make them mine."[17] Such assertive, and potentially forcible, claims on the European woman are never questioned by Fanon or others, while the possibility of a fruitful partnership with a native woman – a native mate for Caliban – is never given serious consideration.

In *The Pleasures of Exile*, for instance, "resistance and liberation are an exclusively male enterprise."[18] Lamming attempts to understand the relation between Miranda and Caliban who, in his version, share "innocence and incredulity" but differ in "their degree of being."[19] Ultimately, however, he privileges "Caliban's history . . . [which] belongs to the future."[20] Miranda, in contrast, is made to depend on her father's view of history and await her future within a patriarchal lineage, whereby "the magic of birth will sail [her], young, beautiful, and a virgin, into the arms of the King's only son."[21] Furthermore, and more crucially, as

Paquet mentions in her foreword, "[finally] like Melville's Ishmael, Caliban is left alone on the island [without the promise of a mate]" and "Sycorax, as a symbol of a landscape and a changing human situation, is a memory, an absence, and a silence . . . [as] Lamming consciously postpones consideration of Sycorax and Miranda's mother as contributing subjects of Caribbean cultural history."[22]

Aimé Césaire's play, *A Tempest* (which I will discuss at length later), also celebrates Caliban's linguistic and political appropriations of Prospero's power, but once again, without radically altering the terms of a patriarchal power struggle in which the woman's presence is incidental or abstract: namely to perpetuate her father's noble lineage by marrying Ferdinand, the ruler of Naples. And Caliban's mother, the "native" Sycorax, figures in the play as a *symbolic* Earth Mother embodied in the natural elements of the island. As a result, while the experience of the play foregrounds a seemingly gender-neutral struggle between master and slave, it is, in effect, predicated on the marginalization of the female figures. Before analyzing the gender politics of Césaire's play any further, I would like to examine the discourse of sexuality in Shakespeare's *The Tempest* and explore how it offers the crucial nexus for Prospero's colonial authority. An analogy for Prospero's imposition of cultural and political organization on the sexuality of his subjects – Miranda, Caliban, and to a lesser extent, Ferdinand – can be found in the structure of the exchange of women as gifts in earlier, "primitive" societies – a structure which served as an idiom for both *kinship* and *competition* among men. In this I hope to show that while Césaire rewrites Shakespeare's play as a third world manifesto of decolonization, he leaves intact the intractable system of gender categories that are the centerpiece of Prospero's ostensibly benevolent mastery.

DESIRING MIRANDA

MIRANDA: Why speaks my father so urgently? This
  Is the third man that e'er I saw; the first
  That e'er I sighed for . . .
FERDINAND: O, if a virgin
  And your affection not gone forth, I'll make you the
  Queen of Naples. (Shakespeare, *The Tempest*, I.ii.445–49)[23]

On the occasion of Ferdinand and Miranda's first meeting, arranged and controlled by Prospero, in act I, scene ii of Shakespeare's play, a curious and telling exchange takes place between the three of them. Miranda articulates her desire for Ferdinand by distinguishing him from the other two men she has known: her father and Caliban. Here, Miranda is unaware of her father's apparently "magical" control of this moment, even as she articulates her desire as a personalized, autonomous experience of sighs and longings. Ferdinand, however, does not look to his heart to understand his attraction for her; instead, he quickly reveals a connection between his sexual desire and the require-ments of a patriarchal lineage: "if a virgin," he asks her, "I'll make you / The Queen of Naples." Prospero, the presiding deity, controls their feel-ings as he finds his power slipping – "this swift business / I must uneasy make" (I.ii.451–52) – while cautioning Miranda against her limited judg-ment: "Thou think'st there is no more such shapes as he, / Having seen but him and Caliban. Foolish wench! / To th' most of men this is a Caliban, / And they to him are angels" (I.ii. 479–82).

In eliding Caliban and Ferdinand in vague comparison to "most of men" – while rhetorically suggesting an identity and difference between them – Prospero points out how he uses Caliban as the less-than-human other in order to define gender (and racial) identity in conveniently elusive terms of what it is *not*. In this gesture, Prospero unwittingly reveals that not only does he fear Caliban's potential for miscegenation with Miranda, but that every man who desires his daughter is potentially a Caliban, unless that desire can be channeled to fulfill the demands of an aristocratic lineage.

While noting the dynamics of Prospero's fatherhood, critics often have observed the play's ambivalence toward motherhood. For instance, Coppèlia Kahn notes that "[Prospero's] only mention of his wife is highly ambivalent, at once commending and questioning her chastity before his daughter: 'Thy mother was a piece of virtue, and / She said thou wast my daughter (I.ii.56–57).'"[24] David Sundelson reiterates this point by suggesting that the "reverence for father Prospero does not extend to mothers. Whatever ambivalence toward them is hidden in Prospero's tale of expulsion, the one mother in the play is unmistakably demonic: Sycorax."[25] She is a "foul witch" (I.ii.263), a "damned witch . . . banished for mischiefs manifold, sorceries terrible / To enter human hearing" (I.ii.264–65). Sundelson then argues, "This demon mother's rage is 'unmitigable' (I.ii.276); only a father could end the torture."[26] Stephen Orgel also persuasively reads the effects of Prospero's ambiva-lence toward wives/mothers: "The absent presence of the wife and mother in the play constitutes a space that is filled by Prospero's creation

of surrogates and a ghostly family: the witch Sycorax and her monster
child Caliban . . . the good child/wife Miranda . . ."²⁷

Caliban as the offspring of this "demon" mother serves appropriately
as an other. Thus, Prospero's (and the play's) view of Caliban as a potential rapist illustrates how the discourse of sexuality underpins colonial
authority. That Prospero assumes authority in terms typical of colonialist discourse is recognized by most postcolonial critics. As one critic
states, "Colonialist discourse does not simply announce a triumph for
civility, it must continually *produce* it [through a struggle with rather than
an assimilation of its others]."²⁸ Hence, interpellated within Prospero's
narrative of sexual and racial control, the identities of both Caliban and
Miranda must constantly be *produced* in terms of sexual struggle in
which, as Prospero's subjects, their sexuality comes under constant surveillance, even as one enables the repression of the other. Both race and
gender conflicts come into play in this three-way dynamic, inhering
within the same system of differences between colonizer and colonized,
yet not without some *dissonances* within the systemic forces. Miranda,
who knows no men (other than her father) between whom she can distinguish, responds unequivocally to Caliban's different appearance,
which seems an inherent sign of his "villainy." In II.ii. she declares to her
father: "'Tis [Caliban] a villain sir, / I do not love to look on" (I.ii.309).
Yet, like a typical colonizer, she also reveals her civilizing impulses
toward Caliban: "I pitied thee, / Took pains to make thee speak, taught
thee each hour / One thing or another" (I.ii.353–55) – simultaneously
holding out little hope of improvement for his "vile race."

Neither Prospero nor Miranda allow Caliban an identity as a desiring
subject who wishes to gain sexual access to Miranda for the legitimate
aim of "peopl[ing] . . . This isle with Calibans" (I.ii.350–51). However,
given Prospero's manipulation of Ferdinand's "wooing," it is clear that
he decides which man is to have access to his daughter. Though Miranda
has a position of colonial superiority over Caliban, she nonetheless has a
marginal role within a *kinship* system in which all the three males are
bonded through their competing claims on her. According to Lévi-
Strauss, Mauss, and others, one of the most striking features of this
system among so-called primitive societies was the practice of giving and
receiving gifts as a part of social intercourse; within this system, the gift
of women was the most profound because the exchange partners
thereby enacted a relationship of kinship.²⁹ Significantly, however, gift
exchange could confer upon its participants a special solidarity as well as
a sense of competition and rivalry. From the perspective of some femi-

nist anthropologists, this system had far-reaching implications for women:

> If it is women who are being transacted, then it is men who give and take them who are linked, the woman being a conduit of a relationship rather than a partner to it. The exchange of women does not necessarily imply that women are objectified . . . But it does imply a distinction between gift and giver. If women are the gifts, then it is the men who are exchange partners. And it is the partners, not their presents, upon whom the reciprocal exchange confers its quasi-mystical power of social linkage . . . [Thus] women are *given* in marriage, *taken* in battle, exchanged for favours, sent as tribute, traded, bought, and sold.[30]

Several contemporary anthropologists recognize the danger of attributing a timeless universality to this concept of a kinship system. For instance, they point to the gender inflections of Lévi-Strauss' reasoning when he says that women should be exchanged as the way only of overcoming the contradiction by which the same woman is, on the one hand, the object of personal desire, and, on the other, the object of the desire of others and a means of binding others through alliance with them. Such a naturalized definition of a woman's role also, critics argue, does not account for some matrilineal, non-Western societies that neither hold proprietorial attitudes toward women nor use them as a means of social and sexual exchange. Despite these limitations of Lévi-Strauss' gendered language, the notion of the exchange of women is nonetheless useful in demonstrating, when applicable, how a specific cultural paradigm organizes and shapes female sexuality and subjectivity.[31]

It is apparent, then, that underlying the dynamics of Prospero's power struggle with Caliban and, to a lesser extent, with Ferdinand, over the two men's sexual claims to Prospero's daughter, lies the social grid of the kinship system. Thus, desiring Miranda makes the noble Ferdinand a suitable exchange partner for her royal father. She is to be the means whereby the royal descendents of the two men will be related by blood. Ferdinand makes apparent that this arrangement is, in effect, an exchange of Miranda's virginity (which her father must guard) for the throne of Naples. This is reinforced at the end of the play, when Ferdinand retrospectively asks *his* father's permission for his marriage to Miranda: "I chose her when I could not ask my father / For his advice" (v.i.190–91).

The marriage of Ferdinand and Miranda typically exemplifies the theory of reciprocity in kinship systems. Marriages are the most basic form of gift exchange, whereby the woman whom one does not take is offered up as a precious gift. Caliban, the seeming outsider among kin,

nonetheless has a role within the system of gender differences underpinning gift exchanges among men. His desire for Miranda leads him to
imagine a kinship with Prospero, even if it means *taking* her forcibly:
"Would't had been done! / Thou didst prevent me; I had peopled else /
This isle with Calibans" (I.ii.349–51). In this scenario, Caliban not only
wishes to create a blood tie with Prospero, but also to use Miranda as a
means of producing male children – a population in the image of
Caliban rather than of Miranda. When Prospero prevents Caliban from
violating the "honour of [his] child" (I.ii.348), he in turn assumes a proprietorial control over his daughter as a sexual gift, which he will later *give*
to the royal Ferdinand.

A central feature of the traditional kinship structure is that *all* levels
and directions in the traffic of women, including hostile ones, are
ordered by this structure. Thus, gift exchange could be an idiom of
rivalry and competition and marriage itself could be highly competi-
tive.[32] In this context, while Prospero believes that Caliban exists outside
of any civilized social forms, the latter is nonetheless Ferdinand's rival in
desiring Miranda, and on the basis of this claim is bonded with the two
other men; an acknowledgement and denial of his desire by Prospero
ironically serves to legitimate Caliban's position as a rival within the
structures of gift exchange. Prospero and Miranda may consider
Caliban "a thing most brutish," but from his perspective, the colonizer
has withheld from him the gift of woman in order to maintain the hierarchical boundaries between them. The basis of the power struggle
between Prospero and Caliban, then, is an implicit consensus about the
role of woman as a gift to be exchanged.

Miranda's role as a gift is further complicated by Prospero's implicit
(and European) fear of a monstrous progeny that could result from a
misplaced gift exchange with a man who is racially marked as other. In
Prospero's eyes the imaginary "Calibans" who could "people" the isle
would connect his lineage to that of Sycorax, whom *he* describes as the
"damned witch" whose "sorceries terrible" banished her from "Argier"
(Algiers). For Prospero (and for European audiences), her magic is antithetical to his supposedly beneficent Art because she embodies an
aberration of nature, both in terms of her sexuality (her impregnation
by an incubus) and her racial identity as a non-European. While
Prospero claims to know the history of her life, his only source is Ariel,
and as one critic points out, "we have no way of distinguishing the facts
about Caliban and Sycorax from Prospero's invective about them."[33]
Given his demonizing rhetoric, it is not surprising that a fear of mis-

cegenation is a crucial trope that structures Prospero's "plot" of selective inclusion and exclusion in which Miranda, Ferdinand, and Caliban figure as prominent characters.

We get a fuller sense of Sycorax's demonization if we consider *The Tempest*'s relation to the poetic geography of the Renaissance (derived from classical and medieval sources), in which European identity is frequently contrasted with images of otherness. According to John Gillies, Sycorax's mythic journey from Algiers to the New World is motivated not so much to find a new "howling wilderness" as to *make* one. Her adoption of "Setebos," a New World "devil" ("my Dam's god"), evokes associations with the name of the demonized god of the "heathen" Patagonian Indians. Thus, in her role as the non-Western other in the collective European imagination, she is like "Ham, progenitor of the Caananite, the Negro and other supposedly bestial and slavish races, . . . an outcast from the world of men, a wanderer beyond bounds and an active promoter of the degeneracy of her 'vile' race."[34]

Prospero's plot of a "happy end," however, does not accommodate the figure of Claribel, who haunts the margins of *The Tempest*. In fact, it is telling that Shakespeare's play, unlike Prospero's script, does not resolve the contradiction between the anxiety of miscegenation from Miranda's potential union with Caliban and the political imperative for a European like Alonso to give his daughter in a marriage across racial lines. References to the forced marriage of Claribel to the King of Tunis in North Africa, which appear early in the play, strike a discordant note in the emerging racial ideology that leads European audiences to rejoice at the play's "happy" marriage at the end – a marriage that preserves the purity of European lineage in the union of Naples and Milan.

That Claribel's match deviates from the cultural norm is made evident by Sebastian when he chides Alonso "That would not bless our Europe with your daughter / But rather loose her to an African" (II.i.129–30) and reminds him that his daughter was divided by her "loathness" for the Tunisian and "obedience" toward her father. Furthermore, Gonzalo's unexplained identification between Claribel and Dido, Queen of Carthage, complicates our view of the racial and gender politics involved in the match. For instance, the fate imposed upon Alonso's reluctant daughter is the one violently resisted by Dido who chose to die rather than marry an African King, Iarbus. According to Peter Hulme, to recall Carthage "is to bring to mind several centuries of punishing wars with Italy . . . when presumably Claribel has been a gift to fend off a dangerous new power in the central Mediterranean."[35]

The references to Dido also evoke contradictory images: that of the widow, and "a model at once of heroic fidelity to her murdered husband and the destructive potential of erotic passion."[36] Overall, while the meanings of this allusion are multiple and remain ambiguous, references to North Africa encroach upon the boundaries of the imaginary Italian states of the Renaissance that defined their culture against "barbarians" like the offspring of the Algerian Sycorax, or in another instance, the "barbarian Moor." While images of the Tunisian queen do not intrude into Prospero's plan of social and sexual organization, they nonetheless open up an imaginary space for viewers (and readers) of the play to imagine the (impossible or repressed) possibility of miscegenation in the service of political expediency, even as the woman's subjectivity continues to be shaped by her status as a gift.

Some political, especially feminist, readings of Shakespeare's *The Tempest* try to open up the play to such dissonances that remain unaccommodated by the play's "happy" conclusion. One such strategy is to read an implicit affinity between Caliban and Miranda in relation to the overarching power of Prospero, whom they designate as a racist patriarch. While acknowledging that historically European women have been complicit with their men in producing the non-European man as a demonized Other and a potential rapist, they attempt to read against the grain of such polarizations. Lorrie J. Leininger's landmark essay, despite its essentialism, is useful in exploring a relationship between Miranda and Caliban, not in sexual terms, but in the context of a mutual recognition of the possibilities of resistance.[37] Thus, Leininger creates an imaginary riposte by Miranda to her father in which she both reveals and disrupts colonial hierarchy as well as the kinship system: "My father is no God-figure. No one is a God-father" (p. 291). Calling for respect for Caliban's non-European ancestry, she also refuses to be used as a means of his oppression:

> . . . men are reminded of Indians when they first see Caliban; he might be African, his mother having been transported from Algiers . . . I will not be used as the excuse of his enslavement . . . I need to join forces with Caliban – with all those who are exploited . . .[38]

Furthermore, Leininger's Miranda repudiates the value placed on her "virginity" both by the kinship system – as a gift exchanged or withheld – and by the colonial institutions based on the "protection" of European women: "I cannot give assent to an ethical scheme that locates all virtue symbolically in one part of my anatomy. My virginity has little to do with the forces that will lead to a good harvest or to greater social justice."[39] Such insights offered by feminist revisions of *The Tempest* make visible the structural contradictions in Miranda's subject-position as "the sexual object of both the Anglo-American male and the native other."[40] And while Miranda ultimately aligns herself to the colonizing father and husband, the play and Leininger also gesture toward an alliance, however problematic, in a childhood "prehistory" when Miranda taught Caliban language, or in a utopian, egalitarian future.

Such feminist possibilities and insights rarely figure in third world, postcolonial versions of the play. A call for decolonization and revolution in a play such as Aimé Césaire's *A Tempest* ironically shows that race and gender struggles occur in antithetical, rather than cooperative relationships. The play enacts a breakdown of colonial hierarchy, but leaves intact the system of kinship between men.

A POSTCOLONIAL "BRAVE NEW WORLD"

PROSPERO: Good God, you tried to rape my daughter!
CALIBAN: Rape! Rape! Listen you old goat, you're the one
  that put those dirty thoughts in my head. Let me tell you something: I
  couldn't care less about your daughter, or about your cave for that
  matter.[41]

Aimé Césaire's Caliban is clearly the protagonist of *A Tempest*. In this telling exchange between him and Prospero, he strongly repudiates the identity of a rapist that he claims *is produced* by his master. Caliban's almost perfunctory dismissal of any possibility of sexually desiring Miranda is put to question in II.i by her description of that "awful Caliban who keeps pursuing me and calling out my name in his stupid dreams" (p. 35). Except for these two moments that leave a lingering sense of ambivalence, the play largely leaves unexplored the issue of power and sexuality as it concerns the relationship between Prospero, Miranda, and Caliban. The latter moment, in effect, seems to deny his identity as a desiring subject, shrugging off "dirty thoughts" not of his own making to become a single-minded prototype of a third world revolutionary. Does his rejection of Miranda as a sexual prize signal a "brave new world" in which the patriarchal kinship bonds between men are dissolved?

Before responding to this rhetorical question, let me first establish *A Tempest*'s dramatic and political credentials. First published in French in the wake of decolonization in 1969, it revised the history of the Caribbean. Calling for a troupe of black actors performing their own version of Shakespeare's play, it was initially produced in Africa, The Middle East, and the Caribbean, as well as in France. It was translated into English by Richard Miller in 1985 and was introduced to New York audiences in a successful, though politically restrained, production in 1991. The spirit of the play derives from the Negritude movement, of which Césaire was one of the founders, with its aim being to reverse the political and linguistic oppression of blacks within colonialism.

Set in a colony – a prototype of a Caribbean or African setting – in the throes of resistance and unrest, the play initially focuses on Caliban's verbal attacks on Prospero's control over language and representation. Here Césaire is clearly sensitive to the way in which the name Caliban/cannibal appears in Shakespeare's play – and in colonial history – "through an imperial and colonial act of translation."[42] Thus, Césaire has Caliban declare his independence in Swahili, "Uhuru!" To which Prospero mutters, "Mumbling your native language again! I've already told you, I don't like it" (p. 11). He wants his native subject to "at least thank (me) for having taught you to speak at all. You, a savage . . . a dumb animal, a beast I educated, trained, dragged up from the Bestiality that still clings to you" (p. 11). Césaire's Prospero is the familiar proponent of the "civilizing mission"; thus, Caliban's rebellion is rightly aimed at Prospero's power of "naming" when he declares, "I don't want to be called Caliban any longer . . . Caliban isn't my name" (p. 15).

Accompanying Caliban's disruptions to the colonizer's language are intimations of an actual resistance movement (as Prospero tells Ariel in III.iii: "Caliban is alive, he is plotting, he is getting a guerilla force" [p. 50]), as well as of an impending black independence in Ariel's concluding resolve to sing "notes so sweet that the last / will give rise to a yearning / in the heart of the most forgetful slaves / yearning for freedom . . . and the lightened agave will straighten [into] / a solemn flag" (p. 60). Prior to his articulation of this "unsettling agenda," Ariel, who is labeled a "Mulatto," plays the historical part of those mixed races, often in the middle of the colonial hierarchy, more able to accept their somewhat limited oppression. Ariel declares that he and Caliban are "Brothers in suffering and slavery . . . and in hope as well . . . [but] have different methods" (p. 20); yet Ariel's vision of brotherhood includes Prospero, and for him any fight of freedom is for his master too – "so that Prospero can acquire a conscience" (p. 22).

The play does not end with an unequivocal victory leading to the expulsion of the colonizer. Rather, it posits a Hegelian dialectic in which Prospero and Caliban remain on the island, with Prospero declaring his power as well as a curious, almost natural bond. "Well Caliban, old fellow, it's just us two now, here on the island" (p. 68). Given this ending, *A Tempest* is commonly staged as a "political comedy" with a humorous rhetorical play on language.[43] However, one cannot overlook the political message of the play: to promote "black consciousness" and rewrite the script of colonial history. At least imaginatively, if not literally, the play creates a different kind of "brave new world" in which the struggle for political and cultural independence is in *process.*

Undoubtedly, Césaire's postcolonial vision (incorporating the philosophy of Negritude) challenges the categories of representation defining the non-European races as inferior and in need of civilization. But while it celebrates a revolution of brotherhood, it holds in place a kinship system in which women figure as gifts or objects of exchange. Caliban's somewhat ambivalent repudiation of Miranda seems to free him from hostility and rivalry toward Prospero and Ferdinand, but in another sense, his gesture can also be read as a symbolic rejection of a potential gift – a daughter who is to be given to some man in marriage. Unlike feminist critics such as Leininger, Césaire, in his revision of Shakespeare's play, makes no attempt to reconceptualize the relationship between Caliban and Miranda, or to suggest any possibilities of a shared resistance to the patriarch. Anxieties about possible miscegenation, so crucial to Prospero's demonization of Caliban in Shakespeare's play, are repressed by Césaire in his diminishment of Miranda's role. Caliban's summary dismissal of any desire to possesses Miranda sexually is a convenient structural device for mobilizing an all-male revolution – one which recapitulates the kinship structure in its most basic form, giving a minimal presence to Miranda.

Thus, a play celebrating the emerging freedoms of the 1960s does not change Miranda's fate. Her marriage is once again *arranged* in a gift exchange that will ensure future peace and stability in a growing nation that will now combine two European city states. Prospero articulates this to Ariel at the outset: "These are men of my race and of high rank . . . I have a daughter. Alonso has a son. If they were to fall in love I would give my consent. Let Ferdinand and Miranda marry, and may that marriage bring us harmony and peace. That is my plan. I want it executed" (p. 16). Though Prospero willfully stays on this island to continue his "civilizing mission," he ensures the consolidation of his kingdom through the alliance of Naples and Milan via the marriage of his daughter. Hence, while Césaire empowers Caliban to cry out unfailingly, "Freedom Hi-Day," we never find out how Miranda's "brave new world" turns out after all.

While Miranda's circumscribed role conveniently fulfills the requirements of a European patriarchy, it is telling that Césaire does not introduce a woman who can be Caliban's "physiognomically complementary mate." Writing in the context of the history of the Americas, and specifically from the perspective of Caribbean women, Sylvia Wynter criticizes Shakespeare's play for its absence of Caliban's mate:

> [The] question is that of the most significant absence of all, that of Caliban's Woman, of Caliban's physiognomically complementary mate. For nowhere in Shakespeare's play, and in its system of image-making, one which would be foundational . . . to our present Western world system, does Caliban's mate appear as an alternative sexual-erotic model of desire . . . an alternative system of meanings. Rather there, on the New World island, as the only woman, Miranda . . . [is] contrasted with the ontologically absent, potential genetrix – Caliban's mate – of another population of human, i.e., of a "vile race" "capable of ill-will."[44]

Reading this absence historically, Wynter (citing Caribbean writers like Maryse Condé) suggests that "the non-desire of Caliban for his own mate, Caliban's 'woman' is . . . a founding function of the 'social pyramid' of the global order that will be put in place following upon the 1492 arrival of Columbus in the Caribbean."[45] In this first phase of Western Europe's expansion into the Americas, given the expanding slave trade out of the "Europe-Africa-New World triangular traffic," Caliban as "both the Arawak and African forced labour, [supposedly] had no need/desire for the procreation of his own kind."[46] It is ironic that these criticisms, revealing the limitations of Shakespeare's play, are also applicable to Césaire's revisionary version. Caliban's revolt can have little impact as long as the absence of a native woman as his sexual reproductive mate functions to negate the progeny/population group comprising the original owners/occupiers of the New World lands, the American Indians.

In conclusion, if Aimé Césaire's A Tempest is widely read as an allegory of decolonization, it fails to address adequately the relationship between liberation movements and the representations of sexual difference. Instead, it shows that if resistance movements are "imagined communities," then such imaginings are frequently based upon particular, and often disempowering, constructions of women's sexuality.[47] As gifts of exchange, or conduits of homosocial desire between men, women taking part in the movements for real national liberation could not escape the determinations of earlier kinship structures. Reflecting this historical trend, Césaire conveniently represents Miranda as the property of the colonizers, but more significantly, displaces the sexual, maternal identity of the "native" woman, Sycorax, onto the idealized abstraction of the Earth as Mother, while denying Caliban a potential union with a Caribbean woman. Finally, Césaire's call for a revolution lacks credibility as he prevents Prospero's former slave from peopling the isle with Calibans.

NOTES

1 George Lamming, *The Pleasures of Exile* (1960) (Ann Arbor: University of Michigan Press, 1992), p. 13.
2 Roberto Fernandez Retamar, *Caliban and Other Essays*, trans. Edward Baker (Minneapolis: University of Minnesota Press, 1989), p. 55.
3 For fuller accounts of *The Tempest* and decolonization, see Eric Cheyfitz, *The Poetics of Imperialism: Translation and Colonization from The Tempest to Tarzan* (Oxford: Oxford University Press, 1991), pp. 42–58. To follow the production of the term, "Cannibal," see Peter Hulme, *Colonial Encounters: Europe and the Native Caribbean 1492–1797* (London: Methuen, 1986), pp. 1–3. Also see Roberto Fernandez Retamar, *Caliban and Other Essays*, pp. 6–21.
4 Cheyfitz, *The Poetics of Imperialism*, p. 42.
5 Retamar, *Caliban and other Essays*, pp. 6–21. Retamar offers a detailed history of the changing political images of Caliban in Latin American history through decolonization.
6 *Ibid.*, p. 14.
7 Lamming, *The Pleasures of Exile*, p. 14.
8 Aimé Césaire, *A Tempest: An Adaptation of The Tempest for Black Theatre*, trans. Richard Miller (New York: Ubu Repertory Theatre Publications, 1969), p. 15.
9 Francis Barker and Peter Hulme, "Nymphs and Reapers Heavily Vanish: The Discursive Con-Texts of *The Tempest*," in *Alternative Shakespeares*, John Drakakis, ed. (London: Methuen, 1985), p. 204.
10 Virginia Vaughan, "'Something Rich and Strange': Caliban's Theatrical Metamorphoses," in *Shakespeare Quarterly* 36.4 (Winter 1985): 390–405.
11 Césaire, *A Tempest*, pp. 67–68.
12 Lamming, *The Pleasures of Exile*, p. 15.
13 Sandra Pouchet Paquet, foreword to George Lamming, *The Pleasures of Exile*, pp. xxi–xxiv, offers a feminist critique of Lamming's postcolonial vision. Specifically, her focus on the missing Sycorax identifies the limitations of the postcolonial revisions of the original.
14 Retamar, *Caliban and Other Essays*, p. 55.
15 See Louis A. Montrose, "The Work of Gender in the Discourse of

Discovery," in *New World Encounters*, Stephen Greenblatt, ed. (Berkeley: University of California Press, 1993), pp. 177–83, for a look at the ways in which the early colonial discourses were gendered, thus feminizing the "New Worlds." His analysis offers a useful model for a rhetorical analysis of the structure of colonial narratives.

16 Malek Alloula, *Colonial Harem* (Minneapolis: University of Minnesota Press, 1987), p. 3.

17 Frantz Fanon, *Black Skin White Masks* (1952), trans. Charles Lamm Markmann (New York: Grove Press, 1967), p. 63.

18 Paquet, foreword, Lamming, *The Pleasures of Exile*, pp. xxi–xxii.

19 Lamming, *The Pleasures of Exile*, p. 114.

20 *Ibid.*, p. 107.

21 *Ibid.*

22 Paquet, foreword, *ibid.*, p. xxii.

23 William Shakespeare, *The Tempest* (1610–11) (New York: Signet Classic/Penguin, 1987). All quotations are taken from this edition.

24 Coppèlia Kahn, "The Providential Tempest and the Shakespearean Family," in *Representing Shakespeare: New Psychoanalytic Essays*, Murray A. Schwartz and Coppèlia Kahn, eds. (Baltimore: Johns Hopkins University Press, 1980), pp. 217–43.

25 David Sundelson, "'So Rare a Wonder'd Father': Prospero's *Tempest*," in *ibid.*, pp. 33–55.

26 *Ibid.*

27 Stephen Orgel, "Prospero's Wife," in *Rewriting the Renaissance: The Discourses of Sexual Difference in Early Modern Europe*, Margaret W. Ferguson, Maureen Quilligan, and Nancy Vickers, eds. (Chicago: University of Chicago Press, 1986), p. 51.

28 I base my analysis of the structure of colonial discourse on Paul Brown's formulation, in "'This Thing of Darkness I Acknowledge Mine': *The Tempest* and the Discourse of Colonialism," in *Political Shakespeare*, Jonathan Dollimore, ed. (Ithaca: Cornell University Press, 1985), pp. 48–54.

29 My application of the exchange of women in kinship systems is indebted to Gayle Rubin's feminist, anthropological analysis, "The Traffic in Women: Notes on a Political Economy of Sex," in *Toward an Anthropology of Women*, Reyna R. Reiter, ed. (New York: Monthly Review Press, 1974), pp. 171–77. For a fuller discussion of Mauss' and Lévi-Strauss's theories by Rubin, see pp. 177–75.

30 *Ibid.*, pp. 174–75.

31 Eleanor Burke Leacock, *Myths of Male Dominance* (New York and London: Monthly Review Press, 1981), pp. 229–41. Leacock discusses the gender inflections of Lévi-Strauss' formulations as well the tendencies of other anthropologists "to seek universals in relations between the sexes," pp. 231–33.

32 Rubin, "The Traffic in Women," pp. 172–74.

33 Orgel, "Prospero's Wife," p. 55.

34 John Gillies, *Shakespeare and the Geography of Difference* (Cambridge: Cambridge University Press, 1994), pp. 140–44. He locates Sycorax within the poetic geography of the period, by drawing on associations (made by Renaissance and earlier geographers and ethnographers) between her and other non-European others.

35 Hulme, *Colonial Encounters*, pp. 111–12.

36 Orgel, "Prospero's Wife," 51.

37 Lorrie Jerrell Leininger, "The Miranda Trap: Sexism and Racism in Shakespeare's *The Tempest*," in *The Woman's Part: Feminist Criticism of Shakespeare*, Gayle Green, Ruth Swift Lenz, and Carol Thomas Neely, eds. (Urbana: University of Illinois Press, 1980), pp. 285–94.

38 Leininger, "The Miranda Trap," pp. 291–92.

39 *Ibid.*, p. 292.

40 Laura Donaldson, *Decolonizing Feminisms: Race, Gender, and Empire-Building* (Chapel Hill: University of North Carolina Press, 1992), p. 17.

41 Césaire, *A Tempest*, act I, scene ii, p. 13. All subsequent quotes will be taken from this edition. Page numbers are noted in parenthesis within the text.

42 Cheyfitz, *The Poetics of Imperialism*, p. 41.

43 D. J. R. Bruckner, Review of *A Tempest*, *New York Times*, October 16, 1991, p. B 1.

44 Sylvia Wynter, "Beyond Miranda's Meanings: Un/silencing the Demonic Ground of Caliban's Woman," in *Out of the Kumbla: Caribbean Women and Literature*, Carole Boyce Davies and Elaine Savoury Fido, eds. (Trenton, NJ: Africa World Press, 1990), p. 360.

45 *Ibid.*, pp. 360–61.

46 *Ibid.*, p. 361.

47 I am indebted to the "Introduction" to *Nationalisms and Sexualities*, eds. Andrew Parker, Mary Russo, Doris Sommer, and Patricia Yaeger (London: Routledge, 1992), p. 13, for this formulation of "imagined communities" derived from Bendict Anderson's useage. Several essays, under the section "Women, Resistance, and the State," examine the relationship between resistance movements and social constructions of women's bodies, pp. 395–424.

CHAPTER 9

Rape, repetition, and the politics of closure in A Midsummer Night's Dream

Laura Levine

At the beginning of act I, scene i of *A Midsummer Night's Dream*, Theseus tells Hippolyta:

> I woo'd thee with my sword,
> And won thy love doing thee injuries;
> But I will wed thee in another key,
> With pomp, with triumph, and with revelling. (i.i.16–19)[1]

He begins the play, that is, by alluding to something like a rape, an originary violence which he says he wishes to transform.[2] What is interesting to me about the speech, however, is the *way* Theseus wishes to transform this violence. He turns to theater, to "pomp . . . triumph . . . and revelling" to turn something like a rape into a legitimate marriage. The question I am going to be examining in this essay is: why should this be? Why should Theseus conceive of theater as a means of transforming sexual violence? The question is doubly puzzling, since a portion of the English Renaissance thought of theater as a *kind* of sexual violence. What does it mean for Shakespeare to show Theseus turning to theater in this way? In a sense, the second question will have to provide a means of answering the first one: in the first part of this essay, I am going to be arguing that Shakespeare shows us Theseus turning to theater to transform sexual violence in order to show the way that theater exactly fails to accomplish such a transformation. In the second part, I am going to be examining the question that this claim logically raises: if theater is not something with the capacity to transform sexual violence, what is it in *A Midsummer Night's Dream*?

Theseus begins the play by asking Philostrate to "stir up the Athenian youth to merriments" (i.i.12) and "pomp" (i.i.15), but no sooner has he made this request, than he himself takes steps to squelch the Athenian youth. For no sooner has he made the request than Egeus appears with Hermia, demanding his "ancient privilege of Athens" (i.i.41), the privilege to "dispose" of Hermia by death if she will not marry Demetrius. He arrives, that is, asking for the same privilege that Theseus himself has had over Hippolyta, the privilege of controlling and directing Hermia's sexuality. And Hermia's language, that she will die before she "yield[s] [her] virgin patent up" (i.i.80), makes clear how close she comes to understanding that privilege as rape. Similarly, Theseus' ruling that Hermia must "die the death, or . . . abjure / For ever the society of men" (i.i.65–66) – the two options are apparently interchangeable – suggests how close Theseus comes to repeating the act he has just repudiated. Theseus even directly implicates his marriage in this repetition of sexual violence when he makes it the deadline for Hermia's decision. "Take time to pause" till "the next new moon," he tells her, "The sealing-day betwixt my love and me" (i.i.83–84). If she can't come to a decision by then she will have to die or wed Demetrius or prepare for all austerity, for single life. Rather than transforming the sexual coercion that he begins the play by promising to get rid of, Theseus immediately repeats it. Rather than undoing an act of sexual violence, he reenacts one. In fact, this sexual violence is embodied in the principle of Athenian law itself. It is the "ancient privilege of Athens" that Egeus begs for when he insists on the right to control Hermia's sexuality, and it is the "law of Athens" that Theseus blames his own ruling on, saying that he himself lacks the power to "extenuate" it. And it is the "sharp Athenian law" that Hermia and Lysander seek to evade when they flee to the forest. Thus, if Theseus begins the play by wishing to transform something like a rape into something like a legitimate marriage, and if he immediately undermines and ironizes that wish by repeating the very act he has sought to transform, the play suggests that that sexual violence is somehow larger and more comprehensive than Theseus himself, that it is built into, virtually the given of life in Athens, the *polis*, itself.

But if the opening of the play depicts sexual violence as being built into (and therefore in some sense a function of) Athenian law itself, the next scenes, the scenes in the forest, characterize it as much more basic and widespread, as being virtually a function of existence itself. Hermia and Lysander flee to the woods to seek a place where the "sharp Athenian law / Cannot pursue [them]" (i.i.162–63). But in the forest, they find a law sharper than the one they are seeking to escape, an authority in "King" Oberon greater than that of "Duke" Theseus, an authority at once more powerful and invasive than the one they've sought to flee.[3] Our expectation, like that of the lovers, is that the forest is going to turn out to be some place other, some place different from

Athens, but the forest turns out to be a mirror image (or worse than a mirror) of Athens itself.

If sexual violence is the given of life in Athens, it is even more so the given of life in the woods. For the hinge on which the plot depends is the Indian child, the "lovely boy" that Oberon wants from Titania. And his means of getting the Indian child is nothing other than the production and manipulation of female sexual appetites. "Thou shalt not from this grove / Till I torment thee for this injury," Oberon says after Titania refuses to hand over the Indian child (ii.i.146–47). But the means of the torment (as well as the means of gaining the child) is the production in her of sexual appetites she will be powerless to resist. "The next thing then she waking looks upon," Oberon says, explaining how the love-in-idleness will work, "(Be it on lion, bear, or wolf, or bull, / On meddling monkey, or on busy ape), / She shall pursue it with the soul of love" (ii.i.179–82). What is striking about this is not simply that Oberon will produce in Titania uncontrollable sexual urges, and not only that these will be as degrading as possible, but that he will seek (specifically) to produce bestiality: "Be it ounce, or cat, or bear, / Pard, or boar with bristled hair . . . When thou wak'st, it is thy dear: / Wake when some vile thing is near" (ii.ii.30–34). Though Oberon calls Titania a "rash wanton" (ii.i.63) and though we are told by Titania herself that the problem is that she has "forsworn his bed" (ii.i.62), it is Oberon who makes Titania into that rash wanton he accuses her of being.

In at least two ways, then, what Oberon does to Titania repeats and amplifies the original violence that Theseus seeks to transform at the beginning of the play: (1) It specifically and elaborately involves the coercion of female sexual appetites, the production of these appetites and direction of them against a woman's will. It is "a kind of rape" not because it involves the penetration of a bodily orifice but because it coerces the woman to obey sexual appetites that are quite literally not her own. (2) In an equally profound way the theft of the Indian child is a violation of the bonds between women (and in that way recapitulates the whole destruction of the Amazons). For at stake in the theft of the Indian child is the destruction of Titania's promise to the votress who was the child's mother. "She, being mortal, of that boy did die," Titania says, "And for her sake do I rear up her boy; / And for her sake I will not part with him" (ii.i.135–37). It is precisely this promise, this bond between the women, which must be destroyed in the course of the play for the plot to advance. For Theseus' sentence cannot be reversed except by Oberon, and Oberon will not budge without the Indian child, and the cost of the

Indian child is Titania's promise to the dead votress. This is the bond that must be destroyed.[4]

It is a bond which itself is deliberately figured as both exotic and eroticized, characterized as it is by the "spiced Indian air," and the privacy of the night the women "gossip" in. It is characterized simultaneously by a kind of limitless play in which, though women imitate the man-made objects of commerce, that imitation is predicated on the knowledge that these objects themselves are at best imitations of the powers of generation reserved specifically for women. "Full often hath she gossip'd by my side," Titania says of the votress:

> And sat with me on Neptune's yellow sands
> Marking th' embarked traders on the flood;
> When we have laugh'd to see the sails conceive
> And grow big-bellied with the wanton wind;
> Which she, with pretty and with swimming gait,
> Following (her womb then rich with my young squire)
> Would imitate, and sail upon the land,
> To fetch me trifles, and return again,
> As from a voyage, rich with merchandise.
> But she, being mortal, of that boy did die. (II.i.125-35)

In this vision of intimacy the votress imitates the world of merchandise, which is itself an imitation of her own fecundity, her own richer cargo. And it is precisely this vision of female plenitude and the largesse it implies – the votress sailing around the world just to fetch Titania trifles – that must be destroyed and rendered impotent in the course of the play for the plot to advance.[5]

This violation is figured in other ways as well. At the end of II.i, Oberon, describing Titania's bower (the same bower Puck will, in III.i, describe as "consecrated" and "close"), says:

> I know a bank where the wild thyme blows,
> Where oxlips and the nodding violet grows,
> Quite over-canopied with luscious woodbine,
> With sweet musk-roses and with eglantine;
> There sleeps Titania sometime of the night,
> Lull'd in these flowers with dances and delight;
> And there the snake throws her enamell'd skin,
> Weed wide enough to wrap a fairy in. (II.i.249-56)

The passage simultaneously evokes a world of erotic release and abandonment (the scents of flowers mingling with spice, the musk, the dances and delight that "lull") and at the same time one of sympathy and protection, the violets nodding (both toward each other in a gesture that implies sympathy, and in sleep), the bank being "over-canopied" in flowers that reach toward each other. Even the description of the snake is not one of animosity or venom, but of vulnerability. Rather than being an emblem of poison or violence, the snake is itself naked, and its skin like the bower itself folds to contain and protect, to house a fairy. Rather than being a phallic image, even the snake, a "her," creates a space of enclosure. It is as if the bower itself creates the same womblike fecundity and protection present in the speech about the votress, as if it were synecdochic for the female body itself.

This is the body that has to be violated in the course of the play. For if the snake is not pictured as venomous, Oberon is: "And with the juice of this," he says of the love-in-idleness, "I'll streak her eyes, / And make her full of hateful fantasies" (II.ii.257–58). A moment later, Puck will redescribe the invasion of what is "consecrated" and "close," describing first the way that Bottom "enter[s]" the "brake" and then the way this image actually invades Titania's sleep:

> Near to her close and consecrated bower,
> While she was in her dull and sleeping hour,
> A crew of patches, rude mechanicals
> That work for bread upon Athenian stalls,
> Were met together to rehearse a play . . . (III.ii.7–11)

It is as if in both of these descriptions what is meant to be "close" or private must be invaded and penetrated, as if the moment of the woman's sexual openness or relaxedness or unguardedness were figured geographically in the bower itself. And it is specifically this "bower", a synecdoche for the woman's body, which must be penetrated and invaded for the plot to advance.[6]

In a sense the story that Oberon tells of the genesis of the love-in-idleness encapsulates the dilemma at the center of *A Midsummer Night's Dream*. Oberon retells to Puck the time he sat on a promontory and heard a mermaid on a dolphin sing "such dulcet and harmonious breath / That the rude sea grew civil at her song" (II.i.150–52). On the one hand, the mermaid's song is so harmonious that it exercises a civilizing power. At the same time, it causes certain stars to shoot "madly from their spheres, / To hear the sea-maid's music" (II.i.153–54). In its beauty and erotic power the song is both civilizing and disordering. It is also the occasion for Cupid's attempt to shoot and seduce the "fair vestal." "That very time I saw (but thou couldst not)," Oberon says:

Flying between the cold moon and the earth
Cupid all arm'd. A certain aim he took
At a fair vestal throned by the west
And loos'd his love-shaft smartly from his bow,
As it should pierce a hundred thousand hearts. (ii.i.155–60)

The shaft misses, "quench'd" in the chaste beams of the moon, but hits
the love-in-idleness instead:

Yet mark'd I where the bolt of Cupid fell.
It fell upon a little western flower,
Before milk-white, now purple with love's wound,
And maidens call it love-in-idleness.
Fetch me that flow'r; the herb I showed thee once.
The juice of it on sleeping eyelids laid
Will make or man or woman madly dote
Upon the next live creature that it sees. (ii.i.165–72)

Just as the mermaid's song is both civilizing and disordering, it is also the
occasion of Cupid's attempted seduction of the vestal, and that seduction is at once both successfully resisted and the occasion of the manufacture of a new aphrodisiac – the love-in-idleness – that will engender
the next coerced love. It is as if every emblem of beauty and eroticism in
the play were also the occasion of a new rape, as if the play were unable
to envision the existence of sexual beauty without imagining as well the
eventual crisis such beauty necessarily engendered.

I do not mean to suggest that such sexual coercion is directed solely
against women in *A Midsummer Night's Dream*, for, in fact, it is a distinguishing feature of the play that every act of sexual coercion begets
another. For instance, the result of Oberon's manipulation and redirec-
tion of Titania's sexuality is her own enslavement of Bottom. "Out of
this wood do not desire to go," she tells him. "Thou shalt remain here,
whether thou wilt or no" (iii.i.152–53). Not only is Bottom chained by
magic to the bower ("Tie up my lover's tongue, bring him silently,"
Titania says [iii.i.201]), but the scene ends by suggesting that sexual
coercion – or what Titania will call "enforced chastity" – is not simply
the condition the play begins with, not simply the condition embodied
in Athenian law, but the given of existence itself. Titania claims that
"every little flower" weeps, "lamenting some enforced chastity"
(iii.i.199–200). In this scene nature itself is pictured as undergoing a
kind of rape to create mood, an erotic setting, the honey bags stolen
from the bees, their "waxen legs" cropped for night tapers and the
wings of butterflies picked for painted fans. As far as I can tell, this is

not a condition that Theseus or anyone else in the play is able to make go away.

If the play begins then with Theseus turning to the revels to try to transform some original violence against women, what it depicts is a world in which this violence is not transformed but repeatedly deepened and amplified, a world in which the parameters of this original violence are always growing. It is in this way (among others) that the play fails to deliver the transformation or resolution or "closure" that Theseus promises.

There is, of course, an argument against this, and I am going to rehearse it briefly in order to say why I do not think it holds. In act IV, Theseus decides to "overbear" Egeus' will (i.179) and allow the lovers to marry whom they please. The argument against what I have been saying is that the lovers do get sorted out. They marry their "true loves," and the play celebrates this marriage in a triple wedding. I shall have more to say later about the instability of this "sorting out," but it seems worth noting here that even the very list of plays Philostrate offers to accompany the celebration ironizes this marriage by reminding us of what Theseus wants to dismiss, the reality of sexual violence. Thus "the battle with the Centaurs, to be sung / By an Athenian eunuch to the harp" (v.i.44–45) – which Theseus only rejects because he's already told it to his love – intrudes into the wedding festivities both a rape and an emasculation.[7] The riot of the bacchanals tearing the Thracian singer, which Theseus only rejects because it was played for him when he came from Thebes as conqueror, intrudes into the festivities the vision of deranged women dismembering Orpheus. It is as if the original rape, the originary violence which Theseus sought to displace, kept returning in the form of the entertainments he banishes and rejects.

So far what I have argued is that sexual violence is not only not healed or transformed in the play, but is actually aggravated and deepened, but what I have not demonstrated is that there is any particular connection between this fact and the play's conception of theater. What I would now like to argue is that the play pictures theater or revelry itself as singularly unsuited to accomplish such a transformation, because of the resemblance theater itself bears to rape in the first place. The information we get about the play's conception of theater comes from two sources which look like diametrical opposites, but which in fact bear witness to the same attitude: the mechanicals who are singularly inept at casting an illusion and the fairies who are equally adept at doing so.

The first depiction of theater that we are given in the play is provided by (and embodied by) the mechanicals, and they are striking for their terror at casting any sort of illusion at all. They are so spooked by the power of casting an illusion that they develop four kinds of alternatives to doing so. The first of these is to simply edit out the representations they take to be dangerous ("I believe we must leave the killing out, when all is done" says Starveling [III.i.14–15]). The second is not to use representations at all, but to use the things themselves that the representations are supposed to stand for – the moon instead of a representation of one (Bottom: "Why then may you leave a casement of the great chamber window (where we play) open; and the moon may shine in at the casement" [III.i.56–58]). The third strategy is an appeal to a sort of figuralism – a man with thorns and lantern to signify the moon, a man with loam and roughcast to signify wall. By avoiding any semblance of verisimilitude, this strategy seeks to avoid the dangers of representation in the first place.

But more insistently than anything else, the strategy the mechanicals adopt is to strip the representation of its representational power by calling attention to its status *as* a representation. Over and over again, the solution Bottom and the others propose to the problem of how to represent things to an audience – especially a gendered audience – is the solution of stripping them of any representational power at all. Thus the solution to the problem of showing a suicide – a problem precisely because such a representation is imagined to be damaging to women – is writing a prologue to tell the ladies it is not really a suicide. "Write me a prologue," Bottom says, "and let the prologue seem to say that we will do no harm with our swords, and that Pyramus is not kill'd indeed; and . . . that I Pyramus am not Pyramus, but Bottom the weaver" (III.i.17–21). Similarly, the solution to the problem of representing a lion on-stage – a problem because of the damage such a representation is imagined to do to the "ladies" – is to have the lion announce he is not really a lion; "half his face must be seen through the lion's neck," says Bottom of the actor (III.i.36–37) and he must say:

"If you think I am come hither as a lion . . . I am no such thing; I am a man as other men are"; and there indeed let him name his name, and tell them plainly he is Snug the joiner. (III.i.42–46)

If all we had of theater in *A Midsummer Night's Dream* were the mechanicals, Theseus' project of turning to the revels to transform an original act of sexual violence would make no sense at all, for in the hands of the mechanicals, theater, at least as we see it in action, is unable to transform even its own dramatic material, let alone the pasts of those who watch it, that is, the "material" of history itself. And yet, in another way, in their conviction that representations exert a transformative power over women, the mechanicals do lend an odd corroboration to Theseus' belief, as if he were not the only person in his culture to believe that women – and thus the histories they've lived through – could be radically altered, reconstituted, by what they see performed in front of them. What is the basis for this belief?

One clue lies in the specific fear the mechanicals exhibit, the fear of presenting a lion to a female audience, though to understand this particular fear we need to identify an analogy the play articulates between representations of wild beasts and the impulse to rape itself. We can see this analogy operating most vividly in Demetrius' threats to Helena as he describes two different kinds of dangers to her virginity. Trying to get rid of her, he vacillates between threatening to leave her to the "wild beasts" and to his own impulses, as if the two were somehow interchangeable. "You do impeach your modesty too much . . . to . . . commit yourself / Into the hands of one that loves you not; / To trust the opportunity of night / . . . with the rich worth of your virginity" (II.i.214–19) he tells her at one moment and at the next threatens, as if the danger were outside in the wildness of the animals rather than inside in the wildness of his own self, to leave her to the mercy of the wild beasts. A moment later, treating the two dangers as if they were synonymous, he adds, "if thou follow me, do not believe / But I shall do thee mischief in the wood" (II.i.236–37). At this moment, the play articulates a tacit analogy between the impulse to rape and the wild beasts that men evoke to represent that impulse. That is, it offers a representational logic which justifies the mechanicals' reluctance to present the ladies with a lion – a lion who will later be said to "deflower" Thisby – by suggesting that what such a representation "represents" is the impulse to rape itself.

But such a representational logic would not explain the mechanicals' larger anxiety about the power of theater unless theater in general were understood to be like the lion, to constitute or enact some sort of "deflowering." And we do find confirmation for this in the other "theater" in the play, the real revelry that goes on in the woods.

Juxtaposed to the mechanicals, of course, is the theatricality of Puck and Oberon that justifies and validates every fear the mechanicals have. This theatricality is characterized not simply by the "revels" that Titania and Oberon keep delaying to perform, but by exactly the illusionism the mechanicals fear. Where the mechanicals are afraid to cast illusions,

Puck and Oberon specialize in doing so. Not only does Puck call himself an actor ("What, a play toward? I'll be an auditor, / An actor too perhaps" [III.i.79–80]) and conceive of the human behavior he watches and manipulates as a "pageant" (III.ii.114), but he embodies the very principle of illusionism itself, sometimes "playing" Demetrius, sometimes "playing" Lysander. Oberon instructs him in the creation of auditory illusions:

> Like to Lysander sometime frame thy tongue;
> Then stir Demetrius up with bitter wrong;
> And sometime rail thou like Demetrius,
> And from each other look thou lead them thus. (III.ii.360–63)

And if the mechanicals, in a sort of encoded delicacy, are careful not to present the image of a "wild beast" to the ladies, Puck's illusionism vacillates between *embodying* those beasts –

> Sometime a horse I'll be, sometime a hound,
> A hog, a headless bear, sometime a fire;
> And neigh, and bark and grunt, and roar, and burn
> Like horse, hound, hog, bear, fire, at every turn – (III.i.108–11)

and producing in women sexual appetites for them. Operating on Oberon's instructions, he seeks specifically to produce in Titania the lust for "ounce, or cat, or bear, / Pard, or boar with bristled hair," seeks specifically to bring about the kind of rape the mechanicals apparently fear. The rationale for their fear of theatrical representation lies, then, in the support the play provides for it, in its depiction of another theater which displays precisely the attributes the mechanicals would avoid.

But if theater as we see it in the hands of the mechanicals is incapable of transforming anything, and theater as we see it in the hands of Puck and Oberon reenacts, rather than transforming, a rape, why does Theseus turn to the idea of theater, to revels in the first place, in order to transform sexual violence? What basis is there in the play for theater or revel to possess any positive transformative power at all?

In one sense there is an obvious answer to this question in the notion of masque and in the revels that Titania and Oberon jointly perform. We are told from the beginning that these revels do have a constitutive power, though we know this only in their absence, only by what happens when they fail to be performed: ". . . the quaint mazes in the wanton green, / For lack of tread, are undistinguishable," says Titania. "The human mortals want their winter here" (II.i.99–101). In the absence of these revels the universe is plunged into both epistemological uncertainty, the impossibility of knowing the differences between things, and ontological uncertainty, the inability for things to actually be different. We could argue, then, that in these revels the play locates the model of transformative theater that Theseus invokes. Since these revels do ultimately take place – midway through act IV, Oberon takes Titania's hands to dance and promises her that "Now thou and I are new in amity, / And will to-morrow midnight solemnly / Dance in Duke Theseus' house triumphantly" (IV.i.87–89) – and the play ends with this dance, it does seem to offer a kind of masque to the anti-masque-like blundering of the mechanicals. We could argue that just as Oberon, telling Titania to strike the music while he removes the ass' head from Bottom, provides a masque-like removal of discord, so the revels that Oberon and Titania perform allow Theseus to realize his plan of wedding Hippolyta in "another key."

But, in fact, it would be difficult to imagine a masque that called more attention to its own incompleteness, its own instability. For if the drops which induce error have been removed from Lysander's eyes, they have not been removed from Demetrius', a fact which suggests the precariousness of the play's resolution and creates the fantasy that were the drops removed from Demetrius' eyes, were he returned to his natural state, the situation – the whole love triangle – could begin all over again. Similarly, it would be difficult to imagine a masque that more insistently exposed itself to be contaminated by the very forces it would seek to tame. This is true not only for the obvious reasons: that Titania and Oberon are specifically implicated in the adulteries of Theseus and Hippolyta, that the "resolution" of the plot is dependent on Oberon, his theft of the Indian child and his exploitation of Titania's sexuality to extract the child from her, but because the play calls insistent attention to the failure of the revels to secure that difference necessary for transformation, that difference that it suggests is the prerequisite for "true love" itself.

Arguing with Hermia at the beginning of the play, dismissing her claim that Lysander is "in himself" worthy, Theseus argues that worth isn't inherent in an individual person but a matter of the value that fathers and rulers confer ("In himself [Lysander is worthy] / But in this kind, wanting your father's voice, / The other must be held the worthier" [I.i.53–55]). His position is only one step away from the rhetoric of ownership as Egeus speaks it: "what is mine, my love shall render him. / And she is mine" (I.i.96–97). In contrast, Hermia argues that human beings are unique, each with an essentially different identity. This is the premise behind her belief in "true love," which presupposes that human beings cannot be substituted for one another, that there is only one "true" self or person that will do.

For the revels to transform the original dilemma at the beginning of the play, then, they would need to bring about an order which corresponded to Hermia's view of things, a world in which ownership gave way to personhood, a world in which persons were different from each other. But Puck, putting in the drops that are supposed to remove "error" from Lysander's eyes, ironizes exactly that possibility and suggests the improbability of such a universe:

> . . . When thou wak'st
> Thou tak'st
> True delight
> In the sight
> Of thy former lady's eye:
> And the country proverb known,
> That every man should take his own,
> In your waking shall be shown.
> Jack shall have Jill;
> Nought shall go ill;
> The man shall have his mare again, and
> all shall be well. (iii.ii.453–63)

To the extent that the words imagine an essential partner, an other half integral and indispensable to the self, they participate in Hermia's notion of "true love." But to the extent that the "proverb" that will be shown is that every man will "take" "his own," Puck's words reinscribe the rhetoric of ownership with which the play began. And to the degree they imagine the future as "Jack" having "Jill," they deindividuate, erode, and erase the differences between the lovers, threaten to make everyone into generic males and females. Not that there were many of these differences to begin with – it seems no mere convention that Egeus has to identify Demetrius and Lysander for Theseus ("Stand forth, Demetrius . . . Stand forth, Lysander.") or that so much is made of the superficial differences between Helena's height and Hermia's shortness, since there is often little else to differentiate them from each other, or that Oberon has no real answer to Puck's "Did not you tell me I should know the man / By the Athenian garments he had on?" (iii.ii.348–49). In their final vision ("The man shall have his mare again") Puck's lines reduce women not simply to possessions, but to the animals they have ostensibly been protected from throughout the play; they imagine a world which is simply the mirror image of Titania's union with an ass.

Beneath the play's masque and its apparent resolution of discord lies a view of theatricality itself as the production of insistent and unmanageable sexual desire, a desire that is inherently animalistic. This is, incidentally, exactly what those who attacked the stage during the period characterized theater as being. For Stephen Gosson, theater whetted "desire to inordinate lust" and reduced the women who watched it to prostitutes, and the men, like Bottom, to braying colts.[8] For both Gosson and Prynne, theater is founded on and in rape, Romulus, having established the first theater "as a horsefaire for hoores . . . to gather the faire women together" so that each of his soldiers "might take where hee liked a snatch for share."[9] And theater itself comes to be synonymous with its origins, for pamphleteers conceive of it as a kind of rape of the mind, a "ravishing" of the senses.[10] In an extended treatment of a production of *Bacchus and Ariadne*, Gosson describes the coercive power of theater to make the spectators compulsively reenact the sexual acts they have seen upon the stage.[11] Prynne says that plays "devirginate unmarried persons."[12] What *A Midsummer Night's Dream* offers in the figure of Theseus turning to the revels, then, is something like the disturbing figure of a double negative. He turns to what is culturally understood itself as a kind of rape in order to conceal and manage his own sexual violence.

NOTES

1 All quotations from *A Midsummer Night's Dream* are taken from *The Riverside Shakespeare*, G. Blakemore Evans, textual ed., (Boston: Houghton Mifflin Co., 1974).

2 While it can be argued that Theseus' opening claim, "I woo'd thee with my sword," does not literally describe a forced penetration, it is not necessary for it to do so in order for what he has done to Hippolyta to constitute rape, for it has become axiomatic that definitions of rape during the period were ambiguous and contradictory, and the central contradiction revolved around tensions between rape as a "crime against property" and rape as a crime against "the person," that is, a view of rape as abduction and a view of rape as violation of a woman's will. My premise in this essay is that *A Midsummer Night's Dream* is caught in a dynamic between these two views of rape; which, both simultaneous and in competition with each other, charge various moments of the play. Thus when Egeus accuses Lysander of stealing Hermia and claims his right to put her to death, he is, in effect, articulating an older view of rape as theft of a father's property, though no contemporary English statute would have allowed him to put her to death, or to do anything more than disinherit her, for an illicit marriage. When Hermia at the same juncture refuses to yield her "virgin patent" up, she

articulates more recent attitudes about rape as violation of a woman's will, attitudes implicit in the play's depiction of Oberon's treatment of Titania (though ironically, by making her lust after Bottom, he puts her in a position which would have exposed her to the consequences of disinheritance, according to an older tradition). As I will suggest, by the time Titania says that every little flower weeps some "enforced chastity" it is as if the threat of sexual violence in the play has become so great that it disrupts all definitions or parameters for containing it.

For the claim (which has become a critical cliché) that the legal view of rape changed from the "medieval period" to the late Renaissance from "a crime against property" to "a crime against the person" (p. 41), see Nazife Bashar's "Rape in England between 1550 and 1700," in *The Sexual Dynamics of History: Men's Power, Women's Resistance* (London: Pluto Press, 1983), pp. 28–42. But Bashar's own shrewd analysis of the discrepancy between the rigors of statute and the laxity of practice belies this claim. Seeking to account for declining conviction rates in the face of increasingly severe statute, Bashar examines the demographics of women who brought rape charges and notes that while most women bringing such charges were older, the only cases to result in convictions involved rapes of children, assumed to be virgins. Bashar's conclusion that "only the rapes that had in them some element of property, in the form of virginity, ended in the conviction of the accused" (p. 42) suggests the degree to which conceptions of property were always embedded in attitudes toward rape, even when formal definitions of the crime seemed to invoke conceptions of personhood. Bashar's work suggests, in fact, the inextricability of the two conceptions from each other, their dynamic effect upon each other.

For ambiguities in statute itself, see, in particular, statutes from 1557, 1576, and 1597 in *The Statutes at Large: From the First Year of King Edward IV to the End of the Reign of Queen Elizabeth.* vol. II (London: Charles Eyre and Andrew Strahan, printers to the King's most Excellent Majesty, 1786). Thus, the first of these seems, on the one hand, to clearly distinguish between rape and abduction (and thus to imply a conception of the difference between woman as person and woman as someone else's property) in punishing the "tak[ing] or convey[ing] away . . . any Maid or Woman Child unmarried . . . out of or from the Possession, Custody or Governance, and against the Will of the Father" with two years imprisonment, and punishing the same act if it results in "deflowering" with five years. On the other hand, the act fails to specify whether it is the violation of the woman's will that accounts for the increased penalty or the loss of the property of her virginity, and the same act makes the woman's will irrelevant in a later section when it spells out the consequences for her if she marries against her father's will. The 1576 act seems to intensify the punishment for rape by taking away the benefit of the clergy for convicted rapists, but even as it does so it implicitly reverts to a conception of rape as theft by repeatedly associating rape with burglary, reiterating the phrase, "Rape or Burglary." The 1597 act, "An Act for taking

away of Clergy from Offenders against a certain Statute made in the third
Year of the Reign of King *Henry* the Seventh, concerning the Taking away
of Women against their Wills unlawfully" enacts its contradictoriness in its
very title, since it simultaneously imagines women as persons with wills
which can be violated and as property which can be "taken away." This act,
ostensibly one of those tightenings of rape law during the period because it
removes the benefit of the clergy, in fact only deals with those who steal
away women with property ("Women as well Maidens as Widows and
Wives, having Substance, some in Goods moveable, and some in Lands and
Tenements, and some being Heirs apparent to their Ancestors, for the Lucre
of such Substance been oftentimes taken by Misdoers contrary to their Will
...")

For legal writers who seem to clearly distinguish between rape and abduc-
tion (and thus crimes against person versus crimes against property) see Sir
Antony Fitzherbert, *The Newe Boke of Justices of the Peas* (1538), in the *Classical
English Law Texts* series (London: Professional Books Limited, 1982), and Sir
Edward Coke, *The Second Part Of The Institutes Of The Lawes Of England* (1642)
(New York: Garland, 1979), though while Coke sees rape as "carnall knowledge of a woman by force and against her will" (p. 180) he is extremely concerned with the dishonour such an act brings to her house and family, and in
that sense does not seem to conceive of her as fully separate from them. The
clearest distinction is provided by *The Lawes resolutions of womens rights* which
identifies "two kindes of Rape," one of which is called "Ravishment . . . but
unproperly," which is "when a woman is enforced violently to sustaine the
furie of brutish concupiscence, but she is left where she is found, as in her
owne house or bed, as Lucrece was, and not hurried away, as Helen by Paris,
or as the Sabine Women were by the Romans," and the other, abduction,
which is "both by nature of the word, and definition of the matter," the
"right ravishment" (pp. 377–78). Though conceptually distinguishing
between abduction and rape, for this text, it is abduction, the stealing away
of the woman, that makes it rape in the first place, hence the endless interest
in entailment and inheritance. See *The Lawes resolutions of womens rights: or,
The lawes provision for woemen. A methodicall collection of such statutes and customes,
with the cases, opinions, arguments and points of learning in the law, as doe properly con-
cerne women. Together with a compendious table, whereby the chiefe matters in this booke
contained, may be the more readily found* (London: printed by the assignes of John
More, esq. and are to be sold by John Grove, 1632).

In other words, even where writers conceptually distinguish between rape
as violation of a woman (a position which implicitly regards woman as
person) and abduction (which implicitly regards woman as property) in
practice these two views get conflated over and over again, in both legal
theory and legal practice during the Renaissance.

In this construction of rape law and rape trial during the period, I am
heavily indebted to Jessica Winston and in particular to her brilliant "More
than Power to Tell: *Lucrece's* Silence and the Definition of Woman," in

manuscript in "Cruelly Penned; Rape and the Subject of Sexual Violence." See as well Barbara Toner's fine chapter on the history of rape in *The Facts of Rape* (New York: Arrow Books, 1982).

3 In my sense of the repressive and invasive power of authority in the play, I differ from both René Girard and Leonard Tennenhouse. For Girard, repressive authority in the play is merely a pretext for mimetic desire's need for obstacles:

> We soon realise that Shakespeare is more interested in this systematically self-defeating type of passion than in the initial theme of "true love," something . . . always in need of villainous enemies if it is to provide any semblance of dramatic plot . . .

> Although the theme of outside interference is not forgotten, it becomes even more flimsy. In the absence of the father figures, the role is entrusted to Puck, who keeps pouring his magical love juice into the "wrong" eyes.

See pp. 189–90 in "Myth and Ritual in Shakespeare: *A Midsummer Night's Dream*," in *Textual Strategies: Perspectives in Post-Structuralist Criticism*, Josue V. Harari, ed. (Ithaca: Cornell University Press, 1979), pp. 189–212. In contrast, for Tennenhouse, authority corrects itself in the course of the play: "the problem authority has to master is a problem with authority itself, authority grown archaic. At the outset the law seems to serve only the will of the father . . . When Theseus overrules the angry father, juridical power can no longer be identified with patriarchal power." See pp. 111–12 in *Power on Display* (New York: Methuen, 1986). I differ from both readings in my sense of authority's real and destructive power throughout the play. Girard seems to me to ignore this power and Tennenhouse to exaggerate its transformation, an exaggeration possible, in part, through a minimizing of the similarities between Theseus and Oberon that facilitates seeing in Oberon an "alternative" to "patriachal power."

My reading of the play as depicting rape as the condition of existence itself differs markedly from four different kinds of readings of *A Midsummer Night's Dream*. It differs most from readings like C. L. Barber's "May Games and Metamorphoses on a Midsummer Night," which sees in the play an "exorcism of evil powers" (p. 139) and in the fairies not the "fairies 'of the villagery,' creatures who . . . were dangerous to meddle with, large enough to harm, often malicious, sometimes the consorts of witches," but "pageant nymphs and holiday celebrants" (p. 144), "creatures of pastoral" (p. 145). See *Shakespeare's Festive Comedy*, (Princeton: Princeton University Press, 1959) pp. 119–62. It differs secondly from those purportedly "darker" readings of the play which seem to me ultimately to back away from the implications of their own arguments and so not to be so dark. See, especially, Michael Taylor's "The Darker Purpose of *A Midsummer Night's Dream*," (*Studies in English Literature*, 9 [1969]: 259–73), which argues that though "Shakespeare's

'darker purpose' is to suggest that the appearance of discord among the
lovers is not appearance only but does, in fact, hint at a more brutal reality,"
Shakespeare doesn't "allow us to experience any more of this dream-as-
nightmare than is sufficient to be grateful for the fact that it is not really
dangerous" (268, 272). See as well David Bevington's "'But We Are Spirits of
Another Sort': The Dark Side of Love and Magic in *A Midsummer Night's
Dream*," which associates Puck with the "irrational and frightening," but sal-
vages Oberon as a ruler "insisting on the establishment of proper obedience
to his authority" (p. 83), in *Medieval and Renaissance Studies: Proceedings of the
Southeastern Institute, Summer 1975* (Durham: Duke University Press, 1978). It
differs, thirdly, from important feminist readings of the play which either
explore the implications of its opening lines and then apply them to the
tragedies, but not to the play itself (see Madelon Gohlke's "I Wooed Thee
with My Sword: Shakespeare's Tragic Paradigms," in *The Woman's Part:
Feminist Criticism of Shakespeare*, Carolyn Ruth Swift Lenz, Gayle Greene and
Carol Thomas Neely, eds. [Urbana: University of Illinois Press, 1980], pp.
150–70) or quite clearly appreciate the destruction of the bonds between
women in the play, but see this destruction as the cost of some positive transformation that nevertheless takes place (see Shirley Nelson Garner's "*A
Midsummer Night's Dream*: 'Jack Shall Have Jill; Nought Shall go Ill,'" *Women's
Studies* 9 [1981]: 47–63). It differs, finally, from crucial readings like Girard's
and Tennenhouse's in its sense of authority's real and destructive power
within the play.

    In contrast to all of these, Louis A. Montrose powerfully identifies that
power, arguing first that Shakespeare's sources "weave the chronicle of
Theseus' rapes and disastrous marriages, his habitual victimization of
women, into the lurid history of female depravity," leaving "traces of those
recurrent acts of bestiality and incest, of parricide, uxoricide, filicide, and
suicide, that the ethos of romantic comedy would evade" (p. 77) and second
that this "weaving" reveals the way that patriarchal norms are themselves
"compensatory for the vulnerability of men to the powers of women" (p.
77). (See Montrose, "*A Midsummer Night's Dream* and the Shaping Fantasies of
Elizabethan Culture: Gender, Power, Form," in *Rewriting the Renaissance*,
Margaret W. Ferguson, Maureen Quilligan, and Nancy J. Vickers, eds.
[Chicago: University of Chicago Press, 1986], pp. 65–87, as well as the
earlier and longer version of the essay, "'Shaping Fantasies': Figurations of
Gender and Power in Elizabethan Culture," *Representations* 1.2 [Spring
1983]: 61–94). Because the two versions of this essay contain slightly differ-
ent emphases, I have quoted each where relevant.

    Where Montrose brilliantly documents the compensatory nature of
patriarchal violence within the play, I am more concerned with the logic of
a world in which rape is simply taken to be a given, the condition of existence itself, and with the way such a world is caught in the relentless repetition of the dilemma it is seeking to transform. I am, in this enterprise, deeply
influenced by Jonathan Crewe's "Shakespeare's Figure of Lucrece: Writing

Rape," in his *Trials of Authorship: Anterior Forms and Poetic Reconstruction From Wyatt to Shakespeare* (Berkeley: University of California Press, 1990), pp. 140–63.

For crucial discussions of narrative strategies for legitimizing and naturalizing rape, see Stephanie H. Jed's *Chaste Thinking: The Rape of Lucretia and the Birth of Humanism* (Bloomington and Indianapolis: Indiana University Press, 1989), pp. 1–17, and Susan Frye's "Of Chastity and Violence: Elizabeth I and Edmund Spenser in the House of Busirane," *Signs: Journal of Women in Culture and Society*, 20.1 (1994): 49–78. Where I focus on the fantasy that theater can be made to legitimize a rape, Jed powerfully demonstrates the ways that the narrative has been made to do so ("If the narrative of Lucretia's rape somehow legitimizes the foundation of Republican Rome, we might wonder if there is some kind of reciprocal relationship: do republican laws and institutions also legitimize the conditions of sexual violence?" [2]).

4 For influential readings of the play which have stressed the destruction of the bonds between women implicit in Oberon's capacity to make Titania break her vow, see Garner, "'Jack Shall Have Jill,'" and Montrose, "'Shaping Fantasies,'" as well as Philippa Berry's *Of Chastity and Power: Elizabethan Literature and the Unmarried Queen* (London: Routledge, 1989), p. 144. I differ from these critics in the reading I offer below, primarily in my sense of the way this violation is part of a chain of sexual violations, a repetition of the original violation which Theseus seeks to dispell.

5 C. L. Barber identifies the same vision of female fecundity at stake in the speech, but not the sense of the way it must be violated for events to progress (see *Shakespeare's Festive Comedy*, p. 137). For Montrose, this sense of female fecundity articulated by the speech is, in large part, what men seek to compensate for. Thus the fantasy of male "autogeny," a fantasy Theseus himself helps articulate at the beginning of the play, is "an overcompensation for the *natural* fact that men do indeed come from women" ("'Shaping Fantasies,'" 72).

6 For an analogous reading (for very different purposes) of the destruction of the wall, see Pat Parker's brilliant "Anagogic Metaphor: Breaking Down the Wall of Partition," p. 48, in *Centre and Labyrinth: Essays in Honor of Northrop Frye* (Toronto: Toronto University Press, 1983), pp. 38–58.

7 Where for Montrose these banished entertainments call attention to the play's tendency toward "mythological suppression" – the suppression of the "acts of bestiality and incest . . . parricide, uxoricide, filicide and suicide," that characterize the play's sources – for me the entertainments are repetitions of an original violation within the text which Theseus seeks unsuccessfully to dispell. See "'Shaping Fantasies,'" 75.

8 See Stephen Gosson, *The School of Abuse* (1579; rpt. London: The Shakespeare Society, 1841), pp. 22, 48.

9 *Ibid.*, p. 19. Prynne repeats the story. See William Prynne's *Histrio-mastix: The Player's Scourge or Actor's Tragedy* (New York: Garland, 1974), pp. 30, 452–53.

10 See Gosson, *School of Abuse*, p. 22, and Anglophile Eutheo (Antony Munday), *A Second and Third Blast of Retrait from Plaies and Theatres* (London, 1580), p. 32 for the claim that the love of theater "ravishes."

11 See Gosson, *Playes Confuted in five Actions*, in Arthur F. Kinney, *Markets of Bawdrie: The Dramatic Criticism of Stephen Gosson*, Salzburg Studies in Literature, no. 4 (Salzburg; Institut für Englische Sprache und Literatur, 1974) pp. 193–94. For my discussion of this passage, see *Men in Women's Clothing* (New York and Cambridge: Cambridge University Press, 1994) pp. 12–13 and (more broadly) pp. 10–25. For critics who examine Gosson for his centrality to an anti-theatrical tradition that articulates the sexual power of theater, see Valerie Traub, *Desire and Anxiety: Circulations of Sexuality in Shakespearean Drama* (London: Routledge, 1992) p. 119 and chapter five, note 2; and Jean E. Howard, "Crossdressing, The Theatre, and Gender Struggle in Early Modern England," *Shakespeare Quarterly* 39 (1988): 418–40.

12 See Prynne, *Histrio-mastix*, pp. 340–41, for the claim that "Stage-Playes devirginate unmarried persons, especially beautifull, tender Virgins who resort unto them."

CHAPTER 10

Subjection and subjectivity: Jewish law and female autonomy in Reformation English marriage

M. Lindsay Kaplan

While marriage functioned, for the most part, as a mainstay of patriarchal control in the early modern period, Reformation reassessment of the structure and meaning of marriage brought about challenges to notions of male dominance and allowed space for female subjectivity and agency. The impetus for these changes, I argue, comes from an engagement with Jewish attitudes on marriage and divorce which influence the ways in which marriage was thought to function. Before the Reformation, marriage and women's subordinate position within it was understood as permanent. The Hebraic concept of marriage, adopted in Protestant treatises and taken up as a model in parliamentary debates about the permanence of the people's subordination to the king, saw it as fully dissoluble. Divorce provided, at least theoretically, a means by which a wife could effect her own release from the control of her husband, and Jewish law thus could be made to serve those who would challenge the gender hierarchy. In advancing this claim, I recognize that this radical potential was never realized. However, I am interested in examining the fissures of patriarchal ideology under stress which allow for counter-patriarchal thought and action, even if women's subordination ultimately remained intact.

An exploration of the history and development of marriage in Christian Europe, with particular attention to its contractual nature, provides a foundation for my discussion of gender conflict in early modern England. From the eleventh century onward, the Roman Catholic Church viewed marriage, in addition to its natural and sacramental aspects, as a contract which could only be formed by the voluntary consent of both parties.[1] However, the consensual component of this process was exercised only at the formation of the contract; once sealed, that is, consummated, it could not be dissolved by either party. The couple could be granted a separation, on limited grounds, by the ecclesiastical court, but the sacramental nature of marriage made dissolution and remarriage an impossibility. The only ecclesiastical recourse for a bad marriage was, under very specific circumstances, annulment due to an improper contracting.[2] This voided the marriage entirely, but often subjected the couple to penitential discipline.[3]

The Lutheran Reformation rejected the Roman Catholic claim that marriage constituted a sacrament, presenting it instead as an earthly institution subject to civil law and authority.[4] This metamorphosis in the conception of marriage affected the structure of the law regulating its constitution and dissolution. Canonical law had heretofore prohibited divorce and remarriage on the basis that marriage was a sacrament that could not be dissolved, emphasizing Jesus' preaching: "What therefore God hath joined together, let not man put asunder" (Matthew 19:6).[5] The reformers saw the *relationship* as constituting the institution, not the reverse; if companionship did not exist between wife and husband, then, in effect, neither did marriage. Divorce and remarriage should be permitted to avoid the problems of adultery and fornication that arose under the canonical system which allowed only judicial separation.

This innovation of the Reform movement signaled a rejection not only of Roman Catholic doctrine, but, in effect, an interpretation of Christian Scripture. Let us return to Matthew 19 and look at how the text represents marriage and divorce. Jesus' pronouncement of husband and wife constituting one flesh is the answer to a question asked by the Pharisees regarding the permissibility of divorcing one's wife for any cause. In response to his statement, the Pharisees cite Mosaic law allowing divorce:

They say unto him, Why did Moses then command to give a writing of divorcement, and to put her away? He saith unto them, Moses because of the hardness of your hearts suffered you to put away your wives: but from the beginning it was not so. And I say unto you, Whosoever shall put away his wife, except it be for fornication and shall marry another, committeth adultery. (Matthew 19: 7–9)

Matthew 5:32, which is almost identical to this last statement, adds "and whosoever shall marry her that is divorced committeth adultery." This teaching challenges the Deuteronomic divorce law (Deut. 24:1) by representing it as an afterthought legislated in response to Jewish inadequacy. In so doing, it forcefully argues against divorce, by which only separation seems to be meant, except in the case of adultery, and, taken in conjunction with Matthew 5:32, prohibits remarriage even in cases of permitted separation.

In advocating divorce, Protestant reformers adopt what is essentially a

Hebraic notion of marriage as a contract that can be completely dissolved – and remade with another party if so desired. "When a man hath taken a wife and married her, and it come to pass that she find no favor in his eyes, because he hath found some uncleanness in her: then let him write her a bill of divorcement, and give it in her hand, and send her out of his house. And when she is departed out of his house she may go and be another man's wife" (Deut. 24:1–2). It is clear from the passage that remarriage is possible after a divorce for either party. While it should be noted that, in spite of Jesus' teaching in the Gospels, the early church did in fact sanction liberal laws of divorce, the orthodox Christian position for the centuries leading up to the Reformation prohibited the termination of an existing marriage followed by the contracting of a new one.[6] The reformers' endorsement of divorce and remarriage in effect privileged Jewish practice over the recent history of the Christian church.[7]

The connection between divorce and Jewish law is even more pronounced if we turn from continental reform to examine the transmission and impact of the Reformation in England. Strikingly, the debate surrounding Henry VIII's desire to divorce his wife and former sister-in-law, Katherine of Aragon, provided the impetus for embracing the Protestant movement. Coincidentally, it stimulated an urgent interest in the interpretation of Mosaic law. The continental reformers generally emphasized a return to the original and unmediated texts of the Bible; in England this royal controversy added fuel to a renewed interest in Hebrew in early sixteenth-century England. Motivated by Katherine's inability to produce a male heir and his intense desire for Anne Boylen, Henry sought to find a means of dissolving his first marriage in order to contract a second. His case was based on the claim that he had violated the law set forth in Leviticus 18:16: "Thou shalt not uncover the nakedness of thy brother's wife." However, this text was seen to be in conflict with the Deuteronomic commandment of levirate marriage (Deut. 25:5): that a man should provide an heir for his dead brother by marrying his brother's widow. The competing texts in Leviticus and Deuteronomy regulating marriage between a man and his (deceased) brother's wife impelled the king to consult, in addition to numerous Christian authorities, the rabbinic community of Venice; Henry insisted on personally reviewing the resulting opinions.[8] The Pope's refusal to grant an annulment resulted in Henry's break from Catholicism and in the establishment of the Protestant Church of England which granted the king's divorce and legitimated his subsequent marriage.

Numerous books published in the century following Henry's divorce explore Hebrew Scripture in general or marriage law in particular.[9] In his *Explication of the Judiciall Lawes of Moses*, one of three books he authored on Hebrew Scripture and law, Scottish theologian John Weemse equates divorce law with nullified Jewish law. Of the three types of law God gave to the Jews – moral, ceremonial, and judicial – only the first is still applicable to Christians. Weemse selects divorce as an example of the voided judicial law, which was established, as it were, reluctantly:

[in order to] permit something for the eschewing of greater evill ... So this Law permitted divorcement for the hardnesse of the peoples hearts, and for the eschewing of greater inconvenience, least hard-hearted men should have killed their wives.[10]

Here divorce epitomizes those particular Jewish laws which are now obsolete for Christians.

Even those early Protestant texts arguing in favor of divorce nevertheless register uneasiness at its basis in Mosaic law. Heinrich Bullinger's *The Christen State of Matrimonye*,[11] published in English in 1541, labors to distinguish between valid Christian reasons for divorce and illegitimate Jewish ones. Bullinger argues that divorce and remarriage are permitted for the innocent party, either husband or wife, in the case of adultery, citing 1 Corinthians 7 and, obliquely, Matthew 19, neither of which actually supports his claim.[12] However, he anxiously limits this permission by contrasting it to inappropriate Judaic practice:

To the maryed/not I/but the lorde commandeth that the wyfe be not divorced from hir man / but yf she be / for anye light cause by anye such Jewesh permission for theyr hardneckednes divorced (for such acshions become not you which ar Christened) yet let hyr abyde unmaried / or els be reconcyled to hyr housband. And lykewyse of the man.[13]

Although Bullinger argues in favor of divorce and remarriage without firm support in Christian Scripture, he nevertheless attempts to distance himself from Jews and the Hebrew text that authorizes his claim.

However, by the middle of the seventeenth century, arguments made in favor of divorce are justified in an explicitly Jewish and rabbinic context. John Milton's 1643 *Doctrine and Discipline of Divorce*[14] startled his contemporaries in advocating divorce (and remarriage) for reasons of incompatibility, a stance based on rabbinic interpretation of the Deuteronomic law.[15] He argues explicitly here that the Jewish law of divorce, far from being abrogated by Jesus, is justified by him:

we have an expresse law of *God*, and such a law, as wherof our Saviour with a solemn threat forbid the abrogating . . . Ye have an author great beyond exception, *Moses*; and one yet greater, he who hedg'd in from abolishing every smallest jot and tittle of precious equity contain'd in that Law.[16]

Some critics of the treatise particularly attacked its authorization of Mosaic law through the New Testament. Henry Hammond attacks the "*special* artifice made use of," by Milton in "bringing back *Christ* unto *Moses*, of interpreting the restraint laid on this matter in the *New Testament*, by *analogie* with the *Judaical permission* in the Old," while Alexander Ross rejects the *Doctrine*'s thesis on the grounds that it is Jewish, not Christian, practice "that a man may put away his Wife, though not for adultery; so taught the Jews."[17]

John Selden, an unparalleled comparative jurist, was a contemporary of Milton and a source of a considerable amount of the poet's rabbinic knowledge.[18] His astonishing mastery of both biblical and rabbinic texts resulted in the publication of seven books on Jewish law, most of which contained discussions relevant to contemporary English political disputes. The penultimate of these works, the *Uxor Hebraica*, or *Jewish Wife*, exhaustively catalogues Jewish laws relating to marriage and divorce and compares them with the marital laws of other societies. In the *Uxor*, Selden employs the sheer magnitude of his data to argue implicitly for the development of divorce law in England. While acknowledging the divine origin of marriage, the comparative nature of the *Uxor* demonstrates that secular custom determines how societies constitute and dissolve marriages.[19] Strikingly, Selden firmly locates his argument for innovation in English divorce law within the structure of not only Hebraic but rabbinic teachings.[20]

The treatises on marriage and divorce in early modern England that associate divorce and remarriage with Jewish law do not so much reflect the practice of contemporary ecclesiastical law as they do a desire to reform the status quo. In spite, or perhaps because of the specific conditions surrounding the English Reformation, marriage and divorce law continued in a state of turmoil for more than a century following Henry's divorce. While England's marriage and divorce law remained the most conservative of any Protestant country in Europe (divorce and remarriage were not officially sanctioned until 1857),[21] the sixteenth and seventeenth centuries marked a period of multiple reforms and proposed reforms of both marriage and divorce.[22] Having sketched out an overview of the development of theories favoring divorce, I would now like to consider in greater detail legislative attempts to implement, and popular arguments in favor of, a more liberal divorce law.

The first post-Reformation attempt to establish divorce law in England was drafted in 1546 by a commission charged in the Act in Restraint of Appeals (1534) to revise canon law. Henry failed to sign the draft before his death, and in 1550 a new commission was appointed which produced the *Reformatio legum ecclesiasticarum*. This proposal provided for divorce and remarriage for the innocent party, wife or husband, in cases of adultery, desertion, and other maltreatment. It languished until 1566 when radical Protestants squeaked it through the Lower House of Convocation before it died. In 1571 the House of Commons set up a commission to review the document, but the proposal was considered too radical; this attempt at ecclesiastical reform died in committee along with proposed modification of divorce law.[23] In fact, the Catholic canon law of divorce was never repealed and to this day the Church of England has never introduced a new code of law to supersede it.[24]

However, the official church position was not monolithically enforced; during the Renaissance it was circumvented informally and during the Interregnum it was temporarily suspended.[25] Additionally, the period produced numerous texts on ecclesiastical reform and marriage which set forth opinions on divorce contrary to current ecclesiastical law. In his *A Declaration of the X Holye Commaundements*, Bishop John Hooper argues for divorce in cases of adultery for both men and women.[26] In 1590, William Perkins publishes his *Christian Oeconomie* (translated from Latin into English in 1609) which argues for divorce for cases of desertion, "intolerable conditions," absence, and adultery without discrimination of sex:[27]

Now in requiring of a divorce, there is an equall right and power in both parties, so as the woman may require it as well as the man; and he as wel as she. The reason is, because they are equally bound each to other, and have also the same interest in one anothers bodie; provided alwaies, that the man is to maintaine his superioritie, and the woman to observe that modestie which beseemeth her towards the man.[28]

John Rainolds wrote his *Defense of the Judgement of the Reformed Churches* in 1597, but it was not published until 1609, because the Archbishop of Canterbury:

thought it not meet to be printed, as containing dangerous doctrine, and breeding sundrie inconveniences, if any weary of wife or husband might, by committing adultery procure freedome of marying whom they list.[29]

The subversiveness of divorce was linked to the challenge radical Protestant reform in general posed to the ecclesiastical status quo. William Whately advanced the innovative argument that certain actions in themselves effectually dissolved the marriage in *A Bride-Bush or Wedding Sermon*:

> Principall [duties] I terme those, by the breach whereof this knot is dissolved and quite undone . . . The first is, the chaste keeping of each ones body each for other . . . Against which duty if either of them shall offend, the party so transgressing, hath committed adultery, broken the covenant of God, remooved the yoke from the yoke fellowes neck, and laide himself open (if the Magistrate did as Gods law commands) to the bloody stroke of violent death . . . The next is cohabitation or dwelling together . . . And if it so fall out, that either partie doe frowardly and perversly withdraw him or herselfe from this matrimoniall society . . . the other is loosed from the former band, and may lawfully (after an orderly proceeding with the Church or Magistrate in that behalfe) joyne him or her selfe to another.[30]

Although Whately is careful to impose some official control over this proceeding, the fact that this redress was not available within English ecclesiastical law suggests that one could avoid that structure and receive this sanction from an independent divine or justice. In another caveat against reckless divorce, he includes an implicit criticism of current ecclesiastical practice:

> Onely we professe, that in cases of this nature, a just and orderly course must bee taken. Every one may not headdily, and upon a sudden, carve to themselves: but seeke direction, and crave helpe from the Church and Magistrate, whose dutie bindes them to provide remedy for such inconveniences.[31]

According to the *Dictionary of National Biography*, *A Bride-Bush* raised a storm of opposition in the church. Whately was convened before the High Commission in 1621, but was dismissed upon retracting his propositions. He printed retractions of his argument in a later edition of *A Bride-Bush* (1624) and in *A Care-Cloth* (1624).

William Gouge's *Of Domesticall Duties*, published a year after Whately was dismissed by the High Commission, presents a similar, but more circumspect, discussion of divorce. In a discussion of the "Common mutuall duties betwixt Man and Wife," he cites desertion as a "vice contrary to matrimoniall unitie."[32]

> That *Desertion* therefore on the delinquents part is such dissolution of mariage, as freeth the innocent parties from the bondage thereof. In many reformed Churches beyond the seas *Desertion* is accounted so farre to dissolve the very

bond of mariage . . . the matter being heard and adjudged by the Magistrate, the marriage bond may be broken, and libertie given to the partie forsaken to mary another. But because our Church hath no such custome, nor our law determined such cases, I leave them to the custome of other Churches.[33]

While repeating, in effect, Whately's opinion on desertion and divorce, Gouge is careful to distinguish, without comment, between the "custome" of other Protestant churches and England's ecclesiastical practice. His discussion of adultery is cautiously vague: "*Adulterie* [is] . . . a vice whereby way is made for *Divorce*: as is cleare and evident by the determination of Christ himselfe."[34] Is he simply saying that Scripture supports judicial separation without remarriage currently available in England, or suggesting that Jesus' pronouncement allows for innovation in current practice? On the punishment for adultery, Gouge is clear that men and women are equally culpable "in regard of the breach of wed-locke, and transgression against God,"[35] suggesting that if the redress were allowed, both men and women would be able to divorce adulterous spouses.

With the onset of the civil war, opportunities for expressing dissent with the status quo, including marriage and divorce law, increased. In January 1643, Parliament abolished the episcopacy and convened the Westminster Assembly later that summer to determine the future of the Church of England.[36] Milton published the first of his divorce tracts one month after the convention of the Assembly, addressing the dedicatory letter to them and hinting in the title-page at the text's import for their deliberations: "The Doctrine and Discipline of Divorce: Restor'd to the good of both sexes, From the bondage of Canon Law, and other mis-takes, to Christian freedom, guided by the Rule of Charity. Wherein also many places of Scripture, have recover'd their long-lost meaning: Seasonable to be now thought on in the Reformation intended."[37] In this treatise, Milton argues that the key to the larger Reformation of the Commonwealth lies in a successful reforming of the laws governing the family:

For no effect of tyranny can sit more heavy on the Common-wealth, then this household unhappines on the family. And farewell all hope of true Reformation in the state, while such an evill as this lies undiscern'd or unregarded in the house.[38]

He advances the radical notion, citing Hebraist Paul Fagius for support, that divorce should be allowed for reasons of incompatibility.[39]

That indisposition, unfitnes, or contrariety of mind, arising from a cause in nature unchangeable, hindring and ever likely to hinder the main benefits of conjugall society, which are solace and peace, is a greater reason of divorce than natural frigidity, especially if there be no children, and that there be mutuall consent.[40]

The parity of the two contracting parties is emphasized both in dissolving an inappropriate marriage and constituting a fit one:

For all sense and equity reclaimes that any Law or Cov'nant how solemn or strait soever, either between God and man, or man and man, though of Gods joyning, should bind against a prime and principall scope of its own institution, and of both or either party cov'nanting . . . [I]n God's intention a meet and happy conversation is the chiefest and the noblest end of mariage.[41]

Either wife or husband is justified, according to Milton's interpretation, in dissolving a marriage that violates the true purpose of the contract, an equitable rapport between the parties. This parity, implicit here, is made explicit in the text's title, which purports to restore divorce "to the good of both sexes."[42]

Selden, whose *Uxor Hebraica* was completed by 1640 (though not published until 1646) was one of thirty laymen selected as a member of the Westminster Assembly.[43] He would almost certainly have influenced the discussion of new divorce regulations introduced in Parliament in the 1640s and 1650s.[44] In the *Uxor* he argues that natural law, which he understands as the biblically derived Noachide commandments, allows to both men and women "the completely unrestricted power to decide to dissolve a marriage."[45] In concluding his impressive catalogue of marriage and divorce laws, Selden circumspectly observes:

if what has been pointed out is correctly reflected upon, it is not hard to ascertain what had to be decided with respect to the several important questions that were wont to be controverted and discussed regarding the law of marriage and divorce, both human and divine.[46]

The proposed Civil Marriage Act (passed in 1653) initially permitted divorce to either spouse on proof of the partner's adultery, but this clause was rejected and excluded from the final form of the legislation.

If opinion in favor of divorce legislation did not succeed in changing the law, the concept of divorce did find support in another parliamentary context in the political debates over the nature of the contract between king and subject. The royalists who first adopted the paradigm of monarch as husband to his subservient people/wife no doubt did so expecting no one to challenge this model, since marriage in early modern England was, with few exceptions, considered permanent. This is why, according to Mary Lyndon Shanley, "The Royalists thought they had found in the marriage contract a perfect analogue to any supposed contract between the king and his subjects, for marriage was a contract, but was in its essence both hierarchical and irrevocable."[47]

However, parliamentarians who challenged absolute monarchy were forced by the terms of the debate to support the claims of the subject, and by analogy the wife, with recourse to divorce law, often associated with the Jews. This argument creates a political interest in exploring and promoting, albeit theoretically, the rights of women in marriage.

The Royalists emphasized traditional notions of the permanent nature of marriage, and the subordination of the wife, when using it as a model for relations between the subject and monarch. In his tract, *Conscience Satisfied*, Henry Ferne argues against the claim that the people retain some reserve of power when they contract with the king to be their ruler:

as if in Matrimony (for the King is also *sponsus Regni*, and wedded to the kingdom by a Ring at his Coronation) the parties should agree, upon such and such neglect of duties, to part a sunder; . . . what our Saviour said of their light & unlawfull occasions of Divorse, *non fuit sic ab initio*, it was not so from the beginning, when God at first joyned man and woman, may be said of such a reserved power of resistance, it was not so from the beginning.[48]

While no clear antecedent for "their . . . Divorse" is expressed, the context of Matthew 19 which Ferne quotes associates this practice with the Pharisees to whom Christ addresses this statement.

If Ferne's reference to the Jews is understated, fellow-Royalist Dudley Digges draws a more explicit connection between Jews and the solubility of marriage. He too challenges the notion that this contract between monarch and people could be rescinded;[49] as he argues in *The Unlawfulness of Subjects Taking up Armes*:

The Jews could have made this plea, grounded in the nature of a Covenant, the breach of which (though instituted by God betweene King and People, *Deut.17*) was no dispensation for them to Rebell, as was evidenced formerly . . . So there is a cont[r]act betweene Husband and Wife, the violation of which on the mans part doth not bereave him of his dominion over the woman.[50]

If Jews who above all other people might have had grounds to challenge the contract, still had no warrant to rebel against *their king*, certainly English subjects do not. Marriage is represented as a contract which the husband/monarch may violate with impunity, while retaining dominance over his wife/subject. The abiding nature of this covenant is presented in terms of the Christian definition of marriage, again with reference to Matthew:

As in Marriage, so in Monarchy, there are two parties in the Contract . . . Consent therefore joynd man and Wife, King and People, but divine Ordinance continues this Union; Marriages and Governments both are ratified in heaven . . . Whom God hath joyned let not man put asunder; They must take their King for better for worse.[51]

The subjection of the wife to the husband is therefore authorized by the permanence of marriage. However, Digges does admit that divorce is sometimes allowed, although he ingeniously turns Jewish law to his own advantage:

It is very observable though it was permitted to the man in some cases, to give a bill of divorce, yet this licence was never allowed to women . . . women cannot unmarry, nor the people unsubject themselves.[52]

While the Deuteronomic text (24:1–2) allows the husband to divorce his wife, this law does not articulate the reciprocal right of the wife, standing here for the people, to divorce her husband. However, Digges' use of Jewish law to invalidate divorce as an option for the subject/wife is the exception that proves the rule, since the majority of the political theorists who discuss divorce law understand it as establishing the right to dissolve a marriage by either participant.[53]

The precise nature of this covenantal or contractual relationship between the king and people or husband and wife becomes the focus of the parliamentary debate. In his tract, *The Wounded Conscience Cured*, William Bridge concedes that partial non-performance of a contract does not completely invalidate the agreement, but he nevertheless insists that the people are entitled to redress their wrongs:

for though the Kings of Israell were Monarches, and immediatly designed by God himselfe to their office, and so one would thinke there should be no need of their comming to the crown by a covenant, yet to shew the necessity of this oath and covenant when they came to their Crownes, they also tooke an oath, and entred into covenant with the people to protect their rights and persons, 1 Chro.11.3.[54]

Bridge in effect reverses the Royalist argument by suggesting that even the kings of Israel, who have the best claim to divine installation, still derive their authority by means of a covenant with the people. Here the kings of Israel and, as we shall see, divorce law, serve as a model for, and not a counter-example to, English monarchy. Bridge continues:

the end of [the king's] trust being to looke to the Kingdome, though there be no such words expressed in the covenant or agreement betwixt the King and his people, that in case he shall not discharge his trust, then it shall be lawfull for the State of the Kingdom by armes to resist, and to looke to their owne safety: their safety being the end of this trust, & *ratio legis* being *lex*, in reason that must be implyed . . .[55]

In other words, although there is no explicit clause in the covenant allowing for resistance, this does not preclude taking action if the contract is broken. The analogy to marriage clarifies Bridge's point:

there is a covenant stricken betweene a man and a woman at Marriage; when they marry one another it is not verbally expressed in their agreement, that if one commit Adultery, that party shall be divorced; and yet we know that that covenant of Marriage carries the force of such a condition.[56]

Bridge assumes the dissolution of a marriage when either party commits adultery. In contrast to English ecclesiastical law, he, like Whately, presents divorce as if it were operative for English Christians.

The anonymously published *Jus Populi*, attributed to Henry Parker, does not make explicit mention of divorce, but the assumptions about the contractual nature of marriage and hence its solubility form the foundation of his argument for parity between the parties:

In Matrimony there is something divine (the Papist makes it sacramentall beyond royall inauguration) but is this any ground to infer that there is no humane consent or concurrence in it? does the divine institution of marriage take away freedome of choice before, or conclude either party under an absolute degree of subjection after the solemniziation? . . . And if men, for whose sakes women were created, shall not lay hold upon the divine right of wedlock, to the disadvantage of women: much lesse shall Princes who were created for the peoples sake, chalenge any thing from the sanctity of their offices, that may derogate from the people.[57]

While not arguing for absolute marital equality, Parker's insistence on the validity of women's rights in marriage bolsters his claim for the people's rights. Parker moves directly from speculating about parity in the marital relation to questioning the divine origin of hierarchy:

government it self in the very constitution of it is so farre from being injoyned as divine upon any persons (not before ingaged by their own, or their Ancestors consent) or from being necessitated by any precept, or president in Scripture, that we rather see an instance of the contrary in the story of *Lot* and *Abraham*. Certainly there was in nature some majority or precedence due either from *Lot* to *Abraham*, or from *Abraham* to *Lot*, (for the rules of order are no wayes failing) and yet we see this is no sufficient inforcement to subject either of these Patriarks to the others jurisdiction.[58]

The expected example of Lot and Abraham, taken from Genesis 13, demonstrates that subjection is not divinely commanded. The proximity of these two examples opens up the possibility for questioning the necessity of a husband's, as well as a king's, superiority.

Milton published his *Doctrine and Discipline of Divorce* (1643, 1644) in the midst of this debate over the nature of the relationship between ruler and subject mediated through the institution of marriage. He emphasizes the political significance of the family by reversing the parliamentary analogy that argued the family provided a model for ruler/subject relations, and instead uses the state as a model for the family in order to justify divorce:[59]

> He who marries, intends as little to conspire his own ruine, as he that swears Allegiance: and as a whole people is in proportion to an ill Government, so is one man to an ill marriage. If they against any authority, Covnant, or Statute, may by the soveraign edict of charity, save not only their lives, but honest liberties from unworthy bondage, as well may he against any private Covnant . . . redeem himself from unsupportable disturbances to honest peace, and just contentment.[60]

Marriage establishes the primary bond of the post-Reformation English family,[61] which domestic manuals, political treatises, and ecclesiastical doctrine assert as "the fundamental social institution; . . . order in families was both necessary for and parallel to, order in the state."[62] The family represented an important tool in church and state governance, hence the personal operated as a version of the political. The difference between domestic sphere and governing sphere was imagined as more a quantitative than qualitative one, as one of scope rather than function. However, if this model invests, albeit theoretically, individuals with political importance, it also seeks to place controls over that potential:

> A family is . . . a little common-wealth . . . a schoole wherein the first principles and grounds of government and subjection are learned . . . So we may say of inferiours that cannot be subject in a familie; they will hardly be brought to yeeld such subjection as they ought in Church or common-wealth.[63]

Domination over the members of the family is necessary precisely because of its political status.

If marriage provides the foundation for this institution of social organization, it also provides a context in which the status and function of gender roles could be formulated. Upon marriage, a woman became subservient to her husband while simultaneously assuming authority over other members of the household – servants, and subsequently, children.[64] Because the wife's status, unlike that of children and servants, involved both authority and subjection, her relationship to her husband was not clear-cut. Marriage manuals represented her obedience to her husband as crucial to the smooth running of a godly household. However, the wife was seen as a partner responsible, in conjunction with her husband, for the economic well-being and order of the home.[65] As William Gouge points out: "the wife is by Gods providence appointed a joynt governour with the husband of the familie."[66] While all the authors on the topic insisted upon the wife's inferiority to her husband, they were hard-pressed to represent her subjection as absolute.

This concern with defining the roles of man and woman in marriage can be seen as a result of the Reformation, when the conjugal relationship, and not the sacramental nature of the union, became the basis of the institution. One particularly important model for a more balanced relation between husband and wife was the Puritan notion of marriage as covenant, based on convenantal models in Hebrew Scripture.[67] This idea develops from Genesis 2:18 in which woman is created as a "help meet" for man. "The character of this mutual help is carefully defined in Puritan treatises and sermons on marriage, so that each partner will know what he [or she] must do. The duties of mutual help in marriage are the terms of the covenant entered into by the spouses upon their marital union."[68]

As might be expected, these mutual duties are so defined to give the husband precedence over the wife. However, the implications of the covenantal aspect of this mutuality suggests a more contractual relation based on consent. The idea of covenant modifies patriarchal power in giving authority to both members of the union, whether it be between God and human, ruler and subject, or husband and wife. As one Puritan divine writes, "We must not make Gods covenant with man, so far to differ from Covenants between man and man, as to make it no Covenant at all."[69] If a human is theoretically entitled to break a covenant with God in the (albeit impossible) event of a divine non-performance of duty, how much more justified is a subject or a wife entitled to dissolve her contract with king or husband, who are clearly inferior to God?[70] What are the implications of this thinking for a society which does dissolve its contract with the king?

Susan Amussen links the disorder which marks the period between 1560 and 1640 with swift social and demographic changes, and argues that the family served as an anchor for this troubled culture:

The attempts to control unruly villagers so common in this period suggests a growing inability to control disorder within the normal local channels. Here the analogy between family and state was particularly useful. As we have seen, although the gender order was challenged, that challenge was never explicit or direct. Women did not ask to govern, claim equality with their husbands or declare the family an irrelevant institution. Challenges to the class order were far more direct. People asserted their social and moral equality with "superiors," they criticized and insulted the local governors and they refused to accept existing hierarchies. Because of the ideological relationship between family and state, the control of gender disorder symbolically affirmed all social order.[71]

However, if the challenges to the family and gender hierarchy were less powerful than those posed to the social hierarchy, they were nevertheless significant. David Underdown argues that "there really was a period of strained gender relations in early modern England, and . . . it lay at the heart of the 'crisis of order.'"[72] In the pamphlet wars of the sixteenth and seventeenth centuries, women responded to, and defended themselves from, misogynist attacks; if they did not completely break away from the gender hierarchy, they nevertheless drew attention to the injustices they suffered under the system.[73] The radical religious sects that flourished in the seventeenth century rejected many social, sexual, and gender systems.[74] The women who petitioned for release of four Leveller leaders in the late 1640s and early 1650s demonstrated impressive political organization and courage – and a selective disregard of expectations for female behavior:

Despite the obligatory curtsy to custom and convention in the protestations of the inferiority with which the women prefaced their petitions, when it came to explaining their actions the women forgot their modesty and came out with bold arguments to justify their activities. They drew on the Bible and secular history for support . . . and [used] arguments which implied equality of the sexes . . .[75]

The violence of the condemnations of these women bears witness to the strength of the challenge they posed to the status quo.

The relation between the family and the state would seem to be symbiotic, both in reinforcing the status quo and in undermining it. While the family served as a hedge against change, it also was influenced by the political ferment of the period. Shanley argues that the use of marriage as a model for political relations changed assumptions about its contractual nature: "if marriage were a 'contractual' relationship, the terms of the contract as well as entry into the relationship were negotiable."[76] Amussen suggests that "discussions of the state and marriage in royalist and parliamentarian pamphlets had a broad social impact," given the widespread political involvement of all classes and their access to political writings.[77] In fact, we find traces of these challenges articulated in glimpses of women's lives in the period. The radical Baptist preacher Mrs. Attaway cited Milton's *Doctrine and Discipline of Divorce* in justifying her decision to leave one husband and marry another,[78] as Thomas Edwards records with distaste in *The Second Part of Gangræna*:

> Mistris *Attaway* the Lace-woman . . . spake . . . of Master *Miltons* Doctrine of Divorce, . . . saying, it was a point to be considered of; and that she for her part would look more into it, for she had an unsanctified husband . . . and how accordingly she hath practiced it in running away with another womans husband, is now sufficiently known.[79]

In this instance, the wife's ability to leave one husband and choose another marks not the exchange of one subjection for another, but her capacity to act autonomously. The issue of a wife's subordination to her husband is challenged in a 1640 debt suit in the Court of Exchequer which in passing notes, and rejects, her attempt to maintain parity with him when she entered into marriage:

> [A wife] (as good authors warrant) is bound to follow her husband, although she be never so right or honourable, and he a vagabond; and if she cannot vow to bind him, much less can she sue him: and a covenant betwixt baron & feme before marriage, that she shall not be subject to him, is void, and contrary to the law of God and nature, and publick honesty.[80]

A more systematic sampling of both ecclesiastical and common law court records is necessary before any assessment can be made about the extent and nature of such opposition to the status quo, but these examples demonstrate that political and ideological debates of the period made themselves felt in the lives of early modern men and women.

If the groundwork for divorce was already laid in Hebrew Scripture and Puritan marriage manuals, and if the logic of divorce was carried out on the national level in the deposition and execution of Charles I, why did domestic divorce fail to follow, especially given the political link between family and state? While the notion of a divorce between subject and ruler had been politically expedient, ultimately the dissolution of a contract between husband and wife was not. Domestic divorce would have provided a means by which a wife could "unsubject" herself from her husband. Concomitant with this reclaiming of power over her person would come the reclaiming of whatever property or assets she brought into the marriage, and control over current earning power, since many women participated in a household economy.[81] If I differ with Amussen in weighing more heavily the threat posed by changes to the gender hierarchy, I agree with her assessment that the family was understood as crucial in establishing the larger social order. Given its importance during a turbulent time, its structure could not be significantly altered and still serve as a stabilizing institution. However, its own permeability in times of crisis exposed it as an imperfect means of controlling the social order. If the family was invested with political importance in order to combat other crises of the day, the political nature of the family made it potentially challenging to the status quo when its own structure threatened to change. Once the political crisis of the civil war subsided, the family was demoted from its position of political efficacy, and threats to the gender order lost their larger social power and significance:

> as the family became a less important part of local government and discipline, women's role in family government lost its public significance . . . The relative absence of conflict about both class and gender after the Restoration rested on this increasing distance between women and men, rich and poor; distance simultaneously made the elite more secure and deprived those they ruled of the proximity – social and economic – necessary for effective challenges.[82]

What kind of challenge did the radical implications of divorce pose if they were not made officially available? Raymond Williams' discussion of challenges to the ruling order suggests a possible answer to this question:

> alternative political and cultural emphases, and the many forms of opposition and struggle, are important not only in themselves, but as indicative features of what the hegemonic process has in practice had to work to control . . . It would be wrong to overlook the importance of works and ideals which, while clearly affected by hegemonic limits and pressures, are at least in part significant breaks beyond them, which may again in part be neutralized, reduced or incorporated, but which in their most active elements nevertheless come through as independent and original.[83]

The extent to which the contractual nature of divorce is incorporated into political theory is an indication of its power; its rejection in the area of gender rleations is a measure of its threat:

> it is a fact about the modes of domination, that they select from and consequently exclude the full range of human practice. What they exclude may often be seen as the personal or the private, or as the natural or even the metaphysical. Indeed it is usually in one or other of these terms that the excluded area is expressed, since what the dominant has effectively seized is indeed the ruling definition of the social.[84]

The privatization of the family that occurs after the Restoration serves simultaneously to limit the influence of challenges to the gender order in the social order, and to unhook the dependency of the social order on the family as a source of either stability or change.

This essay has demonstrated a link between divorce law, rooted in Jewish law, and the possibility for female agency in the early modern period. While liberal feminist critiques of the status of women in the early modern period have tended to link women's subjection to a biblical, which is to say, Hebraic, patriarchal system, I have shown that Jewish law does not bear a causal relation to gender hierarchy, but can serve the interests of those seeking to challenge that dominance.[85] If this challenge was not immediately successful, it was nevertheless significant in encouraging female agency and equality.

NOTES

I would like to thank Barbara Harris and the participants of her Fall 1993 Folger Institute seminar on "Women, Politics and Political Thought in Tudor and Stuart England" for helping to lay the foundations of this essay. I am also grateful to the Folger Institute and the English Department of Georgetown University for funding a course release which greatly enabled my participation in the seminar. Thanks to Jeffrey Shoulson and Robert Viscusi for providing the impetus to produce earlier versions of this essay. I am particularly indebted to the friends and colleagues whose insight and encouragement at various stages of this project proved invaluable: Dympna Callaghan, Michael Ragussis, Amy Robinson, Jason Rosenblatt, and Valerie Traub.

1 John Witte, Jr. "The Transformation of Marriage Law in the Lutheran Reformation," in *The Weightier Matters of the Law: Essays on Law and Religion*, J. Witte, Jr. and F. Alexander, eds. (Atlanta, GA: Scholars Press, 1988), pp. 57–97, see pp. 62, 65. Thanks to Josh Mitchell for this reference.

2 Witte discusses the range of absolute (diriment) impediments which invalidated a marriage, including prior vows of celibacy, contracts with non-Christians, and incest (*ibid.*, pp. 66–67).

3 *Ibid.*, pp. 88–89.

4 *Ibid.*, pp. 71–72.

5 All citations of the Bible are from the King James Version.

6 Witte, "Transformation of Marriage Law," p. 90, esp. note 102.

7 However, this major shift was effected through a reinterpretation – not a direct rejection – of Jesus' teachings, and reformers drew on Roman and early canon law, in addition to Hebrew Scripture, in delineating grounds for divorce (*ibid.*, pp. 90–91).

8 In effect, a conflict over the status of marriage and divorce helped bring about what Cecil Roth described as the rehabilitation of "Hebrew literature from the general discredit which it had suffered in Europe since the rise of Christianity," *A History of the Jews in England*, 3rd edn (Oxford: Oxford University Press, 1989), p. 146. For a more detailed discussion of Henry

VIII's consultations with the Italian Jewish community, see David Katz, *Jews in the History of England* (Oxford: Oxford University Press, 1994), pp. 15–48.

9 Jason Rosenblatt, "Aspects of the Incest Problem in *Hamlet*," *Shakespeare Quarterly* 29 (1978): 349–64, see notes in pages 353–60 *passim*.

10 John Weemse, *Explication of the Judiciall Lawes of Moses* (London, 1632), p. 3.

11 Heinrich Bullinger, *The Christen State of Matrimonye* (1541, rpt. Amsterdam: Theatrum Orbis Terrarum, 1974).

12 Bullinger, *The Christen State*, (pp. lxvi recto, lxvii recto). 1 Corinthians 7:15 does allow for separation from a non-Christian spouse, and suggests the marriage is dissolved, but does not speak of adultery: "if the unbelieving depart, let him depart. A brother or sister is not under bondage in such cases." This verse is used to justify separation in cases of malicious desertion; see Jonathan R. Ziskind, *John Selden on Jewish Marriage Law: The Uxor Hebraica* (Leiden, New York, Copenhagen, and Cologne: E. J. Brill, 1991), p. 24. Note that only the unbeliever can chose to separate from the spouse, the Christian is commanded to remain married (1 Corinthians 7:12–14, 16). Also, it is not clear that remarriage is allowed here, since 1 Corinthians 7:10–11 states that "Let not the wife depart from her husband. But and if she depart, let her remain unmarried."

13 Bullinger, *The Christen State*, p. lxxvi verso.

14 John Milton, *Complete Prose Works*, Don M. Wolfe, general ed., 8 vols. (New Haven: Yale University Press, 1959), vol. ii, pp. 217–356.

15 Jason Rosenblatt has argued in a meticulous and persuasive essay, "Milton's Chief Rabbi," *Milton Studies* 23 (1988): 43–71, that *The Doctrine and Discipline of Divorce* is "the most Hebraic of Milton's prose works" (47). What distinguishes Milton's tracts from those previously discussed is not only that he attempts to reconcile the apparently contradicting texts in Hebrew and Christian Scripture, but, as Rosenblatt demonstrates, he does so with recourse to rabbinic learning (60–61). For an extended consideration of Milton's engagement with Jewish law, see Rosenblatt's *Torah and Law in "Paradise Lost"* (Princeton: Princeton University Press, 1994).

16 Milton, *Complete Prose Works*, vol. ii, pp. 229–31.

17 Quoted in Rosenblatt, "Milton's Chief Rabbi," 58.

18 See *ibid.*, 57–66 *passim*.

19 Ziskind, *John Selden on Jewish Marriage Law*, pp. 19, 22.

20 In this text, as in his other Jewish works, Selden is concerned to show that in most cases, both sacred and secular disputes fall under the jurisdiction of the Jewish secular court, a point which supported his own position that ecclesiastical law in England should be subordinate to the state.

21 Lawrence Stone, *Road to Divorce: England 1530–1987* (Oxford: Oxford University Press, 1990), p. 7.

22 Although actual divorce and remarriage were not officially sanctioned, they existed in a *de facto* form. In his book, *The Family in the English Revolution* (Oxford: Blackwell, 1989), Christopher Durston notes that it "remained virtually impossible to prevent desertion and informal separation" in spite of

the fact that no formal divorce regulations were passed (p. 98). Susan Amussen suggests in *An Ordered Society: Gender and Class in Early Modern England* (Oxford: Blackwell, 1988), that the ecclesiastical separation without possibility of remarriage could nevertheless function as full divorce: "Though remarriage after a separation was officially impossible, the only ecclesiastical penalty was the forfeit of a bond, which became a fine on those who offended" (p. 57). This bond, set at one hundred pounds, was stipulated in the canons enacted by Convocation in 1603–04. Stone remarks that the rule "was ambiguous, since the canon did not explicitly say that such a remarriage was either invalid or adulterous," although these second marriages would probably not hold up in law (*Road*, p. 305). Bigamy was made a felony by 1603 act of Parliament, but it permitted benefit of clergy, so men could avoid hanging (women, however, were not allowed into the clergy and could therefore not claim this benefit). Additionally, this act contained a clause exempting those who were "divorced [i.e. judicially separated] by sentence of the ecclesiastical court," which substantially weakened the power of the law (Stone, *Road*, p. 306). Stone concludes "that despite the tightening of the official legal screws in 1597–1603, the practice of remarriage by a husband after a judicial separation for a wife's adultery still occurred occasionally – or possibly frequently – in the first half of the seventeenth century, with the cautious blessing of at least a few highly respected church dignitaries and theologians" (*Road*, p. 308). Nevertheless, these points should not obscure the fact that at no time before 1857 were divorce and remarriage officially and explicitly sanctioned by law.

23 Chilton Latham Powell, *English Domestic Relations, 1487–1653*, 2nd edn (New York: Atheneum, 1972), p. 63; Stone, *Road*, pp. 301–03.
24 Powell, *ibid.*, p. 61. Of course, a civil code was eventually established in 1857 (Stone, *Road*, pp. 15–16), but England's ecclesiastical resistance to divorce continues to make itself felt in the twentieth century with Edward VIII's abdication of the throne in order to marry divorcée Wallis Simpson, and speculations about Prince Charles' chances of reigning if he wanted to remarry in the light of a possible divorce from his estranged wife.
25 Powell, *ibid.*, 99; Stone, *Road*, pp. 301–8.
26 John Hooper, *A Declaration of the X Holye Commaundements* (n.p., 1548), pp. clxiii–clxvi.
27 Powell, *English Domestic Relations*, p. 80.
28 William Perkins, *Christian Oeconomie*. trans. Thomas Pickering (London, 1609), p. 120.
29 Quoted in Powell, *English Domestic Relations*, p. 82.
30 William Whately, *A Bride-Bush or Wedding Sermon* (London, 1617), pp. 2–4.
31 *Ibid.*, p. 5.
32 William Gouge, *Of Domesticall Dvties* (London, 1622), p. 215.
33 *Ibid.*, pp. 215–16.
34 *Ibid.*, p. 218.
35 *Ibid.*, p. 219.

36 Ziskind, *John Selden on Jewish Marriage Law*, p. 13.
37 Reprinted in Milton, *Prose Works*, vol. II, p. 220.
38 *Ibid.*, pp. 229–30.
39 Cecil Roth describes Fagius as "the famous German Protestant divine and humanist . . . appointed [in 1549] to the chair of Hebrew at Cambridge – the first more or less competent scholar to occupy such a position in England" (*History of the Jews*, p. 146).
40 Milton, *Prose Works*, vol. II, p. 242.
41 *Ibid.*, pp. 245–46.
42 There is some dispute over whether Milton intended that men and women should have equal access to divorce; see Powell, *English Domestic Relations*, p. 96, and Durston, *The Family*, p. 19. Also, I am not suggesting here that Milton was arguing for sexual equality; see *Paradise Lost* book IV, lines 288–311 for his representation of a hierarchical relation between wife and husband.
43 Ziskind, *John Selden on Jewish Marriage Law*, pp. 22, 13.
44 Durston, *The Family*, p. 98.
45 The Noachide laws, which establish the legal status of non-Jews, are derived by the rabbis of the Talmud from Genesis 2:16 (Ziskind, *John Selden on Jewish Marriage Law*, pp. 33, 12).
46 *Ibid.*, p. 508.
47 Mary Lyndon Shanley, "Marriage Contract and Social Contract in Seventeenth-Century English Political Thought," in *The Family and Political Thought*, Jean Bethke Elshtain, ed. (Amherst: University of Massachusetts Press, 1982), pp. 80–95; see p. 81.
48 Henry Ferne, *Conscience Satisfied. That there is no Warrant for the Armes now taken up by Subjects* (Oxford?, 1643), p. 12. There is some question about the provenance and date of this pamphlet which seems to have been published in London, not Oxford, and certainly circulated in some earlier edition or manuscript, since William Bridge's answer to Ferne is published in 1642.
49 Shanley, "Marriage Contract," p. 83.
50 Dudley Digges, *The Unlawfulness of Subjects Taking up Armes against their Soveraigne, in what case soever* (London, 1647), p. 111–12.
51 *Ibid.*, p. 113.
52 *Ibid.*, pp. 113–114.
53 It should be noted that the Deuteronomic law was often interpreted by Christian reformers as applying equally to husband and wife, in contradistinction to Jewish practice. Although the biblical text does not explicitly prohibit wives from presenting a *get*, or bill of divorce, to her husband, it describes the divorce transaction only in terms of the husband's capacity to effect it: "When a man hath taken a wife and married her, and it come to pass that she find no favor in his eyes, because he hath found some uncleanness in her; then let him write her a bill of divorcement and give it in her hand and send her out of his house" (Deut. 24:1). The rabbinic interpretation that a woman cannot give her husband a divorce (although in some

cases she can force him to give her a *get*) remains part of Orthodox Jewish practice up to this day, despite the fact that this causes terrible hardship for women. For a discussion of possible strategies permitted by *halachah* (Jewish law) for remedying this problem, see Rabbi Eliezer Berkovits' (z''l) *Jewish Women in Torah and Time* (Hoboken, NJ: Ktav, 1990), pp. 100–27. Berkovits condemns the contemporary unwillingness in the Orthodox community to redress this injustice, which he sees as running counter to a tradition of *halachic* innovation to improve the status of women.

54 William Bridge, *The Wounded Conscience Cured, the Weak One Strengthened, and the Doubting Satisfied. By way of Answer to Doctor Fearne* (London, 1642), p. 29.

55 *Ibid.*, p. 31.

56 *Ibid.*

57 Anonymous, *Jus Populi. Or, a Discourse Wherein Clear Satisfaction is Given, as well Concerning the Right of Subjects, as the Right of Princes* (London, 1644), pp. 4–5.

58 *Ibid.*, p. 5.

59 Shanley, "Marriage Contract," p. 87.

60 Milton, *Prose Works*, vol. II, p. 229.

61 By primary, I mean first or founding relation, not necessarily the most important, and certainly not the only household connection. While this essay focuses on the heterosexual wife–husband relation, I nevertheless want to point out that a variety of relationships – filial, homoerotic, amicable – based on power, affect, and/or physical attraction exist within a given household.

62 Amussen, *An Ordered Society*, p. 35. This view of marriage as a political and social entity is also advocated by the German reformers (Witte, "Transformation of Marriage Law," pp. 58–59).

63 Gouge, *Domesticall Duties*, p. 18.

64 Since contemporary discussions of the family assume it takes the shape of a household, I follow their lead in focusing my comments on the middle classes and gentry who could afford to employ servants.

65 Amussen, *An Ordered Society*, pp. 41–42.

66 Gouge, *Domesticall Duties*, p. 253.

67 Of course, Catholic doctrine also conceptualized marriage as, initially, a contract; however, once it was properly validated and consummated, it was irrevocable and could not be broken for non-performance. Hence, there is no emphasis on the contractual expectations of wives' and husbands' roles after the establishment of a marriage.

68 James Johnson, "The Covenant Idea and the Puritan View of Marriage," *Journal of the History of Ideas* 32.1 (1971): 107–18, see 108.

69 Quoted in *ibid.*, 115.

70 *Ibid.*, 116. In *The Sexual Contract*, (Stanford: Stanford University Press, 1988) Carol Pateman argues that any contract presupposes an uneven balance of power between the two contracting parties. While I grant this point, particularly as regards early modern marriage, I would counter that the option to dissolve the contract provided women, even if only theoretically, with more leverage than they had previously experienced in marriage.

71 Amussen, *An Ordered Society*, p. 182.
72 David Underdown, "The Taming of the Scold: The Enforcement of Patriarchal Authority in Early Modern England," in *Order and Disorder in Early Modern England*, Anthony Fletcher and John Stevenson, eds. (Cambridge: Cambridge University Press, 1985), pp. 116–36, see p. 136.
73 Katherine Usher Henderson and Barbara F. McManus, *Half Humankind: Texts and Contexts of the Controversy about Women in England, 1540–1640* (Urbana and Chicago: University of Illinois Press, 1985), pp. 24–31.
74 See Phyllis Mack, "Women as Prophets during the English Civil War," *Feminist Studies* 8.1 (Spring 1982): 19–45; Keith Thomas, "Women and the Civil War Sects," in *Crisis in Europe*, Trevor Aston, ed. (London: Routledge, 1965), pp. 317–40; and Christopher Hill, *The World Turned Upside Down: Radical Ideas during the English Revolution* (New York: Viking, 1973), pp. 246–60.
75 Patricia Higgins, "The Reactions of Women, with Special Reference to Women Petitioners," in *Politics, Religion and the English Civil War*, Brian Manning, ed. (London: Edward Arnold, 1973), pp. 177–222; see pp. 214–15.
76 Shanley, "Marriage Contract," p. 81. However, Shanley believes that the arguments of the 1640s played a limited role in moving toward a transformation of the idea of matrimony:

> Parliamentarian and republican writers were forced by these arguments to debate the royalist conception of marriage as well as of kingship. They gradually extended their individualistic premises into the depiction of domestic order. The parliamentarian discussions, however, were beset by various inconsistencies. It was John Locke who, more clearly than his predecessors, saw the implications of contractarian ideas for marriage, and who attempted to solve several of the dilemmas that had beset earlier attempts to compare the marriage bond to the social contract. (p.81)

In focusing exclusively on political treatises, she ignores the evidence of the marriage manuals, some of which do articulate a strong endorsement for parity in divorce. Shanley also supports uncritically the long-term "benefits" of Locke's thinking, which she sees as forming the basis "for liberal arguments about female equality and marriage" (p. 81). Pateman argues that Locke's notion of a compact between husband and wife assumes "a natural foundation for the wife's subjection" (*Sexual Contract*, p. 93); she calls into question a feminism founded in liberal contract theory. While Pateman might also reject my use of divorce as a means of improving the status of the woman in allowing her to dissolve a contract, I concur with her rejection of Locke's contract theory and its implicit power imbalance.
77 Amussen, *An Ordered Society*, p. 61.
78 For more information on Mrs. Attaway, see Richard L. Greaves and Robert Zaller, eds., *Biographical Dictionary of British Radicals in the Seventeenth Century* (Brighton: Harvester, 1982); thanks to Lois Schwoerer for directing me to this source.

79 Thomas Edwards, *The Second Part of Gangræna: Or A Fresh and further Discovery of the Errors, Heresies, Blasphemies, and dangerous Procedings of the Sectarie of this time* (London, 1646), pp. 10–11.

80 *English Reports*, Max A. Robertson and Geoffrey Ellis, eds. (Edinburgh: William Green, 1907), vol. LXXXIII, p. 1065.

81 Stone cites two forces inhibiting divorce reform: anxieties about renewing revolutionary conflict, which occur in 1688 after the establishment of the constitution, and after the French Revolution; and the near sanctification of property rights and male primogeniture (*Road*, p. 350). For an analysis of the ways in which legal devices served to prevent heiresses and widows from obtaining property owed them under common law, see Eileen Spring, *Law, Land, and Family* (Chapel Hill: University of North Carolina Press, 1993).

82 Amussen, *An Ordered Society*, p. 187.

83 Raymond Williams, *Marxism and Literature* (Oxford: Oxford University Press, 1977), pp. 113–14.

84 *Ibid.*, p. 125.

85 For a nuanced and persuasive examination of gender relations in "patriarchal" thinking, see Margaret J. Ezell's *The Patriarch's Wife: Literary Evidence and the History of the Family* (Chapel Hill: University North Carolina Press, 1987). As noted earlier, Shanley locates an emerging feminism not in the divorce debates of the 1640s, but in Locke's contract theory of the 1690s, which she characterizes as rejecting biblical authority:

> This shift to social-contract theory occurred as arguments from natural law began to replace those based on scripture. Scripture had been adequate to prove that God had intended subjects to be subordinate to the prince and wives to be subject to their husbands, but it was not necessary to demonstrate that both kinds of authority were based on free consent. ("Marriage Contract," p. 88)

It is not clear that these points cannot be made with response to Scripture; John Selden, for instance, bases his formulation of natural law on rabbinic interpretation of Genesis (Ziskind, *John Selden on Jewish Marriage Law*, pp. 10–12). Shanley ignores the disturbing implications of Locke's argument that the family was not a political institution (Amussen, *An Ordered Society*, p. 186). The period of inaction on divorce (1660–1850) is concomitant with that of the decreasing power of women as the domestic sphere becomes private and depoliticized.

CHAPTER 11

"Where there can be no cause of affection": redefining virgins, their desires, and their pleasures in John Lyly's Gallathea

Theodora A. Jankowski

Your chast harts my Nimphes, should resemble the Onix, which is hotest when it is whitest, and your thoughts, the more they are assaulted with desires, the lesse they should be affected.[1]

Diana's admonition to her nymphs is not surprising. The goddess' construction as an exemplar of virginity within Greco-Roman mythology (as transmitted to sixteenth-century England) – as well as her location within a play by John Lyly – makes such a response predictable.[2] But the particular definition of virginity, as well as its validation, evident in Diana's speech goes beyond a literary convention. *Gallathea* (1592) is *about* virginity in a way that only works designed to flatter Elizabeth I could be "about" virginity.[3] Yet even though the virgins in this play, as well as Diana herself, flatter the queen of England merely through their intact bodily condition,[4] they represent a decidedly problematical concept of virginity. After all, the play presents a virgin sacrifice – meant to save a society – that is subverted by members of the society expected to be saved by it. And the play ends with the most important human virgins seemingly about to be incorporated into the sexual economy as a result of marriage. If this play is meant either to validate virginity or flatter the Virgin Queen, it is a decidedly curious construct. One thing I would like to argue in this essay is that the condition of virginity, especially during Elizabeth I's reign, could not be anything but a "curious construct."

Virginity plays a vexed role in the patriarchal society of (Protestant) early modern England. Without this necessary premarital condition, young women cannot be married nor – more importantly – can their fathers achieve the (socially and economically) desirable alliances that result from marriage. In this context, then, virginity can be constructed as simply a (biological) condition that all young women should possess to allow them to be successfully married and thus fully incorporated into the sex/gender system[5] of their society. Virginity here is simply a "means" toward an "end" of social integration and conformity. Without virginity, a woman cannot become, or be considered, a legitimate member of society. Therefore, a woman who loses her virginity *before* marriage – and thus renders herself incapable of marriage – becomes a social pariah as well as an economic liability. She is liable to social containment through redefinition as an impure, used, violated, imperfect being whether or not she was a willing participant in the means of her own despoilation. Given the importance of virginity for the functioning of patriarchal society – which would cease without the economic and social connections forged by marriages[6] – virginity gains an almost fetishistic importance in and of itself. The pure, intact, perfect woman marks the perfection of society and her own exemplary place within it. Paradoxically, however, as Hastrup has demonstrated, the virgin cannot retain her fetishistic position as the object of all desire because "a female is not fully specified as a woman until she has been sexually associated with a man. At one level it is the man who spoils the purity of the virgin, but at another level it is only through intercourse with a man that a woman becomes wholly a woman, and thus enters into the pure female category."[7] In order to continue to maintain her importance to her society, the virgin's intact body must be "violated"/sacrificed to assure, and validate, the social/cultural/economic/(political) connections that patriarchal early modern marriage was about. Consequently, this socially-mandated virginity carries within it the seeds of its own destruction. The virgin remains so only *for* a man's/men's needs. Her virginity is *proved* by her husband in the (quasi-)ritual defloration of the wedding night. Paradoxically, though, it is at the point at which proof of virginity is obtained – the rupturing and bleeding of the hymen – that the virgin ceases to exist. A husband does not need a wife to *remain* virgin, only to *be* virgin until proof of that (now non-existent) virginity is accomplished.

The above "narrative" of virginity represents the early modern social construction of the virginal estate.[8] Female virginity was required to ensure the legitimacy of heirs to a male bloodline essential for the reproduction of patriarchal society. Virgins who lived this narrative were valued and assured a place of respect within their society. But what of those virgins whose lives did not replicate their society's trajectory of the ideal virginal existence? Those who were – or allowed themselves to be – sexually violated before marriage were easily reconstructed as social pariahs, actual or metaphorical "whores." *Measure for Measure*'s Juliet, whose visible pregnancy marks her body as non-virginal, clearly shows how a woman could be rendered "whore." Despite the fact that her sexual encounters only involved Claudio, her betrothed, she is equally condemned to death with him although her sin is considered to be "of heavier kind than his."[9] That many contrive to save Claudio's life – but not Juliet's – further locates her outside "polite" society. Similarly, when the Duke tries to determine Mariana's estate, he is forced to conclude she is "nothing then, neither maid, widow, nor wife?" (v.i.183–84). Lucio's "helpful" definition – "she may be a punk, for many of them are neither maid, widow, nor wife" (185–186) – definitely makes the connection that even one sexual experience can shift a woman from the category of "virgin" to "whore."[10] That this play is "peopled" by so many absent, but necessarily obvious, prostitutes serves to drive home the connection still further. The various women in *Measure for Measure* can be seen as deviant "exemplars" of the impure woman upon whose tainted body society could not be built, or as the actual bodies upon which men created (and enjoyed) the concept of "whore."

There was, however, another way in which women could violate early modern society's narrative of virginity: they could refuse marriage *and* the kind of contaminating sexuality that would render them whores. For these women, virginity became the "end" rather than the "means" of their lives, so that their virgin condition marked them, paradoxically, as "deviant." It is more difficult to understand how this sort of deviance was constructed by early modern society, or represented in literary texts of the period. In some cases – such as Moll Cutpurse in *The Roaring Girl* – "deviant" virgins were simply demonized as whores. While the text indicates that Moll is a virgin, her refusal to marry, coupled with her transgressive dress and masculine pastimes, causes virtually all the male characters to regard her as sexually loose. While Moll is an extreme example of such sexual demonization, some Shakespearean virgins are marked as sexually deviant because they either refuse to marry at all – Beatrice; refuse to marry the men their fathers wish them to – Hermia, Desdemona; or use their speech in transgressive ways – Katharine, Isabella. In other cases, the powerfully iconic virginity of Elizabeth I may have diluted the taint inherent in the unusual behavior of such virgins as Helena (*All's Well that Ends Well*), Portia, and Marina.

What increases the difficulty of understanding literary representations of non-marrying virgins is their position relative to desire or pleasure. The virgin's bodily integrity is reinforced by a similar "spiritual" integrity, a purity of thought as well as deed, which suggests that she herself is neither desired nor desiring. Not only does she neither take pleasure not give it, but she appears to be removed from any economy of pleasure. Only when she is "loved" by a potential husband can the virgin be considered as a potential wife, a woman who is allowed the experience of desire and pleasure, though in very circumscribed ways. Even as a bride-to-be, the virgin remains the "object" of the husband-to-be's desire. While she may ultimately experience the wifely pleasures her husband grants her, at no time in her premarital state is she ever allowed the autonomy of being a desiring subject. The virgin is expected to be the object of desire or pleasure, never the subject actively engaged in desiring an other or obtaining pleasure for herself and/or another.

Given the relative complexity of the non-marrying virgin, it was not surprising that there were no "rules" for dealing with those women who chose virginity as an "end." It is difficult to determine how patriarchal society either constructed them or tried to write them into society. One can argue, simply, that they were always considered to be "outside" society in some intrinsic way. The question remains, however, as to whether these virgins existed "outside" society in a demonized realm of the "anomalous" or the "deviant" – and served the patriarchy as important examples of improper behavior – or whether they existed outside society in some separatist context, creating a "world" that existed somewhat in opposition to the "real" one, but, of necessity, touched and influenced by it. If these "deviant" virgins created some sort of separatist enclave/condition, how did it differ from the patriarchal society it was connected to? Or, to ask the question another way, how did the behavior of virgins in *this* world differ from the accepted behavior of virgins in the "real world"? By asking these questions, I am proposing to open a space for consideration of virginal behavior that is *not* patriarchally determined. I would like to look at what characterizes such behavior, and why it might not be acceptable within "real" society. Most importantly, I want to consider how such a restricted world might provide a space whereby virginal women could construct desire/pleasure in ways totally different from – and in opposition to – the patriarchal sexual economy.

John Lyly's oddly constructed paean to virginity, *Gallathea*, provides an interesting place to examine both the implications of virginal desire and the limitiations of patriarchal control over women. Ironically, the fathers' desire to control their daughters' destinies frees the virgins Gallathea and Phillida to explore not only the possibilities of a woman-only society, but of an economy of desire that is similarly woman-centered. In this play, the inhabitants of a certain pastoral region[11] must present "the fairest and chastest virgine" (1.i.42–43) to the monster Agar every five years or Neptune will destroy the country with floods. It is not known whether the sacrifice is killed, eaten, or raped by the Agar, or transported to Neptune for either rape or death. However, the potential for a hideous end for the sacrifice is strong enough for Tyterus and Melebeus, fathers of fair, chaste daughters, to protect their children by disguising them as boys.

The virgin sacrifice acts as a bond between human society and divine agency in the same way as a marriage acts as a bond between two families. As Lévi-Strauss has indicated,[12] the woman's/(virgin's) body is the means by which an economic/social contract is forged between two men (families). Similarly, the body of the sacrificial virgin acts, in Lyly's play, to forge a contract/alliance between men and gods that can be read as a metaphor of marriage. The normal virgin is "rewarded" for keeping her virginity with marriage; Lyly's virgin sacrifice is "rewarded" by saving her society from destruction. Virginity thus is reinforced as a means to an end, never as an end in itself. In either case, patriarchal society can only continue if marriages/sacrifices occur, and they can occur if men/(gods) negotiate them over virgin's bodies. But rather than blatantly announcing that the role of the virgin in patriarchal society is simply that of bargaining chip in a contractual arrangement, early modern English society masks the virgin's role with a love narrative in which her primary gift to her beloved/betrothed is her bodily integrity. The bride's well-preserved and extremely fetishized virginity allows her a valorized position within her society which is ceremonially reinforced by both her marriage and its consummation.[13] A similar valorization of the virgin sacrifice occurs in Lyly's play, for Gallathea argues that her disguise leads to dishonor rather than to the triumphant virtue that sacrifice would (1.i.69–83). Yet despite the importance of the virgin sacrifice for the continuance of society in *Gallathea*, no one seems to realize that Tyterus and Melebeus have secreted their daughters until the Agar refuses Haebe, the (less beautiful) sacrificial virgin presented to it. If Haebe, like the ideal early modern English woman, has preserved her virginity, she *should* be rewarded in the appropriate socially-determined way for this accomplishment. If social salvation through sacrifice replaces marriage in Haebe's society, then her nomination as sacrifice *should* be accepted. She *should* become the exemplar of her society's fetishized virginity. But she does not. Her virgin condition is suddenly made subservient to her beauty and she is refused. Why?

This is a difficult question to answer absolutely, but I would like to suggest a couple of possible responses. Both involve consideration of the most important member of this play's first audience, Elizabeth I. If *Gallathea* was written to flatter, as well as amuse, the Virgin Queen, its ability to do so would be curtailed if a virgin's only destiny were shown to be death. Thus the Agar's refusal to accept Haebe not only saves the character's life, but flatters Elizabeth by demonstrating that, although there may be *many* virgins, only one is special (or beautiful) enough to be the Virgin Queen. That Haebe is willing to accept the *honor* of patriotic sacrifice – even if she feels personally unworthy (v.ii.8–55) – also flatters Elizabeth by validating the personal sacrifices – youth, marriage, children – this ageing virgin has undergone for her country.[14] The failure of Haebe's sacrifice might also represent a "miracle" not necessarily caused by her lack of beauty: the Agar may have been kept away from his virgin by the powerful/magical presence of Elizabeth I in the audience. In fact, the failure of this particular sacrifice leads ultimately, with Diana and Venus' intervention, to the disbanding of the virgin sacrifice as a means of tribute to Neptune. Thus Haebe could be viewed as a saviour of her country for *stopping* the sacrifice, and not as a destroyer of her country for failing to be accepted. But the actual reason for the sacrifice's failure is less important than the results of the failure: one particular form of patriarchal oppression is stopped forever. Virgins' bodies are no longer to be used to forge alliances between men and gods.

The bizarre situation of the virgin sacrifice also serves to point out a major contradiction intrinsic to patriarchy. If individual fathers exercise their rightful power over individual daughters, they can put their entire society at risk, as the society of *Gallathea* is so placed when the sacrifice is refused. By exercising one sort of patriarchal control over their daughters, Tyterus and Melebeus paradoxically free them from another sort of patriarchal control. Thus freed, the daughters are able to experience the world of Diana and her nymphs, a woman-only "corrective" to the early modern sexual economy. While part of the pastoral world the entire play is situated in, Diana's "sweete troope" (1.ii.12) constitutes an essentially separate "society" of virgins. This vision of Diana and her nymphs certainly derives from the Greco-Roman mythological tradition which constructs Diana as a woman-oriented virgin goddess whose effect on men (like Acteon) was both legendary and deadly.[15] She lived and hunted isolated from men with a community of women followers. Although the potential for female–female eroticism certainly exists within such all-women communities,[16] Lyly's play focuses on the loyal and friendly, rather than the erotic, aspects of such a society. Thus while Gallathea

and Phillida cannot actually "belong" to Diana's society because of their
perceived "male" natures (disguise), their actual femaleness and virginity
– coupled with their desire to avoid sacrifice (marriage) – indicate that
they do "belong." Indeed, they become incorporated into the society to
some degree as a result of the nymphs falling in love with them. By act III,
scene i, Eurota and Ramia are infatuated with Gallathea(Tyterus) and
Telusa with Phillida(Melebeus).[17] The cause of the nymphs' lovesickness
is Cupid who, in an attempt to get the nymphs to forsake virginity and
embrace love, has disguised himself as "a sillie girle" (II.ii.1). Interestingly, and despite the effects of the "female" to male cross-dressing in this
play, Cupid's male to "female" cross-dressing does not result in his
becoming an object of affection. His disguise *provokes* love, but not of
himself (or his disguised persona), since the objects of the nymphs'
affections are the "boys" Gallathea(Tyterus) and Phillida(Melebeus). Yet
even though this love *appears* to be male–female love, it is in fact
female–female love, thus reinforcing the fact that, within a society of
virgins, virgins are not only the *objects* of desire but can become desiring
subjects as well.[18]

   This view of nymphs as desiring subjects can be sharply juxtaposed to
the picture of them contained in that portion of Diana's speech with
which I began this essay. As the speech continues, it even more strongly
contrasts the actively desiring nymphs I have been considering to the formerly "chaste" virgins of Diana's train:

> Shall it be said . . . that *Diana* the goddesse of chastity, whose thoughts are
> alwaies answerable to her vowes, whose eyes never glanced on desire, and whose
> hart abateth the poynt of *Cupids* arrowes, shall have her virgins to become
> unchast in desires, immoderate in action, untemperate in love, in foolish love, in
> base love? (III.iv.27, 28–33).

Diana's speech, as well as her dialectical conflict with Venus throughout
the play, serves to isolate virginity – and virgins – from love and desire
and thus reinforces the early modern construction of (biological) virginity that I began this essay by examining. But since most of the virgins in
this play, nymphs and mortals, have separated themselves from the patriarchal sexual economy that has defined virginity in this biological way,
can we continue to use this "patriarchal" definition for the virgin characters in this play? The virgins may, indeed, avoid male desire and male
penile rupture of their hymens. But do they avoid desire altogether?
And, can a virginity which exists exclusively in a non-patriarchal space
claim/hold the same definition it does in patriarchal society? If women

could exist with other women in a "society" with no property to transfer, no fear of pregnancy – and thus no possibility of fetishization of the hymen – would virginity mean the same thing? Would it even exist in a world that lacks the necessary penis to define it?

Once Cupid has been unmasked as the source of love in Diana's pre-viously "chaste" virginal society, he is punished by being set to untie love knots. As the nymphs watch, they comment that some knots untie easily by themselves while others remain fast. The false love knots are shown to be the results of money, force, or male dissembling, all products of the patriarchal sexual economy (IV.ii.37–56). Those that remain fast – the true knots – were made by "a womans hart" (34, 60), or "by faith, and must onely be unknit of death" (49–50). Although the male god Cupid has trifled with the affections of the female nymphs, this act indicates a predisposition to consider women's love truer than men's love. This assumption of female honesty and loyalty is reinforced by the relation-ship between Diana and her nymphs. Although tricked by Cupid, the nymphs never betray or challenge Diana outright and easily return to their previous pursuits once Cupid is exposed. Also, even though two nymphs love the same "boy," Gallathea(Tyterus), they do not engage in a power struggle to gain control of "him." The nymphs never sacrifice their friendship or loyalty to each other, or to Diana, for love.[19] Virginity thus allows women to form a unified society that can clearly (and easily) withstand any sort of disunity (Cupid and love) introduced from the outside. Yet the brief views the play presents of the desiring nymphs do not explain the role pleasure or eroticism plays (or does not play) in this virginal society. To obtain a more detailed view of how desire manifests itself among virgins, I would like to consider how the love between Gallathea and Phillida is represented.

In the context of *Gallathea*, Haebe can be seen as a representation of society's "ideal virgin," a good daughter of the patriarchy. She willingly allows gods and (male) citizens to use her body to forge alliances. She never challenges the uses to which her virginity is put even when she sus-pects that her body may not be the "right" one for the situation. If Haebe is what a virgin *should* be, then how are we to understand Gallathea and Phillida, the two virgins who are removed from the sacrifi-cial/(marriage) economy? On one level, their disguises simply represent the means by which they are able to save their lives. But on a more important level, these disguises foreground the two characters and mark them as distinctly different from the "ideal" virgin of their society,

Haebe. These disguised virgins do not remain simply fugitives from a sacrifice/(marriage). They manage, I would suggest, to completely problematize not only traditional notions of female virginity, but various kinds of social interactions between women as well. Gallathea and Phillida become the locus of many conflicting notions of what virgins "are" within early modern society, and only some of them are related to traditional notions of patriarchal marriage. The instability of the characters' "meaning" is foregrounded in the situation(s) surrounding their disguise. *Gallathea* is one of the few early modern plays that allows a space, however contested, for female–female desire.[20] This "space" is possible not only because of Gallathea's and Phillida's disguise, but because of their stated virginity. The disguise allows the two women to escape from the sacrificial (marriage) economy and interact with each other in a place in which virginity "rules" and creates its own society: the forests the women share with Diana and her nymphs.

Gallathea and Phillida's desire is triggered by a standard device of disguise plays: a character falls in love with a person whose gender, as marked by clothes/disguise, is contrary to the actual gender. In this play, the dual disguise renders the plot doubly complex: two "boys" – really women – fall mutually in love with "boys" who are really women. Unable to reveal their disguised natures, the two women develop a friendship that is initially tempered by the suspicion that the "boy other" each is in love with *may be* really a woman. In act III, scene ii, in the midst of a series of gender-confusing riddles about the possession of virginity, the two women "voice" their suspicions:

> PHILLIDA.   [aside]. What doubtfull speeches be these? I feare me
> he is as I am, a mayden.
> GALLATHEA.   [aside] What dread riseth in my minde! I feare the
> boy to be as I am a mayden. (III.ii.28–31)

By act IV, scene iv, the "fear" generated by that suspicion intensifies:

> PHILLIDA.   Why, what doost thou feare?
> GALLATHEA.   Nothing but that you love me not. *Exit.*
> PHILLIDA.   I will. Poore *Phillida*, what shouldest thou thinke of
> thy selfe, that lovest one that I feare mee, is as thy
> selfe is . . . For if she be a Mayden there is no hope of
> my love . . .   (IV.iv.35–38, 42–43)

This "fear" that both women articulate not only acknowledges the suspicion that their love object is "same" rather than "other," but also validates the woman–woman desire that surfaces between them. Although dressed as boys, each woman knows herself to be a woman and, by this point in the play, is sure that the "boy" she loves is also a woman. Fearful or not, these women have accepted the gender of their love object and are emotionally committed to their desire for a person of the same gender. These virgins have thus redefined themselves as lovers, as well as redefined the terms of their love in a way that opposes it to those masculinist notions of "love" as a contractual arrangement negotiated by men across women's bodies. They seem no longer to be definable as virgins in patriarchal terms, whether that definition refers to the "intact" woman whose virginity is "bounded" by marriage, or the "deviant" woman who allows male violation of her body, extends her virginity to a permanent condition, or chooses a woman as her love object. But *can* love exist between virgins and, if so, what *kind(s)*, and in what context(s) can it be expressed? Even though Gallathea and Phillida actually "desire" a member of the same gender, it is difficult to speculate about just how this woman–woman desire is expected to play itself out. *Have* Gallathea and Phillida "shown" their love, and, if so, *how* have they done so?

Lyly's text is remarkably unstable in this respect. At times we are led to believe that the women *know* they love women – and *act* upon that love. At other times, previously raised expectations are immediately lowered. Gallathea and Phillida's first encounter occurs in Act 2, scene 1 and they are almost instantly attracted to each other. Yet their attraction is revealed within a context that also questions their unstable gender-appearance:

> PHILLIDA.   [aside] It is a pretty boy and a faire, hee might well
> have beene a woman . . .
> GALLATHEA.   [aside] I knowe not howe it commeth to passe, but
> yonder boy is in mine eye too beautitful!
>
> (II.i.19–20, 44–45)

Even though unsure, and puzzled, about the gender of the "other boy," each woman has, by the end of act II, fallen in love and resolved to take some action. Gallathea vows to "follow [her love] into the Woods" (II.iv.12) and Phillida vows to "transgresse in love a little of [her] modestie" (II.v.6–7). An important question to consider is whether she *does* transgress her modesty and, if so, how and to what extent?

The women appear next in act III, scene ii, the riddling scene I mentioned earlier. Although each fears – or suspects – the "boy" she loves to be a woman, the scene ends without either character gaining/revealing "definite" knowledge of this issue. However, unlike scenes iv and v of act ii where the characters went off alone to search and ponder, this scene ends with their exiting together to Phillida's curious speech: "Come let us into the Grove, and make much of one another, that cannot tel what to think one of another" (iii.ii.58–59). Here again the phrase "make much of one another" is inconclusive. What *will* Gallathea and Phillida do in the grove? How much of "making much" is verbal, how much physical? This inconclusive language can lead one to believe that the women will *surely* learn the "truth" of their gender as the result of their "making much." The suspicion that they do find out – or, at least, that they thoroughly enjoy the process of exploration – is reinforced by the fact that the characters are absent until Act iv, scene iv. Yet the beginning of that scene – another set of riddles about "fairness," "boys," and "virgins" – forces us to conclude that whatever "making much" encompasses, for Gallathea and Phillida such "much making" may not result in gender revelation. Each still "fears" the other is a woman, and both leave for more wandering in the groves (iv.iv.32). The two are clearly still infatuated with each other, but whatever pleasures they have shared have not "convinced" them that their love object is a woman. Gallathea and Phillida's consistent desire for each other, coupled with the "fact" that they never seem to "discover" the other's gender, suggests that virginal pleasure is quite different from the sorts of pleasure that are part of the patriarchal sexual economy. To claim that the women's indecision regarding their lovers' gender would mean that they have not seen each other's genitals implies that our notions of pleasure are grounded in a masculinist, scopic focus on genital sexuality. If we believe that "real" sex between men and women must entail penile vaginal penetration, we may be tempted to claim that the virgins do not know their lovers' "real" gender because, having no penis between them, they cannot engage in "real sex" and so avoided any activity that would have revealed each woman's lack of a penis. But can we claim that *all* sexual activity, *all* pleasure requires either a genital focus or "ocular proof" of gender? Are there not pleasures virgins can provide each other which do not require such a masculinist or biological focus? I suggest that *Gallathea* invites us to speculate on the possibility of a kind of desire and an economy of pleasure that is focused on the lovers' *entire* selves rather than that small portion located between their legs.

Thus, when the "truth" of their genders is finally revealed to Gallathea and Phillida in act v, scene iii, their responses demonstrate both the degree of their affections and their (continued) "ignorance" regarding their gender-identity:

GALLATHIA.	Unfortunate *Gallathea*, if this be *Phillida*!
PHILLIDA.	Accursed *Phillida*, if that be *Gallathea*!
GALLATHEA.	And wast thou all this while enamoured of *Phillida*, that sweete *Phillida*?
PHILLIDA.	And couldest thou doate upon the face of a Maiden, thy selfe beeing one, on the face of fayre *Gallathea*?
NEPTUNE.	Doe you both beeing Maidens love one another?
GALLATHEA.	I had thought the habite agreeable with the Sexe, and so burned in the fire of mine owne fancies.
PHILLIDA.	I had thought that in the attyre of a boy, there could not have lodged the body of a Virgine, & so was inflamed with a sweete desire, which now I find a sower deceit. (v.iii.110–21)

Even though this play allows a space for woman–woman desire, the type of desire that occurs is represented as curiously "chaste." Is this because Lyly refuses to countenance the existence of woman–woman desire, or is the only sort of woman–woman desire he can conceive of one that exists within the traditional patriarchal definitions of virginity as an unviolated bodily condition? What does this perception say about the possibility/probability of desire between women?

I want briefly and provisionally to answer this question by recalling the instability of Lyly's text in terms of just how female–female desire/pleasure can be represented. In this context, the text can also be seen to be remarkably unstable as regards the representation of gender itself. One reason we may not be able to mark the boundaries of desire/pleasure is because we are often unable to mark the boundaries of gender in this play. This latter circumstance results from the extraordinary degree of complexity surrounding the disguises. Our first view of Gallathea is as a "boy." That is, the boy actor playing the woman character Gallathea is already dressed as the disguised Gallathea(Tyterus) (i.i.60–61). Thus the "woman" Gallathea is *always* represented on stage as the "boy" Gallathea(Tyterus). Even though we are meant to make the mental jump from boy actor, to (absent) "woman" character Gallathea, to disguised "boy" character Gallathea(Tyterus), all we ever *see* on-stage is a character in male clothing – an actual boy dressed as one – who purports to be a woman/daughter called Gallathea.

In contrast, Phillida *is* represented, at least once (i.iii), as female. A boy actor plays Phillida, yet he wears female clothing, thus *reinforcing* the femaleness of Phillida. Yet, two scenes later, Phillida is also disguised as a boy. Thus, for this character we are presented with the equation: boy actor has become "woman" character Phillida and is now disguised as "boy" character Phillida(Melebeus). For the rest of the play Phillida, like Gallathea, will appear in boy's clothing, will be *seen* as "male," will be called by a male name, yet will be "known" to be "female."

This is not an unusual situation. We go through similar mental contortions whenever we see/read of Rosalind or Viola. Yet if we *see* a production on the twentieth-century stage, where Viola and Rosalind are usually played by women, we must remind ourselves not only of the extinct tradition of boy actors, but also of the homoerotic desire encoded in the various layers of male and female disguise/desire they enact.[21] Yet in terms of *Gallathea*, how is the homoerotic desire for/between boy players to be understood in terms of a love/desire that is expressed by "women" characters? How can we extricate the various layers of same-sex from different-sex eroticism as well as distinguish between the genders involved in the desire displayed in this play? To make sense of what is happening, we need to ask not only how gender is marked, but where we are to draw the boundaries between genders. We are presented with two boy actors playing characters in male dress who do and do not declare their love for each other. This situation appears to be a representation of male–male desire. Yet these characters constantly remind the audience that they are women. Thus, their declarations would appear to represent female–female desire. At the end of the play, a marriage is promised between these same two boy actors in male dress, a situation that appears to represent the "consummation" of male–male desire. Yet we are told that the gender of one character is to be changed. Will the desire then enacted by this couple change to/be read as male–female eroticism? What has finally happened to desire and to our reading(s) of gender in this play?

Although we are initially assured that Gallathea and Phillida are (female) virgins, the cross-dressing conventions of the play serve to foreground the instability of both gender and desire to a much greater degree than many other plays involving cross-dressing. But while all this confusion *does* occur, and while a rhetoric and a plot structure identifying the characters as women *is* present, visual (and auditory) clues indicate that *Gallathea* also presents its audience with a representation of male–male desire. We virtually always see two characters in male dress expressing desire to each other while they address each other with *male* names. This effect of male dress and names seems, at times, to destabilize female–female desire and foreground male–male desire. But I would also suggest that the fact that the play was initially performed by the

Children of Paul's contributes to this sense of gender instability and shifting erotic desire. Like the "play boys" in adult companies, choirboys often became objects of audience members' erotic interest.[22] Yet their relative youth would allow a different sort of desire to be generated. One source of humor in comedies put on by the boy companies was the disparity between the implied sexual "innocence" of the actors and the often bawdy sophistication of the lines they spoke.[23] Such a juxtaposition would foreground the boys' youth and suggest that the desire they generated was pederastic. But was the desire for such young boys primarily felt by men – man–boy desire – or by women – woman–boy desire? Or did the extreme youth of some of the boys allow them (cross-dressed or not) to be considered as "girls," thus suggesting man–girl or woman–girl desire? I do not wish to attempt to answer these questions, but simply to speculate on the various possibilities of desire present – not only in *Gallathea* but between audience members and choirboys – when youth, in addition to costuming,[24] renders gender indistinct. The indistinct gender boundaries displayed within the boy companies generally could have made it more difficult to determine whether male–male or female–female desire (or a combination of the two) was being represented in this particular Lyly play.

However, the presence of male–male desire is distinctly questioned at the point at which the women's female gender is exposed in act v, scene iii. The revelation of the same gender of their love object does not destroy Gallathea and Phillida's desire, though it does serve to elicit on their "fears" regarding a love that both Diana and Neptune define as "unnatural." Further, the sea god reminds us/them that the women's love is

An idle choyce, strange, and foolish, for one Virgine to doate on another; and to imagine a constant faith, where there can be no cause of affection. (v.iii.128–30)

Neptune, the voice of patriarchal society, indicates that the women have made "idle" choices because it is "foolish" for virgins to "dote" upon one another. Humanist philosophy indicated that any love that "doted" was excessive, but I would argue here that Neptune is focusing upon the *gender* of the doters – the same and female – rather than upon a love that is out of control. Further, I call attention to his questioning of the *constancy* of a love between virgins where there "can be no cause of affection." I would suggest that Neptune is pointing out that love and affection can only exist where there is a *penis*, a "cause" of (and "means" for) affection. This pointed reference to the lack of a penis in Gallathea and Phillida's love also reinforces the perception that the desire we have been seeing so much of in bodies whose gender is remarkably shifting and indistinct is *not* male–male desire. Yet despite Neptune's rearticulation of the necessity of gender difference for love to "work" within a patriarchal context, the two women, without fear, have already declared their love:

> GALLATHEA.   I will never love any but *Phillida*: her love is engraven
> in my hart, with her eyes.
> PHILLIDA.   Nor I any but *Gallathea*, whose faith is imprinted in
> my thoughts by her words. (v.iii.124–27)

These declarations show that the virginity in this play is inextricably tied to woman–woman desire in a way that questions both the nature – or "cause" – of male-defined love as well as its use of the virgin body to solve patriarchal social problems. Gallathea's and Phyllida's refusal to relinquish their female–female love reinforces both its strength and the power of women characters to find ways of defining themselves and their affections that are "outside" the patriarchal sexual economy. The transgressive nature of the two characters is reinforced by the fact that male–female desire can be recuperated only by arbitrarily changing one of the women into a *real* boy and thus ending the play with a marriage. But the arbitrary nature of the change – no one knows who will become the "real boy" and the women do not seem to care – serves to call attention to the nature of the marriage being made here.[25] I would argue that Venus' cavalier attitude toward gender – a penis may be necessary to legitimize the union, but the organ here becomes an "add-on" part, sort of like a better-fitting dildo – trivializes the whole notion of the traditional patriarchal marriage.[26] True love determines this union, not a contractual arrangement between fathers. In fact, Tyterus objects to Gallathea being changed to a boy, for the event would disinherit her younger brother. But his objection is disallowed by Venus, who seems to be creating a new sort of "marriage" that is designed to accommodate woman–woman desire and not a patriarchal inheritance scheme.

The transgressive love of Gallathea and Phyllida also raises questions about virginity itself: must it only be defined according to patriarchal norms? Might it be a life choice which *is* an end in itself? Can a virgin life choice enable women to find a way out of the patriarchal sexual economy? In response to these questions, I would suggest that *Gallathea* demonstrates that virginity *can* be defined against patriarchal norms. Virginity *can* be viewed as a means by which women refuse to be part of the sexual economy, refuse to be defined exclusively in terms of their reproductive capabilities, and embrace love relationships which allow these refusals. This definition of virginity carries encoded within it the notion that strong bonds of friendship and affection exist between women that are *not* acknowledged by patriarchal society or the patriarchal narrative, and that these bonds might have an erotic component, might grow into woman–woman desire.[27] According to this definition, being a virgin means that the woman in question defines herself in terms of herself and other women, not in terms of men, male society, or the patriarchal sexual economy.

The importance of female desire in general is reinforced in the epilogue of this play where Gallathea (still presumably in male disguise) urges certain members of the audience to

Yeelde Ladies, yeeld to love ladies, which lurketh under your eye-lids whilst you sleepe, and plaieth with your hart strings whilst you wake . . . Confesse [Cupid] a Conquerer, whom yee ought to regarde, sith it is unpossible to resist; for this is infallible, that Love conquereth all things but it selfe, and Ladies all harts but their owne. (epi. 5–7, 9–12)

Even though Gallathea does not specify whether the ladies should engage in female–female or male–female love, the fact that the women are encouraged simply to love serves again (and finally) to destabilize the notion of patriarchal marriage that frames this play. Women who actually/actively desire (and love) would be unwilling to sacrifice the object(s) of their affections for contractual marriage arrangements made against their wills with those they did not love. Urging women to love in this way also urges them to divorce themselves from the patriarchal sexual economy in a way similar to Gallathea and Phillida, and also similar to (but different from) Elizabeth I herself. The queen's perpetual virginity placed her outside the sexual economy and reinforced her power as an anomalous, though "special," ruler. Her unique virginity, coupled with her incorporation of this bodily condition into a political rhetoric, rendered her society's construction of her "deviance" invalid. In a related way, the virginal "society" in Lyly's play renders the social construction of Gallathea and Phillida's virginity as deviant similarly invalid. The court of the Virgin Queen, especially when considered as a venue for drama, has the potential to seriously question dominant social constructions of virginity and render them at best "curious," at worst dangerously deviant and in need of recuperation.

NOTES

Many thanks to Dympna Callaghan for her help in framing the argument of this essay and to Jean Howard for her (as usual) incisive and probing critique of an early draft.

1 John Lyly, *The Complete Works of John Lyly*, R. Warwick Bond, ed., 3 vols. (Oxford: Clarendon Press, 1902; rpt. 1973). *Gallathea*, vol. II. pp. 419–28, quote, vol. II, p. 454, (III.iv.21–23). All further references to *Gallathea* will be to this edition and will appear in the text.

2 A helpful analysis of how Greek and Roman deities are employed in early modern texts occurs in Peter Saccio, *The Court Comedies of John Lyly* (Princeton: Princeton University Press, 1969), pp. 102–13.

3 The only known quarto of *Gallathea* is dated 1592. Bond, in *Lyly*, vol. II, pp. 419, 427, suggests that Court performance may have occurred on January 1, 1586, 1587, or 1588.

4 Ellen M. Caldwell's work, "John Lyly's *Gallathea*: A New Rhetoric of Love for the Virgin Queen," in *Women in the Renaissance*, Kirby Farrell, Elizabeth H. Hageman, and Arthur F. Kinney, eds. (Amherst: University of Massachusetts Press, 1988), pp. 69–87, exemplifies the kinds of readings possible if Lyly's plays are considered as texts designed to flatter the queen. See also David Bevington, "John Lyly and Queen Elizabeth: Royal Flattery in *Campaspe* and *Sapho and Phao*," *Renaissance Papers* (1966): 57–67; and Joel Altman, *The Tudor Play of Mind* (Berkeley: University of California Press, 1978), ch. 7. While I acknowledge this "genre" of Lyly criticism, I wish to detach my analysis of *Gallathea* from the "inevitable" allegorical connection with Elizabeth I and consider how virginity as a social – as opposed to a political – construct is created and deployed. Obviously, though, one needs to consider Elizabeth as patron of court performance, which I maintain can be done without recourse to an allegorical reading of either Lyly or the queen. The following works consider the "political" aspects of Elizabeth I's virginity: Frances A. Yates, *Astraea: The Imperial Theme in the Sixteenth Century* (London and Boston: Routledge and Kegan Paul, 1975); Louis Adrian Montrose, "'Eliza, Queene of Shepheardes,' and the Pastoral of Power," *English Literary Renaissance* 10 (1980): 153–92 and "'Shaping Fantasies': Figurations of Gender and Power in Elizabethan Culture," *Representations* 1 (1983): 61–94; Leah S. Marcus, "Shakespeare's Comic Heroines, Elizabeth I, and the Political Uses of Androgyny," in *Women in the Middle Ages and the Renaissance*, Mary Beth Rose, ed. (Syracuse: Syracuse University Press, 1986), pp. 135–53; Theodora A. Jankowski, *Women in Power in the Early Modern Drama* (Urbana and Chicago: University of Illinois Press, 1992), ch. 3; Susan Frye, *Elizabeth I: The Competition for Representation* (New York and Oxford: Oxford University Press, 1993).

5 ". . . a 'sex/gender system' is the set of arrangements by which a society transforms biological sexuality into products of human activity, and in which these transformed sexual needs are satisfied," Gayle Rubin, "The

Traffic in Women: Notes on the 'Political Economy' of Sex," in *Towards an Anthropology of Women*, Rayna R. Reiter, ed. (New York and London: Monthly Review Press, 1975), pp. 157–210, quote, p. 159.

6 Frederick Engels, *The Origin of the Family, Private Property, and the State* (New York: International Publishers, 1973), pp. 119–46.

7 Kirsten Hastrup, "The Semantics of Biology: Virginity," in *Defining Females*, Shirley Ardener, ed. (New York: John Wiley), pp. 49–65, quote, p. 58.

8 I have briefly outlined what is the Protestant – although "secular" might be a more all-encompassing term – "discourse of virginity" in early modern England. This discourse is based upon the writings of such authors as: Martin Luther, Heinrich Bullinger, John Calvin, Alexander Niccholes, William Whately, John Wing, William Gouge, John Dod and Robert Cleaver, Richard Brathwait, Daniel Rogers, and Jeremy Taylor. The Roman Catholic "discourse of virginity" – based upon the writings of Paul, Jerome, Ambrose, and Augustine – was quite different from the Protestant, since it also allowed for the possibility of a woman's "perpetual" virginity, a religious "vocation" as a nun. For more detailed explications of the Catholic and Protestant (religious) discourses, including readings of the abovementioned texts, see Theodora A. Jankowski, "'The scorne of Savage people': Virginity as 'Forbidden Sexuality' in John Lyly's *Love's Metamorphosis*," *Renaissance Drama* 24 (1993): 123–53.

I use the term "discourse" in Michel Foucault's sense that categories of discourse create our experience(s) and regulate our world. See Foucault: *The Archaeology of Knowledge and the Discourse on Language*, trans. A. M. Sheridan Smith (New York: Pantheon, 1972), esp. part II; "The History of Sexuality," in *Power/Knowledge: Selected Interviews and Other Writings*, Colin Gorden, ed., trans. Gordon, Leo Marshall, John Mepham, and Kate Soper (New York: Pantheon, 1980), pp. 183–93; *The History of Sexuality. Volume I: An Introduction*, trans. Robert Hurley (New York: Vintage, 1990); and *Remarks on Marx*, trans. R. James Goldstein and James Cascaito (New York: Semiotext[e], 1991).

9 William Shakespeare, *The Complete Works of William Shakespeare*, David Bevington, ed. (New York: HarperCollins, 1992), *Measure for Measure*, pp. 404–43, quote, p. 419, (II.iii.29). All further references to Shakespeare's plays will be to this edition and will appear in the text.

10 Catherine R. Stimpson, "Shakespeare and the Soil of Rape," in *The Women's Part*, Carolyn Ruth Swift Lenz, Carol Thomas Neely, and Gayle Greene, eds. (Urbana, Chicago, and London: University of Illinois Press, 1980), pp. 56–64, makes a similar claim regarding a woman who has been raped: "The fact of having been raped obliterates all of a woman's previous claims to virtue. One *sexual* experience hereafter will define her" (p. 61).

11 The play is set on the banks of the Humber river in Lincolnshire. The Agar is assumed to symbolize the *eagre*, or tidal bore, on the Humber estuary, Saccio, *Court Comedies*, p. 100; Bond, *Lyly*, vol. II, p. 428. Despite this "actual" location, the play also seems to be set in an ancient pastoral landscape, Altman, *Tudor Play*, p. 209. Phyllis Rackin, "Androgyny, Mimesis, and the

Marriage of the Boy Heroine on the English Renaissance Stage," *PMLA* 102 (1987): 29–41, makes an important distinction between the "recognizable sixteenth-century [aspects of] Lincolnshire" of the apprentice plot of *Gallathea* and the "idealized, mythological, and ahistorical" aspects of the Gallathea–Phillida plot (p. 34).

12 For Claude Lévi-Strauss, *The Elementary Structures of Kinship* (Boston: Beacon Press, 1969), marriage is a "total relationship of exchange . . . not established between a man and a woman, but between two groups of men, [in which] the woman figures only as one of the partners" (p. 115). This idea becomes the basis of Eve Kosofsky Sedgwick's definition of male "homosocial" relations in *Between Men* (New York: Columbia University Press, 1985) and *Epistemology of the Closet* (Berkeley and Los Angeles: University of California Press, 1990). See also the following: Heidi Hartmann, "The Unhappy Marriage of Marxism and Feminism: Towards a More Progressive Union," in *The Unhappy Marriage of Marxism and Feminism*, Hartman et al., eds. (London: Pluto Press, 1991), pp. 1–41; Veronica Beechey, "On Patriarchy," *Feminist Review* 3 (1979): 66–82; Gail Omvedt, "'Patriarchy': The Analysis of Women's Oppression," *The Insurgent Sociologist* 13 (1986): 30–50; Rubin, "Traffic".

13 Lynda E. Boose, "The Father and the Bride in Shakespeare," *PMLA* 97 (1982): 325–47, makes important connections between virginity, the female body, and the "ritual" of marriage.

14 Elizabeth I would have been fifty-nine when the quarto of *Gallathea* appeared and anywhere from fifty-three to fifty-five when the play was performed at court.

15 Nancy J. Vickers, "Diana Described: Scattered Woman and Scattered Rhyme," *Critical Inquiry* 8 (1981): 265–79.

16 Valerie Traub, "The (In)significance of 'Lesbian' Desire in Early Modern England," in *Erotic Politics: Desire on the Renaissance Stage*, Susan Zimmerman, ed. (New York and London: Routledge, 1992), pp. 150–69, examines the erotic potential of "monogamous, erotic 'virginity' as the natural expression of love between women" in Diana's community as represented in Thomas Heywood's *The Golden Age*, see especially pp. 159–61. The potential for erotic encounters in various sorts of women-only communities is part of the "myth" of female–female eroticism connected to both actual and literary convents, like Margaret Cavendish's *The Convent of Pleasure*. See also Rosemary Curb and Nancy Manahan, eds., *Lesbian Nuns: Breaking Silence* (Tallahassee: Naiad Press, 1985).

Gregory W. Bredbeck, *Sodomy and Interpretation: Marlowe to Milton* (Ithaca and London: Cornell University Press, 1991), especially pp. 201–13, points out that the pastoral carried encoded within it a discourse of male homoeroticism, especially in "the two major models influencing Renaissance writers, Theocritus's *Idylls* [especially the fifth] and Virgil's *Eclogues* [especially the second]" (p. 20).

17 When disguised, the women are called by their fathers' names.

18 Penelope J. Englebrecht, "'Lifting Belly is a Language': the Postmodern Lesbian Subject," *Feminist Studies* 16 (1990): 85–114, persuasively argues for a rearticulation of the terms Subject–Object – which she sees as "linguistically and socially mediated by the action of the paradigmatically (male) Subject *upon* the (female) Object" – for defining lesbian desire. She sees the "lesbian terms, Subject and Other/self [which she coins, as referring] to operation and are more than interchangeable; they are synonymous" (p. 86).

19 In contrast to my reading of the play, Altman in *Tudor Play* characterizes the result of Cupid's infiltration of the community as "jealous wrangling" among the nymphs curtailed by Diana's "furious" chiding (p. 208).

20 While many important books – by Bredbeck, *Sodomy*; Jonathan Goldberg, *Sodometries: Renaissance Texts, Modern Sexualities* (Stanford: Stanford University Press, 1992); and Bruce R. Smith, *Homosexual Desire in Shakespeare's England* (Chicago and London: University of Chicago Press, 1991) – have recently appeared to supplement Alan Bray's early volume, *Homosexuality in Renaissance England* (London: Gay Men's Press, 1982), and explore male homoeroticism in the early modern period, no book is yet available that explores female homoeroticism. Of the essays (or chapters of books) available, the most important are both by Traub, "(In)significance" and *Desire and Anxiety: Circulations of Sexuality in Shakespearean Drama* (London and New York: Routledge, 1992). See also James Holstun, "'Will you rend our ancient love asunder?': Lesbian Elegy in Donne, Marvell, and Milton," *English Literary History* 54 (1987): 835–67.

21 Most recent critical examinations of cross-dressing on the early modern stage consider the practice in connection with responses to it in anti-theatrical tracts. Additionally, Lisa Jardine, *Still Harping on Daughters: Women and Drama in the Age of Shakespeare* (1983; rpt. New York: Columbia University Press, 1989), argues that the mere existence of the "play boy" marked him not only as an object of erotic interest, but as an object of male–male desire. She also claims that *all* desire manifested between male audience members and actors was (male) homoerotic, a point she specifically makes in connection with *Gallathea* (pp. 9–36, especially pp. 20–21). Laura Levine, "Men in Women's Clothing: Anti-Theatricality and Effeminization from 1579–1642," *Criticism* 28 (1986): 121–43, examines the perceived "unstable" identity of the cross-dressed actor which led to his construction as "monstrous" because he was effeminized by wearing women's clothes (especially pp. 125, 130). Rackin, "Androgyny," maintains that cross-dressing resulted in making gender "doubly problematic" (p. 29). Jean E. Howard, "Crossdressing, the Theater, and Gender Struggle in Early Modern England," *Shakespeare Quarterly* 39 (1988): 418–40, states that the meaning of cross-dressing "varied with the circumstances of its occurrence" and that the "various manifestations of crossdressing in Renaissance culture" allow us to "read aspects of class and gender struggle in the period . . . in which the theater . . . played a highly contradictory role" (p. 418). Stephen Orgel, "Nobody's Perfect: Or Why Did the English Stage Take Boys for Women?"

South Atlantic Quarterly 88. 1 (1989): 7–29, argues for the theater's assumption of "the interchangeability of the sexes" (p. 13), a contention supported by early modern medical treatises. (See also Thomas Laqueur, *Making Sex: Body and Gender From the Greeks to Freud* [Cambridge, MA and London: Harvard University Press, 1990].) These beliefs fed the fear that boy actors might become "as," if not "actual," women, especially as objects of male–male desire. Steve Brown, "The Boyhood of Shakespeare's Heroines: Notes on Gender Ambiguity in the Sixteenth Century," *Studies in English Literature* 30 (1990): 243–63, examines "boys" outside the theater as objects of male–male desire, especially in connection with the use of the term/name "Ganymede" to refer to an "ingle" or "catamite" – young male whore (especially p. 251). (See also James M. Saslow, *Ganymede in the Renaissance* [New Haven and London: Yale University Press, 1986].) Peter Stallybrass, "Transvestism and the 'Body Beneath': Speculating on the Boy Actor," in *Erotic Politics*, Susan Zimmerman, ed. pp. 64–83, considers the various implications for cross-dressing of the play boy's actual body.

22 Pamela Brown, "Boys Will Be Girls: John Lyly's *Gallathea*," unpublished manuscript (1993), suggests that the choirboys' erotic potential was necessary to ensure their success and mentions that they may even have solicited for sex, along with the other whores, in St. Paul's (fols. 3, 5–6).

23 Michael Shapiro, *Children of the Revels* (New York: Columbia University Press, 1977), pp. 106–07. Choirboys began singing at seven or eight years of age and continued until their voices broke, at about thirteen or fourteen (Shapiro, *Children*, p. 8). Pamela Brown, "Boys Will Be Girls," suggests that Diana's scornful references to her nymphs' loves as "pelting boyes, perhaps base of birth" (III.iv.49–50) could be a barbed reference to (male and female) audience members' dalliances with their young servants (fol. 16).

24 Stallybrass', "Transvestism," examination of the (possible) use of prosthetic breasts (or tight lacing to produce a cleavage) by boy actors for "nude" bedroom scenes suggests a means by which these actors might, indeed, be mistaken for "real girls" and thus questions Jardine's, *Still Harping*, contention that *all* desire between early modern audience members and actors was male homoerotic.

25 "For the girls and the gods in *Gallathea*, gender is arbitrary, unreal, and reversible because the vantage point transcends the social to include the realm of fantastic imagination and spirit where androgyny is an image of human self-completion rather than an aberrant social category" (Rackin, "Androgyny," p. 31).

   Altman, *Tudor Play*, seems to challenge the "arbitrariness" of the change by claiming to "know" which woman will become a boy (p. 209). Caldwell, "New Rhetoric," indicates "that desire to be free of either a life-threatening female identity or of a confining male disguise seems to motivate the women far more than the satisfaction of mere sexual passion . . ." (p. 70). She sees the play as a celebration of constancy, rather than metamorphosis (p. 71), despite the fact that she feels the text is "a thinly disguised allegory of a woman's reluctance to face the sexual demands of marriage" (p. 70). I do, however, agree with her contention that the play offers a "personal, not public, reason for marriage" and "seeks to locate a new rhetoric between the extremes of Petrarchanism and common lust . . ." (p. 70).

26 Philippa Berry, *Chastity and Power: Elizabethan Literature and the Unmarried Queen* (London and New York: Routledge, 1989), points out that Venus' act of changing one lover's body could be regarded as "asserting the completeness and authority of the feminine [through] woman's possession of phallic power" (p. 125).

27 Janice G. Raymond, *A Passion for Friends* (Boston: Beacon Press, 1986).

CHAPTER 12

The terms of gender: "gay" and "feminist" Edward II

Dympna Callaghan

On the front of Jonathan Dollimore's *Sexual Dissidence*,[1] a landmark text in queer, theory and criticism, is a remarkable photograph by Rotimi Fani-Kayodo entitled *Station of the Cross, Vatican City* of two people waiting for a train (figure 12.1). One is a beautiful and scantily clad male in late adolescence perched on a wooden barricade, looking directly and enticingly at the camera. The other is a woman, a nun, sitting behind the barricade, slouched over it, her face hidden by her hands, in what resembles a less than pious attitude of prayer, emphasizing the pun of the photo's title on railway stations and the meditation exercise of contemplating Christ's passion and death. The obese nun appears exhausted. The capacious folds of her habit envelop expanses of flesh bulging beneath. For the young man, there is sexual allure in the business of waiting, the hint of the prospect of erotic encounter; the nun, on the other hand, is just waiting, in a pose that strikes the viewer as a continuation of an asexual life at prayer. In this photo, whose subject is erotic anticipation, the youth excites sexual interest, not the nun. In contrast to the dazzling blond beauty of the boy next to her, she is a desexualized object, or perhaps even an object of sexual revulsion. Indeed, the attraction aroused by the highly sexualized young man seems to depend on an indifference to the nun; an indifference that has both positive and negative implications within the terms of the photo to the constitutive difference of gender and its attendant hierarchy.

The photograph seems to be an anti-sexist representation insofar as it substitutes an empowered scantily clad young man for the traditional sultry and submissive gaze of a scantily clad young woman. And feminity in this depiction – weary, and checking for the arrival of the train or perhaps taking a furtive peep at the boy's candid display of his sexuality – is far less prescriptive than either the secular fantasy of the anorexic, sexually available adolescent or the religious image of the ever-youthful virgin-mother. Further, because the young man is coded as the object of

275

Figure 12.1 Front cover of Jonathan Dollimore's book *Sexual Dissidence*, featuring *Station of the Cross, Vatican City*, Rotimi Fani-Kayodo (1991).

gay desire, his gaze disrupts the assumption of the heterosexual male viewer. That is to say, the axis of vision in the picture is gay regardless of the sexuality, or for that matter, the gender of the boy, the photographer, or the viewer. There remains, however, a troublesome interplay between the focus on the male homoerotic and the feminine sub-erotic. For while the photo eschews conventions of patriarchal representation in one sense, it colludes with another of its key aspects – the misogynist specter of physically repellent femininity whose sexuality is covert, cloistered, and conveniently, closeted. Certainly, Rotimi Fani-Kayodo's juxtaposition of the boy to the nun deliberately pressures dominant codes of representation (and thus dominant masculinity). That is, the photo's homoeroticism suggests for the viewer at least the possibility of moving outside an economy of desire constrained by gender and a system of heterosexual alliance; but repositioning woman within such a frame may not move *woman* – who sets up the photo's homoerotic dynamics – outside of the categories of patriarchal culture. Hardly a celebration of feminine amplitude, the picture may indeed leave woman behind as the weighty baggage of a sexually unappetizing order.

Unfortunately, "positive images" of both women and gay men will not rectify the cultural problems around gender and sexuality articulated by the photograph. In an endeavor to address these problems in all their complexity, I want to ask a question of Fani-Kayodo's image: what are the terms of gender here and how do they operate? For gender has its terms, its demands, and it makes them even in those moments when they appear to be held in abeyance by the forces of critical interrogation. We are not obliged to obey these demands, but our capacity for dissidence is dependent upon knowing what they are, and being aware that they are made.

By insisting on the terms of *gender* within *patriarchy*, I invoke concepts which are now often thought to bear an irredeemably monolithic, trans-historical cast. I will define patriarchy as the historically specific distribution of property and power in favor of men, which secures its continuance primarily by means of the discipline of gender in the production of gendered subjects. Far from transcending history, the power asymmetries addressed by "gender" and "patriarchy" are deeply embedded within its historical transmutations. My choice of categories is, then, a response to two topics of heated debate in Renaissance studies, and indeed their extrapolation in the Renaissance context will occupy the body of this essay. These issues are whether the subject, as we currently understand it, endowed with depth, interiority, and self-consciousness, emerged in the Renaissance and whether or not modern sexualities – lesbian, male homosexual, heterosexual – can be discerned before the nineteenth century.[2] I want to return to the categories patriarchy and gender, and situate them in relation to the apparently more flexible concepts of sexuality and subjectivity because women are placed in very different relations than men to the institutions that produce their gender, such as the Church, marriage, property, royal office, and so on. As Foucault points out: "There are two meanings of the word subject: subject to someone else by control and dependence, and tied to his own identity by a conscience or self-knowledge. Both meanings suggest a form of power which subjugates and makes subject to."[3] My contention is that whatever definition of personhood and its attendant sexuality we adopt, the subjugations of gender are asymmetrical.

My argument does not, however, preclude there being a discontinuous relation between sexuality and gender.[4] Indeed, the distinction between gender and sexuality has been one of the most valuable insights of Queer theory. Such a distinction ruptures the "straight," forced symmetry of compulsory heterosexuality, thus making homoeroticism – both male and female – visible and possible. Valerie Traub writes:

> [T]he conflation of gender and sexuality is specious at best. Contemporary lesbians and gay men at various moments have constructed their own erotic significations through the use of a deviant vocabulary: "butch, rough-fluff, and femme," "top and bottom," and sign systems of hanky codes and key signals. It may seem as though the gender polarities that structure these signifying systems remain . . . Not completely, however: while butch/rough-fluff/femme designations continue to conflate gender and eroticism, they recognize a continuum rather than a dichotomy of identifications . . .[5]

Traub disarticulates *gender roles*, not gender as such, from sexuality in order to disrupt heterosexual polarities. This maneuver gives space for resistance to gender without denying the terms that necessitate it in the first place. Indeed, in a more recent analysis of early modern representations of women's desire for one another, Traub demonstrates that the type of female eroticism that provoked official reaction involved the woman's penetrative capacity, either prosthetic or the result of clitoral hypertrophy. What is at issue here, she claims, "is not sexuality but gender."[6] The recognition that there is a distinction – but not a categorical disjunction – between gender and sexuality is vital for heterosexual and lesbian feminists alike because it allows us to address the differences within femininity. As Teresa de Lauretis argues, one of "the most deeply rooted effects of the ideology of gender" is that it "does not address, cannot address, the complex and contradictory relation of women to Woman, which it defines as a simple equation: women=Woman=Mother."[7] The analysis of the effects of the disciplinary mechanism of gender, especially on female homoeroticism, are an integral part of the feminist project. Lesbian inquiry, even in its most separatist vein, registers the iron discipline of gender because male supremacy casts its pall even (or perhaps especially) over women's erotic love for one another.

For Eve Kosofsky Sedgwick, in contrast, sexuality is posited as irreducible to "the terms and relations of gender."[8] Could it be, however, that for all that *Epistemology of the Closet* invites dialogue with its readers and critical engagement with its terms, it is the terms of gender, the very terms Sedgwick seeks to banish, that motivate her decision to privilege "(male) terms of analysis" over feminist ones, "where a distinctively feminist (i.e., gender-centered) and a distinctively anti-homophobic (i.e., sexually centered) inquiry have seemed to diverge . . . this book has tried consistently to press on in the latter direction"?[9] A focus on a male sexuality, I would argue, always subtends the absolute separation of sexuality from gender. It is Sedgwick's focus on men that makes it possible to dispense with gender because, according to cultural comonplace, in the case of men, gender is unmarked while women are *the* gender of culture. For Sedgwick, heterosexist assumptions inhere in the analysis of gender: "[T]he ultimate definitional appeal in any gender-based analysis must necessarily be to the diacritical frontier between the genders. This gives heterosocial and heterosexual relations a conceptual privilege of incalculable consequence."[10] Here Sedgwick conflates the mechanisms of gender oppression with resistance, to them. Lesbian assaults on *hom(m)osexuality*, for instance, Irigaray's attack on the notion that there is only one sex – male – and everything else is merely *different from it*, advance instead the idea that there is a species of difference constituted by radical alterity, namely femininity.[11] That is, the difference between the genders understood from an explicitly feminist perspective can actually work to disarticulate feminine sexuality from the patriarchal imperative. Alternatively, Catharine MacKinnon argues that the emphasis on sexual difference (which is what Sedgwick understands as gender) not only has obscured, but also justified the continuing social inequities meted out to women.[12] These understandings of gender get compressed beyond recognition in Sedgwick so that the history of power relations between genders and attempts "to gain analytic and critical leverage on the female-disadvantaging social arrangements,"[13] in other words, resistances to gender, are read as synonymous with the operations of gender as an oppressive and hierarchical construct – that is, with its instantiation and enforcement. (Thus, endeavors to redress wage disparity are not assertions of heterosexual privilege.) Gender, then, may not be the essentially diacritical difference of culture, but it remains the discipline of sexuality.

Crucially to my purpose, Sedgwick's categorical disjunction between gender and sexuality means that feminist and queer inquiry have divided aims: "The study of sexuality is not coextensive with the study of gender; correspondingly, antihomophobic inquiry is not coextensive with feminist inquiry. But we can't know in advance how they will be different."[14] Sedgwick is, of course, right to argue that gender and sexuality are different, but her remarks imply both a counter-productive divisiveness between queer and femnist work and a sense that sexuality is a free-floating entity. Sexuality has then only a tangential connection to gender, the social and cultural formation that grounds it in history. I will argue, *contra* Sedgwick, that gender always disciplines sexualities, and that this outcome, far from being unforeseeable, has all the banal predictability of patriarchal power. Indeed, libidinal forces are never outside the social, never outside the regime of disciplinarity – a regime that is not merely punitive but also constitutive. That is, whatever the ontological emptiness of gender categories, they continue to exert an implacable political force. Just as proclaiming "color blindness," not as a *goal* of anti-racist politics, but as a practice, overlooks the existence of white supremacy (as when the rhetoric of color blindness is used by unscrupulous politicians to discredit affirmative action policies), the theoretical division of gender from sexuality can obfuscate male supremacy. As Teresa de Lauretis (a theorist who, unlike Sedgwick, perceives that lesbian and feminist inquiry have convergent aims) concedes:

I find it impossible to dismiss gender either as an essentialist and mythical idea of the kind I have just described, or as the liberal bourgeois idea encouraged by media advertisers: someday soon, somehow, women will have careers, their own last names and property, children, husbands, and/or female lovers according to preference – and all that without altering the existing social relations and the heterosexual structures to which our society, and most others, are securely screwed.[15]

This provocative passage comes toward the end of a chapter, and its curious combination of optimism about superficial social arrangements and pessimism about deep structural change is as disconcerting as it is challenging. What, one might well ask, does de Lauretis want? What does it take to change "existing social relations and the heterosexual structures to which our society, and most others, are securely screwed"? The answer is that it takes more than simply power and property changing hands – from men to women, from straights to lesbians – because this is merely an assimilationist strategy. Under this rubric of the extensibility of civil rights, one could, for example, be as "glad to be gay" as "glad to be mad," without much troubling over the qualitative difference between the two marginalized categories. Sexuality is indeed more malleable and open to change and personal rearrangement than gender, as Sedgwick suggests,[16] but this is so only because it is more palatable to the status quo than structural changes in the terms of gender. As de

Lauretis indicates, it is even possible that certain classes of people would be allowed the right to indulge their sexual preferences without affecting the overarching heterosexual structure.

The crucial distinction is not, as Sedgwick suggests, the difference between "the study of gender" and "the study of sexuality," between feminism and queer studies. What is politically significant is the principled difference between being anti-homophobic or anti-sexist, and anti-patriarchal. By "anti-patriarchal" I do no mean opposition to an amorphous rule of the fathers, but a counter to specific distributions of property and power which will bring about the more radical changes implied by de Lauretis' analysis of the limitations of current attempts to integrate gay men and lesbians into mainstream society. The former constitutes a local intervention with inherently (de) limited effects, while the latter entails a double imperative: to annihilate the heterosexism inherent in the social construction of gender and continually to engage with gender as the structure of social inequity.

It is within the critical and theoretical context discussed above that I wish to address the terms of gender in relation to two early modern treatments of the history of Edward II. With the release of Derek Jarman's film (1991), Christopher Marlowe's play, *Edward II* (*c.* 1592),[17] has achieved an almost iconic status in gay criticism, its author identified as proto-Queer, while the "proto-feminist" history *The Raign and Death of Edward II* (written 1626), has provoked an intense debate about whether Elizabeth Cary, Countess of Falkland, was in fact its author. My own position does not depend on Cary's authorship (though for convenience's sake I will refer to the text as "Cary's" throughout): it depends on the feminist interest and investment in Cary having written it.[18] Marlowe and Cary can, of course, only anachronistically be described as "gay" and "feminist," and feminist and queer cultural representations and identities do not have early modern "equivalents."[19] However, one can lay claim to these terms in order to ascertain those continuities that do exist within the sexualised terms of gender. Marlowe was a spy, brawler, notorious atheist, and sodomite, while Cary inhabited that emergent and transgressive identity of woman writer and had the temerity to convert to Catholicism while her subsequently estranged husband was Lord Deputy of Ireland, an act for which he reduced her to such penury that the Privy Council was obliged to intervene on her behalf.

That both authors wrote about Edward II, however, is not in itself remarkable. Edward's reign (1307–27), appears to have been one of perennial fascination. Holinshed's *Chronicles* (1577 and 1587; Marlowe's primary source) and Stowe's *Annals of England* (1580; a secondary source for Marlowe), John Taylor's sonnet on Edward II in *A Brief Remembrance of All the English Monarchs* (1618), Michael Drayton's *Piers Gaveston* (1595) and *Mortimerados* (1596), which he subsequently rewrote as *The Baron's Wars* (1602); and Ben Jonson's unfinished work on Mortimer all told the history of Edward II.[20] That a condensed octavo version of Cary's *Raign and Death* entitled *The History of the Life Reign and Death of Edward II*, was published in the same year that the full-length one saw print (1680) indicates that it was as relevant a political lesson for the late seventeenth century as it had been for the Elizabethan and Jacobean era. Indeed, Marlowe's play, though written during the reign of Elizabeth, has been taken as a commentary on James' problems with his favorites in Scotland. Similarly, Cary, writing in 1626, is thought to be disapprovingly pointing toward James' relation to his favorites in England.[21] Much of the interest in Edward's downfall from Holinshed's *Chronicles* through the late seventeenth century, then, was in its extensible capacity for political allegory. However, the allegorical dimension of Marlowe and Cary's reworking of the past as an intervention in the politics of the present does not take the conventional form of allegorical didacticism directed at an erring ruler. In Marlowe's play, what is at stake is how to demystify Elizabethan erotic politics by making the sovereign a man whose most significant erotic alliances are with male favorites. And what is at issue in Cary's text, which patently disapproves of Edward's misgovernance as Marlowe's does not, is how a wife may legitimately usurp the personal and political sovereignty of her husband. Thus, what distinguishes Cary and Marlowe from other early modern treatments of the story of Edward II as a crisis of sovereignty is that, for them, this crisis hinges on a juxtaposition between representations of femininity and homoerotic masculinity.

Current interest in Marlowe clearly rests on the fact that sexual practices which have been consistently persecuted, suppressed and marginalized since the eighteenth century (and intermittently prior to it) take center stage in *Edward II*, and it may seem perverse to argue that the drama is more about patriarchy than it is about sexuality. But in the play, sexuality is always overtly bound up with dominant institutions and practices of power. Indeed, only the modern ideology of sexuality allows it to be perceived as such – as sexuality, rather than say, patronage – at all. As John Michael Archer argues, Edward's power is a commentary on – though not an allegory of – Elizabeth's court, because the connection is insisted on in Gaveston's remark that London after exile, "Is as Elysium to a new come soule":

> *Edward II* both underwrites the political erotics of Elizabeth's court . . . and criticizes its compulsory heterosociality by imagining a male monarch, courted by male suitors, and threatened by over-mighty male subjects. In doing so, it once again both conceals and reveals the paradoxical link between patronage and homoeroticism as subversive practice and social bond.[22]

While Edward II is not merely a cipher for Elizabeth, there is an undeniable resemblance between Edward and Elizabeth's sovereignty. Marlowe shows that patriarchal sovereignty is never, in practice, a clear and prescriptive relation of domination and subordination (though the ideal articulation of sovereignty nonetheless accompanies the practice).[23] Thus, even the radical ambiguation of sexual dominance or binary differences entailed in the rule of a female or sodomitical monarch indicates the adaptability of patriarchal sovereignty rather than its absolute subversion.

Throughout, the play's ideological project is determined by the juxtaposition of femininity and male homoeroticism, and not merely by the sodomitical exclusion of the feminine, rendering the position of women in this structure a fascinating one. When Edward brands Isabella with adultery, what is at stake is less a matter of personal betrayal than alternative allegiance:

> QUEEN ISABELLA: Thus do you still suspect me without cause?
> NIECE: Sweet uncle, speak more kindly to the queen.
> (II.ii.227–28)

That another woman – the only other woman in the play apart from that backdrop of patriarchal history, the silent ladies in attendance – comes to Isabella's defence is significant. It is she, Edward's niece, the Duke of Gloucester's daughter, who is in a position structurally parallel to that of the Queen. She is introduced in act II, in a scene framed by Baldock and Spenser's talk of the latter's homoerotic attachments to Gaveston. From the perspective of conventional sexual relations, we have here a young woman sadly unaware of court politics who expresses genuine longing to marry her duplicitous beloved: "since he was exil'd, / She neither walks abroad nor comes in sight" (II.i.23–24). She then enters rejoicing at the return of her beloved and reading passages from his amorous missives which, in contrast to the lines from Edward's letter which open the play (*"My father is deceas'd. Come, Gaveston, / And share the kingdom with thy dearest friend"*), are replete with all the tired and overblown rhetoric character-

istic of that genre: "When I forsake thee, death seize on my heart!"
(II.i.63). It is when she has been married to Gaveston, given as a gift by
Edward, that she speaks her one-line defense of Isabella. However,
Edward's niece is not just a gullible young woman to whom sodomy is
unintelligible, but someone who in the next scene actively participates in
the alliances it generates, belying any suspicion that her union with
Gaveston is anything other than felicitous. Her agency and investment in
sodomitical power relations which constitute the status quo become
apparent when she begs patronage for Spenser and Baldock from the
king: "Two of my father's servants whilst he liv'd: / May't please your
grace to entertain them now" (II.ii.240–41). In this episode, Gaveston
and his bride work together, he seconding her request on behalf of
Spenser, with whom we know him to have had a significant personal
connection from the opening of act II: "For my sake let him wait upon
your grace" (II.ii.251). Homoerotic attachment and the apparatus of
heterosexual alliance both enforce patriarchy in attempts to buttress
their own positions.[24]

Male homoerotic bonds are represented in Marlowe's play as within
rather than outside patriarchy, and making them is acknowledged to be
one of its most pervasive practices. When the Elder Mortimer famously
advises his discontented and Machiavellian nephew:

> seeing his mind so dotes on Gaveston,
> Let him without controlment have his will.
> The mightiest kings have had their minions (I.iv.391–93)

he shows homoeroticism and power to be perfectly compatible: famous
men from Achilles to Socrates have had male lovers. Crucially, for
Mortimer these same sex attachments are not sodomitical, as such. For
sodomy, as Jonathan Goldberg's *Sodometries* has so valuably demonstrated, consists of male–male sexual love plus disorder. Archer observes
that Mortimer's speech indicates "an earlier and alien realm of sexual
possibility remote from present realities."[25] In fact, the list of famous
lovers of their own sex suggests what is almost unthinkable at a moment
of intense homophobia such as our own, namely, that overt male sexual
alliances with other men once butressed power far more than they contested it. Younger Mortimer's response affirms that same-sex relations
do not inherently pose a threat to the social order:

> Uncle, his wanton humour grieves not me;
> But this I scorn, that one so basely born
> Should by his sovereign's favour grow so pert. (I.iv.404–06)

It is the combination of homoeroticism and class transgression that makes *sodomy* both visible and transgressive here.[26] Mortimer's riposte is to argue that Gaveston is not a "minion." No servile dependent he; there is nothing diminutive about his social carriage. Yet as he expands upon what he finds so troubling, it is neither sodomy nor class status that bother Mortimer, but Gaveston's mastery of the techniques of self-display that ordinarily constitute authority. In the wrong hands these become foppery:

> While soldiers mutiny for want of pay,
> He wears a lord's revenue on his back,
> And, Midas-like, he jets it in the court,
> With base outlandish cullions at his heels,
> Whose proud fantastic liveries make such show
> As if that Proteus, god of shapes, appear'd. (i.iv.408–13)

In violation of sumptuary propriety and law, Gaveston, as Emily Bartells has observed, stages a spectacle of power.[27] It is a capacity for transformation that Gaveston has signaled at the opening of the play with the expressed purpose of manipulating the King, "And drawing the pliant king which way I please" (i.i.53). This is not the studied indeterminacy of postmodern theories about the performance of identity, but an appropriation of one of the most powerful apparatuses of power, that of spectacle, in order to effect a transformation of class status. This manipulation is quite outside Mortimer's repertoire of Machiavellian strategy, and one for which he will profess not outright envy, but only moral disdain.

It is the malleability of Gaveston's self-representation that makes him so desirable and so beloved of Edward. The political end of this spectacle, according to his own motivation, however, is not consolidation of an already established sovereign power – though this is of course its ultimate effect – but the display of the illicit power of a social climber. Isabella, in contrast, while not desiring control over the forces of cultural and social representation, remains trapped in a residual paradigm of the ritual display of court culture:

> O miserable and distressed Queen!
> Would, when I left sweet France, and was embarked,
> That charming Circe, walking on the waves,
> Had chang'd my shape! or at the marriage-day
> The cup of Hymen had been full of poison!
> Or with those arms, that twin's about my neck,
> I had been stifled, and not liv'd to see

The king my lord thus abandon me!
Like frantic Juno will I fill the earth
With ghastly murmur of my sighs and cries;
For never doted Jove on Ganymede
So much as he on cursed Gaveston.
But that will more exasperate his wrath. (I.iv.171–84)

Isabella claims that the self-destructive histrionics of Juno are the sole
theatricals to which she has recourse. Gaveston's power lies in his access
to representational mechanisms in the play, while Isabella's power
appears to take cover behind the stereotypical constructions of the vic-
timized woman and the abandoned wife. And while these historionics
may have no influence on the king, they certainly have the desired effect
on the barons with whom she subsequently develops an enormously
powerful alliance: "Look, where the sister of the king of France / Sits
wringing of her hands and beats her breast!" (I.iv.188–89); "Hard is the
heart that injures such a saint" (I.iv.191). At this juncture, Isabella may
become an ambivalent figure for the audience – a hapless victim or a
strategic manipulator – depending on how far her performance corresponds with these conventional descriptions. Isabella bases her bid for
power on an older mode of feudal alliance and its attendant ritualized
self-representation, whereas Gaveston relies on making a spectacle of his
sexual access to the king.

   Gaveston endeavors to control how Isabella is represented. He trumps
up the charge that she has committed adultery with Mortimer. In a viru-
lently misogynist episode, the King and Gaveston mercilessly bait
Isabella:

KING EDWARD: Fawn not on me, French strumpet; get thee gone!
ISABELLA: On whom but on my husband should I fawn?
GAVESTON: On Mortimer; with whom, ungentle queen, – I
                say no more – judge you the rest, my lord.
ISABELLA: In saying this, thou wrong'st me, Gaveston.
                                                    (I.iv.146–50)

Edward clearly holds Isabella responsible for the demand for Gaveston's
exile, and argues, very plausibly, that she has the power to revoke it.
Isabella's power lies in her alliance with the barons:

KING EDWARD: by thy means is Gaveston exil'd
                   But I would wish thee reconcile the lords,
                   or thou shalt ne'er be reconcil'd to me.
QUEEN ISABELLA: Your highness knows, it lies not in my power.
KING EDWARD: Away, then! touch me not. – Come, Gaveston.

QUEEN ISABELLA: Villain, 'tis thou that robb'st me of my lord.
GAVESTON: Madam, 'tis you that rob me of my lord.
QUEEN ISABELLA: Wherein, my lord, have I deserv'd these words?
                 Witness the tears that Isabella sheds,
                 Witness the heart that sighing for thee, breaks,
                 How dear my lord is to poor Isabel!
KING EDWARD: And witness heaven how dear thou art of me.
                 There weep; for till my Gaveston be repeal'd
                 Assure thyself thou com'st not in my sight.
                                                   (1.iv.156–70)

Gaveston's attempts at presenting to Edward a sexually repellent Isabella are enormously successful. Throughout the play, we get a sense of Edward's physical revulsion for Isabella as opposed to his physical intimacy with Gaveston: "Touch me not," "Com'st not in my sight." "My lord" clearly belongs to "my Gaveston": "He claps his cheeks, and hangs about his neck, / Smiles in his face, and whispers in his ears" (1.ii.51–52). Sexuality is not the issue here, so much as access to the king's body, and in early modern England these could take the form of any number of lowly or exalted relations of service, none of which were necessarily or inherently eroticized. Isabella's power lies, then, in a genuinely powerful alliance with Edward's political opponents.

Isabella trades her covert alliance with the barons for the less politically potent influence to be had from sexual access to a man, Young Mortimer: "The Prince I rule, the queen do I command" (v.iv.46).[28] When Isabella returns to England, she briefly rallies before the assembled multitude at Harwich, trying unsuccessfully and belatedly to retain her grasp on power, this time through public address. While her previous speeches have been private and often soliloquized lamentations on her loss of Edward's love, she begins this speech, all too soon interrupted by Mortimer, in the manner of Elizabeth I's address to the troops at Tilbury:

> Now, lords, our loving friends and countrymen,
> Welcome to England all, with prosperous winds!
>   . . . a heavy case
> When force to force is knit, and sword and glaive
> In civil broils makes kin and countrymen
> Slaughter themselves in others, and their sides
> With their own weapons gor'd! But what's the help?
> Misgoveren'd kings are the cause of all this wrack;   (iv.iv.1–9)

The speech is a vivid description of civil war as self-mutilation, and it prophetically invokes the *contrapasso* of Edward's own final disfigurement, "With their own weapons gor'd!" Despite the fact that this is the most stringent and comprehensive critique of Edward's reign in the play, it is also the moment when the queen loses her power to Mortimer. Once Isabella enters the domestic sphere as Mortimer's surrogate wife, all her power over the instruments of representation is lost. After Harwich, all Isabella's performances are strictly controlled by her lover: "Finely dissembled! Do so still, sweet queen" (v.ii.76). The fifteen minutes of fame atop Fortune's wheel are allotted to Mortimer, not Isabella. He justifies his *coup*, not as Isabella has done as a matter of dire exigency, but as an act of belligerent indignation against sodomitical sycophants who "havok England's wealth and treasure." Silence is enforced upon Isabella, and the sense that it may be coercively enforced is indicated when she tells her son, "I dare not speak a word" (v.iv.96).

Edward's misogyny, of course, is superficially premised on the notion that Isabella has cuckolded him with Mortimer. For everyone but Edward, the real issue is that a male consort has power, which Isabella by virtue of her gender alone cannot have in a culture that defines femininity and power as mutually exclusive, antithetical entities, brought together only in enormous contradiction and with a vast national apparatus of mythology-as-ideology in the figure of the Virgin Queen. "Mortimer / And Isabel do kiss while they conspire. / And yet she bears a face of love, forsooth" (IV.v.21–23).

The conclusion of Marlowe's play shows the restoration of patriarchal order with the final emphasis on dynastic continuity: "Ah, nothing grieves me, but my little boy / Is thus misled to countenance their ills!" (IV.iii.51–52). This "little boy" has an unnerving awareness of posterity:

> The king of England, nor the court of France,
> Shall have me from my gracious mother's side,
> Till I be strong enough to break a staff. (IV.ii.24–26)

When young Edward comes to power, the juxtaposition of femininity and masculine homoeroticism gives way to a familial and dynastic configuration, that is, to the renegotiated and reinforced terms of gender – but only at the price of the chilling spectacle of Edward III's allegiance to his father before the gory head of the decapitated Mortimer, and the rebuke and imprisonment of his mother: "Sweet father, here unto thy murder'd ghost / I offer up this wicked traitor's head" (v.vi.99–100). Edward thus renounces his mother and pleads allegiance to his dead father before the image of what is, in Freudian terms, his own displaced castration, the severed head. Dynasty reasserts itself through gender's disciplinary mechanisms:

                              Accursed head,
      Could I have rul'd thee then, as I do now,
      Thou hadst not hatch'd this monstrous treachery! (v.vi.95–97)

Sexual and dynastic control are consolidated here by addressing
Mortimer as the formerly unruly member of the body politic. Mortimer
is feminized, first in the sense of being symbolically castrated, and secondly, in being capable of gestation and generation. Curiously,
Mortimer, the closest approximation we have in the play to the idea of
dominant masculinity, becomes a figure who has been unnaturally
impregnated by treachery. Symbolically, then, Edward III is asserting his
own desire to subjugate, "Could I have rul'd thee then." Gregory
Bredbeck has brilliantly argued that "Sodomy does not create disorder;
rather disorder demands sodomy."[29] In this sense, castration, the inau-
gural and ultimate discipline of gender, articulates itself simultaneously
with the homoerotic practice of government: men on top – of a hierarchy of other men. Thus, sodomy converts its disorderliness into a dominant practice rather than a subversive identity, and as Archer points out,
"finally it is regicide and not sodomy that is fully recognized and punished."[30] So, having banished his mother and promised her execution,
Edward directly addresses two symbolic absences – the dead head and
his dead father.[31] The last word of the play is "innocency," the new king's
exculpation from the sins of his predecessor: "I offer up this wicked
traitor's head; / And let these tears, distilling from mine eyes, / be
witness of my grief and innocency" (v.vi.100–03). Edward's testament
constitutes both the punishment and repression of sodomy, the figure of
regicide, because Mortimer, in having Edward impaled by Lightbourne,
becomes figuratively the instrument of sodomy, that unnatural instrument now cut off and bleeding before the new king. As Judith Haber has
powerfully argued, Marlowe's play is about the submission to history
defined as the dominant ideology. Her paradigmatic example of this is
the manner of Edward II's murder: " [N]ot only is the manner of
Edward's murder literally true but, in its logical 'punishment-fitting-the-
crime' aspect, it is a figure *for* the literal truth, the intelligible, the deter-
minate, the (patri) lineal, the causal – the historical."[32]
      In contrast to Marlowe's play, in which Isabella is hastily dispatched to
the tower to leave the scene free for the continuation of Edward III's
kingship, Cary places central importance on Isabel and on her reactions
to the execution. Phyllis Rackin argues that most Renaissance history
"was not simply written without women; it was also written against
them."[33] Cary's text is exceptional in offering as it does a female per-

spective on turbulent historical events. In part, her narrative form, rather than Marlowe's dramatic one, allows Cary full access to Isabel's subjectivity. Certainly, Cary's turgid history is enlivened by Isabel's appearance. From this point on, Edward ceases to be the text's protagonist, and instead, Isabel's response to events is vividly imagined and recorded. Cary becomes Isabel's advocate and records the history from her point of view.

The notorious "invisibility" of the manner of Edward's death, which Cary dwells on with salacious relish, replaces the conventional invisibility and erasure of the feminine typical of male-authored texts. In a sense, Cary uses sodomy to make femininity visible:

The historians of these times differ both in the time, place, and manner of his Death; yet all agree that he was foully and inhumanly murther'd, yet so that there was no visible or apparent signe which way 'twas acted . . .
The Queen, who was guilty but in circumstance, and but an accessory to the intention, not the Fact, tasted with a bitter tune of Repentance, what it was but to be quoted in the Margent of such a Story; the several relations so variously exprest of their Concessions, that were the Actors and Consenters to this deed, differ so mainly that it may better be past over in silence, that so much as touch'd; especially since if it were in that cruel manner, as is by the major part agreed on, it was one of the most inhumane and barbarous acts that ever fell within the expression of all our *English* Stories; fitter rather to be pass'd over in silence, than to be discours'd, since it both dishonoureth our Nation, and is in the Example so dangerous. It seemes *Mortimer* was yet a Novice to Spencer's Art, of that same *Italian* trick of Poysoning, which questionless had wrought this work as surely, with less noise, and fewer agents. (p. 155)

What is significant in Cary's account is that a king who has insistently somaticized sovereignty, is disciplined by a practice which at once reproduces his crime *and* erases it. The somatization of sovereignty thus vies with the mythic notion of divine right, which continues irrespective of the mortal body of any individual king. The invisibility of the manner of death parallels Isabel's status as a marginal inscription on both the crime and its history. Further, its marginal, erasable status parallels the status of the feminine where female subjects, no matter how saturated by their gender, nonetheless, leave no impression on the patriarchal record. In accordance with the Foucaultian paradigm of discourse repression and production, the murderous act itself must not be spoken of, but is endlessly talked about as that about which one must be silent. For an act without apparent trace (historically and perhaps corporeally), it has left an indelible mark. As Cary rightly points out, poisoning would have been the discreet way to kill the king, so clearly the main goal was not discretion. The phrasing of the passage is such that Mortimer sounds unschooled in some *sexual* "Italian trick" of Spencer's.[34]

Cary's text has a moral project – the outright condemnation of Edward and justification of this wife's treason – as Marlowe's does not. Regicide is evil, but Cary leaves us in no doubt that in this instance it was fully justified:

> But you may object, He fell by Infidelity and Treason, as have many other that went before and followed him. 'Tis true; but yet withal observe, here was no second Pretenders, but those of his own, a Wife, and a Son, which were the greatest Traytors: had he not been a traytor to himself, they could not all have wronged him. (p. 160)

Cary's *Raign and Death* makes clear from the outset that Edward is degenerate and that women are not morally culpable in his downfall; and in so doing, she enfranchises the domestic sphere:

> Neither was this degenerate Corruption in him transcendent from the womb that bare him, since all Writers agree his Mother to be one of the most pious and illustrious pieces of Female-goodness that is registered in these memorable Stories of all our Royal Wedlocks. (p. 2)

The source of Edward's perversion is "Gaveston his Ganymede, a man as base in birth as in condition" (p. 4), "his left-handed Servant" (p. 24). Cary clearly disparages Gaveston because she regards sodomy as an inherently degenerate practice, and, in the rhetoric with which she rationalizes this position, sodomy is posited not as a personal idiosyncracy of Edward (or, as in Marlowe's Old Mortimer's speech, of monarchs in general), but as a structural weakness in the system of absolute monarchy: "[It] is the general Disease of Greatness, and a kinde of Royal Fever, when they fall upon an indulgent Dotage, to patronize and advance the corrupt ends of their Minions, though the whole Society of State and Body of the Kingdom run in a direct opposition" (p. 16). Edward fails to display his proper sovereignty to his people:" [T]he King appear'd so little himself, that the Subjects thought him a Royal Shadow without a Real Substance" (p. 20) and publicly "he slubbers o'er his private Passion" (p. 23). That is, though Cary's formal charge against Edward is that he has confused private desire with public government – "his private Appetite should subscribe to publick necessity" (p. 9) – there is an implicit suggestion that with sodomy it could not be otherwise. Such a suggestion leads Cary to posit in somewhat contradictory fashion a norm of male sexual behavior that is not absolutely "heterosexual." Excessive love, rather than specifically homosexual desire, becomes the object of her critique: "Such a masculine Affection and rapture was in those times without president, where Love went in the natural strain, fully as firm, yet far less violent" (p. 28). This excessive love constitutes effeminacy, and as Alan Sinfield reminds us, effeminacy, though it rarely correlates with same-sex passion in the Renaissance to the degree that it does in accounts of Gaveston, is founded in misogyny: "the root idea is of a male falling away from the purposeful reasonableness that is supposed to constitute manliness, into the laxity and weakness conventionally attributed to women."[35] Cary overturns this convention and makes Isabel the corrective to effeminate sovereignty.

When Isabel escapes the snares of Spencer to France with Mortimer, we are told "his Craft and Care, that taught him all those lessons of Cunning Greatness, here fell apparent short of all Discretion, to be thus overreached by one weak Woman" (p. 92). Baldock too falls prey to the error of underestimating her: "*Alas, what can the Queen a wandering Woman compas, that hath nor Arms, nor means, nor Men, nor Money?*" (p. 93). Even though Cary has made clear earlier that the queen indeed "had cast a wandering eye upon the gallant *Mortimer*" (p. 89), once his wife has flown, Edward's public taints upon her reputation are ridiculed by Cary:

[A] Declaration is sent out to all the Kingdom, that taints the Honour of the Queen, but more his Judgement. The ports are all stopt up, that none should follow: a Medicine much too late; a help improper, to shut the Stable-door, the Steed being stol'n: but 'tis the nature of a bought Experience, to come a day too late, the market ended. (p. 94)

Spencer's conflict with Isabel is described in terms of a contest of wits between Eve and the serpent: "*Spencer*, that was as cunning as a Serpent, findes here a female Wit that went beyond him, one that with his own Weapons wounds his Wisdome" (p. 91). Spencer has, however, wit enough to fear Isabel: "He knew her to be a Woman of a strong Brain, and a stout Stomack, apt on all occasions to trip up his heels, if once she found him reeling" (pp. 86–87). Cary intervenes here to rewrite history and place the queen's power over Spencer in the most positive possible light – not as devious manipulation but as political ingenuity.

Cary's Isabel is a warrior queen who frequently outwits the men around her, and whose paramour is barely mentioned. Indeed, Mortimer is little more than an accessory to Edward's downfall. Isabel presents the major *political* challenge to Edward's reign; her sexual liaison with Mortimer is of remarkably little significance. She is the self-composed diplomat, who overcomes her passion for revenge and assuages

Mortimer, restraining him from rash action, as she strategizes their return to England (p. 104). Far less the spurned wife than the rebellious queen, "Her Army still grows greater, like a beginning Cloud that doth fore-run a Shower" (p. 123), Isabel gains a specifically military victory, "the Queen having thus attained to the full of her desire, resolves to use it to the best advantage" (p. 127). It is Isabel, and not Mortimer, who defeats Edward, who can only hope in vain for mercy at her hands (p. 125). She heads for London in a victorious parade whereupon "A world of people do strain their wider throats to bid her welcome" (p. 128). Cary argues for women's statecraft and intellectual capacities, "Thus Womens Wit sometimes can cozen Statesmen" (p. 109), instead of offering a defensive apologia for traditional female virtues.

There can be no question that the female-authored Isabel is the plucky victor whereas Marlowe's Isabella functions as the rather stereotypically forlorn queen who cannot survive without male support. Rejected by Edward and then her brother, Valois, Marlowe's Isabella finally turns to Mortimer. While this does not, of course, mean that positive images of women necessarily make for more radical or even better texts, it does show how history is read differently by an author who foregrounds female political agency. For all that, Cary's championing of Isabel is an argument for a strong, ideal patriarchy. Had Edward exercised proper manly power, there would have been a perfect balance between the reciprocal duties of sovereign and subjects:

> The *power Majestick* is or should be bounded; and there is a reciprocal correspondence; which gives the *King* the obedience, the subject equal right and perfect justice, by which they claim a property in his actions if either of these fall short, or prove defective by wilful errour, or by secret practice, the State's in danger of a following mischief. (p. 68)

But Edward, as well as being the possessor of "many *puny* vices" is also a "cruel Tyrant" (p. 74) in the "bloody Hurly-burlies" (p. 76) of the realm.

Contrary to the claims of feminist critical appraisals of the text, it is not an heroic nature that allows Isabel to resist tyranny. Rather, her resistance – aligned with that of Edward's subjects – comes about as a natural effect of the King's weakness:

> Though in a sinking greatness all things conspire to work a fatal ruine, yet in our Story this is the first president of this nature, or where a King fell with so little Honour, and so great an Infidelity, that found neither Sword or Tongue to plead his quarrel. But what could be expected, when for his own private vanities and

Passion, he had been a continuall abetter of unjust actions, and had consented to the Oppression of the whole kingdom, and the untimely Death of so many Noble Subjects? (p. 137)

In sharp contrast to the bowmen and pikes who take up Edward's cause in Marlowe, Cary leaves Edward without even the semblance of military support. Again, private vanities as such are not the issue but, rather that "all things at home, under his Government, were out of rule and order; and nothing successful that he undertook by forraign Employment" (p. 39). Edward has virtually ceded all power to Gaveston, "He thus assuming the administration of Royal affairs, his Master giving way to all his actions" (p. 53). Cary states that it was "not altogether improbable" that this was the result of witchcraft, "for never was Servant more insolently fortunate, nor Master unreasonably indulgent" (p. 49). It is the kingdom which must pay for Edward's excesses, "making the Subject groan under the unjust Tyranny of an insolent oppression" (p. 40).

But the pseudo-sexual instrument of this disorder is not the phallus, the patriarchal organ of government, so to speak, but the tongue, by which Edward is sexually manipulated first by Gaveston, and then by Spencer. A loyal subject declares: "*I am no tongue man*" (p. 55) while the evil of the realm is seen to emanate from the tongue: "Admission of the Royal ear to *one Tongue* only, ties all the rest" (p. 62).[36] Spencer, like his predecessor, "made his tongue a guide to lead his actions" (p. 86). Even though Edward is the "feminine" recipient of the tongue, the Machiavellianism of those who manipulate with it is almost feminine power gone public – that is, the influence of the "*Harpy* with his *Lycean* eyes" (p. 54), which in the properly ordered state is normally kept within the confines of the private realm.

When the queen manufactures a spectacle of her power, Cary voices her one criticism of Isabel, which is that she leads Spencer in triumph:

[h]e is led through each Town behinde the carriage . . . Certainly, this man was infinitely vicious, and deserv'd as much as could be laid upon him, for those many great and insolent Oppressions, acted with Injustice, Cruelty, and Blood; yet it had been much more to the Queen's Honour, if she had given him a quicker death. (p. 128–29)

This is an astonishing moment in the narrative: not only is Isabel's honor totally divorced from the question of chastity, but also the death sentence she has meted out to Spencer is corroborated. The style of Isabel's justice, however, is severely criticized – specifically, the way she grasps the reins of representation. Spencer deserves death, but one more fitting his class position, "Though not by Birth, yet by Creation he was a Peer of the Kingdom" (p. 129). Cary continues, "it was at best too great and deep a blemish to suit a Queen, a Woman, and a Victor" (p. 129), but then, as she adds in a passage about Isabel's execution of Arundel on the following page, "we may not properly expect Reason in Womens actions" (p. 130). In Cary's narrative, the queen and Mortimer reign on unpunished. In this sense, Isabel's victory is the antithesis of conventional patriarchal history where "Depicted as blank pages awaiting the inscription of patriarchal texts, silenced by the discourse of patriarchal authority, the women could never tell their own stories,"[37] and yet her role is to consolidate the powers she ostensibly challenges.[38] Cary presents Isabel as a figure of legitimate resistance to cruelty and wantonness, whose only real sin is not adultery but her display of Spencer and her own power after she defeats him. Women too, it seems, can be the instruments of strong patriarchy, and the unpunished victory is a fantasy of how they can be absorbed within it.

I have been pursuing the juxtaposition of male homoeroticism and femininity in order to determine where such a configuration places women, and I want to conclude by exploring that juxtaposition in the context of Jonathan Goldberg's illuminating study, *Sodometries*. This pioneering book, among other things, valuably endeavors to disclose the limits of feminist discussions which treat "gender as if the only forms of power involved were those that determine the inequality between the sexes (arguments . . . which collapse questions of sexuality in to questions of gender)."[39] Goldberg's valid and significant objective here is to make homoeroticism visible in the Renaissance, a visibility contingent upon the degree to which it can be made distinct from gender. He argues that feminist critics in particular have ignored the homoerotic. For example, he criticizes Lisa Jardine's *Still Harping On Daughters*: "For her, there are no women in Shakespeare, simply boys travestying the woman's part. (Transvestism is a travesty of women; homosexuality is the proper name for this)."[40] Given the systematic subordination of women, however, there can be little wonder that feminist critics lack faith that women would have been well represented on a stage that excluded them. Yet, Goldberg claims that attention to women's subordination is *in itself* tantamount to homophobia. A focus on the restrictions of gender, which, it must be emphasized, constrain women more than men, is seen itself to perpetuate those restrictions. Thus, in criticizing the way feminist critics subsume sexuality under the category of gender, Goldberg reverses the maneuver and collapses gender into sexuality. Crucially, that sexuality is ungendered. The result is a postmodern rendition of the allegedly gender-neutral, universal subject – man; nothing less than a covert return to masculinity.[41]

Heterosexuality, defined as "the relations between men and women,"[42] flattens out, so that the specificity of feminine sexuality, whether heterosexual or homoerotic, gets lumped in with masculine heterosexuality. The trajectory of his argument leads Goldberg in his analysis of Marlowe's *Edward II* to make the astonishing claim that Isabella is a sodomite: "A sodomite, then, in Stubbes's sense of the term, but not a boy. For what Marlowe intimates, insofar as it is possible to think of Isabella as a sodomite, is that the possibility for 'strong' female behavior lies outside of marriage and its regularization of gender."[43] While technically, Isabella as an adulteress, could be considered a sodomite, there is a danger that in making sodomy a privileged category of indeterminacy – "beyond any ontological category"[44] – untrammeled by allegedly restrictive understandings of gender, femininity loses its coherence and specificity. Sodometries for Goldberg are not so much sites of resistance as sites of the dissolution of all order: "The identity that Marlowe gives to the sodomite is a fully negativized one against which there is no positivity to be measured."[45] In this, we have moved not just beyond restrictive understandings of gender but beyond gender altogether. The logic behind this strategy is that gender is restrictive and sexuality needs to be liberated from it, a logic which obscures the fact that sexuality is produced under the discipline of gender.

Phyllis Rackin has argued in her analysis of Shakespeare's history plays that "In the central scene of historical representation, women have no place."[46] Marginal as the roles of wife, mother, and England's queen may be, even these dynastic roles are unavailable to Marlowe's Isabella – Kent even wins her son from her in act v. Marlowe's queen is caught in the interstices of male power, never really able to wield it on her own behalf. Isabella's adultery, far from being an act of *resistance to* the constraints of marriage is rather a last ditch resistance against her *exclusion from* conjugality. The price, then, of Goldberg's insistence on sexuality as distinct from gender is the erasure of the discipline of gender *and* the possibility of a specifically female resistance.[47] In Goldberg's reading of the relation between the feminine and the male homoerotic, then, women disappear. In Marlowe and Cary's texts, in contrast, both male homoeroticism and gender hierarchy become hyper-visible in the exacerbated conditions of Edward's reign.

I began with the institutional imaginary of the photograph of a well-known book cover, in a well-known patchwork of symbolic distributions, not only because it vividly exemplifies recurrent tensions between femininity and homoerotic masculinity, but also because it makes visible some of the covert operations which structure representational processes in patriarchy. Of particular concern in this regard is the way femininity and homoerotic masculinity are set against one another. This manifests itself as an unsettling alignment between feminism and homophobia, homoeroticism and misogyny, and does so in spite of the shared political agenda of much feminist and queer theory. Such an opposition constricts interventions and isolates their effects so that work against either sexism or homophobia produces interventions that may challenge certain practices within patriarchy, but not the structure itself, and only serves, however unwittingly, inadvertently, or reluctantly, to reproduce the patriarchal order.

The configuration of sexuality and gender, male homoeroticism and feminity, as juxtapositions rather than antagonistic antitheses, I hope, suggests a contiguity which recognizes that "divide and conquer" is one of patriarchy's most enduring strategies. I hope also to register that there is a powerful patriarchal projection which saddles woman with both the mark of gender and blame for its discipline; by extension, feminism is seen as having a unique investment in enforcing gender's terms. As psychoanalytic theory has demonstrated, it is femininity that threatens to disrupt gender, while the Law of the Father sets the terms.

NOTES

I with to thank my coeditors and David Hawkes, David Riggs, Jean Howard, Forbes Morlock, Michael Schoenfeldt, and Joel Simon for their astute comments on this essay.

 1 Jonathan Dollimore, *Sexual Dissidence: Augustine to Wilde, Freud to Foucault* (Oxford: Clarendon Press, 1991).
 2 Alan Sinfield, *Cultural Politics – Queer Reading* (Philadelphia: University of Pennsylvania Press, 1994), p. 14.
 3 Michel Foucault, "The Subject and Power," in *Michel Foucault: Beyond Structuralism and Hermeneutics*, Hubert L. Dreyfus and Paul Rabinow, eds. (1982; Chicago: University of Chicago Press, 1983), p. 212.
 4 In psychoanalytic theory the sociological distinction between sex and gender has long been discredited. See Jacqueline Rose's introduction to *Feminine Sexuality: Jaques Lacan and the Ecole Freudienne* (London: Macmillan, 1982). In her essay "The More Things Change," in a special issue of *Differences* on queer theory: 6. 2/3 (1994), Elizabeth Weed takes a different view of Sedgwick's position:

[I]t is tempting for feminists to suspect that what we are seeing is somehow the chiasmic revenge of sex: sex, having been once displaced by gender, now returns the favor. Things are more complicated, of course. Sedgwick's "sexuality" is not – or is not only – [Gayle] Rubin's "sex." The latter refers to the relatively restricted notion of sexed reproduction whereas sexuality is that Foucaultian phenomenon produced by the densely entangled discourses of religion, science, and the sciences of man, with its historically privileged relationship to identity, truth, and knowledge. Intervening in these entangled discourses, Sedgwick wants to keep the slippery terms of sex, gender, and sexuality from always sliding into one another, so that sex is not always already chromosomal difference and reproduction, so that acts and sensations of "sex" are not always caught in a gendered genital economy, and so that sexuality can be inflected outside the homo–hetero axis. It is, then not quite right to say that Sedgwick seeks to disengage sexuality from gender. More accurately, the analytic space she opens up looks to drive a wedge not simply between sexuality and gender, but between sex-sexuality and sex-gender. (249–50)

Weed complicates the category of sexuality, but leaves gender untouched. The issue for me, however, is not so much the slippage from one category to another – gender-into-sex-into-sexuality – but the rigidity of gender as the disciplinary structure of patriarchy rather than its analytic framework.

5 Valerie Traub, *Desire and Anxiety: Circulations of Sexuality in Shakespearean Drama* (New York: Routledge, 1992), p. 101.
6 Valerie Traub, "The (In)Significance of 'Lesbian' Desire," in *Queering the Renaissance*, Jonathan Goldberg, ed. (Durham: Duke University Press, 1994), p. 69.
7 Teresa de Lauretis, *Technologies of Gender: Essays on Theory, Film, and Fiction* (Bloomington: Indiana University Press, 1986), p. 20.
8 Eve Kosofsky Sedgwick, *Epistemology of the Closet* (Berkeley: University of California Press, 1990), p. 16.
9 *Ibid.*, pp. 5–16.
10 *Ibid.*, p. 31.
11 See Luce Irigaray, *This Sex Which Is Not One*, trans. Catherine Porter with Carolyn Burke (Ithaca: Cornell University Press, 1985).
12 Catharine MacKinnon, *Feminism Unmodified: Discourses On Life and Law* (Cambridge MA: Harvard University Press, 1987), pp. 32–45.
13 Sedgwick, *Epistemology of The Closet*, p. 28.
14 *Ibid.*, p. 27.
15 de Lauretis, *Technologies of Gender*, p. 21.
16 Sedgwick, *Epistemology of The Closet*, p. 34.
17 Christopher Marlowe, *The Complete Plays*, ed., J. B. Steane (1969; rpt. Harmondsworth: Penguin, 1986).
18 Cary, Elizabeth, *The Raign and Death of Edward II* (London: J. C. for Charles

Harper et al., 1680); STC. 313, and *The History of the Most Unfortunate Prince King Edward II* (London: A. G. and J. P., 1680), STC 314. The text is extant in two versions, the former a long version, with many formal resemblances to dramatic structure, such as several speeches in blank verse. I refer to this text throughout my essay. See Tina Krontiris, *Oppositional Voices: Women as Writers and Translators of Literature in the English Renaissance* (New York: Routledge, 1992), p. 160. An essay by Donald Stauffer in 1935 sought to establish Cary's authorship, "A Deep and Sad Passion," in *The Parrott Presentation Volume*, Hardin Craig, ed. (New York: Russell and Russell, 1935), pp. 289–324. That the *Raign and Death* has been almost completely accepted into the canon of early modern women's writing is evidenced by the fact that it has been examined in recent important treatments of women writers of the period, such as Krontiris' *Oppositional Voices* and Barbara Lewalski, *Writing Women In Jacobean England*, (Cambridge, MA: Harward University Press, 1993). Patricia Crawford notes in "Women's Published Writings 1500–1800," in *Women In English Society 1500–1800*, Mary Prior, ed. (New York: Methuen, 1985), pp. 211–31, that Wing attributes the text to Henry Viscount Falkland, that the text has also been attributed to Elizabeth, and that in an unpublished paper, Daniel Woolf suggests it may be a forgery of the exclusion crisis period (p. 262). See Tina Krontiris' argument for Cary's authorship in "Style and Gender in Elizabeth Cary's *Edward II*," in *The Renaissance Englishwoman In Print: Counterbalancing the Canon*, Anne M. Haselkom and Betty Travitsky, eds. (Amherst: University of Mass Press, 1990), pp. 137–39. See also Isobel Grundy, "Falkland's *History of* . . . *King Edward II*," *Bodleian Library Record* 13. 1 (1988): 82–83. Barry Weller and Margaret Ferguson, who remain skeptical about Cary's authorship, provide an excellent summary of the issues in their introduction to *The Tragedy of Mariam, The Fair Queen of Jewry* (Berkely: University of California Press, 1994), pp. 12–17. Diane Purkiss thoroughly elucidates the problems concerning Cary's authorship without trying to resolve them. However, she chooses to include *Edward II* in her edition of the "plays" of Cary, published with the poetry of Aemilia Lanyer, in *Renaissance Women: The Plays of Elizabeth Cary, The Poems of Aemilia Lanyer* (London: William Pickering, 1994), see especially pp. xxi–xxx. Christopher, Marlowe, *The Complete Plays*, J. B. Steane, ed. (1969; rpt. Harmondsworth: Penguin, 1986).

19   For the debate on historicizing the category of homosexuality since Foucault's claim that it emerged only in the nineteenth century, see: Terry Castle, *The Apparitional Lesbian: Female Homosexuality and Modern Culture* (New York: Columbia University Press, 1993), chapter 1; and Claude Summers' introduction to *Homosexuality in Renaissance and Enlightenment England: Literary Representations in Historical Context*, *Journal of Homosexuality* Vol. 23. 1/2, 1992 (New York: Haworth Press). See also in that volume, Joseph Cady, "'Masculine Love,' Renaissance Writing, and the 'New Invention' of Homosexuality," pp. 9–40. I would argue that in some sense the debate is based on the erroneous assumption that Foucault is speaking only of homo-

sexuality. Since homosexuality is what defines and produces the discrete category of heterosexuality, it is more accurate to say sexuality itself can be
dated as a recent event.

20 For an excellent analysis of other treatments of Edward II, see Gregory
Bredbeck, *Sodomy and Interpretation* (Ithaca: Cornell University Press, 1991),
pp. 48–9. Bredbeck does not, however, mention Cary. John Taylor, *A Briefe
Remembrance of All the Englishe Monarchs* (London, 1618), sig. B4; Michael
Drayton, *The Works of Michael Drayton*, J. W. Hebe, ed. (Oxford: Basil
Blackwell 1961); Ben Jonson, "Mortimer His Fall," in *Ben Jonson: Works*, C.
H. Herford and Percy Simpson, eds. (Oxford: Clarendon Press, 1929–52)
vol. VII, pp. 58–59.

21 See Krontiris, *Oppositional Voices*, p. 91. One of James' Scottish cousins, Esmé
Stuart, was, like Gaveston, actually banished from the realm. See Jonathan
Goldberg, *Sodometries: Renaissance Texts, Modern Sexualities* (Stanford: Stanford
University Press, 1993), p. 271.

22 John Archer, *Sovereignty and Intelligence: Spying and Court Culture in the English
Renassance* (Stanford: Stanford University Press, 1993), p. 77.

23 For Dollimore, who uses both lesbian and gay texts to extrapolate his thesis,
the epistemological and political rupturing wrought by a repeated unsettling
of the opposition between dominant and subordinate "operating in terms of
gender" is what constitutes sexual dissidence (*Sexual Dissidence*, p. 21).

24 Goldberg notes the play allows for "ways of conceiving sexual relations and
gender construction that cannot be reduced to the normative structure of
male/female relations under the modern regimes of heterosexuality"
(*Sodmometries*, p. 129).

25 Archer, *Sovereignty and Intelligence*, p. 81.

26 Sharon Tyler notes that Marlowe emphasizes that Gaveston is low-born
even though his sources do not, "Bedfellows Make Strange Politics:
Christopher Marlowe's *Edward II*," in *Drama Sex and Politics*, James
Redmond, ed., Themes in Drama 7 (Cambridge: Cambridge University
Press, 1985), p. 57.

27 Emily Bartells, *Spectacles of Strangeness: Imperialism, Alienation, and Marlowe*
(Philadelphia: University of Pennsylvania Press, 1994), pp. 143–72.

28 Of course even as an adulteress, the queen remains dangerous. Phyllis
Rackin has argued that women in patriarchal historiography represent a
physicality that men can neither capture nor control, and that the adulterous woman in particular threatens to disrupt and destroy the dynastic
scheme and "at any point could make a mockery of the whole story of patriarchal succession." *Stages of History: Shakespeare's English Chronicles* (Ithaca:
Cornell University Press, 1990), p. 160.

29 Bredbeck, *Sodomy and Interpretation*, p. 77.

30 Archer *Sovereignty and Intelligence*, p. 86.

31 Judith Haber remarks about Edward III's threatening his mother with
execution: "His painfully firm resolution is particularly striking in a play in
which almost everyone has been presented as 'slack' or 'drooping,'"

"Submitting to History: Marlowe's *Edward II*," in *Enclosure Acts: Sexuality, Property, and Culture in Early Modern England*, Richard Burt and John Michael Archer, eds. (Ithaca: Cornell University Press, 1994), p. 179.

32 *Ibid.*, p. 180.
33 Rackin, *Stages of History* p. 160.
34 I will use Cary's spelling of "Spencer" throughout my discussion of her text.
35 Sinfield, *Cultural Politics*, p. 15. For an analysis of motifs of clothing and the body in relation to effeminacy, see Gregory Woods, "The Body, Costume, and Desire in Christopher Marlowe," in *Homosexuality in Renaissance and Enlightenment England*, Summers, ed., pp. 24–25.
36 Edward, however, actively employs, as well as being passively manipulated by, the politics of the tongue: "Thus *Kings* can play their parts, and hide their Secrets, making the Tongue the instrument of sweetness, when that the Heart is full of bitter Gall and Wormwood" (p. 64).
37 Rackin, *Stages of History*, p. 147.
38 Dollimore points out: "dissidence may not only be repressed by the dominant (coercively and ideologically), but in a sense actually produced by it, hence consolidating the powers which it ostensibly challenges (*Sexual Dissidence*, p. 27).
39 Goldberg, *Sodometries*, p. 21.
40 Lisa Jardine, *Still Harping on Daughters: Women and Drama in the Age of Shakespeare* (1983; rpt. New York: Columbia University Press, 1989). Goldberg, *Sodometries*, p. 113.
41 Goldberg, *Sodometries*, p. 106.
42 *Ibid.*, p. 107.
43 *Ibid.*, p. 123.
44 *Ibid.*, p. 121.
45 *Ibid.*, p. 124.
46 Rackin, *Stages of History*, p. 147
47 Challenging new historicist notions of containment, Barbara Lewalski argues that Cary's history, like the writings of Jacobean women in general, is inherently a text of resistance:

Although these writers were subsequently ignored or suppressed, I take it that their literary gestures of resistance matter . . .

. . . Attention to these women writers will also help us recognize that authorship may be the process as well as the product of asserting subjectivity and agency. (*Writing Women in Jacobean England*, p. 11)